*Cities after the Fall of Communism*

# Cities after the Fall of Communism

## Reshaping Cultural Landscapes and European Identity

Edited by John Czaplicka,
Nida Gelazis, and Blair A. Ruble

Woodrow Wilson Center Press
Washington, D.C.

The Johns Hopkins University Press
Baltimore

EDITORIAL OFFICES

Woodrow Wilson Center Press
Woodrow Wilson International Center for Scholars
One Woodrow Wilson Plaza
1300 Pennsylvania Avenue, N.W.
Washington, D.C. 20004-3027
Telephone: 202-691-4029
www.wilsoncenter.org

ORDER FROM

The Johns Hopkins University Press
Hampden Station
P.O. Box 50370
Baltimore, Maryland 21211
Telephone: 1-800-537-5487
www.press.jhu.edu/books/

© 2009 by the Woodrow Wilson International Center for Scholars
All rights reserved
Printed in the United States of America on acid-free paper ∞

2 4 6 8 9 7 5 3 1

*Library of Congress Cataloging-in-Publication Data*

Cities after the fall of communism : reshaping cultural landscapes and European identity / edited by John Czaplicka, Nida Gelazis, and Blair A. Ruble.
   p.  cm.
Includes bibliographical references and index.
ISBN 978-0-8018-9191-5 (hardcover : alk. paper)
  1. Cities and towns—Europe, Eastern. 2. Post-communism—Europe, Eastern. 3. Architecture—Europe, Eastern. 4. City planning—Europe, Eastern. I. Czaplicka, John. II. Gelazis, Nida M. III. Ruble, Blair A., 1949–
  HT145.E75C57   2008
  307.760947—dc22

2008036155

 Woodrow Wilson International Center for Scholars

The Woodrow Wilson International Center for Scholars, established by Congress in 1968 and headquartered in Washington, D.C., is the living, national memorial to President Wilson.

The Center is a nonpartisan institution of advanced research, supported by public and private funds, engaged in the study of national and world affairs. The Center establishes and maintains a neutral forum for free, open, and informed dialogue.

The Center's mission is to commemorate the ideals and concerns of Woodrow Wilson by providing a link between the world of ideas and the world of policy, by bringing a broad spectrum of individuals together to discuss important public policy issues, by serving to bridge cultures and viewpoints, and by seeking to find common ground.

The conclusions or opinions expressed in Center publications and programs are those of the authors and speakers and do not necessarily reflect the views of the Center staff, fellows, trustees, advisory groups, or any individuals or organizations that provide financial support to the Center.

The Center is the publisher of *The Wilson Quarterly* and home of Woodrow Wilson Center Press, *dialogue* radio and television, and the monthly newsletter "Centerpoint." For more information about the Center's activities and publications, please visit us on the web at www.wilsoncenter.org.

Lee H. Hamilton, President and Director

Board of Trustees
Joseph B. Gildenhorn, Chair
David A. Metzner, Vice Chair

Public members: James H. Billington, Librarian of Congress; G. Wayne Clough, Secretary of the Smithsonian Institution; Bruce Cole, Chairman, National Endowment for the Humanities; Michael O. Leavitt, Secretary of Health and Human Services; Condoleezza Rice, Secretary of State; Margaret Spellings, Secretary of Education; Allen Weinstein, Archivist of the United States; Mark R. Dybul, designated appointee of the President from within the federal government

Private citizen members: Robin Cook, Donald E. Garcia, Bruce S. Gelb, Sander R. Gerber, Charles L. Glazer, Susan Hutchison, Ignacio E. Sanchez

# Contents

Acknowledgments ... ix

Introduction: What Time Is This Place? Locating the Postsocialist City ... 1
*Nida Gelazis, John Czaplicka, and Blair A. Ruble*

**Part I. European Cities Old and New:
Re-creating Medieval Histories**

1 The Changing Face of Vilnius: From Capital to Administrative Center and Back ... 17
   *Irena Vaisvilaite*

2 The Novgorod Model: Creating a European Past in Russia ... 53
   *Nicolai N. Petro*

3 Wrocław's Search for a New Historical Narrative: From Polonocentrism to Postmodernism ... 75
   *Gregor Thum*

**Part II. Architecture and History at Ports of Entry**

4 Mapping Tallinn after Communism: Modernist Architecture as Representation of a Small Nation ... 105
   *Jörg Hackmann*

5 The Persuasive Power of the Odessa Myth ... 137
   *Oleg Gubar and Patricia Herlihy*

6 Traveling Today through Sevastopol's Past:
   Postcommunist Continuity in a "Ukrainian" Cityscape    167
   *Karl D. Qualls*

7 Locating Kaliningrad/Königsberg on the Map of Europe:
   "A Russia in Europe" or "a Europe in Russia"?    195
   *Olga Sezneva*

**Part III. Cities at a New East-West Border**

8 Kharkiv: A Borderland City    219
   *Volodymyr Kravchenko*

9 L'viv in Search of Its Identity: Transformations of the
   City's Public Space    255
   *Liliana Hentosh and Bohdan Tscherkes*

10 Łódź in the Postcommunist Era: In Search of a
   New Identity    281
   *Joanna Michlic*

11 Szczecin's Identity after 1989: A Local Turn    305
   *Jan Musekamp*

Conclusion: Cities after the Fall    335
   *Nida Gelazis, Blair A. Ruble, and John Czaplicka*

Contributors    347

Index    353

# Acknowledgments

Many of us have traveled back and forth many times to the cities addressed in this volume since the late 1980s. Along with the social, political, and economic upheavals, we have noticed the constant reorganization of the urban landscapes there and wondered how they were related. While each new monument, café, or shopping mall would surprise the intermittent visitor, locals seemed to incorporate seamlessly these new structures into their lives, rarely remarking upon them if at all. Nevertheless, the transformation of material culture in each of these cities is linked to profound shifts in how each community views its past, present, and future.

This volume is the concrete result of the views and ideas that developed from a conference organized jointly by the Center for European Studies (CES) at Harvard University and the Kennan Institute of the Woodrow Wilson International Center for Scholars. The meeting was convened by John Czaplicka and Charles Maier of CES and Blair Ruble of the Kennan Institute and was sponsored by the Minda de Gunzburg Center for European Studies, the Harvard Ukrainian Research Institute, the Goethe Institute in Boston, and the Woodrow Wilson Center. The conference, titled "Cities after the Fall: European Integration and Urban History," was organized through the work of John Czaplicka and Lisa Eschenbach at CES, and with the assistance of Edita Krunkaityte of the Kennan Institute.

The conference included several people whose contributions were not included in this volume, but were nonetheless greatly appreciated by the editors. We are indebted to Peter A. Hall, director of the Minda de Gunzburg Center for European Studies; Charles Maier, Leverett Saltonstall Professor of History at Harvard University; Wolfgang Kil, a journalist and architectural critic in Berlin; Jacek Dominiczak of the Academy of Fine Arts in

Gdansk; and Janis Dripe, an architect and former chief of protocol of the Republic of Latvia.

Finally, we owe a debt of gratitude to the authors of each of the chapters included in this volume. These contributions, which give this book its depth and color, represent many years of focused research devoted to a specific time and place. The cities they have studied will continue to shift and change, and their development—like the works of these authors—ought to be followed closely.

Washington, D.C.
August 2008

*Cities after the Fall of Communism*

# Introduction: What Time Is This Place? Locating the Postsocialist City

*Nida Gelazis, John Czaplicka, and Blair A. Ruble*

Writing about the symbolism of space and time that had been used to characterize American cities, Anselm Strauss once posed a deceptively simple question: What time is this place? The question introduced an analysis of how Americans had endowed their cities with symbolic and material references to the past and future in order to orient themselves in times of rapid urban transformation.[1] Answering this simple question about situating a city in history and projecting its future has become central for those reimagining and remaking the cities of the former Soviet Union and postcommunist Central and Eastern Europe.

Imagine how much more complex and disorienting have been the broad transformations of postcommunist cities. Since 1989, the residents of these cities have experienced rapid and simultaneous spatial-temporal, geocultural, geopolitical, and economic transformations, many of which are still taking place.[2] Gentrification, the commoditization of urban space, demographic change, postindustrial economic transition, and democratization have all changed—and are still changing—the images and appearances of the cities throughout the region. At the same time, new senses of place and new place-based identities have developed within the frameworks of ethnic and national revivals, the turn toward a united Europe, and globalization. The trajectory of postsocialist development points variously in global, European, national, local, and personal directions, and these crosscutting vectors of identity guide the processes of cultural, economic, and political reorientation. Any momentary assessment of where, how, and when the cities of the region are defining themselves as these processes unfold is full of complexity and contradiction, which is mirrored in the concrete reshaping of the cities themselves.

Much of the push and pull on the urban fabric in Eastern Europe during the past eighteen years has been conceptual as well as physical, and related to the selective appropriation of local heritage and history. Which heritage is recognized and how the history of a city is being constructed reveal a great deal about the aspirations of its people—or of its cultural and political elite. The abridged stories of the urban past and the preferred projections of the urban future presented in the chapters in this volume suggest how the citizens of Tallinn, L'viv, Odessa, and the other cities examined here are trying to project themselves into the postcommunist marketplace of ideas and images. In these projections, one clearly recognizes multiple orientations and contradictory influences.

Each of the eleven chapters in this volume focuses on a postcommunist city with a particularly interesting story to tell: Vilnius, Novgorod, Wrocław, Tallinn, Odessa, Sevastopol, Kaliningrad, Kharkiv, L'viv, Łódź, and Szczecin. In choosing these cities, the question "What time is it?" was again deeply relevant. Before 1991, all these cities were in two countries—either in Poland or the USSR. The border between Poland and the USSR was porous in comparison with the borders, both real and virtual, between these two countries and the West. In different ways and under unique circumstances, each city had reacted to the common forces of Sovietization to which they were subjected. Communist ideology, though variously interpreted, was the shared principle guiding the work of urban planners, architects, and historians across the region. By January 1992, however, the ideological tether between these cities was severed when the two countries that had held these cities became six.

Now, more than a decade later, these eleven cities have been remade, and their stories have been retold according to a number of new and old ideologies and aspirations. Each chapter that follows can be seen as a sort of narrative vector analysis of each city's unique path and the forces that have contributed to its trajectory in its country. And each of the six countries where the cities are now located—Estonia, Latvia, Lithuania, Poland, Russia, and Ukraine—has likewise been defined in the reorganization of the cities studied here. Moreover, the dichotomy of the pre-1991 period has reemerged in a new form. Rather than sets of Polish and Soviet cities, two new sets have been created: those cities that belong to the European Union, Vilnius, Wrocław, Tallinn, Łódź, and Szczecin; and those that do not, Novgorod, Odessa, Sevastopol, Kaliningrad, Kharkiv, and L'viv. This new dichotomy can help scholars understand perceptions of "Europeaness" in the postcommunist space and how cities have chosen whether or not to incorporate "European" norms.

The postsocialist character of these eleven cities is being reformulated in a mixed groping for a new past and a new future, and this duality is expressed through architecture that embodies the new political culture and society.[3] In Vilnius, the Renaissance Grand Duke's Palace is being reconstructed, while the glass-and-steel ensemble of a high-rise civic center has been built across the Neris River. In its Italianate style, this reconstruction of the Lithuanian palace at once refers to the origins and European heyday of its city and embodies national Independence. The modern edifices posed opposite the palace, meanwhile, embody the desire to plug into the new global economy through the establishment of a modern service sector and financial industries.

Of course, such urban admixture is nothing new; all cities are composed in the aggregate of varying times and places and people. Yet there is something very new and distinct in the postcommunist transition as urban communities work their way through overlapping economic, political, cultural, demographic, and spatial transitions. What Henri Lefebvre, Michel Foucault, and others have called a *heterotopy* resonates with the complexity of this postsocialist (and as some might propose, postmodernist) situation of competing interests and times.[4] Place *and* time are, simply put, only the coordinates of history, while *making* history and telling it are about projection and orientation, about historical models and models for the future. Building and redesigning, conserving, and renovating are political acts *making* history in these cities. Such acts are the focus of consideration in this volume.

## New Historical Narratives

The residents of postsocialist cities project their future through history as much as they project their future against history. These projections are broad combinations of fact and fiction, as certain historical narratives are elevated over others (even if they contrast strongly with current demographic, political, and economic realities). To see how now overwhelmingly monoethnic cities—such as L'viv, Łódź, and Wrocław—celebrate pasts of great diversity or how certain aspects of local Polish history are ignored or denied in Vilnius is to begin to understand the conflicted history of Central and Eastern Europe and its present resonance. The counterfactual in representing local history derives from a past of shifting borders and transient political and cultural hegemonies. Tidying up such confused pasts has meant streamlining the often-proclaimed postcommunist "return of history" and turning toward myth in a capitalist and postmodern present. This contemporary mythmaking assumes concrete form in restored and reconstructed buildings or in the referencing of a particular tradition.

For instance, Kaliningrad seeks to define itself as the center of contemporary and historical Europe by putting Russian speakers in historical costumes to celebrate the legacies of Immanuel Kant and the Europe of the Enlightenment. Elsewhere, architects and archaeologists scour the local landscape for pasts to rebuild in precise replica, as with the reconstruction of the Grand Duke's Palace in Vilnius. Among the many challenges of such efforts is that the historical examples often have little to do with current reality. The ancestors of peasants from the Central Volga have little to do with Kantian philosophy, while Poles as well as Lithuanians are of great significance to the actual history of the palace in Vilnius. Conversely, how is one to understand the pilgrimage of newlyweds to the grave of Kant in the newly reconstructed gothic cathedral of Kaliningrad instead of to some memorial dedicated to the "Great Patriotic War"?[5] Similar questions are posed by each of the contributors to this volume. The search for a "new historical narrative" for Wrocław that Gregor Thum delineates in chapter 3 below is a red thread that winds through the individual contributions. The path of that search is being paved in the physical terms of brick and mortar and of glass and steel.

The change in meaning attached to places—and the decisions made to conserve, restore, or reconstruct certain historic structures—are part of a process of projecting both new and old images of the city to forge a postsocialist identity. As each municipality decides which extant historical structures to keep in place—and which to demolish—local leaders are adding or subtracting concrete support for one or another historical narrative of place. To build a castle in Vilnius or an Orthodox church in Novgorod is not just to reconstruct a destroyed historic structure. Such historical replicas communicate traditional civic values, indicate urban origins, and may even serve to suggest models of conduct in the present. The impetus for their reconstruction derives variously from the need for political legitimization and a reassertion of local identity and autonomy, which are supported in the concrete recognition of former urban achievements and the retrieval of the "radiant past."[6] The choice of a particular urban past has great implications for the city's present and future identity.

For example, in chapter 6 below, Karl Qualls tells us how the city of Sevastopol has chosen to preserve its grand memorials—reminders of the city's heroic role in Imperial Russian and Soviet history—even though it is now a city in Ukraine. He argues effectively that the idea of a "Ukrainian city" can seem foreign to the residents of a city where Russian history and the Russian language dominate, and where the nearby Tatar settlements serve as heritage-bait for tourists. In chapter 8, Volodymyr Kravchenko, examining Kharkiv, another Russo-Ukrainian city, describes a city poised on the border in its identity building. The continued embrace of Soviet-era monuments and street names sustains a Russian rather than Ukrainian presence. Meanwhile, the European turn in Kaliningrad described by Olga Sezneva in chapter 7 can be understood as an attempt to establish a local genealogy linked to a German and European, rather than Russian, place. Going back to the future in Europe is achieved by folding German history into the common history of all Kaliningraders.

In chapter 2, Nicolai Petro offers a variation on the same theme, in Novgorod the Great, one of the most important cities of medieval Rus'. Its municipal leaders are trying to look ahead by recalling their particular Hanseatic and mercantile history. This particular past provides historical legitimacy for democratic institutions and strengthens the projection of the city into the center of Europe. Yet nothing in the region is quite as simple as political leaders might wish, for the simultaneous restoration of the city's many Orthodox churches to their former splendor recalls an indigenous and peculiarly Russian past. The embrace of Sevastopol's heroic defense of Russia and the Soviet Union, Kharkiv's vitality as a center of Soviet industrialism, and Novgorod's membership in the Hanseatic League all provide meanings—quite different meanings—to guide each city's contemporary residents into its post-Soviet future.

Nostalgia certainly drives some of this postsocialist historical revival of the respective Hanseatic, Hapsburg, industrial, and Kantian "Golden Ages" of Novgorod, L'viv, Łódź, and Kaliningrad—and similar Golden Ages in other postcommunist cities.[7] Yet more is at work. What in these "pasts made present" might engender nostalgia? Though a city's chosen pasts may have very little connection to its contemporary residents, they still have everything to do with their current orientation and aspirations for the future. To return to Strauss and his ideas about the imagery of cities, this process of conceptual appropriation is a central aspect of civic promotion and boosterism with repercussions for the character and form of the postsocialist city.

Rebuilding a centuries-old church that was destroyed three-quarters of a century ago, the contributors to this volume argue, is highly instrumental and future-oriented. As Petro writes, this is a nostalgia that purposefully links "old symbols to new policies." This is a nostalgia that is about seeking a radiant future just as much as recreating a radiant past. In chapter 10 below, Joanna Michlic suggests as much when describing how the image of the promised land that recalls Łódź's industrial past is being employed in the present. In the same vein, the multicultural heritage of cities such as Tallinn, L'viv, and Vilnius serves as a historical platform for projecting integration into a new Europe. But instrumentally reviving images of an urban past can become as much a burden as a resource, as Oleg Gubar and Patricia Herlihy reveal in their discussion in chapter 5 of the "persuasive power of the Odessa myth." One must wonder how the glorious Soviet and Russian pasts of Kharkiv and Sevastopol, respectively, will affect the future of Ukraine. Such considerations are especially apropos when legends of past urban grandeur reveal the poverty of contemporary projects of revival and renovation. Myths put to ideological purpose can stifle the very future that is being embraced.

## Bleak Histories and Current Confrontations with the Past

Myths are attractive in part because the recent history of Socialism and Communism has been so bleak. Moreover, postsocialist ambitions often seem too distant to be appreciated, despite the remarkable transformation of the past decade and a half. A review of urban history over the past century throughout the region conjures up images of revolution, war, genocide, forced migration, rapid industrialization and deindustrialization, colonization, and resettlement. Understandably, postcommunist cities seek to reclaim an exemplary past that preceded all the carnage and dislocation. The radical discontinuities of local history mark urban bodies that had been fed the potent medicines of political, economic, racial, and social ideologies. These potential panaceas led only to physical devastation combined with the purging of collective memories and populations.

The violent "cures" born of ideology involved war, interethnic conflict, authoritarian rule, and many successive five-year plans that radically changed the region's cities. They were converted into fortresses, outposts, and Socialist showcases; were forced to quickly industrialize; and were subjected to the political and ethnic cleansing of their populations. Their active citizens were removed and eliminated, at worst, or disenfranchised and brought under centralized control, at best. A succession of populations were shifted in and out of the cities. These cities' histories were rewritten, in some cases many times over.

In these cities today, as citizens and visitors walk down streets, the outcomes of such radical cures stare them in the face. They confront ever-changing street and place names. To research the history of their city, they have to know its toponymic history. Lemberg became Lwow, which became Lvov and later L'viv, all in one century alone. Wilno became Vilnius, and Königsberg became Kaliningrad. These changes on maps and signs are meant to—and, in fact, do—proclaim the transfer of a country, a state, a region, a city, a neighborhood to a new country or regime.

Nomen est omen. More than the name plates changed in the multiple occupations and reoccupations of historical urban settlements. In the Soviet period, new cities were built alongside the old, with little or no relationship to the structures of the past. The "historic" city was often neglected, unlike in the West, which eradicated historic buildings and structures in the name of "renewal." In the East, it is an irony of history that such neglect, which meant to make history vanish, would ultimately help to conserve the historical "substance" that now literally invites attempts to return to some "radiant past." It is the once modern and subsequently dilapidated Socialist city that now *belongs* to history.

The structural changes in the city shrink in significance when compared with the demographic changes that are part of Central and Eastern Europe's bleak recent history. Entire ethnic and socioeconomic groups were expunged from the urban present—not just the urban past. The successive names given the main streets of many of the cities examined here during the twentieth century—Lenin Street, Hitler Avenue, and Stalin Boulevard—mirror the succession of violent regimes. Only after the fall of the latest authoritarian regimes could such central arteries be rechristened "Freedom Prospect." Along with projecting new urban identities, today's freely elected municipal authorities have another challenge on their hands—to confront the bleak history of Europe's twentieth-century heart of darkness.

## Righting Wrongs?

The various projects of historical urban reclamation described in the chapters that follow entail more than constructing a promising new identity. In some instances, the new street signs, rebuilt churches and civic centers, and re-*embourgeoisment* of the historic city is about trying—however clumsily and sterilely—to right the wrongs of the past century. Contemporary commemorative practices—the building of monuments and museums, the celebration of new holidays, the development of conservation projects, the renamings—are very uneven in their emphases.

In chapter 1 below, Irena Vaisvilaite describes how a museum in Vilnius dedicated to the anti-Soviet resistance by the Lithuanian people tames the city's tortured past by relegating it to a distant view. The historical importance of Jewish culture in Vilnius finds expression in the Vilna Gaon Jewish Museum, which recognizes both the horrific suffering of Lithuania's Jews in the a once-vibrant Jewish community and its contribution to the city.[8] In contrast, the Soviet era is everywhere present in the architecture and in the names of streets in Kharkiv. As Kravchenko discusses in chapter 8, the city stands today as an urban monument to the early Soviet era.

All commemorative acts, no matter how concrete or extensive, cannot recover the demographic mix that had characterized many of the cities considered here. The radical and purging processes of national and ethnic "consolidation" administered to places such as L'viv, Wrocław, and Vilnius made them part of the "new" Europe composed of ethnically homogenous states. This fact gives the lie to the now-fashionable—and thoroughly nostalgic—pretense of multicultural urban societies in a current version of "Europe." In chapter 11 below, Jan Musekamp is right to refer to this as a "facade" in his discussion of Szczecin. In cities that retained some ethnic diversity, such as Tallinn, the multicultural mix and cultural hierarchies shifted drastically as they were forcefully incorporated into the Soviet Union. Russian "settlers" or "colonists," depending on the perspective, changed the complexion of these cities and are now *indigenous* to them.

Other cities—such as Novgorod, Vilnius, Kaliningrad, and Wrocław—had been radically transformed in their form, character, and function long before they began the postsocialist process of fashioning new cultural-geographic and geopolitical identities. After the forced resettlement and industrialization of the Soviet era, the dissolution of the Soviet Union ushered in just one more stage in a succession of drastic transformations in the image and perception of each city. Postsocialist-era shifts in the meanings have had some immediate physical repercussions. Churches used as warehouses or museums dedicated to atheism have been returned to their ecclesial bodies and restored to their original functions. Cyrillic signs brought into the streets of Tallinn and Vilnius after the Baltic states were incorporated into the Soviet Union have been removed, though the Russian populations remain. Some of the Soviet-built architecture in the central city districts has been demolished and replaced in an attempt to quickly gain distance from the ancien régime. Much of the initial physical realignment of the postsocialist city was slowed by the drastic economic restructuring.

*Demontage* was the order of the day in the first years after the end of Communism. Above all, the contributions to this volume demonstrate the new role of choice in configuring the past and the future that now lies in the hands of the postcommunist municipalities, their populations, and the new economic powers in place. Indeed, the transition from Communism to capitalism has given city leaders and builders the opportunity to ask the question "What time is this city?" Their answers reveal tremendous diversity.

## New Markets

Visitors to cities on what was the other side of Europe before the fall of Communism may still harbor images of Socialist cities colored in the industrial shades of gray and brown and accented with occasional dashes of red—quite a contrast to the splash of multiple colors in the capitalist cities that have succeeded them. Urban appearances have greatly changed with the introduction of economic and political choices. The introduction of markets of all kinds, from the street to high finance, has made the cities of Central and Eastern Europe appear and feel more complex, vivid, and variegated. How very different the display of brand name sports shoes and jerseys arrayed in newly designed storefronts in a faraway place like contemporary Sevastopol seem from the shortage-plague markets of the old Eastern Bloc with their limited assortments of shoddy consumer goods. Yet many of the tantalizing consumer goods on display there or along the boulevards of Vilnius or L'viv are there only for nouveaux riches and the new tourists who can afford them. A new and striking inequality is visible in the dress of people walking by cafés in contemporary East Berlin or Warsaw, or in the storefronts and apartment buildings nearby. This fundamental change in social reality reflects equally basic changes in the economic framework that have affected the physical and social fabric of the city.

This new capitalist reality produces alliances rarely seen in Western Europe and North America. For example, as Jörg Hackmann demonstrates in chapter 4 below, heritage preservation and "progressive modernism" are allied in Tallinn because both are seen as cultivating a fresh representation of a *modern* Estonia. But modernism in Kharkiv's city planning and architecture, acquired while the city was the capital of Soviet Ukraine, has quite a different meaning. It derives, as Kravchenko notes in chapter 8, from the attempt to shape the New Man of the Socialist society. The city's dominant architecture of utopian pretensions represents a great accomplishment of Ukrainian and Soviet planning. We see in these contrasting examples how architectural style and types are mixed and matched in an era when nearly all previous symbolic cues have lost meaning.

Part of the contemporary story is to use the symbolism of the built environment to put a community on the map of "Europe." L'viv markets itself as the Florence of Ukraine, whereas Szczecin is in the process of restoring elements of architectural historical distinction to its waterfront. Neither of these cities prints propaganda about its mass housing projects of Soviet vintage. Rather, their leaders and residents want to be seen as having taken a "European turn" (e.g., the one Thum notes for Wrocław in chapter 3) or a "local turn" (e.g., as noted by Musekamp in chapter 11), which employs architectural elements and styles and urban images as signs not only of distinction but also of belonging to Europe.

This positioning throughout history—the reorientation of symbolic space in the city—reaches back to a time before Socialism in a search for historical models that bridge the interlude of Soviet Socialist domination. Sevastopol and Odessa no longer flout their being awarded the Golden Star of Hero of the Soviet Union.[9] The independent interwar years for Baltic cities, as Hackmann notes in chapter 4, provide a different safe harbor of meaning. In L'viv, as Liliana Hentosh and Bohdan Tscherkes reveal in chapter 9, the Hapsburg city of the late nineteenth and early twentieth centuries stands above the twentieth century's contest for dominance among Poles, Ukrainians, and Russians. In L'viv and Vilnius, monuments to the city's founder (Prince Danylo and Grand Duke Gediminas, respectively) reach back to lay the groundwork for the contemporary legitimacy of Ukrainian L'viv and Lithuanian Vilnius.

## Aspirations for the Future—Questions for the Present

The changing meaning and perception of the cities described in this volume depends on a selective cultivation of the urban past, a past whose unabridged version is full of abrupt and violent disjuncture and discontinuity. As local political, business, and cultural leaders and entrepreneurs seek to redefine their communities in a period of transition from a Socialist past to a capitalist present, they offer diverse answers to the question "What time is this city?" Their differing answers display a need for political legitimization, a pragmatic bent, hopes for the future and, sometimes, a willingness to confront some of the darker aspects of local history. The diversity of responses reflects the presence of deep-seated ambiguities felt by many in the region about the "new" Europe and the "old." What should become apparent in reading the chapters of this volume is that the variety of responses to new urban realities indicate the formation of new identities and are attempts to situate place in a new geopolitical context. The symbolism of place has a larger spatial dimension of great pragmatic as well as theoretical import. How these cities represent themselves resonates with all the larger facets of geopolitical transition.

The Baltic cities of Tallinn and Vilnius, now under the umbrellas of NATO and the European Union, demonstrate their relative success in a capitalist context by competing with one another in building modern complexes and skyscrapers. Elsewhere—as in the Russo-Ukrainian cities of Odessa, Sevastopol, and Kharkiv—the new demonstrates far less emotional impact than the old. Soviet symbolism combines with Russian Imperial models to produce an alternative to overt Ukrainianization. Meanwhile, cities with strong regional identities—such as L'viv, Novgorod, and Kaliningrad—are looking even further back in time, to when they were cities quite unlike those of the present, to find the inner resources to enable them to move from the margins of Europe to its center. In the new geopolitical framework, Polish cities such as Wrocław and Szczecin have tentatively approached their historical and largely German "other" in limited patterns of recognition and reinterpretations of the historic city. In Łódź and many cities, the rapid deindustrialization of the postsocialist era has relegated a central element of urban identity to the past and opened up land for future development. Uncertainties about such future development are still pervasive in many of the cities considered here.

How each of these cities reorients itself with regard to the past and future relates directly to its struggles with the contemporary realities of markets and elections that are part and parcel of postcommunist existence. The forces of capitalism and newly formed political constellations are refashioning these cities and promoting new urban imagery and identities—even if they sometimes seem arbitrary. What had been a function of ideology is now one of the proverbial marketplace of ideas.

The remarkably brief period of the most recent radical transformation in urban character, identity, and form "after the fall"—of Communism, of the Berlin Wall, of authoritarian and centralized regimes, of command economies—deserves attention by policymakers and scholars alike. The contributors to this volume seek to initiate this investigation by exploring how each city being examined is attempting to situate itself in a new world order. However radiant these cities' futures may be, the search for their radiant past continues apace. What time is this city? However this question is answered, it locates each city in the *present* discourse of urban life.

## Notes

1. See Anselm Strauss, *Images of the American City* (New Brunswick, N.J.: Transaction Books, 1976; orig. pub. 1961); especially see chapters 2 and 8, which respectively discuss the "symbolic time of cities" and the role of "era and geography in urban symbolism."

2. Alan Dingsdale has appropriately referred to the "new geographies of postsocialist Europe" to raise the question about the new conceptualization for the territory of Eastern Europe and the former Soviet Union. Referring to localities, such as cities he writes: "The conjunction of democratisation and marketisation created localities in new forms of individual and environmental development. Localities were produced by myriad individual decision-makers with contrasting interests and purposes in a multi-scalar renegotiation of places of complex connectivities." Alan Dingsdale, *Mapping Modernities: Geography of Central & Eastern Europe* (New York: Routledge, 2001), 176.

3. The concept of architecture as political culture has perhaps been best summarized in two volumes of essays : *Architektur als Politische Kultur: Philosophia Practica,* ed. Hermann Hipp and Ernst Seidl (Berlin: Dietrich Reimer Verlag, 1996); and *Politische Architektur in Europa vom Mittelalter bis heute: Repräsentation und Gemeinschaft,* by Martin Warnke (Cologne: Dumont Buchverlag, 1984). The subtitle of Warnke's volume, "Representation and Community," points to the hinge pins of this collection.

4. See Henri Lefebvre, *Révolution urbaine / The Urban Revolution* (Minneapolis: University of Minnesota Press, 2003). The term "heterotopy" is also used by Michel Foucault (in *The Order of Things,* in 1967; see transhttp://www.foucault.info/documents/heteroTopia/foucault.heteroTopia.en.html), but Lefebvre's usage relates more thoroughly to the city. It is worth stressing that the urban heterotopy composed of different places within a place (the city) is at once heterochronic as each of the multiple places refers to a distinct time or temporal dimension. One can further elaborate on the concept of heterotopy in this particular context by referring the unused spaces of industrializa-

tion that "opened" so dramatically after the dissolution of the Soviet Union and its economic system.

5. One might further ask how the ethnic German from Kazakhstan and southern Russia who came in the 1990s might pose an effective link to the history of Balitic Germans.

6. For a discussion of the concept of the "radiant past," see Margart Paxson, *Solovyovo: The Story of Memory in a Russian Village* (Washington and Bloomington: Woodrow Wilson Center Press and Indiana University Press, 2005), 90–119.

7. Svetlana Boym has dealt with the literary and cultural concept of "nostalgia" in such urban circumstances and in an especially effective way with regard to Saint Petersburg and Moscow. Svetlana Boym, *The Future of Nostalgia* (New York: Basic Books, 2001). In the context of the postsocialist city, that concept is but one of many significant facets affecting the instrumental use of heritage and history.

8. Important here is the specific reference in this museum to the "righteous ones," Lithuanians who saved Jews, and to the idea of tolerance, embodied in the "Tolerance Center," which is a branch of the museum. Another branch of the museum, the Paneriai Memorial Museum, commemorates victims of the genocide during World War II at the site of their murder. At various inconspicuous sites throughout the city, the borders of the old Jewish quarters are marked. In some places, Hebrew lettering shines through to the surface. And a modest plaque has been erected to commemorate the Great Vilna Gaon, Elijahu ben Solomon Zalman (1720–97), the luminary among the many Talmudical scholars; this plaque is shown in figure 1.10 below.

9. Serhii Plokhy, "The City of Glory: Sevastopol in Russian Historical Mythology," *Journal of Contemporary History* 35, no. 3 (July 2000): 369–83.

# Part I

# European Cities Old and New: Re-creating Medieval Histories

# 1

# The Changing Face of Vilnius: From Capital to Administrative Center and Back

*Irena Vaisvilaite*

Vilnius, one of the Baltic region's most vibrant cities, is booming. And for the past ten years, it has experienced particularly interesting patterns of development. In fact, one could say that its recent development reflects several different epochs of the city's history. The unique mix of historical eras these developments evoke, as well as the unique history of Vilnius, reflects the ways in which the process of urban development is both similar to and different from what is going on in other history-rich postcommunist cities. As in most postcommunist societies, Vilnius's developers and city planners have turned to history to find or define the city's cultural identity, which is fused to a vision of its future and embodied in recent concrete urban developments and government policies.

The restoration of Lithuania's independence in 1990 and the subsequent reestablishment of Vilnius as its capital, after a hiatus of more than two hundred years, entailed revising and reevaluating not only the plans for new development in the city but also the existing urban fabric. Throughout the twentieth century, Vilnius's political and cultural history was the subject of incessant debate. Inherent in this debate are the many narratives of the city's history, which, depending on what era is seen as the most important, changes the city's character substantially, and which in turn cannot help but be reflected in its development.

The earliest references to a city called Vilnius can be found in the letters of Grand Duke Gediminas in 1323.[1] At that time, Vilnius was the capital of a pagan state, which hosted German and Rutenian communities and had a Christian prayer house. By the fifteenth century, Jewish, Karaite, and Tartar communities had been established in the city. When Vilnius became one of the two capitals of the Polish-Lithuanian state in the sixteenth century, the city's Polish-speaking population began to grow substantially, and thus, by the eighteenth century, Polish was its predominant language.

Like other medieval Central European capitals, Vilnius developed two centers: the center of sovereigns, and the center of townspeople. The former consisted of the Lower Vilnius Castle and Vilnius Cathedral, while the focal point of the latter was the Town Hall next to the city parish church (figure 1.1). At the end of eighteenth century, the cathedral, Town Hall, and the Bishop's Palace were rebuilt in the neoclassical style, and open squares were created next to the buildings to emphasize their importance.

## The Development of Vilnius before 1990: From Capital to Administrative Center

Vilnius's era of urban reform before 1990 ended with the division of the Lithuanian-Polish state. Most of the Lithuanian territories of the defunct state were annexed by Tsarist Russia, including Vilnius. Vilnius was no longer the capital but simply an administrative outpost of the Russian Empire, and the Russian authorities began new urban development projects in the city that emphasized the city's Orthodox and Russian elements. This policy was expressed in monuments built in its main squares honoring Russian rulers and their appointees in Lithuania. Remnants of the city's past as the capital of a large empire were destroyed. Most notably, the Grand Duke's Palace and the City Wall were reduced to rubble and removed piece by piece.[2] Russian and Orthodox influences were manifested primarily through the construction of an Orthodox church dedicated to the patron saints of the Romanov Dynasty at the city's highest elevation and the creation of a new axis for the city—the Avenue of Saint George, patron of the Russian state—connecting Vilnius Cathedral to the Neris River. This avenue, the name of which would change

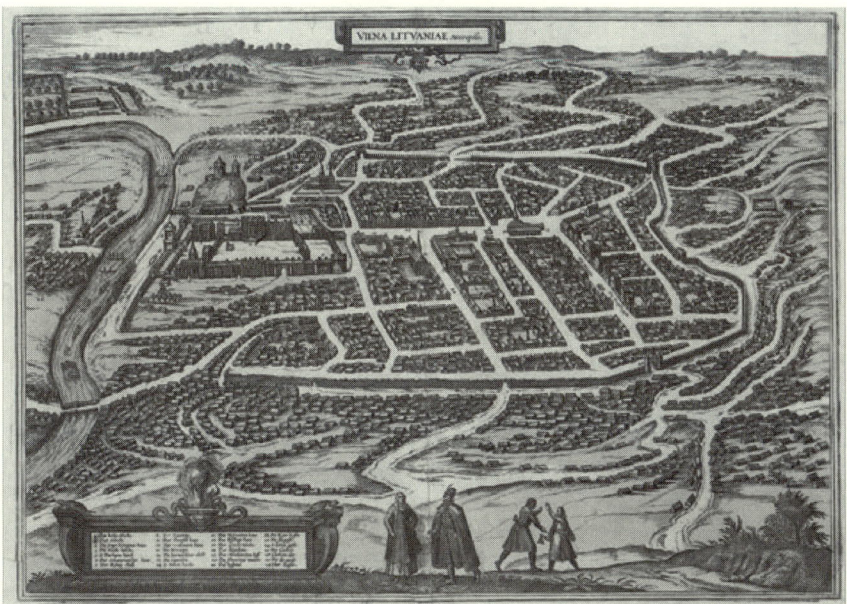

Figure 1.1. The old city plan of Vilnius from Braun's atlas. Photograph by Vidmantas Jankauskas.

every time political power changed hands, was crowned by the magnificent Orthodox Church of the Apparition of the Holy Mother of God, which was constructed to counterbalance the Catholic cathedral. At the same time, this period saw the development of a modern high Polish culture, the formation of the Lithuanian and Belarusan national revival centers, and the mushrooming of Jewish cultural and political organizations.

As the Russian Empire was crumbling at the beginning of the twentieth century, the rise of nationalism and aspirations for sovereignty by the empire's constituent nations ignited a fierce conflict between Lithuanians and Poles over Vilnius. Lithuania declared its independence and created its new state on February 16, 1918. Poland annexed Vilnius and its region by force in 1920.[3] Thus, just as Vilnius was attempting to recover its status as the capital city of the newly independent Lithuanian state, it was again demoted to serving as an administrative center for the *vaivadija* (voivodship, province). In the meantime, Lithuania's state administration was moved to Kaunas. Lithuania did not give up its claims to Vilnius, which made Lithuanian-Polish relations tense throughout the period between the wars.

With the military victory in place, the Polish government moved quickly on urban reconstruction to highlight Vilnius's Polish features and its links to Polish history. Conscious efforts were made to delete traces of Imperial Russia from the city's architecture. In Vilnius, these initiatives did not achieve the scale they had in Warsaw. For instance, not a single Russian Orthodox church was pulled down, although these that had originally been Catholic churches and had been transformed by the Russians into Orthodox ones, they were returned to the Catholic community. Rather, the process was limited to the consistent removal of monuments that had been erected by the Russian government. The heart of an active Polish statesman, Jozef Piłsudski, was buried in Vilnius with the intention of building a statue as a monument. Piłsudski was born not far from Vilnius and had consistently pursued the reestablishment of the old Commonwealth of Poland-Lithuania. Ultimately, however, the idea of his monument in Vilnius was hampered by political vicissitudes.

Polish historians and art historians at Vilnius University (long a stronghold of the Polish cultural elite) initiated careful research into the city's history and architecture with the objective of restoring and rebuilding some of its historically important buildings, such as the cathedral and the Grand Duke's Palace. However, due to the escalating war and Poland's weakening hold on the Vilnius region, fairly few of the construction plans were ever implemented. Nevertheless, the historical research and analysis conducted at that time had a lasting impact on the debate over the city's history.

Polish rule of Vilnius ended when the Soviet Union attacked Poland in 1939 and offered Lithuania an agreement that would hand back control over the Vilnius region to the Lithuanians. Lithuania accepted this offer but, by 1940, the Soviet Union had annexed Lithuania and Vilnius became the capital of a Soviet republic. After Germany attacked the Soviet Union in 1941, control over Vilnius again changed hands, and it was administered by the Nazis for the subsequent four years. Of all previous struggles for control over the city, Vilnius suffered from this occupation the most, for these years saw the establishment of the Vilnius ghetto, from which members of Vilnius's Jewish community were sent to death camps and shooting fields, and which resulted in the tragic decimation of the Jewish community and its cultural heritage.[4]

The Red Army entered Vilnius again in 1944, and military operations damaged part of the Old Town. The war was immediately followed by a mass migration of Poles from Vilnius (and elsewhere in the Soviet Union) to Poland. At the same time, many Jews who had survived the Holocaust left Vilnius as well. Thus, in the space of four years, the Polish and Jewish populations of Vilnius vanished and were gradually replaced by Lithuanians, Belarusans, Russians, and nationals from other Soviet republics.

The Soviet administration planned and carried out the material reconstruction of the city. It demolished the war-damaged old synagogue of Vilnius and decided against the reconstruction of the ruined quarters of the Old Town. It closed the majority of churches, synagogues, and prayer houses of various faiths, as well as Catholic and Orthodox monasteries. And it eliminated the historic cemeteries situated within the city and nationalized private residences.

The Soviet development of the new city center started at the main street of the New Town, which was renamed Stalin Avenue. The Soviet authorities fashioned a former marketplace along this avenue into an open square and erected a statue of Joseph Stalin in its center. After 1956, Stalin Avenue and Stalin Square were renamed after Vladimir Lenin, and a statue of Lenin replaced the one of Stalin. Lenin Square became the most important center for all types of official ceremonies, and state institutions were concentrated around it.

The Soviet administration had planned to eliminate the Old Town completely in the 1950s, thereby obliterating all traces of history (figure 1.2). It closed the cathedral and planned to use the large structure as a garage. It had intended to pull down the Town Hall, and it used the Bishop's Palace as a Soviet Army officers' club. Historic street names were changed to reflect the Soviet reality. For example, Pilies (Castle) Street in the Old Town was renamed Gorky Street, after the Soviet writer Maxim Gorky. In 1953, a new master plan for the city was developed, which induced first gradual and then rapid construction of districts of multiflat houses and factories around the old center of Vilnius (figure 1.3).

Before the plan to destroy the Old Town was implemented, however, the approach to historic city districts and buildings had changed, in tandem with the changing ideology of the early 1960s. Instead of pulling down historic monuments, the Soviets "neutralized" them by emphasizing their aesthetic, rather than historic, aspects. Thus, Vilnius Cathedral and a few other churches as well as the old Town Hall were converted into art museums and again opened to visitors. The Provost's House of Vilnius Cathedral, which had once been home to a number of famous personalities from Lithuanian history, was reconstructed and promoted as a fine example of Gothic and Renaissance architecture.

In the 1970s, efforts were made to improve the image of Vilnius through the consistent reconstruction and modernization of the neglected and dilapidated Old Town. Recreational and cultural institutions—such as a youth

Figure 1.2. A drawing of the new center of Vilnius—Stalin Square—in the planned reconstruction of Vilnius, 1953. Courtesy the Municipality of Vilnius.

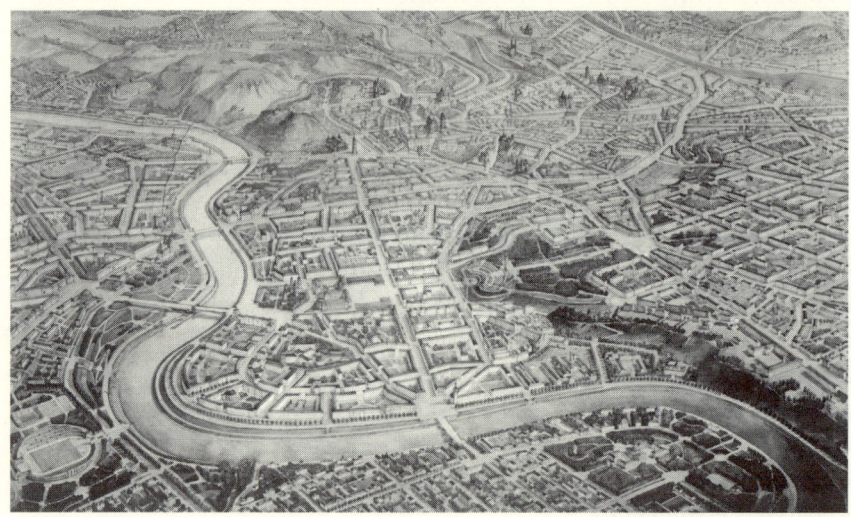

Figure 1.3. A panoramic drawing of the planned reconstruction of Vilnius, 1953. Courtesy the Municipality of Vilnius.

theater, a puppet theater, and an exhibitions hall—were relocated in the Old Town. The Monument Restoration and Design Institute of the Lithuanian Soviet Socialist Republic conducted architectural studies of buildings in the Old Town to document their artistic value. Restored houses in the Old Town were converted into comfortable contemporary apartments. Attracted by the ambience of the Old Town—with its narrow streets, picturesque interior courtyards, and dramatic views from top-floor windows—many artists began moving there, often opening workshops and studios. Nevertheless, the vast majority of the Old Town remained unrestored and living conditions there were primitive, often cut off from essential utility networks. To accelerate the Old Town's renaissance, the authorities paid less attention to the historically accurate reconstruction and the retrieval and restoration of old architectural elements, preferring to simply construct buildings approximating traditional architectural forms.

Despite the historical and architectural studies conducted by the Monument Restoration and Design Institute, the restorers of the Old Town avoided making specific allusions to the historic families or ethnic groups that had lived in its buildings, or putting accents on the history of buildings and quarters that would link them to their past functions. For instance, the historic Jewish quarters were among the first to be restored, yet there was no indication given to identify the former ownership of those buildings. Nor was there any mention of the ghetto set up by the Nazis that had occupied these same quarters. Because the majority of Vilnius's inhabitants at that time were first-generation newcomers and because prewar publications about the city were hardly accessible,[5] the history of its quarters and buildings rapidly fell into oblivion. The Old Town became merely an architectural museum: full of beautiful buildings, but without clear markers identifying their historical uses or inhabitants.

A number of publications and newspaper articles praised the architectural features of the newly restored quarters, such as tiny walk-through backyards, narrow winding alleyways, and sculptural walls.[6] A few "medieval" restaurants and cafes were opened in the Old Town during this period. For the most part, they occupied basement spaces and became very popular because of their warm ambience. The Soviet Union's tourism program grouped Vilnius together with Riga and Tallinn as cities that represented "Western" styles of architecture, from the Gothic, Renaissance, and Baroque periods. Yet, in the 1960s and 1970s, tourism from the Western world was very restricted in Vilnius. Most of the city's visitors were Americans of Lithuanian origin.

In the 1970s, some of Vilnius's historically Lithuanian features were revealed, and the University of Vilnius became a locus of this activity. To celebrate the university's four-hundredth anniversary in 1978, the authorities commissioned a number of artworks to commemorate people who had helped to preserve Lithuania's language and culture. The baroque church of Vilnius University was restored after a long period of neglect. It was turned into a museum of scientific thought. The old university palace was restored, too. Paintings, tapestries, and murals were commissioned to decorate the walls of these buildings. Some of the most important of these are the gallery of sculptural portraits featuring university professors from the sixteenth through the nineteenth centuries, by the sculptor Konstantinas Bogdanas; a monumental fresco that relates the history of the university with its key figures, on the ceiling vaults of the university bookshop, by Vytautas Kmieliauskas; and tapestries on a Lithuanian folksong theme, by the textile artist Ramutė Jasudytė, which decorates the university rector's office.

At the same time, this initiative endeavored to conceal the Polish contribution to the University of Vilnius, especially during the interwar period, when the university was completely Polish. This resulted from a tacit agreement between the university's intellectuals and the Nomenklatura, who shared a negative view of the Polish occupation of Vilnius. Both Poles and Lithuanians are extremely sensitive about this issue, because it was a historic turning point for the city. No one likes to broach the topic of the city's tragic demographic changes during those years, or to address the circumstances under which it was returned to Lithuania. Rather than contend with the Lithuanian-Polish conflict, which led to a complicated history of resistance and collaboration with both the Nazis and the Soviets, the Lithuanian cultural elite and artists were keen on symbolically anchoring Vilnius to its Lithuanian heritage, rather than to its Polish or Jewish communities, in the city's restoration projects.

In the early 1970s, Justinas Marcinkevičius published the poetic drama *Katedra* (The Cathedral), in which Vilnius Cathedral was depicted as a symbol of Lithuanian ethnicity and a pantheon of historic Lithuania. Like many other contemporary works, it ignored the multiethnic and multifaith character of the Lithuanian Grand Duchy, which included the area that is now Belarus and a part of present-day Ukraine. During the Soviet period, this aspect of Lithuanian history could be addressed only indirectly through poetry or art, but not in historical studies. Probably the most interesting example of this is the historical novel *Pogodalis,* by Petras Dirgėla, published in 1978. It raises the question of why the Great Duchy of Lithuania never became a maritime power and instead focused on conquering the eastern Slavic lands rather than turning to the West.

The 1970s also saw a renewed interest in modernizing the city of Vilnius. In contrast to the 1950s plan, the updated 1978 Master Plan for Vilnius envisioned creating new districts rather than destroying the cherished Old Town. According to the new Master Plan, the city center would to be moved from the Old Town, and the new buildings that would make up the new center would encompass both banks of the Neris River. First, a new community center was developed on the bank of the river opposite the Old Town (figure 1.4). The series of new structures included a large department store and household services center and the Museum of the Revolution. Two hotels were built in this area, one of which was the city's first high-rise building, Hotel Lietuva, which became the architectural apex of Vilnius. Later, the hotel was balanced by high-rise apartment buildings that were constructed in the surrounding areas. The ideas represented in the new Master Plan reflected a substantial reshuffling of the urban space, which focused on the development of new residential districts around the city. The Neris River was transformed from setting the city's margins into an internal town river

Figure 1.4. A model of the design for the new center of Vilnius on the right bank of the Neris River, 1974. Courtesy the Municipality of Vilnius.

Figure 1.5. A model of the two new centers of Vilnius, 1980s. Courtesy the Municipality of Vilnius.

(figure 1.5). The river's edge became a picturesque riverbank, which wound through the city, creating the illusion of a channel system. To connect the old city center with the new residential districts, a new road network was developed and bridges were constructed.

Within the new city center, new large-scale public, political, and cultural buildings were constructed. For example, the Palace of the Supreme Council of Lithuania (architect, Algimantas Nasvytis), the Central Committee of the Lithuanian Communist Party (architect, Vytautas Čekanauskas), and the Opera and Ballet Theatre (architect, Nijolė Bučiūtė) were scattered along the bank of Neris River next to a footbridge that connected the two parts of the new center.

As new districts and buildings sprang up throughout the 1970s, the Old Town's City Hall became the core of a cultural district, which included the newly built Art Exhibition Center, the Youth Theater, and a reconstructed Cinema Maskva (Moscow). The museums were concentrated around the cathedral, which had housed the Gallery of Art since the 1960s. The History Museum and Museum of Applied Arts were situated nearby. As old buildings were transformed to serve new purposes in the Old Town, a number of portrait monuments were constructed on small squares throughout the city, dedicated to various Lithuanian Communist Party leaders. This was followed by the installation of several sculpture groups and memorials to celebrate important personalities from Lithuanian national culture. Thus, the city's new monuments and sculptures offered hints of its Soviet and national context, which had been stripped away before.

The construction of private residences was banned within the Old Town and the new city center of Vilnius. Therefore, most people lived in the new residential districts, which with every new plan and initiative grew in concentric circles from the city center. The urban reconstruction of Vilnius was not unique in the Soviet Union, in which all Soviet republic capitals and major cities were undergoing planned changes. In the general context of the Soviet Union, Vilnius was often recognized for architectural design and the overall high quality of its urban renewal projects. In fact, the designers of the new residential district of Vilnius received Soviet Union awards. In 1968, the architects Birutė Kasperavičienė, Bronius Krūminis, and Vytautas Zubrus, the designers of the first residential district Žirmūnai in Vilnius, were given the USSR State Prize. It was the first time a prize of this rank had been awarded for the idea of urban development and construction of communal housing in the Soviet Union. It very much boosted the prestige of Lithuanian architects. In 1974, the architects Vytautas Čekanauskas, Vytautas Balčiūnas, Vytautas Brėdikis, and Gediminas Valiuškis received the Lenin Prize for the residential district of Lazdynai in Vilnius.

Thus, in the postwar period, Vilnius's radical demographic and political changes were reflected in the city's changing material culture. In the absence of the Poles and Jews who had once shared the city with Lithuanians, by the 1970s and 1980s, Vilnius had become a typical Soviet capital, in which elements of ethnic culture and history were obscured and in which urban plans and reconstruction focused on creating a modern Soviet city. These plans changed with every ideological shift, and Vilnius adopted the identity of an administrative center and an outpost of the larger Soviet Union, looking to Moscow for direction. Yet aspirations for the economic autonomy of Lithuania, triggered by Mikhail Gorbachev's perestroika, soon developed into a movement for national and state independence, which was followed first by symbolic, and then actual, separation from the Soviet Union. This political shift launched a new phase of redevelopment in Vilnius.

## From Administrative Center to Capital

In the process of breaking free from the Soviet Union, the nations of Lithuania, Latvia, and Estonia regained the statehood they had lost in 1940. Among the many other changes brought about by the breakup of the Soviet Union, the capitals of these three former Soviet republics once again gained the status of independent state capitals. In Vilnius, practical political steps taken to re-create the state capital spurred the initial changes in material culture. From 1988 to 1991, Soviet monuments were pulled down and removed. Street names from the interwar period were reinstated to replace those that had been changed by the Soviets, and new streets were named after Soviet dissidents and national heroes.

As new state institutions were created, projects to restore the symbols and monuments associated with the independent Lithuanian state became a priority. Special attention was given to the most important symbols of the interwar state, such as the monuments symbolizing Lithuanian Independence in 1918 and those representing the leaders of the national revival movement and other historical personalities. Because the majority of such monuments had been destroyed by the Soviet regime, most of them had to be reconstructed.

The projects to reerect the monuments were initiated by so-called initiative groups of citizens and of cultural and political figures. The reconstruction usually was based on existing pictures. For example, the monument to Duke Vytautas the Great in Kaunas was reconstructed on the basis of photographic records. Sometimes the remains of the destroyed monuments would be found. In other cases, it was possible to use existing models, as was the case with the monument in the town of Širvintos, which was dedicated to the victims of the battle for the Lithuanian Independence. This monument, originally created by the renowned sculptor Robertas Antinis, was recreated by his son from the models his father had preserved. Probably the most important memorial site in Lithuania, the complex dedicated to the Unknown Soldier in the courtyard of the History Museum in Kaunas, was also recreated from photographs and old blueprints.

In general, government institutions in post-Soviet states returned to the buildings from which they had operated before 1940. The Soviet authorities had been eager to obliterate every memory of the Baltic states' independence and had therefore changed the function of those buildings, often downgrading their prestige by turning them into schools or headquarters of nongovernmental organizations. Yet this general process of reclaiming former government buildings was somewhat different in Vilnius compared with Tallinn and Riga. Due to the Polish occupation of the region surrounding it, Vilnius was not a capital during most of the Independence period. Therefore, the architectural symbols of the first Republic of Lithuania—namely, the Presidential Palace, Parliament, Government, and State Bank buildings —were situated in Kaunas, the provisional capital. Thus in 1990, when Lithuania proclaimed the restoration of its independence, there were no buildings to which the Seimas (Parliament) could return. Instead, the Seimas continued to work from the building of the Supreme Council of the Soviet Republic of Lithuania. Similarly, in 1991, the Government of the Republic of Lithuania settled in the former palace of the Central Committee of the Lithuanian Communist Party.[7] These decisions were practical, because these buildings were readily available for the new government institutions to occupy. But by using the Soviet buildings, the new democratic regime maintained some continuity with the Soviet regime, which was troubling to some. In 2004, discussions were initiated by Parliament members regarding adapting of the Seimas building to better suit a Parliament that actually functioned, in contrast to its predecessor, which had a merely decorative function.

The Palace of the Supreme Council of the Lithuanian Soviet Socialist Republic—which was designed by Algimantas Nasvytis and Vytautas Nasvytis and constructed in 1980, and which currently houses the Seimas—was originally intended as a venue for the semiannual meetings of the Soviet (quasi-)Parliament. The assembly of the deputies—selected along the lines of gender, nationality, education, and profession—and the single-party and trade union membership voted for the projects of predrafted and already-discussed laws, and the sessions lasted no longer than several days. Thus most of the volume of the building is dedicated to representational purposes; it features a hall similar to a theater foyer and grand, lofty staircases that do not actually reach all the floors. The General Assembly Hall and other larger conference rooms have no source of natural light. Most offices are cramped with room only for a table and a chair. Thus, the building is really not designed to accommodate a busy and intense work routine for Parliament.

Since 1991, Parliament has relocated some of its functions into adjacent structures that formerly housed the Finance Ministry of the Lithuanian Soviet Socialist Republic and the Trade Union Central Council. The Chancellery, Press Center, and technical services of Parliament are now located in these buildings. In 2006, the Parliament of the Republic of Lithuania decided to ask the government to fund the construction of new conferencing premises.

As Lithuania began its integration into the international community, it was urgently necessary to find buildings and premises for new ministries and embassies.[8] It then became obvious that Vilnius had long been a provincial town, ruled as it was from the outside from the nineteenth century to the beginning of the twentieth century. There was a clear shortage of reasonably modern embassy buildings, and although there were magnificent mansions from the seventeenth and eighteenth centuries (when Vilnius was a capital of the Grand Duchy of Lithuania), these buildings were old and in disrepair, and it was impossible to renovate them quickly.[9]

Instead, new authorities were situated in buildings that reflected the times of the Russian Empire, Polish rule, and the Soviet period, while embassies were offered private villas built in the nineteenth and twentieth centuries, the majority of which were situated in the residential districts of Žvėrynas, Antakalnis, and Naujamiestis (New Town), which were favored by the Soviet Nomenklatura.[10] As these districts filled with foreign representations and ambassadorial residencies, the prestige that these districts had during the Soviet era was reinforced.

The French and Swedish governments purchased sixteenth- and eighteenth-century buildings on the central street in the Old Town to house their embassies, and they invested much time and money to restore the buildings and to make them functional, representative spaces in the very heart of Vilnius. Embassies and cultural centers operating under the auspices of foreign representations made an important contribution to the internationalization of the city.[11] As a result, the foreign owners of the properties in the Old Town led the city's changing orientation. Thus, the French and Swedish governments had more influence than any entity based in Lithuania on the initial renovation projects in the city.

## Nation Building

The first step in urban planning that was connected with nation building was the design contest for the monument to Grand Duke Gediminas, who moved the capital of Lithuania from Trakai to Vilnius in the fourteenth century and is considered to be the founder of Vilnius. It was decided by the state to build a monument in Cathedral Square, near the land of the former Lower Castle. The first phase of the design contest received a number of project proposals, which revealed a divergence between Romantic and modern interpretations of history. The contestants representing the Romantic trend found inspiration in the concept of the nineteenth-century monument. They presented ideas for figurative monuments of representational character enacting the story of the founding of Vilnius and showed the duke as its founder.

Another group of contestants offered a modern, abstract type of design—symbols that did not present a finite interpretation of the event. Patriotic citizens and politicians who were involved in the evaluation process rejected the modern forms offered by these artists and supported the traditional, representative monument for the "founder of the capital." Thus, the Romantic interpretation prevailed, and after heated discussions and two more design contests, the project by Vytautas Kašuba (1915–97), a sculptor who had lived most of his life in exile, was selected (figure 1.6).

The erection of the Gediminas monument in Cathedral Square was seen as restitution of the square's prominence in the city, which had long been usurped by Lenin Square during Soviet rule. After the removal of the statue of Lenin, the former shrine for the official authorities was downgraded to become just another city square and was not very popular among the citizens. The square was once again given its original name, Lukiškių aikštė (after a former suburb of Vilnius). Under the rule of Tsarist Russia, the market square was used as an execution site for the participants in the 1863 uprising. The former KGB Building located next to the square currently houses

Figure 1.6. The monument to Grand Duke Gediminas, 1998. Sculptors: Vytautas Kašuba, assisted by Mindaugas Snipas. Photograph by Vidmantas Jankauskas.

the Museum of Anti-Soviet Resistance. Along the lines of this anti-Soviet theme, organized groups of resistance members and Soviet political prisoners proposed redesigning the square to make it the site of a Freedom Monument and, accordingly, changing the name to Freedom Square. The Municipality of Vilnius has organized a competition to select a redesign and monument project. Two rounds of the competition have taken place, and the third is still in progress. The debate about the concept of the future monument is very similar to the one that preceded the building of the monument to Duke Gediminas. The initiative groups, on the one hand, are promoting the idea of a figurative, representational piece embedded in the sculptural tradition of the nineteenth century. Art critics, on the other hand, are encouraging the participants to look for forms that would send a message independent from the period of Soviet domination. It remains to be seen who will win this round.

After a referendum on the issue, the Seimas restored the institution of the presidency in 1992,[12] which automatically triggered the need to find a space for the President's Office and residence.[13] In the absence of a suitable historic building, a group of historians, architects, and archeologists suggested reconstructing the Lower Castle—the former residence of the Lithuanian dukes, which had been destroyed in the late eighteenth century.[14] This idea enjoyed wide public support, because people identified the reconstruction of the Duke's Palace with the restoration of Lithuanian independence. In a sense, it is thought that the reconstruction of the palace would help Lithuanians "recover" their lost history and heritage, which had been repressed by the Soviet regime.[15]

Situating the President's Office in the restored palace was intended to enhance state building in Lithuania.[16] By returning the original function to Cathedral Square—which had been the center of political power in the city—Vilnius could also reclaim its status as the capital of a nation. According to supporters of the initiative, rebuilding the Grand Duke's Palace in the Central European Renaissance style would not only serve as a monument to the statehood of Lithuania but also symbolize Lithuania's strong connection to Europe.[17]

Archeological excavations at the sites of Vilnius's destroyed castles had been under way since 1980, and a few buildings, such as the Arsenal, had been reconstructed in the late 1980s. During the Soviet period, the Lithuanian public closely followed the findings of the archeological explorations of the cathedral's catacombs and the remains of the Grand Duke's Palace. A group of archeologists involved in the research found evidence that Vilnius had already been a capital city dating before the reign of Gediminas, dating back to the times of King Mindaugas (1203–63), the first known monarch of Lithuania. Thus, rebuilding the Lower Castle meant in fact rebuilding the oldest cradle of the Lithuanian state. This idea was further emphasized by the new name given to the project, the Reconstruction of the Palace of the Sovereigns, despite the fact that historians had always referred to the structure as the Grand Duke's Palace. Presumably, for the proponents of the project, "Sovereigns" is preferable because it emphasizes the sovereignty and independence of the Lithuanian nation.

At the beginning of the national revival movement, the idea of reconstructing the Palace of the Sovereigns was supported by many archeologists, historians, nationalist politicians, and older citizens. Émigré organizations were particularly supportive as well. However, the idea also had its opponents; a group of young cultural historians criticized the idea of rebuilding the palace because there were insufficient historical data necessary to reconstruct the building, which had been destroyed two hundred years ago. Moreover, they argued that the reconstruction process itself would tear up the authentic remnants of the palace, which were still being studied by archeologists. A number of solutions for conservation of the sites were offered.

These controversies, in addition to meaning that the construction of the palace would take many years, prompted the then-president of the Republic of Lithuania, Algirdas Brazauskas, to give up on the idea of having the President's Office in the territory of the Lower Castle. Instead, he initiated the plan to renovate and convert the former Bishop's Palace of Vilnius, which had housed some government and public institutions during the nineteenth and twentieth centuries,[18] into the presidential residence and office. Upon completion of its renovation, the Bishop's Palace was inaugurated in 1996, and thus it became the first building representing the state after many decades.[19] This was balanced with another space for official events across town, which was next to the Parliament Palace. Cathedral Square, by contrast, remained a town square, where no official events are held, only public concerts on special occasions.

The idea of restoring the Palace of the Sovereigns did not fall into oblivion, however. Supporters of its restoration continued to exploit the arguments of the symbolic importance of the project. They emphasized that with the restored Palace of the Sovereigns, Lithuania would become a full-fledged member of the family of countries in Central Europe, with a capital and an old residence of sovereigns. However, there was no agreement regarding the purpose of the palace. Archeologists and historians were interested in the palace as an essential representative element of Lithuanian history, while the Lithuanian diaspora wanted to see exhibits representing the history of the state in the palace. Different initiative groups proposed staging "live historical performances" for young people and tourists. The administrators of the National Art Museum, who were ardent advocates of the restoration idea, supported the idea of using the palace to house an art museum, and that the state would allocate additional funds to supplement its collection with authentic art works from the sixteenth and seventeenth centuries.[20] There were some expectations that it would be possible to raise private funds for restoration, but in the end very few donors were found. Stakeholders managed to persuade the government and Parliament that the restored Palace of the Sovereigns would be suitable for holding state celebratory events as well.

In 2001, the so-called Lithuanian Millennium Program was launched, which was approved by the government to prepare for the thousandth anniversary of the first mention of Lithuania's name in a description of the

Figure 1.7. The construction of the Palace of the Sovereigns, 2005. Photograph by Vidmantas Jankauskas.

martyrdom of the missionary and archbishop Bruno (Saint Boniface) in the annals of the Quedlinburg Convent. State funding for the restoration of the Palace of the Sovereigns was an important part of the program, according to which its restoration must be completed by 2009. The palace is intended to host all official events that cannot be held in Parliament or the President's Office (figure 1.7).

## The Old Town: Museum or Theme Park?

The heritage protection movement was one of the most important public phenomena of Gorbachev's perestroika and glasnost. This movement sought to undo the damage done by Soviet-era revisionism and propaganda by striving to restore historical truths and resisting the ideology-based management of the nation's heritage. From an ideological point of view, Vilnius's Old Town was a minefield; the mere existence of its buildings reminded people of many things that the watchdogs of ideology had tried hard to conceal, namely, the rich political, religious, and diverse ethnic history of Vilnius.

Under glasnost, the heritage protection movement focused on two things: the meticulous restoration of the architectural heritage of Vilnius, and restoring the historical context of its buildings. The movement's leaders believed that Vilnius's Old Town was a unique territory that needed to be protected from economic activity as well as from inconsistent or historically inaccurate restoration projects. This was done primarily through their own propaganda projects, which focused on educating the general public. One such initiative was the book *Dingęs Vilnius* (Vanished Vilnius), by the architectural historian Vladas Drėma, which was published in 1991. In it, Drėma describes buildings in the Old Town that were destroyed or have vanished. The book's plentiful illustrations succeeded in stirring up a desire to bring Vilnius back to where it was before all the painful changes of the nineteenth century. This desire was well in line with the claims of "restoration" or "restitution" of the state and society of Lithuania that prevailed in the early years of Independence. This period of historical reconnection coincided with the restoration of many institutions and organizations that had functioned before 1940. People were talking about "returning" to Europe and the "restoration" of democracy and property rights. Therefore, the ideas of "restoration" and "restitution" also came up often in the ongoing conversation on urban development.

This vision, however, had to be adjusted to take into account the consequences of privatization, the decentralization of the city's administration to the municipality, and the economic hardships of the first years of Independence. In 1990, Parliament passed the Law on Local Governance, according to which the responsibility for urban development and planning rested with the municipalities. Thus, the responsibility for Vilnius's Old Town was shifted from the state authorities to the city's municipal government.

Meanwhile, the process of privatizing residences was initiated, enabling tenants to become owners of their apartments. This process in turn created a vibrant real estate market in Vilnius, and, consequently, skyrocketing prices for apartments in the Old Town, which was one of the most prestigious locations in the city. The buyers of the buildings in the Old Town were mostly owners of the first private restaurants and hotels. Thus, from the Old Town's humble beginnings in 1990, when it only had two hotels and ten restaurants and cafes, in fifteen years, its number of hotels increased fivefold and it had nearly a hundred restaurants, cafes, and bars.

Before 1940, quite a large share of the real estate in the Old Town belonged to various religious communities, and it was restored to those communities by the state in the early 1990s. As a result, a large share of the Old Town's properties ended up in private hands. These properties, especially buildings used for worship, had been severely neglected during the Soviet period, and resources to rebuild them were scarce. Thus, to raise funds to restore their houses of worship, religious communities began renting out their restored properties. Overall, the resident population in the Old Town decreased, while commercial activity became more intense, which made it necessary to coordinate heritage protection and commercial activities and also to clearly differentiate the responsibilities of the state and those of private persons.

Unfortunately, the Municipality of Vilnius did not possess adequate experience with heritage protection or sufficient administrative capacity to confront the many issues that had been raised. Municipal offices had very small budgets, and some institutions that had existed during the Soviet period had been substantially reorganized or abolished. Meager state financial resources during the first years of Independence affected the provisions of the first Law on Immovable Cultural Heritage, whereby a large part of responsibility for research and reconstruction of architectural heritage was shifted to the owners' shoulders. Thus, the restoration and modernization of the Old Town, once a government function, was transferred to private hands. The law, however, failed to clearly allocate responsibility for the supervision of reconstruction and research, and it mandated only insubstantial fines from those who violated it.

The State Heritage Protection Commission was set up by Parliament in 1994, to advise the government and Parliament on heritage protection issues. The commission's decisions are not binding, because it does not have any tools to directly affect the actions of both private and public persons or to implement its proposals, most of which survive on paper only. As a result, arbitrary behavior in restoring the Old Town became the norm, which produced a number of reconstructions, extensions of buildings, and adjustments for commercial purposes—which showed little or no concern for historical accuracy or cultural preservation. The worst manifestations of such arbitrary behavior were the enlarged windows of retail shops situated on the ground floors of buildings, added extensions in interior courtyards and in attics, and the construction of a variety of structures used for advertising. Despite the objections of cultural activists, heritage buildings were used to house businesses that were incompatible with the historical purposes of those buildings. The situation was aggravated by the slow and irrational stocktaking by the government of Vilnius's material culture and slow progress in setting requirements for the use and privatization of heritage sites.[21] Lithuania's economic boom in recent years has led to so many arbitrary decisions concerning the Old Town that it has necessitated making amendments to the Law on Immovable Heritage, which were finally adopted in 2004, after long and heated arguments with owners over the uses of material culture. The new law provides for much stricter sanctions for violating heritage protection laws, but it also provides reimbursements for heritage protection expenses from the state budget.

Heritage protection specialists have been berating the rapid pace and poorly managed renovation of the Old Town, which threatens its overall architectural coherence, especially in the context of the rapidly disappearing undeveloped areas—another peculiarity of Vilnius—where citizens used to have orchards and gardens. Increasingly, more architectural forms and details are emerging that are completely foreign to the Old Town.[22] The restaurants, as well as linen and amber shops, focus on luring tourists with architectural ornaments characteristic of wooden rural architecture, in stark discord with the architecture of the stately houses of the nobility and wealthy citizens that line the streets of the Old Town. Fast food chains opt for flashy, colorful shop windows and signs (figure 1.8). Luxurious boutiques selling clothing from famous European designers have enlarged shop windows and employ modern architectural forms. In the summer of 2006,

Figure 1.8. A chain fast food restaurant in the center of the Old Town on Pilies Street. Photograph by Vidmantas Jankauskas.

the monument protection community was outraged by the removal of an entire section of a wall, which was replaced by the clothing shop "Class," with a glass wall incorporating black marble columns with golden capitals, a detail totally foreign to the modest architecture of Town Hall Square. Ongoing criticism, protests, and allegations of corrupt practices in issuing advertising permits have forced the Department of Cultural Heritage Protection under the Ministry of Culture to replace the head of the Vilnius Heritage Section.

The idea of restoring the Old Town, which emerged at the same time as the idea of restoring the Palace of the Sovereigns, has undergone an interesting process of evolution. Heritage protection enthusiasts wanted to highlight the oldest layer in Vilnius, the loss of which was related to the changes introduced by the authorities of Tsarist Russia in the early nineteenth century—namely, removing the ruins of the Palace of the Sovereigns, the City Wall of Vilnius, and other historically important but neglected buildings. In traditional historiography, these objects are related to the Lithuania state's times of prosperity, and therefore the desire to get them back was only natural. The restoration of the Palace of the Sovereigns has already advanced; research on the City Wall is still ongoing, but the idea of rebuilding the entire wall—initially very attractive to many citizens—does not garner much support nowadays.

In 1994, the Old Town was recognized by UNESCO and placed on its World Heritage List. In their petition for this recognition, the Lithuanian heritage protection specialists emphasized that during the period between the thirteenth and eighteenth centuries, Vilnius was a prominent regional center, linking Lithuania with the region that today includes Belarus, Ukraine, and Poland. The idea of proposing the Old Town for the World Heritage List came about in 1989, in the midst of the movement for independence; it was meant to emphasize that Lithuania is part of the cultural and political space of Europe.

In 1996, Lithuanian experts (together with experts from the World Bank, Denmark, Scotland, and Norway) drafted a strategy for reviving the Old Town, which provided that the Old Town must become a protected memorial of history, urban development, and culture. After the government approved the strategy, its implementation was started in 1998. A total of €20 million was spent to fund different programs under the strategy until 2003. The majority of this amount was used by the Municipality of Vilnius for improving the general infrastructure of the Old Town, rather than for the purposes of researching or adjusting the heritage objects. The municipality used the funds to install street lights, create public spaces (particularly in Cathedral Square and its surroundings), reconstruct the avenue crossing the New Town, fix cobblestone streets, and restore facades. The reconstruction of the historic Town Hall Square was also started. All these initiatives improved the appearance of the Old Town and made it more secure and attractive for tourists.

Yet none of the funds were used to improve the internal infrastructure of the Old Town, leaving this expensive task to private owners. This is why the development of the Old Town has been far from even in recent years; private buildings have been undergoing rapid renovations, but municipal buildings look shabby.

Seeking to attract private funds, the municipality set up the Vilnius Old Town Renovation Agency. This agency developed a program, which was named Vanished Vilnius after the book by Drėma mentioned above. The program provided for the restoration of the city's historic Jewish quarters and encompassed a program of handcrafts, ethnographic trades, and fairs. This program was intended, according to the municipality, "to promote prosperity of handcrafts and ethnographic fairs in the Old Town of Vilnius, to revive bygone traditions of trades and handcrafts, to promote establishment of artisan workshops, shops, live museums and ethnographic pubs in the Old Town by making efficient use municipal property in the Old Town."[23]

The heritage protection movement in Lithuania highlighted the multinational character of Vilnius. The restoration of the historic Jewish quarters is intended to serve as a reminder of the rich history of the Jewish community in Vilnius. For this purpose, an information billboard was put up on the site of the Old Synagogue of Vilnius, and a decision was made to reconstruct two of the Jewish quarters that were demolished between 1944 and 1956.[24] The reconstruction of one of them is about to be completed—it will look the same as it did before 1940. However, only the external architectural features of the quarters are being reconstructed from the available designs and pictures; the top floors of former houses for poor people will be used for luxurious condominiums with garages in the basement, and premises on the first floor will be rented for commercial purposes (figure 1.9).

Figure 1.9. The reconstruction of one of the Jewish quarters, 2005. Photograph by Vidmantas Jankauskas.

This reconstruction of the Jewish quarters has been the subject of much criticism. Heritage protection specialists have demanded that the unearthed seventeenth- and eighteenth-century basements be preserved, and the tenants in the surrounding houses have complained about damage to the green spaces in the nearby parks, which are not numerous in the Old Town, and about the excessive density of the rebuilt houses. Critics have been pointing out that the reconstruction of the Jewish quarters is yet another commercial project enabling investors to profit from skyrocketing real estate prices (in 2004, prices for housing in Vilnius increased by 30 percent on average). The authorities issued a call for tenders to reconstruct the Old Town, and they leased the land in the Jewish quarters for a period of ninety-nine years to the successful tender. For the purposes of memorializing the Jewish past of the quarters, a part of the premises on the ground floor in one of the reconstructed buildings will be transferred to the municipality, which subsequently will hand it over to the Vilna Gaon Museum of Jewish Culture. The museum is planning to set up an exhibition of the twentieth-century Jewish art. It is worthwhile mentioning that the ever-intensifying commercialization of the Old Town has already led to more and more objections from the community against the construction of new buildings there. The project to reconstruct the second Jewish quarter has been much criticized as well, because implementing the project would eliminate even more green space along the Old Town's main street and produce yet another luxury apartment complex.

Recently, heritage protection specialists have been concerned that the municipality's Old Town renovation program has digressed somewhat from its original goals. One example of this is what has happened in the quarter of historical trades along the former City Wall. The original program intended that it be used for year-round fairs, so the quarter would manifest "the suburban culture and interaction between town and country." Though the Old Town Renovation Agency has leased premises in or near the Old Town at preferential terms to eleven galleries of handcrafts and trades (e.g., stained glass; historical smithery; workshops for making *verbos,* the intricate flower arrangements used for Palm Sunday; Easter eggs; and amber galleries), the workshops are not well placed to attract tourists, and there is little information about them. Instead, the neighboring land plots have been prepared to be leased for the construction of private houses, "provided that there will be spaces designed for the presentation of historical trades."

Unfortunately, the majority of the so-called revival projects intended to combine history and commerce have nothing to do with the history of the city of Vilnius or its traditions, and they have largely failed to ensure the proper revival and presentation of these traditions. The reasons behind this failure come down to the Old Town Renovation Program itself, which has never clearly distinguished Vilnius's history and traditions from those of the rest of Lithuania. Thus, for instance, the idea of reviving historic cuisine has thus far been limited to the fast food chain "Čili," which opened a branch in the Old Town featuring a few traditional rural Lithuanian dishes on its menu and a pseudohistorical interior design. Another example is the fairs and festivities arranged in the Old Town, which are based on rural and ethnic Lithuanian traditions rather than on the cosmopolitan customs of the historic city. No efforts are being made to revive the traditions of Polish, Russian, Tatar, or Jewish Vilnius or to highlight the histories of these communities in Vilnius. The whole of the city's rich Jewish history is acknowledged only by the memorial plaque for the Great Vilna Gaon, Elijahu ben Solomon Zalman (figure 1.10), on Švento Ignoto Street, which commemorates the Zionist Congress attended by Theodor Herzl, and by memorial plaques to the victims of the Holocaust.

Despite the fact that various state institutions and nongovernmental organizations are making efforts to consistently commemorate all the locations in Vilnius related to Lithuanian history, during a period of fifteen years, very few plaques have been put up to honor outstanding personalities of Belarusan, Polish, or Russian origin. This is largely due to an attitude that these ethnic groups themselves should determine where and how their heritage should be preserved and should finance their own initiatives. Meanwhile, some members of Parliament have proposed an entire program of monuments aimed at the "Lithuanization" of Vilnius by installing ornaments and monuments that point to the history of Lithuania as a whole, not just Vilnius.[25] Of course, these initiatives exclude from this interpretation of Lithuanian history the histories of people from other nations who have been living in Lithuania for ages. As a result, Vilnius is still perceived as the capital of ethnic, rather than historic, Lithuania.

Making an assessment of the developments in the Old Town over recent years, more and more voices are demanding a stronger role for the state in preserving the neighborhood's historical and cultural heritage. Critics emphasize that the municipality is interested, first and foremost, in the income generated from leasing real estate in the Old Town and only secondarily in preserving the value and shaping the image of the Old Town. The municipality is often criticized for incompetent decisions, and allegations of corruption are also abundant.

Figure 1.10. The memorial plaque for the Great Vilna Gaon, Elijahu ben Solomon Zalman. Photograph by Vidmantas Jankauskas.

In response to this criticism, the Municipality of Vilnius formed the Heritage Protection Unit in 2004. The unit is responsible for drawing up, together with the city's Urban Development Department, a detailed plan for the Old Town through 2011, including a plan for developing its monuments. Presentations of some parts of the draft plan to the Old Town community have incited protests against the intended further development of the area. One recourse has been to approach UNESCO experts, who have commented on the menacing changes that the plan would make in the neighborhood's urban fabric, and the approval of the detailed plan has been postponed.

## Capital of Lithuania and Regional Center?

What has been happening in Vilnius's Old Town in recent years is part of the process of the city's general development. Privatization, the transition to a market economy, and the strengthening of local government have encouraged rapid, and rather laissez-faire, development. In 1988, the ban on the construction of private houses was lifted, resulting in the rapid expansion of Vilnius's suburbs and the transformation of former collective garden territories into neighborhoods of private houses. The booming construction of single-family homes required the expansion of the official city boundaries. Having nearly halted due to economic difficulties between 1991 and 1993, the construction of residential multiflat buildings started slowly moving from a standstill; and since 2000, the development of residential construction has accelerated at a high rate, helping to revitalize some parts of Vilnius that had been abandoned since 1991. For example, residential developments have replaced the former Soviet military base, which was situated close to central Vilnius. Yet, because they are seeking to maximize their profits, construction companies are not investing in the development of infrastructure and landscaping. The absence of centralized planning has resulted in a lack of kindergartens and schools to accommodate these new neighborhoods. Thus, these new districts of single-family housing lack a broader urban development plan.

In Soviet times, Vilnius had no small shops or private service business. The needs of the citizens had to be met by shopping and domestic service centers. Although many small entrepreneurs appeared after 1991, there were no essential changes in the Soviet situation. Since 1995, Vilnius has seen the rapid growth of large shopping complexes on its outskirts with various kinds of shops and entertainment centers. Chains of privately owned shopping centers have pushed small businesses located in the city center out of the market. Thus, families living in the center usually shop in the complexes on the outskirts, leaving central Vilnius largely to tourists.

Recent architecture in Vilnius has tended to be emphatically "cosmopolitan" and sterile. The choice of such architectural designs has been dictated by the taste of investors and the desire of architects to speak "the common European" language. New structures, with their neutrality and generic similarity to what is being built in other European capital cities, stress that Vilnius and Lithuania are indeed part of Europe.

The Urban Development Department of the Vilnius Municipality tries to maintain an ambitious urban development approach in central Vilnius. Shaping this part of the city is associated with the aim declared by the municipality to make Vilnius a regional center of business, political life, communication, and culture by 2015. This aim is being pursued through Vilnius's yearly participation in the Cannes Architecture and Investment Fair and attempts to attract as many international events as possible to the city. For this purpose, the municipality has supported the construction of a new sports arena and is planning to build a new stadium, convention center, and entertainment park. Funds from the private sector have been attracted to these projects, but substantial municipal and state funds are also being sought. As a result of the efforts made by the municipality and with the approval of the Ministry of Culture, the Council of Europe has chosen Vilnius to be a European Culture Capital in 2009.

The municipality's idea for the new city center is to create the image of a vigorous and modern city. The Vilnius Master Plan from 1978, which first envisaged the city center spreading on both sides of the Neris River, was used as the basis for drafting the new Master Plan. This plan, which was developed and introduced to the public in 1998, aims to shape the right side of the river as "the new mount of Vilnius" through the construction of high-rise buildings. Next to the privatized and renewed former Intourist state-owned Hotel Lietuva, the new Europos Square was developed, with office buildings rapidly being erected around it (figure 1.11). One of the most prominent is the new Vilnius City Municipality Building. An additional bridge was built to facilitate traffic from the Old Town to the other side of the river (figure 1.12).

The relocation of the Municipality Building from the nineteenth-century building on Gediminas Avenue in the historic center to the opposite bank of the Neris River was the first step in implementing the plan to relocate state institutions from historic buildings to new specifically designed office buildings and to sell the state-owned buildings in the historic city center, where property values are much higher. Therefore, high-rise buildings designated for both business and residential use are planned adjacent to the new Municipality Building, along the main transport artery that starts in the Old Town. This area has until recently been largely one of single-floor wooden houses and industrial structures; thus, the contrast between the old architecture and the new glass-and-steel skyscrapers is extremely sharp (figure 1.13). The completed buildings are nearly double the height originally envisaged in the 1978 Master Plan, and they pierce the skyline of Vilnius—which, according to the requirements of heritage conservationists, was supposed to be dominated by the tower of the Upper Vilnius Castle (figure 1.14).

The development of the right bank of the Neris River has raised heated debates throughout the city. Those concerned about the preservation of historic Vilnius have been outraged by the change in the scale of the city, as the new high-rise buildings have dwarfed the towers of the old city. However, a significant proportion of Vilnius's citizens have a positive view of the new part of the city and approve of its further development.[26]

The nature of the debate surrounding a "Vilnius of skyscrapers" also depends on the broader cultural context. Soviet cultural ideology attributed

Figure 1.11. Europos Square, showing the new Municipal Building, 2005. Photograph by Vidmantas Jankauskas.

Figure 1.12. The Bridge of Mindaugas, connecting Cathedral Square and the new center of Vilnius, 2005. Photograph by Vidmantas Jankauskas.

Figure 1.13. Old and new on the right bank of the Neris River. Photograph by Vidmantas Jankauskas.

Figure 1.14. The right bank of the Neris River, showing the new skyline of Vilnius, 2005. Photograph by Vidmantas Jankauskas.

skyscrapers to the capitalist lifestyle, and the United States in particular. This ideology, and contact with the German and French intellectual traditions, conditioned the typical view of the older-generation intelligentsia toward the United States as a country with no respect for cultural tradition, history, and one's roots but only with a prospering business and consumer culture. Yet even this social group appreciates the freedoms and rights enjoyed by U.S. citizens. For the majority of the Lithuanian population, their experience of the United States is largely known through the vigorous community of political refuges that fled communism in 1944, and therefore is first and foremost associated with success and well-being. The viewpoint of the younger generation toward the United States was reinforced by the difficult transitional period, when Lithuania was working toward accession to the European Union and NATO. U.S. support for membership in these organizations and the model of the liberal market economy that was established in Lithuania have made the United States an ideal for Lithuanians' own political and economic ambitions. This is why the citizens of Vilnius perceive skyscrapers in "the new Vilnius" as symbolic of modern life, progress, and economic ambition. And the "newness" of the architecture, materials, and technologies used for these skyscrapers is accentuated by their placement next to the concrete blocks of Soviet architecture—symbolizing the coveted well-being and renewal of life.

It is significant that the first major event in the new Europos Square was the concert to celebrate Lithuania's accession to the European Union on May 1, 2004. Cultural events, city celebrations, and festivals supported by the municipality generally begin in this square. There is also an indoor sports arena near the square, and there are plans to build a stadium, an entertainment center, and a convention center next door. Thus, the aim here is to create a dynamic public space that will attract citizens not only during the day but also in the evening.

The planned relocation of state institutions to new buildings on the right bank of the Neris River would have an impact on the historic part of the city. Currently, many state institutions are located in the so-called New Town, the nineteenth-century city. The value of property there is particularly high, necessitated by the high demand for land to build apartment buildings and hotels. If the space currently occupied by offices became available, the new buildings would significantly increase the vitality of the New Town because, despite all efforts, this part of the city empties out in the evenings, while life bustles in the Old Town, where most restaurants and cafes are located. To bring more life to the New Town, its central street is closed to car traffic by the municipality in the evening and on weekends, turning it into a pedestrian zone.

Since 1998, the community has become increasingly active in Vilnius's planning processes. Its contribution is felt in its demands on the city government to pay attention to not only the macro but also the micro fabric of the city. Though municipal planners are concerned with major city zoning measures and planning ceremonial and public spaces, community demands are most often oriented toward the improvement of living conditions. Citizens demand to preserve and regenerate green spaces, resist overly dense developments, and would like to have control over what types of businesses move into their neighborhoods. Very often, such aims are presented under a heritage conservation cover, demanding the preservation of Vilnius as it was—"untouched." The facts that citizens are essentially supportive of the city's renewal, while also wishing to preserve the city just as it was, are not necessarily contradictory. While engaged in updating the functions of various neighborhoods and buildings, one may also desire to retain something of the essential features of Vilnius—the diversity of ways of life and the openness that have left visible marks on its fabric.

Even in the most recent city plan, the development of postcommunist Vilnius has relied heavily upon earlier development ideas. On the one hand, attempts have been made to give the city back its history, though the interpretation of this history has been largely influenced by the debates of the first half of the twentieth century regarding the city's ethnicity. On the other hand, there have been attempts to create a new, modern city using guidelines mapped during in the Soviet era that were aimed at separating the old part of the city, with all its history and symbolic representational spaces, from the new city center, where daily public life will focus. Thus, the idea of creating two city centers, which is typical of Central Europe, has been revived on a new level. However, heated discussions about this idea will continue for quite some time.

## Notes

1. See the most recent critical edition of the Gediminas letters: S. C. Rowell, trans. and ed., *Chartularium Lithuanie res gestas magni ducis Gedeminae illustrans* (Vilnius: Vaga, 2003).

2. V. Urbanavičius, ed., *Vilniaus Žemutinės pilies rūmai* (Vilnius, 1999).

3. On the Vilnius question, see T. Snyder, *The Reconstruction of Nations: Poland, Ukraine, Lithuania, Belarus* (New Haven, Conn.: Yale University Press, 2003), 52–72.

4. S. Atamukas, *Lietuvos žydų kelias* (Vilnius: Alma littera, 1998); N. Schoenburg and S. Schoenburg, *Lithuanian Jewish Communities* (Northvale, N.J.: Jason Aronson, 1996); M. Greenbaum, *The Jews of Lithuania: A History of a Remarkable Community 1316–1945* (Jerusalem: Gefen, 1995).

5. Books and periodicals published from 1918 through 1940 were securely locked away in special library units in the Soviet Republic of Lithuania; to access them, a special permit from the security services was required.

6. J. Glemža, *O pamiatkovych upravach architektonickych pamiatok v Litowskiej SSR,* Ochrana pamiatok 7 (Bratislava, 1971); R. Kaminskas, *Praeities paminklai ir šiandiena* (Vilnius, 1983).

7. On November 7, 1991, the Law on the Takeover of Property of Lithuanian Communist Party and Communist Organizations was enacted.

8. The first foreign representation in Vilnius was that of Sweden. It was opened on August 27, 1991, in a small Old Town flat in Vilnius. During Soviet times, the Ministry of Foreign Affairs had three employees and an office in a small villa. When the staff of the ministry started growing rapidly, the ministry was moved to the building of the Council of Ministers of the Soviet Republic of Lithuania.

9. Residences of the prominent old Lithuanian families—Sapiegos, Radvilos, and Sluškos—were handed over to the army or turned into prisons in the nineteenth century. Historical and art research of those residences was conducted during the times of the Polish Republic, but they were not renovated. The Soviet authorities did not take care of the residencies for ideological reasons rather than a shortage of funds.

10. From 1950 to 1989, the construction of private houses was banned in Vilnius, and only multiflat buildings were built. The single-family homes and villas of the end of the nineteenth and beginning of the twentieth centuries were nationalized by the Soviet authorities. In an attempt to provide reasonable accommodation for embassies, in 1991–92 various institutions and organizations were relocated from "embassy-type" buildings to other premises.

11. It should be noted that in the vicinity of embassies, national restaurants and cafes started emerging, a completely new phenomenon in Vilnius. Thus, Italian and French cafes appeared close to the centers of Italian and French culture, a few Italian shops were established in the neighborhood of the residence of the Italian ambassador, a Ukrainian restaurant was opened next to the Ukrainian Embassy, etc.

12. The Law on Presidential Elections was enacted by Parliament in December 1992. The first presidential elections took place in February 1993.

13. The office of the elected president was first located in one wing of the Parliament Building. Such logistic agglomeration of two state powers started drawing criticism in no time.

14. The defense wall of the Lower Castle of Vilnius, a number of other buildings in the territory of the castle, and the Vilnius city wall were pulled down in 1799 in attempts to modernize the city of Vilnius. Patriotic historiography predominantly claimed that by doing so, the Russian Empire was seeking to delete all traces of Lithuanian and Polish statehood. See J.Kłos, *Wilno: Przewodnik Krajoznawczy* (Wilno, 1937), 28.

15. The Soviet Union made efforts to create a joint history of the state by highlighting the link of small individual national states with Russia and by hushing up the history of their independent statehood. Academic studies of the Great Duchy of Lithuania and its culture were restricted for fear that such studies might step up the nationalistic inclinations of Lithuanians, Belarusans, and Ukrainians. The history of Soviet Lithua-

nia was also poorly studied, and thus 1986–87 marked the beginning of intensive studies of the Grand Duchy of Lithuania, repeating the publication of previously banned historical studies produced in 1922–40 in Lithuania and in 1945–90 in exile.

16. During Soviet times, the castle of the old capital of Lithuania—Trakai—was reconstructed, with struggling and many ideological hardships. In the national revival of the mythology of the nineteenth century, this castle serves as a symbol of majesty of the old state—the Grand Duchy of Lithuania. Lithuanian Communist Party leaders had to be on the defensive against the Kremlin over this decision. Therefore, the reconstruction of the Grand Duke's Palace was presented as the act of creating the nation and as a natural consequence of regaining the sovereign statehood of Lithuania.

17. During the years of the national revival in the nineteenth century, the Grand Duchy of Lithuania was identified with the ability of the Lithuanian nation to create and maintain its own state. When a new wave of the national revival movement started in the 1980s, the role of the Grand Duchy was interpreted in a slightly new light, mostly because of the efforts of Lithuanian intellectuals abroad. The Grand Duchy became an example of peaceful coexistence of cultures and faiths, a state that emphasized multinational nature and religious tolerance—a state with a *modern* tradition of statehood. During its first years of Independence, the tolerance and ancient origins of Lithuanian statehood were very much emphasized by politicians.

18. The headquarters of the governors of the Russian Empire were established in the former Bishop's Palace at the beginning of the nineteenth century. From 1922 through to 1939, it was the Palace of the Polish Republic. After World War II, the purpose of the building was changed several times, until finally the House of Artists settled there.

19. The Square of the Presidential Palace was turned into a representational space where the state flag flies during state holidays and an honor guard is posted. Official state receptions are held in the interior courtyard of the palace.

20. Until 1987, the National Art Museum had its exposition in the nationalized Cathedral of Vilnius. When the cathedral was reopened for worshippers, the museum lost its representational exhibition space in the historic center of the city.

21. The Government of Lithuania approved the Provisions of Heritage Register only in 2005.

22. R. Čepaitienė, *Vilniaus senamiesčio sampratų raida: Miestų praeitis* (Vilnius, 2004), 49–57.

23. See http://www.vsaa.lt.

24. One of these quarters—bordering Rūdininkų, Dysnos, and Ašmenos streets—was damaged during the war and was pulled down by the Soviets; another one—between Šv. Jono, Gaono, and Švarco streets—was almost completely destroyed during the war and was cleared away by the Soviets. See http://www.vsaa.lt.

26. The proposal was made to Parliament by a Social Democrat, Vytenis Andriukaitis, in 2004.

26. In a survey of Vilnius's citizens in April 2005, more than half the respondents had a positive view of developing the right bank of the Neris River, 16 percent had a negative view of the renewal of Vilnius in this area, 18 percent were neutral, 62 percent indicated that they support further development on the right bank and new investment, 16 percent expressed their disapproval, and another 17 percent indicated a neutral position with regard to further development on the right bank. See http://www.vilnius.lt/doc/Atsk-VNOsaviv.doc.

# 2

# The Novgorod Model: Creating a European Past in Russia

*Nicolai N. Petro*

> The arrow of our geopolitical compass is turning. Time is moving forward so fast that the past has become increasingly relevant.
>
> —Vladimir Kagansky[1]

## Novgorod in Russia's Memory

Once regarded as the cradle of Russian democracy, commerce, and learning —"our own Russian Florence," as Prince Eugene Trubetskoi once dubbed it—Novgorod has for centuries served as a beacon for Russian reformers. Since the collapse of the Soviet Union, the region's leaders have used the historically based myth of the medieval Novgorod Republic to promote local reforms. Before describing how they have done so, we must briefly explain the political significance of the Novgorod myth by delving back into the city's unusual civic history.

From its inception, the two most distinctive features of Novgorod were its ethnic diversity and confederated system of administration. The city's earliest records describe it as a mixed community of Slavic and Finno-Ugric peoples. The names of two of the city's five boroughs, as well as several elected officials, are clearly of Finnish origin.[2] Perhaps the need to keep such a diverse constituency together first led settlers to adopt the intricate network of formal and informal institutions that preserve popular sovereignty and the republic's independence for more than four centuries. These included the popular selection of princes, the election of magistrates (*posadniki*) as well as their counterweights, the people's tribunes known as *tysiatskye,* and neighborhood assemblies that sent delegates to the citywide popular assembly known as the *veche.* The Novgorod Republic's political ideal was one of local self-sufficiency, which modern-day Europeans would recognize as subsidiarity.[3]

The ultimate seat of civic authority was the citywide town meeting known as *veche,* a body similar in origin to a parliament. It ratified treaties, invited princes, declared war and peace, set taxes, conducted foreign relations, and served as the supreme court for public disputes. Much of its time, however, was consumed by the election (and removal) of the city's two executive officers—the city magistrate and the people's tribune, who were elected simultaneously each year. An additional constraint on abuses of power was provided by the custom of requiring that all state documents (except trade agreements) carry the archbishop's blessing, given in the presence of both the magistrate and people's tribune, and witnessed by the official representatives of all five boroughs.[4]

The Cathedral of Saint Sophia served as the de facto State House of the republic, intertwining church and civil administration in accordance with the Byzantine view that good government required the consent of both the people and the Church. The archbishop of Novgorod had his own military regiment, and he was also occasionally asked to administer particularly difficult border territories. The Church in Novgorod also took an unusually active role in commerce, with Novgorod's priests and deacons being active entrepreneurs and traders.[5] As one historian put it, the Church in Novgorod blessed the accumulation of wealth, participated in it, and helped to administer it for the republic.[6]

That wealth was legendary. At the height of the Hanseatic League, Novgorod was its fourth-largest trading port, with commercial ties comparable to those of Venice and Genoa (archeological excavations in the city have revealed coinage from England, Persia, and even African cowry shells).[7]

During the fourteenth and fifteenth centuries, there were two or three permanent foreign trade settlements in Novgorod, hosting as many as 150 to 200 foreign merchants annually (not including up to two assistants for each merchant).[8] With a main market that, in the sixteenth century, reportedly hosted 1,500 shops for a population of only 35,000 to 40,000, trade had a perceptible impact on the city's quality of life and created a prosperous class of burghers, traders, and artisans (figure 2.1).[9]

Having come into contact with Western Europe quite a bit earlier than Moscow thanks to this trade, Novgorod played a central role in the spread of Latin learning in Russia. The first translation of the Bible into modern Russian and the first Russian encyclopedia both appeared in Novgorod. Russia's first Greco-Slavonic Academy was opened in Novgorod in 1706 by two graduates of the University of Padua. They subsequently prepared

Figure 2.1. Residents of Novgorod still commonly speak of living on either the "Sophia side" or the "trade side" of the river. Both are seen here, on the cover of a collection of postcards from "Lord Novgorod the Great." Saint Sophia's Cathedral is in the foreground, and the white colonnades across the river show Prince Yaroslav's Court, the site of a large public marketplace during the Middle Ages. Photograph by A. Kochevnik; used by permission of the city administration of Novgorod the Great.

teachers for the country's first fourteen grammar schools.[10] All these developments have led some historians to surmise that, had Novgorod avoided annexation by Moscow, Russia would have opened up to the West two or three centuries earlier.[11]

Even so, by the end of the fifteenth century, a fortunate location on the trade route from Northern Europe to Constantinople, and a political culture that rewarded economic entrepreneurship and gave the lower classes a modest influence on government, had allowed Novgorod to amass a territory nearly half the size of European Russia—the largest state to emerge in Europe since the Holy Roman Empire. Just as important, despite repeated attacks from Mongols, Swedes, Teutonic, and Livonian crusaders, it managed to preserved a republican form of government for more than four hundred years, until it fell to Ivan III, grand prince of Muscovy, in 1471.

That, however, is not the end of Novgorod's remarkable story. The deeply ingrained notion of local self-government survived. In the seventeenth-century street elections, the election of the city magistrate, and even town meetings, slowly reasserted themselves over the Muscovite administrative system.[12] Novgorod even retained its own exchequer and monetary system.[13] Thanks to these, the city's political system survived well into the seventeenth century, as evidenced by the fact that at its first opportunity to leave Muscovy—the Swedish invasion of 1611—Novgorod opted for separation and welcomed the Swedes.

Dim echoes of popular resistance to Muscovite rule lingered on even into the nineteenth century (figure 2.2). When Tsar Alexander II instituted the "Great Reforms" of 1864, calling for the creation of institutions of local self-government in cities and villages, Novgorod was one of the first regions to petition that the principle of self-rule be extended to the national level as well.[14]

As the centuries passed and Novgorod's political and cultural distinctiveness dissipated, the symbols and values of the Novgorod myth retained a surprising potency in Russian literature. They even emerged as a dominant theme in the Decembrists' uprising against Tsar Alexander I.[15] Since then, they have become a fixture of political reform efforts, even into the twentieth century.

It is therefore not surprising to find that in post-Soviet times the Novgorod myth has been picked up by scholars, writers, and political activists. Russia's foremost medieval archeologist, Valentin Yanin, has suggested that Novgorod has a stronger claim to being the forerunner of today's Russia than Kyiv because, while Muscovy inherited its centralized form of gov-

Figure 2.2. The monument to one thousand years of Russian history, erected in 1862, stands in the center of Kremlin Park and remains the most widely recognized symbol of Novgorod. It commemorates Russia's leading statesmen, writers, religious, and military leaders but, in deference to local sensibilities, omits Ivan the Terrible. Photograph by Nicolai Petro.

ernment from Kievan Rus', Novgorod preserved its political pluralism and strong commercial ties with the West.[16] Lest his point be lost on the current political elite, Yanin adds: "Our current rulers could learn quite a bit from the history of ancient Novgorod."[17] Many popular writers and essayists have highlighted Novgorod's political significance for the present, suggesting that the true "Slavic path of development" was not Muscovy but Novgorod, with its extensive regional pluralism in politics and commerce.[18] In May 1999, Vladimir Ryzhkov, then a young, aspiring politician, and now a leader of the political opposition in the federal parliament, actually proposed moving Russia's capital to Novgorod because it was "the birthplace of Russian republicanism."[19]

Today's writers and historians appeal to Novgorod's distant past for the same reasons that their ancestors did—because it brings present-day political debates into sharper focus. The impact of the Novgorod myth has been most pronounced, however, in the city where the visible architectural symbols of the past survived to make it, in the academician Dmitry S. Likhachev's words, a living lecture hall.[20] It is to this past, or rather to its popular image, that local leaders turned when the ideals of the Soviet era shattered.

## The Medieval City as Modern Political Symbol

The regional elite's usage of the Novgorod myth has gone through three distinct phases. First, the Novgorod City Soviet vigorously publicized the Novgorod Republic as a model, thereby helping to delegitimize the Soviet era. Second, civic leaders linked symbols from Novgorod's medieval past to a new, long-term vision for the region. Finally, having become conscious of the political utility of Novgorod's symbols, the local government openly embraced them to build public support for new policies.

### *Creating a Better Past*

Because the Cathedral of Saint Sophia was synonymous with the independent spirit of the Novgorod Republic, it is not surprising that in Soviet times it became a prime target of the atheist regime and was eventually closed in 1929. Perestroika, however, allowed local religious activists to challenge the status of Russia's oldest cathedral and, when the Diocese of Novgorod and Staraya Russa was reconstituted in July 1990, these became outright demands that Saint Sophia be reopened as an active church (figure 2.3).

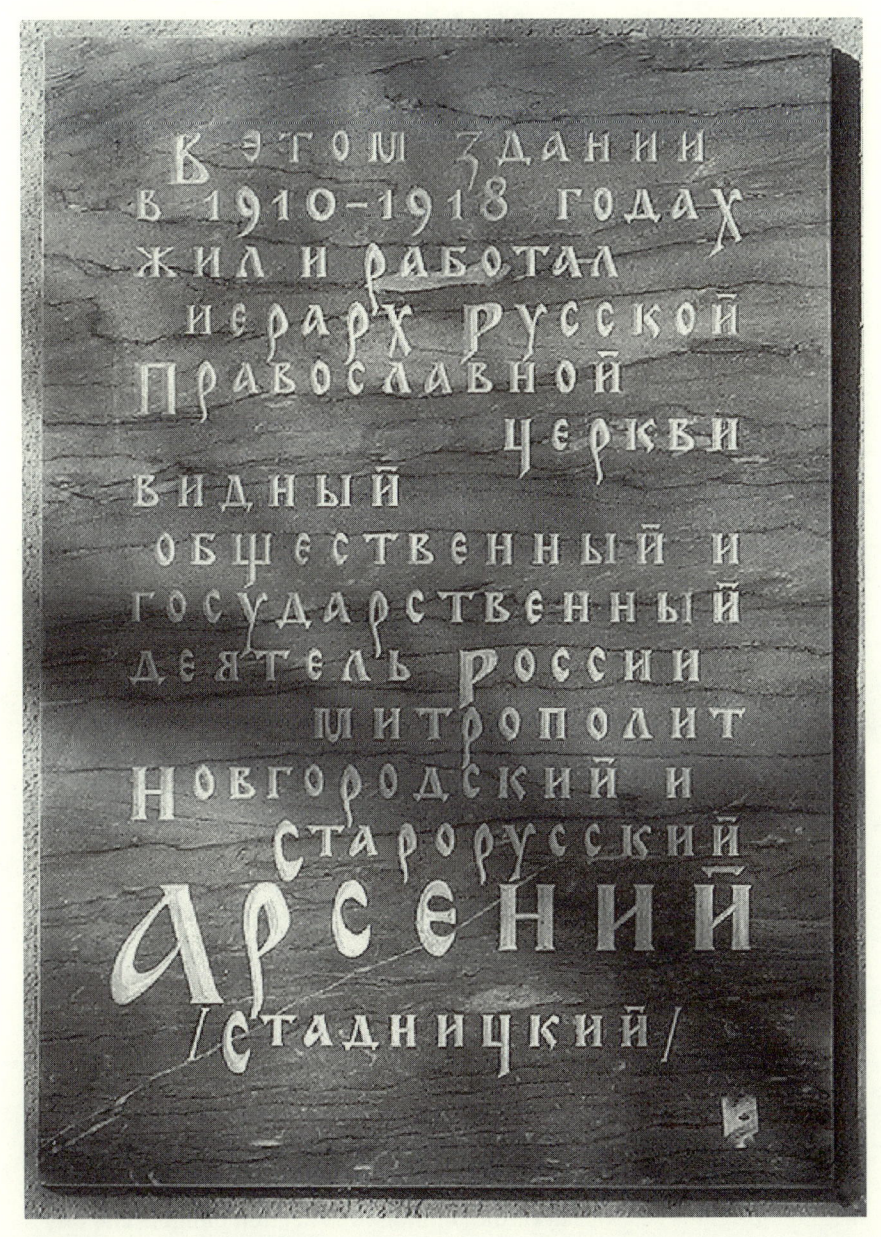

Figure 2.3. A plaque in Kremlin Park, put up shortly after the fall of Communism, commemorates the metropolitan of Novgorod, Arseny Stadnitsky, who led the diocese from 1910 to 1918. He was arrested in 1919 and subsequently exiled; the plaque refers to him as a "prominent social and political personality of Russia." Photograph by Nicolai Petro.

The issue was embraced by many different segments of Novgorod society. Russian nationalists saw it as a means of reasserting Russia's cultural sovereignty, local democrats supported it as a way of undermining the Communist Party of the Soviet Union, and reform-minded Communists pointed to it as proof of the party's ability to change with the times.

Saint Sophia began to receive an inordinate amount of local press coverage that stressed its role as the symbolic unifier and protector of Novgorod. In 1989 the Novgorod Writers' Union founded a new weekly newspaper, called *Veche,* that served as a forum where diverse segments of the local intelligentsia could popularize key components of the Novgorod myth and appeal for public action. Thanks largely to the efforts of this broad local constituency, on August 16, 1991, the Cathedral of Saint Sophia was restored to the Russian Orthodox Church. The significance for the political life of the region of this early successful collaboration among civic groups is hard to overestimate. It has come to be regarded in the region as a model for church-state relations, and it is commemorated annually in the local media, not just as a church holiday but as a turning point in the region's history.

The role of the Orthodox Church at this very critical juncture serves to underscore an aspect of Russia's contemporary cultural (and political) landscape that is often overlooked: its "clericalization." One critic of this phenomenon, Vladimir Kagansky, complains that things have gotten so out of hand in today's Russia that a cityscape is now widely regarded as "truly cultural" only to the degree that it has been clericalized. He has aptly referred to the reconstruction of old churches and monasteries as "the most important visual sign of the new era," particularly when seen against the backdrop of a decaying city infrastructure. The result is not only a stunning new visual symbolism but also new patterns of social behavior, with routines that transform the entire city.[21]

One certainly sees evidence of this within the city limits of Novgorod the Great, as the city was known in its earlier glory and is now again known. The mayor and City Council have cosponsored the construction of a magnificent new cathedral in the city's most populous district, promoted supported religious programs on local television, and subsidized an "experimental" religious school out of the municipal education budget. The city's many public festivals and commemorations still begin, as usual, in the center of the city in Kremlin Park, but now they are typically preceded by a brief liturgy at Saint Sophia, which is advertised right alongside the public event. All in all, more than one hundred and ten Orthodox churches have been reopened in the Novgorod region over in the past decade, more per capita than in any other region in Russia.

Looking back, we can say that the success of these early reformers in wresting control of the city's main historical and cultural icon from "Moscow" was a turning point. It galvanized local reformers into run for public office, and in September of 1989 the reformist electoral association Veche captured nearly one-third of the seats in the regional legislative assembly, and nearly half the Novgorod City Soviet. The leadership of the new Novgorod City Soviet of People's Deputies openly identified itself with the Novgorod myth and, for nearly four years, conducted an intense media campaign to educate the populace about the virtues of republican Novgorod.

The main instrument of this campaign was the city newspaper *Novgorod*, which is distributed free of charge to every family. In its premier issue, the editors promised to devote special attention to local history, and they appealed to the intelligentsia to "help us become aware of our historical past and, by connecting it with the present, more clearly see the road ahead."[22] The chair of the City Soviet, Oleg Ochin, expressed deep regret at how much of Novgorod's ancient heritage had been lost, and then launched into a panegyric that leaves the reader with no doubt about where the new city leaders intended to look for guidance:

> What a sense of pride those Novgorodians must have had in their contacts, not only with their own countrymen, but with the foreigners who came here in large numbers ... curious about the people who had placed such a rich city among the marshes and decorated it with magnificent cathedrals, who ruled over an expanse larger than most in Europe, and were nearly all literate, ... a people who knew the value of free speech and who, unlike the Church obscurantism and court intrigues that held sway in Europe, created a unique democratic construct—the Novgorod state, a republic in the Middle Ages. In my opinion, we have yet to fully appreciate the historical importance of this phenomenon, which can and must serve as an inspiration for the tasks before us.[23]

The City Soviet's most striking initiative was purging the city of all its Soviet-era street names. A local history professor turned City Council member, Vasily Andreyev, cultivated the idea in the public's mind for more than a year, writing dozens of articles and appearing on local radio and television shows, calling Soviet-era street names a "blasphemy, a violent offense against our native history."[24] Andreyev urged his fellow citizens to get rid of these "faceless" names and restore the "true" names of historical Novgorod.

Andreyev's efforts bore fruit on January 4, 1991, when, by a two-thirds majority, the City Soviet restored the pre-1917 names of all the streets in the historical Novgorod (figure 2.4). In one fell swoop, the names Lenin, Bolshevik, Komsomol, Proletariat, Soviet, and Worker's were stricken from

Figure 2.4. The street signs bearing the new, post-Soviet names restored by the City Council in 1991 explain the origins of the street name—in this case, the former Church of Saint John the Baptist. Photograph by Nicolai Petro.

the city map in what remains to this day the most comprehensive cultural de-Sovietization of any city in Russia.[25]

What made the Novgorod City Soviet unusual even during the anticommunist euphoria of 1989–91 was that it did far more than just decry the Soviet past. It linked reforms to a particular period from Novgorod's past. Though the City Soviet did not achieve everything it set out to do, it brought to a decisive end the communist claim to be the sole legitimate interpreters of Russia's past, thereby encouraging people to consider options outside their immediate Soviet-era experience.

## Linking Old Symbols to New Policies

The young governor of the Novgorod region, Mikhail Prusak, turned to the local university for guidance on how to link the symbols of Novgorod's past to his current policy agenda. As he remarked candidly at the time, "Our people do not as yet recognize the importance of our past; that is why we created the university to help us."[26]

"The Novgorod Project: A Leap into Postindustrial Society" was one such initiative, specifically designed to mobilize the public in support of making Novgorod's medieval history the centerpiece of regional development. The project notes that the world is moving into a "postindustrial" phase that emphasizes cultural and intellectual products. This emphasis on cultural paradigms could be quite advantageous for Russia if, rather than imitating the development path taken by the West, it relies on traditional Russian communitarianism, collective action, and cooperation to "leap" directly into postindustrial development.[27]

The key to empowering postindustrial values is greater regional autonomy, which will spawn civic initiative in support of local historical preservation. Modernization efforts should therefore be targeted at increasing sociocultural diversity and cultural pluralism, and in Novgorod should focus on creating a technology infrastructure that would "incorporate the historical-cultural heritage of the Novgorod region."[28]

Novgorod State University and local Novgorod television are to be the main actors in a strategy designed to "incorporate the historical-cultural heritage of the Novgorod lands in intensive cultural, educational, and practical methodological usage, and to broaden the access of diverse groups of actual and potential users to cultural-historical materials."[29] The final report was widely distributed among local officials, but after the bankruptcy of the project's major investor, it was shelved and apparently forgotten by all but senior university officials.[30]

Apparently, however, the report's recommendations continue to provide a broad direction for policy. Tourism, touted as central to postindustrial society, has been officially designated one of the region's key cultural and investment initiatives. Telecommunications became a top priority, so much so that in 1997 Prusak boasted that Novgorod had the nation's third most highly developed telecommunications infrastructure.[31]

In 1995, the building housing the former Institute of Marxism-Leninism was converted into a training center for local civil servants, with special emphasis on the history and traditions of the Novgorod region. Each year nearly twelve hundred public and private managers take short training courses at the center, now known as Dialog. Ultimately, its director hopes to establish a regional school of public administration that applies Novgorodian traditions, history, and culture to the solution of civic problems.[32]

Meanwhile, the local television station, Slaviya, has made local culture and history a mainstay of its programming. In addition to regular programs like *Historical Monologues,* it has produced several feature films that focus on Novgorod's cultural and political heritage, including *Lord Novgorod the Great* (2001) and *The First Republic* (2002–3), a five-part series devoted to the lessons that the "Novgorod model" holds for Russia today.

The station's managing director, Victor Smirnov, a widely published historical novelist, is quite unabashed about his personal sympathies for republican Novgorod. Asked, during a recent television interview, which side he would have supported during the fifteenth-century *veche* debate between the supporters of union with Moscow and the pro-Lithuanian party headed by Martha the Magistrate. Smirnov replied that "as a patriot of Novgorod" he would certainly have sided with Martha. Though history favored another path, he concluded that Novgorod now has a chance for a bit of "historical revenge," by showing that its reliance on local traditions is a better model for Russia today.[33]

Despite scarce funding, the university has set up its own Center for the Study of Culture to explore the impact that Novgorod's history and traditions are having on contemporary political and spiritual life, a project that in 2001 evolved into the Novgorod Interregional Institute for the Social Sciences.[34] The institute plans to organize conferences, seminars, and symposia that focus particular attention on the cultural legacy of Novgorod as it applies to politics, economics, and public administration. According to its mission statement, "Russian statehood originated in a specific region: the

Russian Northwest. Elements of social and political democracy first appeared here, in the territory of Novgorod, and they remained alive here despite our checkered historical development. This is reflected in the heritage of the democratic 'Veche Republic' and in the European political identity of the local population."[35]

## The Political Utility of Symbols

The very effort to conceive a "Novgorod Project" helped key segments of the local elite formulate a long-term development strategy rooted in the Novgorod myth. It described in elaborate detail how Novgorod's symbolic resources could be used, so that when opportunity arose, the blueprint was already at hand. By the end of the 1990s, Governor Prusak and his closest advisers openly referred to that blueprint as the "Novgorod model"—a direct, modern extension of the principles of the Novgorod Republic:

> The Novgorod model demonstrated its viability, giving the world a unique culture that created enormous spiritual and material wealth. History, however, decreed that the country should take another path. The eastern tradition, represented by the principality of Vladimir-Suzdal', and later Moscow, gained the upper hand. The Novgorod Republic was forcibly destroyed and yet, over the course of centuries, it has continued to exist in people's memory. Today this model has a new historical opportunity. Our generation can return to the principals of our ancestors, but on a new basis. Self-government, elections, public accountability of authority, private property, individual liberty—the very cornerstones of the Novgorod Republic—are regaining their former significance.
>
> On January 27, 1998, a joint session of the city and regional Dumas took a truly symbolic step. The deputies unanimously resolved to restore Novgorod's previous historical name—Novgorod the Great. In making this decision, the deputies not only rectified an historical injustice but reaffirmed their commitment to the principles our ancient city once lived by. Without foisting our views on anyone, it seems to us that it is precisely in these principles that we must seek the roots of that national idea that the new Russia so desperately needs.[36]

The fact that, as Governor Prusak likes to put it, "in Novgorod tradition lives" has also had policy implications.[37] Before reviewing the administration's programs in support of small business, for instance, Prusak reviewed sixteenth-century records indicating that there had once been more weavers in Novgorod than in Kazan, Tula, Ustyug, and Mozhaisk combined. Because of this tradition, he felt it would make sense to fund a regional program to revive local linen weaving.[38] When the research center Dialog was given the task of developing the region's housing reform program, it first conducted a study of communal living arrangements in the city from the twelfth to the seventeenth centuries, with appendices and charts comparing those eras to the present.[39] At a conference on local self-government co-sponsored by the regional administration, the mayor of Novgorod the Great underscored the importance of territorial self-administration for his city by pointing out that it is fully "in keeping with centuries of Novgorod traditions and customs."[40]

Governor Prusak's very public conversion to the Novgorod myth has, naturally, also encouraged other government officials to embrace the imagery of Novgorod's past. Historical analogies that would seem far-fetched in other regions are quite common in Novgorod. Thus, in describing how the Novgorod Regional Duma differs from those of other regions, chairman Anatoly Boitsev draws attention to fact that the final budget hearings are open to the public and broadcast live on television and radio. "If there is a modern *veche* in Novgorod today," he concludes "this is it."[41] For the late mayor of Novgorod the Great, Alexander Korsunov, the city's efforts to promote trade and close ties with the West shows that "the spirit of our ancestors has been preserved."[42] In the last interview he gave before his untimely death in 2002, he eloquently summarized his personal vision of Novgorod's historical significance:

> While people in the capitals spar with each other in search of "high political ideals" that will satisfy their ambitions, we can wait. With more than eleven centuries of experience, we have no need to rush. Here in Novgorod the Great is the one, true, centuries-old pillar of tradition, of culture, of principles and government experience that we can all count on. Sooner or later they will come here for the right decisions.
>
> Our task lies not in adopting fleeting goals. Ours is a special trust. We are not closed to contemporary trends, but rather follow our ancient Novgorod traditions in being active and entrepreneurial, some might even say excessively so. I recommend to all who feel "lost," and particularly to those whose decisions affect the lives of millions—come here, feel the real roots and voices of those who came before us. That will be enough.[43]

## Reintegrating Novgorod into Europe

A very significant role in the public's acceptance of this Novgorod model was played by the new, locally oriented school curriculum introduced in 1996. From the seventh through the eleventh grade, students in the region study Novgorod's history for one hour a week. The curriculum is designed to promote "patriotic qualities" among schoolchildren but, as distinct from Soviet times, these now include "a Novgorodian and Russian self-awareness ... [and] an ability to compare our own national, European, and regional histories, and discuss different versions of historical events."[44]

The ultimate purpose is to "Novgorodify" the entire school curriculum. As the principal of School No. 22, Svetlana Matveeva, points out, "not only the study of history, but also literature, geography and biology here is tied to local materials."[45] The deputy director of the Novgorod City Educational Committee, Svetlana Shubina, argues that "children must be given every opportunity to understand the region they live in, what the value orientations of our region are, and how these can them help in life."[46]

Many extracurricular programs are organized around the city's archeological excavations, which are prominently featured in the local press. Programs like "City under the City," "I Am a Novgorodian," and "Be a Magistrate [*Posadnik*]" link contemporary civic education to the city's past by taking students to the digs and asking them to imagine what their role might have been in the cultural and political life of medieval Novgorod.[47] Recently the Novgorod region's Committee on Education has even introduced a preschool component aimed at "resurrecting the national-cultural traditions of the Russian people through a focus on the historical and ethnographic past of the Novgorodian land."[48]

This educational curriculum is supplemented by a vast array of local cultural and volunteer organizations. During the school year, more than three thousand students each month visit the region's history museums and participate in a wide variety of educational programs designed to promote local civic identity, many with names like "Voyage to the Past" and "My City."[49]

More recently, the city has built on the recovery of its lost heritage with a number of initiatives designed to anchor it more firmly in Europe. One such initiative is the pairing of city administrators from Novgorod the Great and Strasbourg under the Technical Assistance for the Commonwealth of Independent States (TACIS) City Twinning Program, an initiative of the European Commission that promotes democratic structures and effective administration at the local level. After an initial round of meetings and visits in 1997 and 1998, the Novgorod city administration endorsed two cooperative projects. The first, known as Strategic Action in Tourism and Urban Reforms in Novgorod's Economy (SATURNE), was completed in 2001. It has led to the establishment of Russia's first-ever central tourist information office and to the cooperative publishing of information (figures 2.5 and 2.6).

A second cooperative project, called Dialog, is designed to adapt French municipal-level innovations to the needs of Novgorod the Great. Over the course of the past decade, the once tightly centralized municipality of Strasbourg has been experimenting with shifting certain functions from the mayor's office to local boroughs. The Novgorod city administration found this idea very much to its liking and, with the assistance of experts from Strasbourg, has set up two similar subdivisions, referred to as "minimayoralties." They deal with whatever issues that local residents find most

Figure 2.5. The Novgorod region has invested heavily in resurrecting its tourist infrastructure, and it was one the first Russian cities to open a single, central information center for tourists visiting the region; known as the Red Hut (Krasnaya izba), it is located in the heart of Kremlin Park. Photograph by Nicolai Petro.

Figure 2.6. In 2001, the city of Novgorod the Great partnered with the French city of Strasbourg. The municipalities shared their experiences in civic administration and tourism. Their cooperation on tourism resulted in a joint brochure, whose cover is shown. Reproduced by permission of the city administration of Novgorod the Great.

pressing. In addition, they serve as a convenient forum for discussion of the city budget, following up on citizens' complaints, improving coordination with local law enforcement, and providing citizens with advice and information on their legal rights. In sum, they act as advocates on behalf of residents to the municipal, and sometimes even the regional, bureaucracy. The local councils of mini-mayoralties include a variety of representatives of social, municipal, commercial, and noncommercial organizations. As of March 2004, two mini-mayoralties have become operational, one in the historic Trade Side of the city, where 7,000 people live, and the other in the newer Western region, where some 30,000 people live. Several more are planed over the coming years.

Finally, there is a project that has been in the works for nearly a decade, known as "The Route from the Varangians to the Greeks." The phrase, originally mentioned in the Russian Primary Chronicle, refers to the river route that once connected Constantinople with the Baltic Sea. Trade along this vital network of rivers helped established Novgorod as a major port during the Middle Ages.

The idea of revitalizing this route originated in 1997, and it has received new impetus since Novgorod joined the New Hanseatic League, an association of over two hundred cities from sixteen countries that promote trade and tourism among its members.[50] Reestablished in 1981, and chaired by the mayor of Lübeck, former towns and Hansa offices are invited to participate in the league's annual "Hanseatic Days." Novgorod the Great was the first Russian city to join the reconstituted league, and it has been designated the host of the league's gathering for 2009.

In preparation for this grand event, the city is seeking funding for an ambitious proposal to create a pedestrian mall and international trade complex that would serve as a permanent exhibit of its Hanseatic ties. The idea, in essence, is to create small versions of the permanent trade representations that medieval Novgorod once hosted, this time in the very heart of its downtown. Locations would be leased to the various Hanseatic partners to promote themselves and their commercial wares, while at the same time providing a convenient and attractive location where Russian tourists could get a "taste of Europe." Tellingly, the proposal is subtitled "Forming a Model of European Integration with the Participation of the Russian Federation."

Although each of these projects is still in its very early stages, together they show a strong desire by local elites to build up Novgorod's European identity and to have the city and the region viewed as Russia's gateway to Europe.

Between 1994 and 2004, the Novgorod region obtained more foreign direct investment per capita than any region of Russia but Moscow. Fully a quarter of the region's factory workers are now employed by foreign companies. The Novgorod elite's confidence in its ability to compete in a global marketplace is reflected in the late Mayor Korsunov's comment that, as far as Novgorod was concerned, Russian membership in the European Union and the World Trade Organization could not happen quickly enough.[51] Underlying this remarkable success in redefining the region's future in European terms lies an astute usage of local historical symbols and myths to ease the way.

Vladimir Kagansky, an astute observer of Russia's modern cultural landscape, has written about how the once totally familiar and ahistorical Soviet landscape has quite unexpectedly, for many locals, come alive with pre-Soviet cultural symbols. Politically and culturally, this sudden flood of local history has often led to very messy attempts to return all the past all at once. As Kagansky expresses it: "History once stood before us as a closed corridor; suddenly it became possible, inevitable, necessary, and even tempting to enter any door and decorate those rooms anew."

In many regions, this has led to serious social conflict. In Novgorod it has not, and the reason seems to be the early emergence of an elite consensus on which version of the past to prefer. This provided a socially receptive environment for the emergence of a view of Novgorod in the twenty-first century as a place that was more "Scandoslavia" than it was "Eurasia."[52]

Despite this striking success, however, it is hard to imagine the Novgorod myth ever becoming a source of serious political opposition to Moscow. Despite occasional attempts in the Russian media to portray Novgorod's policies as the antithesis of the policies of Vladimir Putin, Putin's agenda in fact astutely incorporates key elements of the Novgorod myth, most notably a clear embrace of a European identity for Russia. It would thus be more accurate to say that the Novgorod myth offers a conceptual framework through which the rest of the country could identify itself with Europe, while preserving a distinctly Russian cultural identity.

## Notes

1. Vladimir Kagansky, "Teoretiko-geograficheskie miniatyury," *Russkii zhurnal*, May 8, 1998, http://www.russ.ru/journal/odna_8/98-08-05/kagan1.htm.

2. Dmitry S. Likhachev, *Razdumya o Rossii* (Saint Petersburg: Logos, 2001), 197,

198; Henrik Birnbaum, *Novgorod in Focus: Selected Essays* (Columbus: Slavica Publishers, 1996), 21.

3. Theodor Schilling, *Subsidiarity as a Rule and a Principle, or: Taking Subsidiarity Seriously,* Jean Monnet Working Paper 10, 1995; http://www.jeanmonnetprogram.org/papers/95/9510ind.html.

4. O. V. Martyshin, *Volnyi Novgorod: Obshchestvenno-politicheskiistroi i pravo feodalnoi respubliki* (Moscow: Rossiiskoe pravo, 1992), 175–76, 189.

5. Ibid., 161, 210.

6. E. A. Gordienko, *Novgorod v XVI veke i ego dukhovnaya zhizn* (Saint Petersburg: Rossiiskaya akademiya nauk, 2001), 294.

7. Elena A. Rybina, *Torgovlya srednevekovogo Novgoroda: Istoriko-arkheologicheskie ocherki* (Veliky Novgorod: Novgorodskii gosudarstvennyi universitet imeni Yaroslava Mudrogo, 2001), 98; Likhachev, *Razdumya,* 142.

8. Rybina, *Torgovlya srednevekovogo Novgoroda,* 178, 209.

9. Birnbaum, *Novgorod in Focus,* 72.

10. Svetlana A. Kovarskaya, "Dukhovno-obrazovatelnye traditsii v sotsiodinamike kultury Velikogo Novgoroda," *Vestnik Novgorodskogo gosudarstvennogo universiteta: Seriya "Gumanitarnye nauki,"* November 2000, 9, 12.

11. Birnbaum, *Novgorod in Focus,* 165.

12. V. A. Varentsov, "Struktura upraveleniya Novgorodom v XVI veke," *Vestnik Novgorodskogo gosudarstvennogo universiteta: Seriya "Gumanitarnye nauki,"* May 1996, 41–42.

13. V. A. Varentsov and G. M. Kovalenko, *V sostave Moskovskogo gosudarstva: Ocherki istorii velikogo Novgoroda kontsa XV–nachala XVIII vv.* (Saint Petersburg: Russko-Baltiisky informatsionnyi tsentr "BLITs," 1999), 8, 108.

14. Svetlana A. Kovarskaya, "Novgorodskoe zemstvo v dorevolutsionnoi istoriografii," in *Proshloe Novgoroda i Novgorodskoi zemli: Materialy nauchnoi konferentsii 11–13 noyabrya 1998 goda,* ed. Vasily Andreyev (Novgorod: Novgorodskii gosudarstvennyi universitet im. Yaroslava Mudrogo, 1998), 128, 129.

15. A. Z. Zhavoronkov, ed., *Novgorod v russkoi literature XVIII–XX vv.* (Novgorod: Novgorodskaya pravda, 1959), 8–9.

16. Peter Ford, "Medieval City Holds Key to 'Russian Idea,'" *Christian Science Monitor,* June 5, 1997; "Historian Champions Medieval Novgorod as Model for Russia's Democratic Development," *Jamestown Foundation Monitor,* May 7, 1997.

17. Aleksandr Ivanov, "Veche zamolchalo," *Expert: Severo-zapad,* November 27, 2000.

18. Gennady Lisichkin, *Est li budushchee u Rossii* (Moscow: Kultura, 1996), 164; Paul Goble, "Eye on Eurasia: The Novgorod model," UPI, March 25, 2005, reprinted in *Johnson's Russia List* 9103, http://www.cdi.org/russia/johnson; Moris Simashko, "Pyatyi Rim," *Oktyabr* 7 (2001); Sergei Filatov, "Kareliya: Pravoslavno-luteransoe pogranichya," *Druzhba narodov* 5 (2000); Igor Chubais, "Razgadannaya Rossiya," *Russkiy zhurnal,* July 3, 2001, http://www.russ.ru/politics/meta/20010703-chub.html.

19. "Vopros: kuda by stolitsu perenesti?" *Kommersant-vlast,* May 5, 1999.

20. Likhachev, *Razdumya,* 148.

21. Vladimir Kagansky, "Klerikalizatsiya," *Russkii zhurnal,* April 13, 2005, http://www.russ.ru/culture/20050411.html.

22. "Zdravstvuyte!" *Novgorod,* October 30, 1990.

23. "Kakaya vlast na dvore," *Novgorod,* October 30, 1990.

24. Vasily Andreyev, "Chto v imeni tebe moem . . . ?" *Novgorod,* January 4, 1991.
25. Some Soviet-era names remain in the regions of the city that were built in Soviet times.
26. Mikhail Prusak, opening remarks to the eightieth anniversary of the founding of the Communist Youth League, Novgorod, Novgorod Political Archives Fund, October 29, 1998; from the author's personal notes.
27. Petr Shchedrovitsky and Valentin Tolstykh, *Novgorodskii Proekt: Proryv v postindustrialnoe obshechestvo* (Moscow: Gorbachev Foundation, 1995), 11–14.
28. Ibid., 39.
29. Ibid., 45–46.
30. President Vladimir Soroka committed the university to helping to "formulate and realize" this program as part of its efforts to help improve local self-government. Vladimir V. Soroka, "Mesto i rol sistemy obrazovaniya v mestnom samoupravlenii Novgorodchiny," in *Mestnoe samoupravlenie v Rossii: Istoriya i sovremennost,* ed. B. N. Kovalyov (Novgorod: Novgorodskii gosudarstvennyi universitet im. Yarolsava Mudrogo i Administratsiya Goroda Novgoroda, 1997), 17.
31. *Novosti,* November 28–December 3, 1997, citing a speech by Mikhail Prusak of November 14, 1997; available at http://www.novgorod.ru.
32. Interview with Alexander I. Zhukovsky, director of the Dialog regional municipal research center, Novgorod the Great, April 9, 2002.
33. Viktor Smirnov, interviewed for the program *Sophia* on Novgorod television, rebroadcast July 27, 2003. Smirnov was also the ghostwriter for Prusak's 1999 political autobiography *Reform in the Provinces.*
34. Svetlana Kovarskaya, director of the Center for the Study of Culture at Novgorod State University, personal correspondence, May 17, 2002.
35. Sergey Devyatkin, "Novgorod Interregional Institute for the Social Sciences," author's personal copy.
36. Mikhail M. Prusak, *Reformy v provintsii* (Moscow: Veche, 1999), 94–96.
37. Mikhail Prusak, interviewed by Nikolai Svanidze on the Russian national television channel "RTR" for the program *Pered zerkalom,* February 27, 2000, available at http://niac.natm.ru.
38. Mikhail Prusak, "Vidnye ekonomisty, gosudarstvennye i obshchestvennye deyateli o sobytiyakh poslednikh let," in *Rossiiskoe predprinimatelstvo: Istoriya i vozrozhdenie* (Moscow: Russkoe delovoe agentstvo, 1997), 1.
39. A. N. Panov and S. G. Ovcharov, *Stanovlenie kommunalnogo khozyaistva Novgoroda Velikogo v XII–XVI vekakh* (Novgorod: Severo-zapadnaya akademiya gosudarstvennoi sluzhby, 1997).
40. Aleksandr V. Korsunov, "Reforma Mestnogo samoupravleniya—shag k pravovomu gosudarstvu," in *Mestnoe samoupravlenie,* ed. Kovalyov, 12.
41. Vitaly Eryomin, "Obsuzhdenie budzheta—vkhod svobodnyi," *Rossiiskaya Federatsiya segodnya,* special edition, "Molodost drevnego Novgoroda," January 2002, 13.
42. Kathy Lally, "A Russian Journal," *Baltimore Sun,* September 20, 2000.
43. "Mer Velikogo Novgoroda Aleksandr Korsunov: Lyudei ne obmanesh,'" July 30, 2002, available at http://www.pravda.ru.
44. *Programma kursa 'Novgordika,'* facsimile copy obtained at the Novgorod regional library, no date or author.
45. Gennady Naryshkin, "Obrazovanie i patriotism," *Novgorod,* May 29, 1997.
46. Ibid.

47. Dasha Galkina, "Shkola 'Veche,'" *Novgorodskie vedomosti,* December 26, 2000.
48. Father Alexei Moroz, "O problemakh sovremennogo doshkolnogo i shkolnogo vospitaniya," *Novgorodskie eparkhalnye vedomosti* 5 (May 1999): 3.
49. "Novgorodskii opyt organizatsii bibliotek prodemonstriruyut uraltsam," *Novgorodskie vedomosti* (August 9, 2000).
50. "The New Hanseatic League," http://hanza.gdansk.pl/nhanza_a.html.
51. "Mer Velikogo Novgoroda Aleksandr Korsunov: Lyudei ne obmanesh," July 30, 2002, available at http://www.pravda.ru.
52. Dmitry S. Likhachev, "Nelzia uyti ot samikh sebia . . . ," *Novyi mir,* June 1994, 113–14.

# 3

# Wrocław's Search for a New Historical Narrative: From Polonocentrism to Postmodernism

*Gregor Thum*

The epilogue to a 2001 survey of Wrocław's history, written by a team of historians from the University of Wrocław, begins with a puzzling statement: "The seemingly simple question of whether Wrocław is a Polish or a German city is difficult to answer."[1] One wonders who would ever ask such an either/or question with respect to Wrocław, which had been German Breslau until 1945. Yet within the Polish context, this statement by Wojciech Wrzesiński was a confession. The then-chairman of the Polish Historical Association and one of Wrocław's leading historians of the older generation was implicitly declaring that what Polish historians have been saying about Wrocław since the end World War II was wrong: Wrocław was not Silesia's capital before 1945, when the Allies decided to move Poland 150 miles to the west, a partly Polish city.

Had this clarification come a decade or two earlier, it would have been a revelation. It would have challenged the official interpretation of Wrocław's history in Communist Poland, according to which the border shift of 1945 was the culmination of a long-term historical development that brought a basically Polish city, together with the rest of the "Recovered Lands," home to Poland. In the 2001 survey of Wrocław's history, however, Wrzesiński and the publication's other authors were simply confirming what Wrocław's inhabitants have come to understand since 1989; they were signaling that even professional historians were distancing themselves from the myth of the "Recovered Lands," the purpose of which had been to legitimize Poland's postwar borders in the west and the Polish presence in cities like Wrocław.

The myth lost its political function with the fall of Communism and its international consequences. As soon as reunified Germany once and for all recognized its postwar borders—both in the Two-Plus-Four Agreement with the former World War II Allies and in a separate treaty with Poland in 1990–91—there was no longer any need for Poland to defend the territorial changes of 1945 with questionable historical arguments. And more than that, the myth of the "Recovered Lands," based on the suppression of the region's German past and an overemphasis on all things Polish, harmonized neither with the German-Polish reconciliation since 1990 nor with Poland's desire to join the European Union—which was driven by a belief in a common European heritage and multinational cooperation.

In particular, for younger Polish Wrocławians—who never doubted the permanence of the German-Polish border, who naturally identified with the city where they had spent their childhood, and who embraced the prospect of their country joining the EU—the hitherto Polonocentric reading of Wrocław's past was hardly appealing. Slogans like "Return to the Motherland" (Powrót do macierzy) or "Piast Wrocław" (i.e., Piastowski Wrocław, referring to the Polish dynasty ruling Silesia in the Middle Ages) sounded like other propaganda slogans from Communist times. Most people in Wrocław were eager to leave them behind as quickly as possible.

Yet what happens when the local myths, upon which Polish Wrocław was built after 1945 and with which its inhabitants had been living for three generations,[2] suddenly become dysfunctional? Wrocław, which was reinvented after 1945 as a Polish city by its new inhabitants, is currently in the process of being reinvented a second time. It is the purpose of this chapter to shed light on this breathtaking mental and physical transformation, in the course of which the largest city in western Poland and presumably one of the most dynamic places in postsocialist Europe is acquiring a new identity. It is too early to make any final judgments. We are dealing with an ongoing, open-ended process. However, against the backdrop of the postwar myths, we can identify the elements of a new historical narrative and the impact it is having on Wrocław's rapidly changing physical appearance.

## Wrocław's Eternal Polishness and the Contradiction between Two Modes of Memory

During the conference of Potsdam in the summer of 1945, it took the Allies no more than the stroke of a pen to cede Breslau, together with most of Germany' territories east of the Oder-Neisse line, to Poland. The actual transformation of German Breslau—with more than 600,000 inhabitants, the largest German city east of Berlin—into Polish Wrocław took decades. Within only two years, the Polish authorities had managed to get rid of the 250,000 Germans who had survived the war in Breslau or returned after the city's surrender on May 6 and to replace them with a similar number of Polish settlers from all parts of prewar Poland. But this radical population exchange did not mean that the Polish settlers would consider Wrocław their permanent home.

Postwar Wrocław was anything but a welcoming place. During the siege of the "fortress Breslau" in the final months of the war, more than 60 percent of the city had been destroyed. The Old Town was in ruins, and entire neighborhoods in the south and the west were uninhabitable due to the degree of destruction. In addition, hordes of looters had descended on Wrocław after the war and deprived the city of much of what the war had left intact. The Polish migrants arriving in the city not only found a devastated place but also one that unsettled them with its strikingly German appearance. Until the summer of 1946, when the deportation of the German population to postwar Germany was in full swing, Germans still constituted the majority of the population. Also, Wrocław's Prussian-German looking architecture, German street signs, German monuments, and German inscriptions at every turn reminded the incoming settlers that it had until recently been a German city. Thus it was for many a foregone conclusion that the borders drawn in Potsdam had a merely provisional status and that, sooner or later, Wrocław would be returned to Germany. As a result, the Polish settlers tended to consider their stay in the city as temporary.

Accordingly, Wrocław's new inhabitants hesitated to invest money and time in the maintenance of their houses and apartments. The wartime destruction was followed by postwar neglect. In 1955, an internal report for the Polish government came to the conclusion that "due to a certain haphazardness of the reconstruction, . . . Wrocław makes on its inhabitants and on strangers the impression of a dilapidated city."[3] Photographs taken in the city in the mid 1950s show a place where the war seemed to have ended only recently. The Polish government had contributed to this disastrous situation. Despite efforts to repair a number of buildings to meet the demands of the Polish administration and other Polish institutions in Wrocław, the government tolerated the demolition of entire neighborhoods in the early 1950s to support the reconstruction of Warsaw with bricks from Wrocław.[4]

Wrocław's revival began in the second half of the 1950s, after the government in Warsaw had decided to provide the necessary funds for the comprehensive reconstruction of Wrocław's city center with its famous historical landmarks: the gothic town hall, the magnificent baroque structure of the university, numerous old churches and monasteries, the city palaces of the Silesian aristocracy, and the splendid houses of the city's merchants surrounding the large market squares Rynek and Plac Solny. However, this reconstruction would hardly have had the desired effect without convincing the city's new inhabitants that the border and population shifts of 1945 were irreversible, and that Wrocław had a future as one of the leading cities in Poland. In this process, during which the Polish settlers slowly began to identify with Wrocław, the myth of the city's eternal Polishness emerged.

According to this new master narrative, created mainly by Polish professional historians and promoted through the propaganda apparatus of the Communist government, Wrocław did not become Polish because of arbitrary political decisions at the end of World War II. The postwar settlement was interpreted as the result of a long-term historical development that brought old Polish land, after centuries of "foreign rule," back to Poland. The historians did not deny the presence of Germans in Wrocław before 1945, but they marginalized their significance by presenting them as a small ruling class that contributed little to the city's development. The Poles, conversely, were depicted as the city's only native element. They allegedly maintained Wrocław's Polish character despite all efforts to Germanize the city.[5]

To adapt the city's appearance to this historical narrative, the Polish authorities enforced the thorough "removal of traces of Germanness" as soon as the Germans had left. By 1948, Wrocław had been cleansed of German street names, German monuments, and an enormous number of German inscriptions everywhere in the city. Countless store signs had to be removed, along with advertising slogans on facades, labels on technical devices, the signs for "warm" and "cold" or "free" and "occupied" in public bathrooms, and the epitaphs and other German inscriptions in the city's many churches. At least in the public space, nothing should recall Wrocław's German past.[6]

The authorities even liquidated the German cemeteries and turned them into parks, although with a delay of twenty years because of resistance among the Polish population against the desecration of graveyards. In general, however, Wrocław's new inhabitants accepted the de-Germanization of the public space as willingly as they embraced the myth of Wrocław's eternal Polishness. Joanna Konopińska, a history student arriving from Poznań in the fall of 1945, wrote in a January 1947 entry into her diary: "Almost every newspaper reminds us of the necessity to remove German inscriptions from government buildings, store signs, wherever you find them. Nothing to say against that, since encountering foreign inscriptions at every turn reminds us permanently of the Germanness of this city that we want to consider to be our city, a Polish one."[7]

Yet the removal of German traces was both a comprehensive and limited operation. Though the buildings' surfaces could be cleansed of German inscriptions, their architecture continued to testify to the city's non-Polish past. In addition, inside the buildings, fixtures and furniture, dishes and tools —all that Wrocław's former inhabitants had to leave behind—remained. With respect to these things, any iconoclastic desire failed because of the dire postwar realities. Poland had been devastated during the war, and its population was impoverished. Therefore, the people of Wrocław were more than happy if they found their new houses and apartments equipped with the most necessary things. Interestingly enough, these items continued to exist, sometimes until today. Given the usually poor quality of Socialist products, household articles from prewar Germany became quite popular in Poland. People tried to hold on to these things as long as possible and referred to them as *poniemiecku,* meaning both from the German time and of high—nonsocialist—quality.

As a consequence, the private space was filled with those obviously German things. They continued to testify to a local past that was denied in public. To openly address this schizophrenia, however, would have meant breaking a taboo in Communist Poland. Not until the 1990s could this contradiction so typical of daily life in the "Recovered Lands" be discussed in public. In 1993, the Wrocławian Stanisław Nowicki wrote in retrospect:

> I lived in a German house, in which generations of children came into this world and old German men departed from life. I slept in a German bed, looked at German pictures on the wall, bathed in a German bathtub, ate from German plates and out of German pots, played with German sabers, wrote with a German fountain pen and German ink, leafed through German books.... Sometimes the thought came to mind—Jesus! We are living among stolen objects![8]

The contradiction between a public space cleansed of everything German and a private space riddled with items reminiscent of the German past leads us to the two modes of collective memory described by Jan Assmann with respect to ancient civilizations.[9] He distinguishes between "cultural memory," shaped by the specialists from above as part of a publicly celebrated master narrative, and "communicative memory," circulating in everyday communication but not necessarily part of the master narrative. He understood cultural memory as primarily engaging a distant past, whereas communicative memory centers on more recent historical experiences. As applied to postwar Wrocław, the myth of a city that had been Polish from time immemorial corresponds to Assmann's definition of cultural memory. Whereas Wrocław's cultural memory denied the city's German past, that past maintained its place in the city's communicative memory due to the German material legacy in the city's private sphere.

In Wrocław, cultural memory and communicative memory thus did not just poorly correspond but even stood in direct contradiction to each other, causing a highly unstable relation between the two modes of memory. Yet it seemed to work as long as the city's inhabitants were willing to overlook these contradictions. As long as the Poles in Wrocław did not yet feel fully at home at their new living place and therefore needed the myth of the Polish city psychologically, they did not address the implausibility of the Polish myths. Needless to say, the position of both the West German government and influential expellee organizations that the German/Polish border drawn in Potsdam had only a provisional status—and that, according to international law, the former German territories east of that border were still part of Germany—ensured that Polish Wrocławians would not challenge the myth of the Polish city. After all, this narrative served their own vital interest. Asked in those days whether Wrocław is a German or a Polish city, they would have answered: a Polish city!

## The Need for a New Master Narrative

The international situation affecting Wrocław's status changed long before 1989. In December 1970, the West German chancellor, Willy Brandt, recognized the inviolability of the Polish/German border during his state visit to Warsaw, a step that was embedded in a broader détente policy between East and West and in West Germany's desire to normalize relations with its Socialist neighbors. This important step in German-Polish relations gave the inhabitants of the former German territories reason to believe in the permanence of the postwar settlement and stop fearing a revision of the border. But the Communist government did much to maintain the impression among its citizens that German revanchism was still a threat. After all, this perceived threat had been serving as the strongest argument for Warsaw's alliance with Moscow and the supremacy of the Communist Party in Poland. Yet the authority of the Polish Communists soon began to erode, and fear of German revanchism began to decline.

During the 1980s, a growing number of critical intellectuals in Wrocław began to question the postwar master narrative. As was the case elsewhere in Eastern Europe, intellectuals in opposition to the Communist regimes developed an interest in forgotten or suppressed local histories as a way of distancing themselves from official state ideologies. In Wrocław, they more and more associated the myth of the Polish city with Communist propaganda, even though the myth itself was rather nationalistic in content.[10] According to the Germanist Marek Zybura, the suppression of Wrocław's German past was increasingly perceived as "a moral and intellectual scandal."[11] Polish Wrocławians could learn all about the archeological traces of early Slavic settlement in Wrocław and its medieval architecture but nothing of its nineteenth- and twentieth-century tenement blocks and villas, public buildings and storehouses, industrial architecture, and railway stations. The history of the Prussian-German city, the place where people were actually living, remained a blank spot. Knowledge of Wrocław's modern history was limited to the activities of its small Polish minority.

The revolution of 1989, the end of censorship, and a rapidly developing public sphere in Poland allowed the taboos of Wrocław's past to be addressed in public. Andrzej Zawada, a professor of Polish literature, called Wrocław as "a city whose memory has been amputated. I only became accustomed to this city with difficulty because its debility troubled and tormented me at every turn. . . . Wrocław's past was covered up, just like a family member's offensive origins in one of the so-called better families."[12] Public statements like these—questioning the extent to which the cultural appropriation of Wrocław by its Polish inhabitants has been successful so far—indicated that this very appropriation had reached a new, perhaps final, stage. In the wake of the fundamental changes of 1989, Wrocławians collectively embarked on a search for a local identity capable of integrating those aspects of the city's past that had been denied and suppressed. Their search is the attempt to form a cultural memory that is compatible with the communicative memory of Wrocław's citizens.

Unlike after 1945, the development of a new local master narrative is taking place within the framework of an open discourse, where access is free to anyone. The professional historians, once the custodians of Wrocław's master narrative, have lost their control over the interpretation of the past. Today, everyone has a voice in the process of reinterpreting local history, from scholars and intellectuals, to writers, journalists, and politicians, to architects, preservationists, hotel managers, and tourist guides. Its most important medium are the local newspapers, along with an impressive number of new books written for a broader readership interested in new interpretations of the local past.

In 1996, the city's ambitious and skillful mayor, Bogdan Zdrojewski, tried to accelerate this process by asking the well-known Oxford University historian Norman Davies to write a new history of Wrocław. As a British citizen, Davies seemed to offer distance from the partiality of German or Polish historians regarding the Silesian city, and his international prestige promised to be an effective way to promote Wrocław both inside and outside Poland. One might interpret this approach as reminiscent of the days of the People's Republic of Poland, when the government was used to promote the correct interpretation of history. But despite the government's significant financial and political support for Davies's book,[13] which was published simultaneously in Polish, English, and German, it did not provide a new master narrative. When it came out in 2002, it was only one among many new interpretations of Wrocław's history published in Polish.[14] Davies and his cowriter Roger Moorehouse had to join a quite polyphonous choir that no conductor was able to control any longer. Yet despite this choir's creative chaos, we can identify several recurrent motifs that constitute the main elements of Wrocław's emerging new self-image: the bourgeois city, the German city, the city of Polish expellees, the anticommunist city, and the European city.

## The Bourgeois City

As elsewhere in Eastern Europe, the fall of Communism in Wrocław triggered a bourgeois revolution. This revolution was accompanied by the rediscovery of nineteenth-century architecture and urban planning—a phenomenon, however, that has its parallel in Western Europe—and a growing appreciation for the solid design of the nineteenth century so strikingly different from late Socialism's frugal style, and the tendency to search the bourgeois past for models of a postsocialist life style. The rediscovery of the Old Town is the most obvious sign of the bourgeois turn in Wrocław.

After having been dormant for decades, Wrocław's Old Town is experiencing a striking renaissance. Accompanied by a comprehensive renovation and reconstructions of various historical elements, the Rynek became once again the center of public life in Wrocław (figure 3.1). Starting from there, the architectural upgrading financed both by the emerging market economy and the efforts of the municipal government has been spreading to the adjacent streets and squares, bringing ever larger parts of Wrocław's historic center back to life.

This urban renaissance would not have been possible without the enormous efforts to rebuild the historic center in the second half of the 1950s. One could argue that the current renovations and reconstructions are merely completing what the People's Republic left unfinished. However, the process is marked by an important shift in the urban topography. In Socialist Wrocław, the city's most valued parts were Cathedral Island and Sand Island in the River Odra (Oder), with their gothic churches and the seat of the catholic bishopric. These islands could most easily be linked to the myth

Figure 3.1. The Rynek, the largest of the Wrocław's three historic market squares, has become the center of public life in the postsocialist city. Photograph by Gregor Thum.

of the always-Polish city and its persistent bonds with Poland long after Silesia had become a province of the Holy Roman Empire.

The actual center of the city of Wrocław, with its three large market squares, was historically much more problematic both from the standpoint of Socialism and of Polish nationalism. Already in the Middle Ages, it had been shaped by German-speaking merchants and patricians, who also dominated the City Council. Though the reconstruction of this part of Wrocław could hardly be avoided without giving up the goal of bringing the war-torn city back to life, the urban planners and architects of the 1950s tried to at least deemphasize its "Germanness." They strove for the reconstruction of a Wrocław around 1800, when the baroque ensembles of the Hapsburg period had not yet been transformed into the modern Prussian-German city destroyed in 1945. In addition, the historic center was deprived of some its central functions and converted into a residential area with a limited number of stores and restaurants at street level. As in many Socialist cities, Wrocław's Old Town seemed to be an inhabitable museum of architecture rather than a large city's commercial and administrative center.

Immediately after 1989, Poland's emerging market economy took over the Old Town. In particular, the historically reconstructed market squares, Rynek and Plac Solny, attracted an ever-growing number of cafes, restaurants, pubs, stores, banks, and offices. The municipal authorities supported this movement back to the historic city center with comprehensive restoration efforts. Today, as shown in figure 3.1, the Rynek, with the famous gothic Town Hall, is once again the city's center for communication, trade, entertainment, tourism, and administration. And it has also become Wrocław's most important public space, where citizens meet each other, where urban festivities or political rallies are held, and where the city presents itself to the outside world. Though Saint John's Cathedral, symbolizing Wrocław's Polishness, was the city's most appreciated historical landmark before 1989 and used to be prominently placed on the covers of its tourist guidebooks, the gothic Town Hall has now surpassed the cathedral in popularity. No other building would better represent the restored self-confidence of postsocialist Wrocław. Thus, since 1996, a stylized image of the Town Hall has served as the city's official logo.

## *The German City*

In Warsaw and Krakow, the search for the presocialist past has led to a rediscovery of the Polish bourgeoisie. In Wrocław, it has inevitably led to encounters with the city's German past. Therefore, the post-1989 curiosity of Wrocław's citizens regarding German Breslau is as much the result of the improving Polish-German relations as it is the consequence of the bourgeois turn in a city that had only a German bourgeoisie. Today, German Wrocław has become accessible to everyone through a wave of illustrated books that display a past that had been hidden for more than half a century.[15] German epitaphs have been returned to the original places from which they had been removed after the war. We can even find restored German inscriptions on house facades—something entirely out of the question before 1989 (figure 3.2). Also striking is the reconstruction of the Friedrich Schiller monument in Wrocław's largest park—no matter that monuments to Schiller constituted an important part of the German national cult in the nineteenth century.

On the occasion of Wrocław's millennium in 2000, the local edition of the *Gazeta Wyborcza,* Poland's leading newspaper, published a series of translated articles from pre-1945 Wrocławian newspapers in an attempt to provide a glimpse of daily life in German Wrocław. The historian and journalist Beata Maciejwska was one of the driving forces behind a campaign that intended to strengthen the local identity by uncovering the city's German past. A similar curiosity for the German city drove Marek Krajewski, a professor of Latin at the University of Wrocław, who embarked on a career as a crime novelist in the late 1990s. His debut novel, *Death in Breslau,* which became a bestseller in Wrocław, was the first of his series of "Breslau" thrillers.[16] These novels are all set in Breslau, and they seek to re-create as precisely as possible the topography of the pre-1945 city. In addition, *Death in Breslau* challenged the once-homogenizing stigmatization of Germans as Nazis by strongly differentiating the book's characters. Alongside committed Nazi adherents, Krajewski introduced the novel's protagonist, the detective Eberhard Mock, who passionately abhors the fascist rulers—and is, by the way, a bourgeois figure through and through.

In keeping with this effort to destigmatize German Wrocławians, Polish Wrocław began to honor a growing number of former German citizens, such as the writer Karl von Holtei, an admirer of Silesia's Polish culture; the Jewish physicists and Nobel Prize winners Max Born and Fritz Haber; the Lutheran theologian Dietrich Bonhoeffer; and the beatified Roman Catholic philosopher and nun Edith Stein—the last two of whom were murdered in the resistance against Hitler. Whoever enters Wrocław's old Town Hall, which is today part of the city museum, might be struck by the gallery of busts of "Great Wrocławians," who include a significant number of Ger-

Figure 3.2. After the thorough removal of all "traces of Germanness" from the public space after the war, some of those traces have recently been restored, reminding the citizens of Wrocław of their German past. Photograph by Gregor Thum.

mans. The purpose of this collection, initiated in 1997, is to pay tribute to famous Wrocławians regardless of their nationality. In the words of Maciej Łagiewski, the director of the city museum and one of the most important protagonists of Wrocław's postsocialist identity, "the coexistence of the busts of famous Germans and Poles in the Gallery of Wrocław documents that the common German-Polish cultural heritage is recognized and that the upholding of the city's traditions did not experience a [lasting] rupture."[17]

Yet the display of these outstanding figures of German Wrocław, who today have been so happily absorbed into the local collective memory, also raises unsettling questions. Had these Germans been present in Wrocław at the end of the war, they would have been expelled from the city. It seems as if Wrocław society must still come to terms with the extreme discontinuity in local history caused less by the border shift than by the expulsion of the city's inhabitants. When Polish intellectuals recently suggested that Wrocław, instead of Berlin, should become the seat of the contested documentation center dealing with the history of forced migrations in Europe, the reaction in Wrocław was rather cool. The city was not prepared to be too closely associated with this issue, which is still highly charged emotionally, despite the fact that Wrocław's entire postwar history was shaped by these forced migrations.

So although present-day Wrocław willingly acknowledges the city's German past and goes out if its way to preserve its legacy, the expulsion of its former inhabitants is not officially commemorated. Remarkably, however, the large new monument to Bolesław Cardinal Kominek unveiled on Sand Island in 2005 refers to Kominek as the initiator and author of the famous letter Poland's catholic bishops wrote to their German colleagues in 1965, hoping to open the door for a reconciliation between Poles and Germans after the horrors of the World War II. The monument's German-Polish inscription quotes the letter's most famous sentence: "We forgive and we ask for forgiveness." In this indirect sense, Wrocław even has a monument that refers, albeit indirectly, to the atrocities committed during the expulsion of the Germans.

Many of the outstanding figures of German Wrocław, who have lately found their way into the pantheon of the Polish city, were Jews or Wrocławians of Jewish background. Yet, in general, the city's Polish society does not embrace its Jewish past with the same enthusiasm as its German past. This is all the more striking because the significance of the city's Jewish history is hard to overestimate. Until 1933, its Jewish community was the third largest in Germany and contributed enormously to its intellectual, cultural, and economic life.[18] After 1945, a vibrant Jewish life reemerged due to the migration of thousands of Polish Holocaust survivors to Wrocław.[19] But it did not last, because postwar anti-Semitism, in particular the anti-Semitic campaign of the Warsaw government in 1968, drove the remnants of Poland's once-large Jewish community out of the country.[20] Wrocław's Jewish community shrank to a small group of mostly older people, who were unable to sustain much of a Jewish cultural life in the city.

Due to the lack of public interest in Wrocław's Jewish past, the renovation of the Stork Synagogue, a beautiful classicist building and the city's only remaining synagogue, has dragged on for many years. The old Jewish cemetery south of the Old Town, one of Central Europe's most impressive Jewish cemeteries, has been a historical landmark since the 1980s. But the slow pace of its restoration and its rather halfhearted promotion compared with the city's other landmarks does not reflect its actual historical significance. When it comes to the city's Jewish history, a fairly small group of Wrocławians as yet take an active interest—although this group is growing and there are the first signs of a Jewish cultural revival similar to Krakow's.

In this respect, Wrocław is no different from other places in Poland. Polish society obviously has a much harder time coming to terms with Jewish-Polish history than with German-Polish relations. In the latter case, the asymmetry of guilt, with the Germans so clearly on the heavy end, seems to make it easier for Polish society to put the painful memories aside and reach out to the German side. But with respect to Polish-Jewish relations, this asymmetry of guilt is reversed. Against this backdrop, any evidence of Jewish history in Poland is a reminder of the skeletons still in the closet, a case already made by Jan Gross.[21] The reluctance to embrace Wrocław's Jewish legacy is not necessarily a sign of anti-Semitism in the present. But it clearly testifies to the city's hesitance to face the past's anti-Semitism.

## *The City of Polish Expellees*

About 20 percent of the Polish settlers in postwar Wrocław came from the "Kresy," Poland's eastern territories annexed by the Soviet Union in 1945 and cleansed of most of their ethnically Polish population. About half of these were former citizens of Lwów (L'viv), East Galicia's mainly Polish-Jewish metropolis, with its famous university and other important cultural institutions. Lwowians constituted only a tiny minority of Wrocław's postwar population, but they provided a good deal of the city's intellectual elite.

In the 1950s, more than 60 percent of the professors at Wrocław's universities had previously taught at Lwów's Jan Kazimierz University,[22] and we can find Lwowians in leading positions in many other institutions of Wrocław's intellectual life.

The idea that Polish Lwów had some afterlife in postwar Wrocław was supported by the relocation from Lwów to Wrocław of large parts of the Ossolineum, which is at the same time a library, archive, and publishing house, as well as one of Poland's most prestigious cultural institutions. Its transfer to Wrocław contributed significantly to the city's transformation into a leading center of cultural life in postwar Poland.

Wrocław's most popular monument, to the Polish poet Alexander Fredro, was transferred from Lwów as well. It was unveiled in 1897 on Lwów's market square, and in 1956 it found a new home on Wrocław's Rynek (figure 3.3). Until 1989, the monument's inscription avoided any reference to its original location in Lwów. This issue was politically sensitive. Everyone in Wrocław knew about the annexation of Eastern Poland through the Soviet Union in 1945 and the region's subsequent de-Polonization. But with respect to the Soviet ally, open references to the loss of the Kresy and the expulsion of the Poles from the east would have violated a taboo.

Similar taboos also explain the complicated history of Wrocław's *Panorama of Racławice*. This monumental painting, displaying the battle between Polish insurgents under the command of the national hero Tadeusz Kościuszko against Russian occupation forces in 1794, was unveiled in Lwów on the occasion of the battle's hundredth anniversary. After World War II, the Soviet authorities had little use for a panorama glorifying an anti-Russian revolt and thus in 1946 decided to hand the painting over to Poland, together with the holdings of the Ossolineum. But because of its politically sensitive content, the *Panorama* was not reinstalled before 1985, when its patriotic and anti-Russian message perfectly fit the political atmosphere of those years. Today, the *Panorama* is one of Wrocław's top attractions, a monument both to Poland's tradition of resistance against foreign rulers and Wrocław's Lwowian connection.

The relocation of some Lwowian institutions to Wrocław and the actual share of people with an East Polish background among the city's current population cannot fully explain the many references to Lwów and the Kresy in present-day Wrocław. Wrocławians like to talk about their ancestors from Eastern Poland. Statistically, however, more Wrocławians have parents and grandparents from the voivodship of Poznań or Warsaw than from the Lwowian voivodship. Though one of Wrocław's most famous restaurants

Figure 3.3. The Alexander Fredro monument, shown here, originally stood on the market square in Lwów. In the 1950s, it was transferred to Wrocław. Thus, the monument not only refers to the popular playwright but also to the fate of the Poles expelled from the East after 1945. Photograph by Gregor Thum.

serves Lwowian cuisine, no one thought of opening a restaurant offering specialties from Poznań or Łódź. Despite the fact that 80 percent of the settlers in postwar Wrocław were migrants from Central Poland, people are much less inclined to talk about those ancestors.

Apart from the fact that the expellees from Eastern Poland had a much greater impact on Wrocław's cultural life than their numbers would suggest, there are probably two reasons for the striking importance of the Kresy myth in present-day Wrocław. First, the Kresy have achieved almost mythical status in Poland. After half a century of banning all Kresy references from the public—with the exception of some indirect forms like Wrocław's Fredro monument that did not name its original location—the fascination with the Kresy among both younger and older Poles is hardly surprising. There is a strong desire to catch up, to learn what life was like in Poland's former East, to correct the distorted image of the Kresy in Communist Poland, and to make up for the denial of public mourning over the collective loss.

Second, the rise of the Kresy myth is also a reflection of the expulsion of the Germans, which has become an important issue again in reunified Germany as well as in Polish-German relations. The fact that the German population had to leave the territories ceded to Poland in 1945 was not denied in Communist Poland. But the transfer of the German population was described in such a vague and selective way that the unrestricted information regarding the sheer scale of the operation and its violent character came as a shock to Polish society after 1990. After half a century of never questioning the legitimacy of the resettlement—with the exception of the aforementioned letter of the Polish bishops from 1965, which failed to gain any public support in Poland—Poles suddenly heard their compatriots talking about Polish guilt.[23]

In Wrocław, the suddenly accessible information regarding the situation of Germans in the city after the war and their inhumane treatment before their deportation seriously undermined the myths of Wrocław's glorious "return to the Motherland" and the heroic memories of the so-called pioneers who came to the city in 1945. The invalidation of these myths through the unpleasant facts of the Polish takeover in Wrocław is an additional explanation for the rise of the Kresy myth. Unlike the myths of the Polish pioneers in postwar Wrocław, references to the loss of Polish land in the east are compatible with the growing international awareness of the horrors of the forced migrations in the wake of the wars in Yugoslavia.

By pointing to the fate of the Kresy, Polish Wrocławians both build a bridge to the German expellees and their experience and also rebuff the demands of the hardliners among the expellees, who continue to talk about compensation. In Wrocław, the implicit message of the Kresy myth is clear: We Polish Wrocławians are expellees as well. We feel sympathy for those expelled from our city, but we do this by sharing their destiny. It is this equality of experience that makes it easier for Polish Wrocławians to acknowledge the suffering and lasting pain of the German expellees. That only some of the city's inhabitants really share this experience is of minor importance as long as Wrocław society collectively identifies with the fate of the Polish expellees.

## The Anticommunist City

The commemoration of the Kresy also has an anticommunist component. The Soviet government annexed Eastern Poland and drove out the Polish population by means that today we would brand "ethnic cleansing." The existence of so many Lwowian institutions in Wrocław makes Wrocław a living memorial to the loss of the Polish East and to the inhumanity of the Soviet policy.

The number of anticommunist monuments in Wrocław is constantly rising. In 2000, a large monument was unveiled in close proximity to the *Panorama of Racławice* to honor the 22,000 Polish prisoners of war murdered by the NKVD in Katyn and elsewhere in the western Soviet Union during the spring of 1940. The construction of this monument, initiated by the Lower Silesian Society of the Families of Katyn, was not motivated by any specific link of those events to the city of Wrocław. But a monument to the victims of Katyn, who uniquely symbolize Poland's brutal oppression by the Soviet Union, suits the attempt to rebrand Wrocław, once the Polish Communists' big hope and always central to Communist propaganda,[24] as a city of anticommunism.

Monuments of a different sort, although part of this very rebranding, are the ever-growing number of bronze dwarfs populating the streets of Wrocław. They refer to the Orange Alternative, an anarchic movement under the leadership of "Major" Waldermar Fydrych that emerged among Wrocław's students in the early 1980s. Whereas the Solidarity movement challenged the Communist government through open political opposition, the Orange Alternative mocked real existing Socialism with witty street happenings in the second half of the 1980s. These happenings, often taking place during Socialist holidays, made fun of Socialist symbols and celebrations and sought to break the passivity of the population.[25] Their main symbol became the red-hatted dwarfs that appeared as graffiti everywhere in the city during the 1980s.

Unlike the Solidarity movement, which was a nationwide phenomenon, albeit with a strong base in Wrocław, the Orange Alternative was really rooted in Wrocław. Therefore, the commemoration of the Orange Alternative was a perfect tool to emphasize Wrocław's anticommunist credentials and, at the same time, distinguish the city from other places in Poland. Moreover, the Orange Alternative was known far beyond Poland, was anticommunist without being politically divisive, and was witty and imaginative, which added to its attractiveness in postsocialist Wrocław. The municipal government designated a prominent location on Świdnicka Street for a monument to the Orange Alternative: a dwarf standing on a thumb. In addition, it has turned the dwarf into Wrocław's mascot. Today, popular sculptures of the dwarfs can be found everywhere across the Old Town, sleeping on sidewalks, climbing street lamps, or busy in other activities of that sort (figure 3.4).

The emphasis on Poland's anticommunist tradition in Wrocław's postsocialist collective memory bears the risk of distorting local history. Without questioning that Communism was imposed in Poland and that its opponents were brutally persecuted, there was also considerable support for many of Communism's political and economic goals.[26] In Wrocław, many of the settlers who came to city were attracted by the promise of social advance, equality, and the idea that Wrocław would become a laboratory for a better Polish society—more just, more modern, and more economically successful. Many of Wrocław's postwar housing projects were built precisely in that spirit, which holds great promise for a society still aware of the great social disparities and the poverty of the lower classes in prewar Poland.

The glorification of all forms of anticommunist resistance led to a disregard for some of the actual achievements of the People's Republic of Poland. Most Wrocławians highly value the results of the historical reconstruction of parts of the Old Town in the 1950s, despite the fact that these reconstructions mirror the traditionalism and nationalism of the Stalinist period. Yet they strongly associate the more international architectural style of the 1960s and 1970s—which had its breakthrough in the wake of de-Stalinization—with Socialism, and accordingly they treat buildings in this style with contempt. Much of what was built in those years is indeed mass architecture without great aesthetic ambition. Nevertheless, there are important exceptions.

When the rebuilding of the third of Wrocław's great market squares, Nowy Targ (New Market), started in the 1960s, a radical revision of Poland's

Figure 3.4. The ever-growing number of dwarfs in the Old Town, like this one, evoke the history of the Orange Alternative. Photograph by Gregor Thum.

building policy in reaction to the traditionalism of the Stalinist years and new economic necessities allowed for a reconstruction in a modern style. The architects tried to reproduce not the forms but the character of the historic square with the means of contemporary architecture. In the 1990s, the much more vibrant life of the two other market squares, both of which had been reconstructed in a historical style, led to the plan to replace the "Socialist" architecture of Nowy Targ with a more "historical" architecture of the prewar time.

Yet, two decades after the end of Communism, the historical distance has grown enough to spark resistance against the plans regarding Nowy Targ.

A group of art historians and preservationists led by Agnieszka Zabłocka-Kos oppose the tendency to tear down even the good examples of architecture built by the People's Republic. They call instead for an open debate about what parts of the architectural legacy of Socialist Wrocław deserve the status of protected historical landmarks.[27] Any such discussion is of course a debate about history itself. The debate regarding the reconstruction of Nowy Targ, which probably would not have emerged with that intensity a decade ago, might indicate that the anticommunist iconoclasm of the post-1989 years is fading and giving way to a more balanced view of the Socialist past.

## The European City

One of the strongest elements in Wrocław's new self-image is that of a European city shaped by various cultural influences in the Polish-Czech-German borderland. Not only the new interpretations of Wrocław's history written by local historians promote this image; the municipal government also portrays Wrocław as the multicultural European city par excellence. Typical are statements like the one in a brochure produced for Wrocław's Expo 2010 campaign: "Wrocław's history, full of changes, has contributed to the development of an open-minded and multicultural city, a city where various European traditions are blended and tied together."[28] The city's official slogan, a quotation from a speech Pope John Paul II gave during the Eucharistic World Congress in Wrocław in 1997, plays the same tune: "Wrocław: City of Encounters" (Wrocław: Miasto Spotkań).

With this shift toward a broader European identity—which is also a marketing tool to support Wrocław's ambition to host international events like the World Exhibition or European Union institutions like the planned European Institute of Technology—Wrocław's Hapsburg heritage has gained particular relevance. The Hapsburg Empire is an ideal historical reference point for Wrocław's attempts to rebrand itself as a multinational, European metropolis. No wonder the city is paying growing attention to its architectural legacy from the Hapsburg era. The grandiose Aula Leopoldina in the University of Wrocław's main building, an impressive baroque palace that originally hosted a Jesuit college founded by Emperor Leopold I, has now become the favorite venue in the city for international meetings. To emphasize its Hapsburg origins, the university recently restored the original Hapsburg eagles on the Aula Leopoldina's front door, which had been replaced by Polish and Silesian eagles after 1945, as well as the "Emperor's

Portal," the university's main entrance, which is richly decorated with two-headed Hapsburg eagles.

Through this strong emphasis on its European heritage, Wrocław may seem less Polish than before. Conversely, the European framework allows for an acknowledgement of the substantial German contributions to Wrocław's development without making it look like a historically German city that just happened to recently become Polish. As long as the city's Germans are just part of a multinational history, their presence poses few problems for the changing collective memory. Representing Wrocław as a European city bridges the contradictions between the German and Polish interpretations of local history.

Unlike the Hapsburgian legacy, Wrocław's rich Prussian heritage has yet to be fully discovered. Due to the century-long demonization of Prussia as an anti-Polish state and the precursor to Nazi Germany's eastward expansionism, Prussia still has a rather negative image in Poland. However, there are signs that sooner or later Wrocławians will also integrate the Prussian past into the multicultural vision of their city. The precondition is a reevaluation of Prussia as historical phenomenon, a process that has recently made some headway.[29] Because Poland occupies the largest part of Prussia's historic territories and carries on a good deal of its legacy, it is not unlikely that Poland will play a more important role in this process and overcome the anti-Prussian sentiment of the past. Then Wrocław's self-image would receive another important element.[30]

Needless to say, the European reinterpretation of Wrocław's history and the emphasis on the city's multicultural past provide all that is needed for a new myth. Pointing to the city's multiculturalism can also help smooth over the tragedies of its twentieth-century history. Its slogan, "City of Encounters," can sound sarcastic when applied to a local past where different cultures used to replace each other with deadly violence. First, Nazi Wrocław evicted Poles and Jews and sent thousands of Jewish citizens to the death camps. Then Polish Wrocław drove the German citizens out of the city and cleansed it of German traces. If the tragic events surrounding 1945 are placed within the framework of the numerous political changes the city has witnessed throughout its history, the rupture of 1945 may appear less dramatic and unique than it actually was. By emphasizing its multicultural past, the city risks burying the tragedies of its past under European kitsch.

Multiculturalism as the proclaimed essence of Wrocław raises questions in another way as well. Modern Wrocław is not a place where various ethnic groups live together. The city's inhabitants are almost exclusively Catholic Poles. In fact, we would have a hard time finding a large European city that is less multicultural than Wrocław. The Wrocław-based columnist Klaus Bachmann, who has been criticizing the city's "multicultural legend," observes that its self-ascribed "tolerance" does not cost anything. According to him, the city must first prove itself by accepting its increasing number of Chinese, Japanese, and Korean immigrant workers, who are about to really make it more multicultural.[31]

One might agree with Bachmann that the litmus test for a truly multicultural city is the integration of foreign immigrants—something Polish Wrocław was not challenged to do in the past. However, one should not underestimate the degree of tolerance the city has in fact shown in the past eighteen years. When Wrocławians stress their city's multiculturalism, they mean their new willingness to embrace its non-Polish past and their desire to define its future in a broader European instead of just Polish framework. In this sense, Wrocławians have come a long way since 1990. Their recognition of their city's German past and their hospitality toward visitors who lived in it before 1945, their erection of monuments honoring citizens of German Wrocław, their acknowledgement of the tragedy of forced migration—all are remarkable. So far, these developments have not been matched by any other city in Central and Eastern Europe with a similar history.

## Conclusion

What happened, however, to the old myth of the Polish city from time immemorial? Was it replaced by the building blocks, described above, of Wrocław's new self-image? In the fall of 2007, the city received a new, quite imposing monument: an equestrian statue showing the Polish king Boleslaw Chrobry, symbolizing medieval Poland in about the year 1000, when it pushed its borders westward, approximately to the line where they run today. In addition, Chrobry created a Polish bishopric in Wrocław in 1000, the earliest date of local history recorded in a written document. In this capacity, Chrobry was always the central figure not only for the myth of Wrocław's Polishness but also for the myth of the "Recovered Territories" in general. Since 1945, numerous other Chrobry monuments have been built, and many streets and squares have been named after him in Poland's western territories.

There was always an idea to create a large Chrobry monument in Wrocław, and it is surprising that this idea was not acted on by Communist Poland. After 1989, the never-realized project was taken up by a private foundation named Pro Wratislavia, a creation of the late 1990s sponsored by a number of Polish corporations, the Warsaw Ministry of Culture and National Heritage, and Wrocław's municipal government. However, Pro Wratislavia's proposal for a Chrobry monument on Świdnicka Street, Wrocław's Fifth Avenue, triggered serious criticism. The proposed monument was attacked for its old-fashioned representation of Chrobry with an equestrian statue, for its traditionalist aesthetic, for its proposed location in the heart of the former Prussian city instead of a historically more appropriate place near the Cathedral of Wrocław, and for its overly patriotic message exactly there where the equestrian statue of the German emperor, Wilhelm I, had once stood. The whole project appeared to many like a relapse to the time before 1989, a retro-monument in the style of the People's Republic of Poland.

In the face of these objections, the fact that Pro Wratislavia's eventually succeeded in building the monument to Chrobry demonstrates the persistence of postwar myths in postsocialist Wrocław. But the monument also testifies to the fundamental changes since 1989. First, the monument's supporters had to endure the public criticism of its opponents. Therefore, they could never claim that the monument expresses the feelings of all Wrocławians. Second, the nationalist message a Chrobry monument of this size, shape, and location inevitably conveys is tightly framed by a European rhetoric. According to Pro Wratislavia, Wrocław "has the right . . . to underline the merits of the Polish monarch," who deserves a place in the "pantheon of outstanding figures of Europe of that time." Interestingly enough, we do not find any references to the myths of the "Recovered Lands."[32] Instead, the monument's trilingual, Polish-Czech-German inscription turns Poland's national hero into an early figure of European integration: "Bolesław Chrobry, the first crowned monarch of Poland, ally of the Papacy and the [Holy Roman] Empire in the spirit of a united Europe in the year 1000."

The fact that postsocialist Wrocław has been creating monuments both to Chrobry, who symbolizes the historical legitimacy of the 1945 border and population shifts, and to the citizens of German Wrocław like Bonhoeffer, Stein, and von Holtei, who cast doubt on that very legitimacy, is not the sign of confused local minds. Instead, it is convincing evidence that a democratic society has emerged in postsocialist Wrocław that is able to live with different, occasionally contradictory readings of the past. The polonocentric myth has not disappeared. Its monuments and memorial plaques are still in place. But they now must compete against the many perspectives on Wrocław's past and the numerous new monuments and plaques that have been created since 1989. Wrocław's self-image has lost the homogeneity of the Socialist era.

Wrocław's government is eager to promote a European Wrocław and the tolerant "City of Encounters." After all, this image is most conducive for a city that must compete in a European and global market for foreign investment, EU funds, international events, and institutions like the European Institute of Technology. But despite this fact, the government has not been able to impose a new official reading of Wrocław's history—if it ever intended to do so. Thus, there is also no oppositional reading of the city's history. In the realm of Wrocław's collective memory, the binary construction "official/oppositional" has become a phenomenon of the past. Each Wrocławian carries his or her own version of Wrocław in his or her mind. Everyone picks from a rich and diverse local history—whatever suits. Today, all the city's monuments, both old and new, do not collectively convey a single, simple message. Wrocław has become a postmodern place.

## Notes

1. Wojciech Wrześinski, "Posłowie," in *Historia Wrocławia*, ed. Wojciech Wrześinski et al. (Wrocław: Dolnośląskie, 2001), vol. 3, 172.

2. Gregor Thum, *Die fremde Stadt: Breslau 1945* (Berlin: Siedler, 2003); Polish edition: *Obce miasto: Wrocław 1945* (Wrocław: Via Nova, 2006); an English edition is scheduled to be published by Princeton University Press in 2010.

3. Prezydium MRN Wrocławia (ed. Komitet Budownictwo), "Plan etapowy m. Wrocławia 1956–1960," *Urbanistyki i Architektury* (Archiwum Akt Nowych we Warszawie, KBUA 11/115), December 1955, 13.

4. Jakub Tyszkiewicz, "Jak Rozbierano Wrocław," *Odra*, no. 9 (1999): 17–21.

5. Thum, *Die fremde Stadt*, 304–37.

6. Ibid., 338–92.

7. Joanna Konopińska, *We Wrocławiu jest mój dom: Dziennik z lat 1946–1948* (Wrocław: Dolnośląskie, 1991), 94.

8. Quoted by Marek Zybura, "Breslau und Wrocław," in *Erinnern, vergessen, verdrängen: Polnische und deutsche Erfahrungen*, ed. Ewa Kobylińska and Andreas Lawaty (Wiesbaden: Harrassowitz, 1998), 377; English translation by John Czaplicka.

9. Jan Assmann, *Das kulturelle Gedächtnis: Schrift, Erinnerung und politische Identität in frühen Hochkulturen*, 2nd ed. (Munich: C. H. Beck, 1997), 48–59.

10. José M. Faraldo, "Medieval Socialist Artefacts: Architecture and Discourses of National Identity in Provincial Poland, 1945–1960," *Nationalities Papers* 29, no. 4 (2001): 605–32; Marcin Zaremba, *Komunizm, legitymacja, nacjonalizm: Nacjonalistyczna legitymacja władzy komunistycznej w Polsce* (Warsaw: TRIO, 2001).

11. Zybura, "Breslau," 377.

12. Andrzej Zawada, "Bresław," in *Bresław: Eseje o miejscach* (Wrocław: Okis, 1996), 52.

13. Norman Davies and Roger Moorehouse, *Microcosm: A Portrait of a Central European City* (London: Jonathan Cape, 2002).

14. See Michał Kaczmarek, Mateusz Goliński, Teresa Kulak, and Włodzimierz Suleja, *Wrocław: Dziedzictwo wieków* (Wrocław: Dolnośląskie, 1997); Teresa Kulak, *Wrocław: Przewodnik historyczny* (Wrocław: Dolnośląskie, 1997); Adam Galos, ed., *Historia Wrocławia*, 3 vols. (Wrocław: Dolnośląskie, 2002); and Beata Maciejewska, *Wrocław: Dzieje Miasta* (Wrocław: Dolnośląskie, 2002). Significant contributions to new interpretations of the local history are also in *Encyklopedia Wrocławia* (Wrocław: Dolnośląskie, 2000); and *Atlas Architektury Wrocławia*, 2 vols., ed. Jan Harasimowicz (Wrocław: Dolnośląskie, 1997–99).

15. Maciej Łagiewski, *Breslau gestern: Wrocław wczoraj* (Gliwice: Wokół Nas, 1996); Stanisław Klimek, *Wrocław: Fotografie z okresu międzywojennego* (Wrocław: Via Nova, 2004).

16. Marek Krajewski, *Śmierć w Breslau* (Wrocław: Dolnośląskie, 2000).

17. Maciej Łagiewski, *Große Breslauer: Die Galerie der Büsten im Breslauer Rathaus* (Wrocław: Muzeum Miejskie Wrocławia, 2004).

18. Till van Rahden, *Jews and Other Germans: Civil Society, Religious Diversity, and Urban Politics in Breslau, 1860–1925*, trans. Marcus Brainard (Madison: University of Wisconsin Press, 2008).

19. Bożena Szaynok, *Ludność żydowska na Dolnym Śląsku 1945–1950* (Wrocław: Uniwersytet Wrocławski, 2000); Leszek Ziątkowski. *Dzieje Żydów we Wrocławiu* (Wrocław: Dolnośląskie, 2000).

20. Bożena Szaynok, "The Role of Anti-Semitism in Postwar Polish-Jewish Relations," in *Anti-Semitism and Its Opponents in Modern Poland*, ed. Robert Blobaum (Ithaca, N.Y.: Cornell University Press, 2005), 265–83.

21. Jan T. Gross, *Fear: Anti-Semitism in Poland after Auschwitz—An Essay in Historical Interpretation* (Princeton, N.J.: Princeton University Press, 2006).

22. On postwar Wrocław's social composition in detail, see Irena Turnau, *Studia nad strukturą ludnościową polskiego Wrocławia* (Poznań: Instytut Zachodni, 1960).

23. See Klaus Bachmann and Jerzy Kranz, *Przeprosić za wypędzenie? O wysiedleniu Niemców po II wojnie światowej* (Kraków: Znak, 1997); also see the German translation: Verlorene Heimat, *Die Vertreibungsdebatte in Polen* (Bonn: Bouvier, 1998).

24. Padraic Kenney, *Rebuildung Poland: Workers and Communists 1945–50* (Ithaca, N.Y.: Cornell University Press, 1997); Jakub Tyszkiewicz, *Sto wielkich dni Wrocławia: Wystawa Ziem Odzyskanych we Wrocławiu a propaganda polityczna ziem zachodnich i północnych w latach 1945–1948* (Wrocław: Arboretum, 1997).

25. Bronisław Misztal, "Between State and Solidarity: One Movement, Two Interpretations—The Orange Alternative Movement in Poland," *British Journal of Sociology* 43, no. 1 (1992): 55–78.

26. Kenney, *Rebuildung Poland;* Jan T. Gross, "War as Revolution," in *The Establishment of Communist Regimes in Eastern Europe, 1944–1949*, ed. Norman Naimark and Leonid Gibianskii (Boulder, Colo.: Westview Press, 1997), 17–40.

27. Beata Maciejewska, "Architektura z czasów PRL jak cenny zabytek," *Gazeta Wyborcza* (Wrocław edition), December 28, 2007; Agata Gabiś, "Ocalić od zapomnienia," *Gazeta Wyborcza* (Wrocław edition), January 4, 2008; Beata Maciejewska, "Co

z Nowym Targiem: Zburzyć czy zostawić?" *Gazeta Wyborcza* (Wrocław edition), May 7, 2008.

28. "Veranstaltungskomitee Expo 2010," in *Weltausstellung EXPO 2010 in Breslau* (Wrocław: Veranstaltungskomitee Expo 2010 in Wrocław, 2000).

29. Christopher Clark, *The Iron Kingdom: The Rise and Downfall of Prussia, 1600–1947* (Cambridge, Mass.: Belknap Press of Harvard University Press, 2006); Basil Kerski, ed., *Preußen: Erbe und Erinnerung—Essays aus Deutschland und Polen* (Potsdam: Deutsches Kulturforum östliches Europa, 2005).

30. For an important first reevaluation of Wrocław's Prussian period from the standpoint of an art historian, see Agnieszka Zabłocka-Kos, *Zrozumieć miasto: Centrum Wrocławia na drodze ku nowoczesnemu city, 1807–1858* (Wrocław: Via Nova, 2006).

31. Klaus Bachmann, "Tolerancja kosztuje," *Gazeta Wyborcza* (Wrocław edition), April 15, 2007.

32. See http://www.prowratislavia.org/dla_chrobry.htm.

# Part II

# Architecture and History at Ports of Entry

# 4

# Mapping Tallinn after Communism: Modernist Architecture as Representation of a Small Nation

*Jörg Hackmann*

During the twentieth and early-twenty-first centuries, many cities in Central and Eastern Europe have faced waves of intense debate about old and new cityscapes. New concepts of urbanism and capitalist demands have met increasing interest for the preservation of old urban structures. Although the preservation of monuments is partly in line with the conservative ideas of *Heimatschutz,* it has become obvious during the last decades that such a black-and-white picture of allegedly conservative heritage protection, on the one hand, and progressive modernism, on the other, are not adequate. In fact, both strains of urban development are closely intertwined. Two major consequences of World War II have enhanced and complicated this general observation for the cities between Szczecin and Narva: destruction during and after the war, combined with massive changes in urban population caused by deportations, the murder of Jews, war losses, and, finally, postwar immigration.

## What Time and Where Is Tallinn?

The ways of dealing with these facts in architectural and urbanist notions and accompanying discussions differ considerably from city to city. Therefore, this chapter does not treat Tallinn (the historical Reval and capital of Estonia) as a case study of urban transformations since 1945, but, rather, considers it a unique place of cultural reorientation after the definite end of the postwar era. To analyze this process more closely, I start this study with the question "What time is the city?"[1] By transposing this question to the various times of reference that have led the perception of the city since the 1990s, three answers, conceived as Weberian ideal types, may be suggested: First, the time, at least mentally revived, is the presocialist city. For the Baltic states and Estonia in particular, such an attitude primarily refers to the interwar period of independent statehood and especially to classical international modernism as a dominating architectural style.[2] In the case of Russian cities, say Saint Petersburg, the time of reference lies in an even earlier period, before World War I in the mythical year of "1913." In Saint Petersburg, as well as in Riga,[3] we find Art Nouveau, Jugendstil, as the focal point of cultural reorientation. Second, the time of the city may be "postsocialist" in the narrow sense that Socialist structures are still the dominant ones. This perception may refer to the technical standard of infrastructure as well as to the lack of new architecture,[4] or, in the case of Moscow, even to the revived praise of the Stalinist high-rise buildings. Finally, in a second reading, time may also be regarded as "postsocialist" in that Socialist urban structures are being replaced or pushed aside by new structures. More specifically, one might call this a time of postsocialist capitalism. In Tallinn, one will see this last approach to the city as having become the most influential—one that demands new architecture in addition to the adoption of as few regulations for development as possible. Administrative regulation was widely perceived as an element of the Socialist past that from which Estonia escaped after the peaceful revolution in 1991. Nevertheless, the aforementioned approaches have also made an impact on the city and should be considered in this analysis.

In reference to Tallinn and other Central and Eastern European cities, the capital cities in particular, one may also ask: Where is the city? Where is it placed on the mental maps of the inhabitants, particularly of those involved in the architectural reconfiguration, as well as of foreign visitors and observers? This is an important question because Tallinn was on the periphery of the Soviet Union, often difficult to locate on a map and even more difficult to identify with the Hansa town of Reval. However, since the 1990s, Reval/Tallinn has become a major tourist destination for Northern Europeans (especially Finns) as well as for tourists from the West. At the same time, Tallinn, like many former Socialist cities, is a shrinking city; its population declined approximately 17 percent, dropping from about 479,000 to 396,000 between 1989 and 2004.[5]

These introductory remarks reveal that architectural and urban development in Tallinn cannot be separated from the political and social changes that have been going on since the late 1980s. In fact, architecture may be regarded as a major field of representation for an Estonian society in the process of departing from its Soviet past. The public discourse on architecture—even long before the end of the Soviet Union—primarily referred to the Estonian nation as an ethnic unit. Since the late 1980s, all larger architectural projects (and even some private ones) have been, in one way or another, related to the reconfiguration of a modern society striving to depart from the impact and sphere of Socialism. In this respect, questions about the ethnicity of architects and commissioners, about the models of architecture they emulate, and about the representation of types of architecture in publications are of some interest.

## Architecture and Nationalism

The representation of a nation, or more generally society, in terms of architecture requires some remarks on (neo)nationalism and the ongoing ethnic discourses in Estonia. In this chapter, I argue that there is no direct relation between the sometimes fierce debates on "ethnic democracy" in Estonia[6] and "ethnicity" as a feature in architecture. One might counter, of course, and argue that striving for an "Estonian architecture"[7] implied an ethnicist argument to the exclusion of non-Estonian architects. In fact, the ethnicist notion of architectural development in Estonia seems to have been shaped by the impact of Socialism, thereby calling for analysis against the historical background. If one takes the architects' ethnic background as the major issue in determining Estonian or non-Estonian architecture, one would neglect the semiotic relation between architecture and national representation. A similar shortcoming may be noticed in identifying two further elements as major sources for representing nationality in architecture: folk architecture, and a historicism based on style elements ascribed to national heritage. John Czaplicka's argument that vernacular architecture in Eastern European cities should be analyzed in a broader context, including modernist architecture, needs to be underlined for Tallinn.[8]

With respect to vernacular and national notions of architecture, the breach of 1991 is also of major importance for another reason: In contrast to Soviet times, when there was hardly any private or social activity not controlled by the state, most of the building activities in postcommunist Tallinn are no longer shaped by state or public institutions; hence, there is no simple relation between architecture and the message of the commissioning state, city, or other public institution. Therefore, one must take into account the extent to which buildings of nonpublic commissioners, such as businesses and also private houses, may be included in such a survey.[9] If one were to exclude this category, this chapter would abruptly end right here. A more balanced method requires us to start from an analysis of the concrete changes in architecture and urban structures and relate them to the debates surrounding the urban fabric and architecture in the given cities; that said, one should take a careful look at the degree to which these discourses are related to the perspective of nationalizing representative elements in the physical environment.[10]

## Tallinn: A Twofold History?

To explain the postcommunist developments in Tallinn, some general outlines on the development of the city's topography are given first (see figure 4.1): The medieval structure of Reval, with the castle and the palaces of the nobility on Toompea (German: Domberg; English: Cathedral Hill) and the lower burghers' town, including the town walls, remained largely unchanged during the nineteenth and twentieth centuries. The authenticity of these structures was a major reason for the addition of Tallinn to the UNESCO World Heritage List in 1997.[11] The only significant new element dated before 1945 to conflict with the medieval urban plan is the Orthodox Alexander Nevsky Cathedral on Toompea, erected in 1894 and 1900 by Mikhail Preobrazhenskii. Until 1940, only individual buildings inside the Old Town were replaced. Even the air raid of 1944, which destroyed several blocks of the Old Town south of the Town Hall Square around Saint Nikolai's Church as well as parts of the nineteenth- and twentieth-century quarters around the "Estonia" theater,[12] did not seriously affect the historical topography. The quarters surrounding the medieval town were erected subsequently, following the end of the fortress status of Reval/Tallinn after the Crimean War (1853–56), the deconstruction of the ramparts (1857–64), and the railway connection to Saint Petersburg in 1870.[13] The city saw dynamic expansion in the decades before 1914, in line with the rise of the Estonian population, which in 1904 achieved the majority in the City Duma. However, Eliel Saarinen's master plan for the development of Great Tallinn,[14] as well as

Figure 4.1. A map of Tallinn's city center, 2005. Reprinted, by permission, © 2005 by E. O. Map.

plans for a large city hall on the spot of today's Viru Hotel,[15] went unrealized, as did plans for rebuilding Vabaduse Väljak (Freedom Square) into a site for state representation by the independent Estonia in the interwar period.[16]

As in many other towns in Central and Eastern Europe, Reval/Tallinn had to deal with ethnically motivated "competing visions" of urban history and topography starting in the late nineteenth century.[17] In vernacular visions of the Germans and Estonians alike, the Old Town of Reval was perceived as German,[18] whereas the old suburbs were regarded as Estonian. The competing ethnic biases also shaped the desire and attempts to express nationality in architectural development before 1914, most clearly visible in the theater buildings. Though the German Theater of 1906–10, built by Nikolai Vasil'ev and Aleksei Bubyr from Saint Petersburg, followed a national romanticist style first promoted by Eliel Saarinen in 1900, the Estonia Theater, built on a neighboring spot by the Finnish architects Armas Lindgren and Wivi Lönn in 1910–13, used a neoclassical style (figures 4.2 and 4.3).[19]

This traditional scheme of competing perceptions has continued in the German writings on Reval almost until today. But the Estonians adopted the Hansa town as a part of their own history once the Germans were driven from the country in 1939–40, and the Socialist suburbs began to fill up with Russian-speaking immigrants. Therefore, in Tallinn the sense of divided history was less acute than in Polish cities in the newly gained western territories,[20] such as Wrocław, Gdańsk, and Szczecin, or in the former Polish cities, such

Figure 4.2. The German Theater, 1906–10. Architects: Nikolai Vasil'ev and Aleksei Bubyr. Reprinted by permission of the Museum of Estonian Architecture.

Figure 4.3. The Estonia Theater, 1910–13. Architects: Armas Lindgren and Wivi Lönn. Reprinted by permission of the Museum of Estonian Architecture.

as Lwów/L'viv or Wilno/Vilnius. For Tallinn as well as for Riga, we might rather speak of urban history with a broad historical perspective versus the narrow perspective of Soviet urban history.

## Late Soviet Architecture and Its Impact on Postsocialist Tallinn

Although there have been many plans for an urban reshaping of Tallinn since 1945,[21] the situation was different from Riga, where the first steps toward breaking the old town apart by a huge axis across the former Town Hall Square had already been made. In the case of Riga's Town Hall, Soviet urbanism collided with a notion of historical topography, which was based on plans to reconstruct the ensemble of historic buildings including the famed House of the Black Heads, whose ruins were demolished in 1948.[22] Erecting new buildings on this spot or leaving it empty for reconstruction was a major issue of debate in Riga for decades. In Tallinn, conflicts were not that acute. Although there had been several Soviet projects outside the city center in the 1950s, significant changes to Tallinn's urban fabric did not appear until the late 1960s.[23] For almost twenty years, two high-rise buildings—the first ones in Tallinn—would dominate the city's skyline beyond the Old Town and the Toompea District: The first of these is the Viru Hotel, by Henno Sepmann and Mart Port, built by a Finnish company in 1969–72.[24] Consisting of two large connected vertical slabs with a monolithic concrete framework (figure 4.4), it clearly followed traditions of the International Style. The second, albeit less significant, high-rise building was the Olümpia Hotel, completed in 1980 by Toivo Kallas and Rein Kersten for the sailing competitions of the Moscow Olympic Games of 1980. Another building created specifically for the Olympic Games, the Kultuuri- ja Spordipalee (Palace of Culture and Sport, today Linnahall / City Hall) was erected in the harbor area (figure 4.5). This multifunctional convention center comprises a large auditorium with some 4,600 seats and an ice rink. Completed by Raine Karp and Riina Altmäe in 1981, the Linnahall is a large but rather shallow and symmetrical building, the outer walls of which are covered with uncut regional limestone. The building was designed to open up "cultivated" public access to the Baltic Sea by way of two monumental flights of stairs.[25] The architectural task was demanding, because the build-

Figure 4.4. The Viru Hotel, 1964–72. Architects: Henno Seppman and Mart Port. Reprinted by permission of the Museum of Estonian Architecture.

Figure 4.5. Tallinn City Hall, 1975–80. Architects: Raine Karp and Riina Altmäe. Reprinted, by permission, from *Entsüklopeedia Tallinn* (Tallinn: Eesti Entsüklopeediakirjastus, 2004), volume 1, page 297; © 2004 by Eesti Entsüklopeediakirjastus. Photograph by Peeter Säre.

ing had to bridge railway tracks leading to the harbor and was not allowed to block the extraordinary view of the medieval city from the seaside. The Kultuuri ja Spordipalee was also designed as the culminating point of a band of Socialist modernist buildings (never realized) that was to lead from the Viru Hotel at Viru Väljak to the harbor.[26]

Raine Karp,[27] the same architect who worked in the central architectural office of the ESSR, Eesti Projekt, also designed two large buildings in the center of Tallinn: the Communist Party's political instruction center known as (new) Sakala Keskus (Sakala Cultural Center, 1982–85) and the Rahvusraamatukogu (National Library) (figure 4.6). The Sakala Cultural Center vis-à-vis the Communist Party's Central Committee Building[28] (now the Ministry of Foreign Affairs) on Teatri Väljak (Theater Square) was designed to become the center of Socialist Tallinn. Built as a convention center for the Estonian Communist Party in a postmodernist mode, it alluded to a sacral building with outside buttresses resembling French Gothic style and even features a bell tower.[29] The largest and most important of the buildings of the late Soviet period is the Rahvusraamatukogu (National Library). The competition for its design was held in 1982, and construction began in 1984 on an irregular site behind Kaarli Kirik (Charles' Church) and the Soviet monument to the liberators of Tallinn in 1944, known as the Pronkssõdur (Bronze Soldier), which was relocated in April 2007. The library's structure was not completely finished until 1992, after the end of the Soviet Republic of Estonia. As in the case of the Sakala Cultural Center, one clearly notices sacral architectural features. However, this time the outside of the building, facing the neo-Gothic Charles' Church, resembles a temple—as is partly the case with the Linnahall. The library's vestibule contains not only a monumental staircase climbing the full height of the building but also a multitude of arches and arcades, which contribute a castle- or cloister-like aspect to the interior. Once again, Karp chose local dolomite blocks of irregular size for the walls of the building. Given that this building has been called "the most perfect realization of postmodernism in Estonia,"[30] one can conclude that international trends were already present in Estonia during the Soviet period and wonder about their meaning, which will be addressed below.

The building of the National Library in particular is important for our discussion—not so much for its architectural quality but for its example of transitional architecture.[31] It shows the continuity of postmodernist architecture from late Socialist years to the period of reestablished national statehood. If one interprets it as a temple of the Estonian book, then it is obvious that lending such national structures a sacral character was not an invention of the post-Soviet period. This indicates that ethnicity had already

Figure 4.6. The Estonian National Library, 1984–92. Architect: Raine Karp. Reprinted by permission of the Museum of Estonian Architecture.

played an important role within the framework of officially approved architecture in Soviet times; hence, processes of renationalization or reethnicization cannot be separated from their Soviet prehistory, even if the extent of irony intended by such designs remains under discussion.

## Restored Architecture and Restored Nationality

In Karp's buildings, these allusions to a (mythical) past, albeit ironical in tone, lead to the first major feature of the post-Soviet development: the restoration of architectural monuments, primarily discussed here as an expression of local identity rooted in history before the Soviet era. The major reason for restoring old monuments was to recall the interwar era of Estonian nationhood and statehood. Though one needs to discuss whether such a historical notion was also inherent to the mythical and sacral character of the aforementioned buildings by Karp, in the case of restoring monuments of architecture, the meaning was much more unambiguous and concrete. Restoring buildings clearly connected to the first instance of Estonian nationhood—ones derided by Soviet ideologues as relics of the feudal past, like castles, churches, and manors—sent a clear message. The restoration of castles of the Teutonic Order, manor houses throughout Estonia, or the Old Tallinn Town Hall (Vana Raekoda) not only contradicted Soviet ideology but also indicated that earlier nationalist perceptions of them as symbols of the "seven hundred years of darkness" before the founding of Estonia had disappeared.[32] This type of restoration activity, which began in the Soviet era, underwent dynamic growth in the 1980s.[33] It continued beyond the caesura of 1991 and continues today, although the restoration seems to have lost some of the importance that it had in the early 1990s. The most significant examples of this restoration are the Riigikogu Hoone (Parliament Building) on Toompea and the Estonia Theater.

The Riigikogu Hoone, built by Herbert Johanson and Eugen Habermann in 1920–22, is situated in the building and grounds of what was once the castle of the Teutonic Order and later the residence of the tsarist governor; its current form was shaped from premises devastated by fire in February 1918. The interior—the Assembly Hall, in particular—is an extraordinarily fine example of expressionist architecture and, as such, a rather untypical example for state representation (figure 4.7).[34] The dramatic ceiling and the window jambs feature zigzag motifs; a stark contrast of colors was provided by the lemon ceiling, ultramarine walls, and brown window jambs. Such a modernist solution may be explained by the fact that there were no historical traditions other than mythological ones to represent the new Estonian statehood. After changes during the Soviet period, such as the strange idea of placing a bust of Lenin into the zigzag element above the door at the front wall, the detailed restoration of the Parliament Building was finished in 1997 —more than a historical approximation, it provided a precise reconstruction of the original color schemes as well as of the wooden interiors.[35]

The second example, the Estonia Theater, may be regarded as the most important building of the (ethnic) Estonian population, at least for the few years before the emergence of Independent Estonia in 1918–19. Without political institutions and edifices with which they could identify, the Estonians expressed their cultural identity instead through the buildings of voluntary associations such as the Wastastikune Krediidi Ühisus (Mutual Credit Society) built by Eliel Saarinen opposite the Estonia Theater in 1912.[36] The Estonia, commissioned by a choral society of the same name, was erected not only as a concert and theater hall but also as a house for the society, with club rooms, shops, and the like.[37] After the damage suffered during World War II, the building was restored and partly remodeled by Alar Kotli in the years 1945–51.[38] This remodeling starkly changed the interior of the building,

Figure 4.7. The Assembly Hall of the Estonian Parliament Building, 1920–22. Architects: Herbert Johanson and Eugen Habermann. Restored in 1997 by Mart Kalm and others. Photograph courtesy of the photographer, Kaido Haagen.

adding Socialist emblems throughout and ceiling paintings with Socialist motifs in the theater hall.[39] A subsequent restoration that began in the late 1980s and ended in 1997 not only removed the Socialist decor—although the Socialist painting on the theater hall's ceiling remained—but also added a room for chamber music, which had been planned but not realized in the 1930s.[40] Thus, the restoration could be seen as carrying forth the unrealized plans of the first independent Estonian state;[41] the result, however, is a hybrid one.

Of course, there are many more facets to this complex work of restoration. On the one hand, it is rooted in policies of the Soviet period; in 1966 the Tallinn city center, like Riga, was put under state protection.[42] And even before that, restoration work had begun on the Old Town Hall in the 1950s.[43] On the other hand, the impetus for restoration came from many private initiatives and encompassed all types of buildings,[44] from those built in the medieval period to those built during first era of Estonian Independence. Early modernist and functionalist buildings—such as the abovementioned building of the Mutual Credit Society by Saarinen (restored

1996), or the Kunstihoone (House of Arts) by Anton Soans and Edgar Kuusik (built 1934, restored 1994)—are of particular importance,[45] because they were the subjects of a broad public discourse among Estonian art historians and architects, which was initiated by Leo Lapin.[46] The periodical *Ehituskunst* (Art of Building), published since 1981, has dedicated much space to functionalist architecture and to photographs of the original shapes as well as the contemporary situation of these buildings.[47] It seems that the architecture of classical modernism in Estonia had already become a major subject in the debate about architectural heritage that is discussed below.

## Neglected and Transformed Spaces

The broad and scrupulous restoration work done on the aforementioned buildings contrasts with the neglect, devastation, and demolition visited upon unused Socialist and even presocialist industrial areas, such as in the harbor area of Tallinn and outlying areas and in many public buildings. In some instances, the benign neglect that leads to deterioration must also be regarded as a conscious strategy for clearing space for new buildings. In general, the adaptation and reconstruction of presocialist industrial and Socialist public buildings remains the exception in Tallinn. In the harbor area, as well as in the case of a large paper factory on Tartu Maantee (Tartu Road),[48] the results of decay are clearly visible. The above-mentioned City Hall, although still in use, offers another significant example of neglect: It lies away from the new centers of development and has hence become marginalized. Its exterior staircases of dolomite staircases are in a state of ruin and and no longer offer a convenient approach to the Baltic.[49]

The most important of these partly devastated areas is the industrial area between the booming harbor and Narva Maantee (Narva Road), as it links the passenger ferry terminals with the big hotels of the Kesklinn (City Center). Although there is no master plan for this region,[50] there are some public and private examples of the adaptation of single buildings to new purposes deserving of our attention. The most significant is the Museum of Architecture (Eesti Arhitektuuri Muuseum) in the former salt storage of the Rotermann Factory (Rotermanni Soolaladu), a limestone building of 1908, which was restored by Ülo Peil in 1996. Another example is the Optiva Bank (formerly Forekspank) Building, which was reshaped from a Socialist industrial building—a radio plant—in 1996–97 by Marika Lõoke and Jüri Okas, who covered it with a curtain facade of steel and glass (figures 4.8 and 4.9).[51] As a third example—not as prominent but certainly not un-

Figure 4.8. A Socialist radio plant before being rebuilt into a bank building (shown in figure 4.9). Reprinted, by permission, from *Maja,* number 4 (1997): 35. © 1997 by AS Solness.

Figure 4.9. The rebuilt radio plant (shown in figure 4.8), originally called the Forekspank Building, 1996–97, and now the Optiva Bank Building. Architects: Marika Lõoke and Jüri Okas. Reprinted, by permission, from *Maja,* number 4 (1997): 35. Photograph by Kaido Haagen; © 1997 by AS Solness.

typical—the Centraal Hotell on Narva Maantee might be mentioned. Initially, it consisted of a typical Socialist workers' apartment block in an industrial courtyard, to which a new apartment section was added. In recent years, new office buildings have slowly transformed this postsocialist industrial desert. As a further example of the transformation of a Socialist building, the Melon Shopping Center on Estonia Puiestee (Estonia Alley), may be mentioned; the facade (dating to the late 1950s) of the former Estonian Energy Administration Main Office has been covered with a glass curtain. Inside, the building has been almost totally emptied, making it obvious that this transformation is dominated by features of new architecture.

## Post-1991 Architecture

Having focused on the discussion of late Socialist architecture as well as the restoration activities on public buildings in particular, the picture changes significantly when one looks at the main trends of new architecture since 1991.[52] Here, commercial buildings are most prominent. First place undoubtedly goes to bank buildings, such as the Ühispank Tower (by Raivo Puusepp, 1995–99), a significant pyramidal high-rise building with a glass facade. Indeed, the fact that it is taller than the previously dominating Socialist hotel buildings mentioned above seems to have driven the commissioners, and it was enthusiastically appreciated as symbol of Estonia's economic success.[53] Even more controversial than the architecture, however, is its impact on the urban fabric. Unlike the situation in Riga and Tartu, where single high-rise buildings were erected on empty spaces on riverbanks across from the respective Old Towns, the Ühispank Tower was built on a historic site. Thus, Mart Kalm speaks of a "brutal neglect of public interests," as the building required construction of a new street across the old churchyard of Jaani Seegi Kirik (Saint John's Hospital Church) (figure 4.10).[54] Banks and office buildings around the "Freedom Square," though having no similar impact on the city's skyline, are also clear landmarks of the new era: the Kawe Plaza Building by Henno Sillaste, finished in 1998, and the Tallinn Bank Building by Aare Saks, completed in 1997. Though the latter tries to adapt to the surrounding buildings of the 1930s, the Kawe Plaza Building, built to occupy a unique triangular site and characterized by its entirely glass facade, is a completely new element in that part of the city.

Besides those bank and office buildings, it is once again hotels that constitute the next important group of postsocialist buildings. Apart from adap-

Figure 4.10. The Tallinn business area in 2000. The old wooden buildings in the center were later removed for the new Tartu Road between the Stockmann and Ühispank buildings. Photograph courtesy of the photographer, Peeter Säre.

tations of pre-1940 and Socialist hotels (as in the case of the renovated Viru Hotel and the Palace Hotel, as well as hotels in restored buildings in the Old Town), several new hotels have been erected. The most significant of them is the Radisson Hotel by Vilen Künnapu and Ain Padrik, built in 1999–2001, in close proximity to the Ühisbank Building and a focal point at the end of Laikmaa Tänav (Laikmaa Street); the Radisson, too, surpasses the heights of the older hotels and thus shifts the high point of the skyline to the new buildings of the post-1991 era (figure 4.11).

Shopping centers constitute the third important group of new buildings. Not only have they emerged as huge shopping malls on the outskirts of Tallinn, but also within the downtown area. The most controversial project has been the De la Gardie Kaubamaja, a department store by Andres Alver and Tiit Trummal, completed in 2000, built on an empty site along one of the major streets in the Old Town, thus disguising a Stalinist hotel behind it. The facade is designed as three different vertical sections to coincide with the former separation of three houses. However, this allusion is a purely structural one, as the building incorporates no historicist elements at all. In

Figure 4.11. The skyline of Tallinn in 2004; a view from Toompea. In the center is the tower of the Old City Hall. The other main buildings, from left to right: the Viru Hotel (1964–72, by the architects Henno Seppman and Mart Port), the City Plaza Office Building (2002–4, by Andres Alver and Tiit Trummal), the Ühispank Building (1995–99, by Raivo Puusepp), the SAS Radisson Hotel (1999–2001, by Vilen Künnapu and Ain Padrik), and Maakri Maja (2002–3, by Raili Kadarik and Priit Ehala). Photograph by Jörg Hackmann.

addition, the view through the glass elements makes it clear already from the outside that the inside of the building is treated as one undivided cube. The most important of these shopping centers, however, is the Viru Keskus (Viru Center) by Vilen Künnapu and Ain Padrik, finished in 2004. The transformation of the parking lot behind the Viru Hotel into a mall connected to the hotel was not a surprising idea, because even Soviet plans had contained some kind of a building adjacent to the hotel. But the impact of the mall clearly goes beyond the building of the center itself, as it expanded across the street to include the Soviet Kaubamaja, a department store, built in 1954–60. It is now connected to the new center by a broad, covered pedestrian bridge, an addition that totally neglected and deformed the original facade, thus reducing the old department store to a mere annex of the new center (figure 4.12). On the opposite side of the street, the Soviet-type Teenindusmaja (House of Services) of 1974 has been transformed into another hotel (Tallink) with a new, expressive facade structured on the lower stories using organ-pipe-like elements. Without a doubt, the urbanity of a big city was meant to be achieved on Laikmaa Street between the Viru Center and the Tallink Hotel, the high-rise Radisson Hotel and the City Plaza office building (by Alver and Trumal) at its end; one has such an impression upon entering from the harbor area, the main gateway for tourists to Tallinn (figure 4.13).

Many more examples of modernist architecture—in the harbor area, for instance, as well as commercial buildings (not least by automobile dealerships)[55] on the outskirts—might extend this list of commercial buildings. In any case, this sketch even as it stands reveals that architectural development in Tallinn is now directed by commercial interests and rules, not by state or communal authorities. This development is also reflected in recent publications on Estonian architecture, such as *Vaba Eesti Ehitab* (Free Estonia Is Building)[56] and the Estonian architectural review called *Maja* (House).[57]

At this point, my previous statement that there are no new (noncommercial) public buildings in post-Soviet Tallinn must be slightly modified. Some

Figure 4.12. The Viru Center and the old Soviet Kaubamaja (department store) in 2004. Photograph by Jörg Hackmann.

Figure 4.13. Laikmaa Street in 2004. On the left is the Tallink Hotel. On the right is the Viru Center (2002–4), and in the center is the SAS Radisson Hotel (1999–2001)—both by Vilen Künnapu and Ain Padrik. Photograph by Jörg Hackmann.

new public buildings, primarily related to commerce and communication, such as the ferry terminals in the harbor area, do indeed exist. The KuMu Art Museum on the eastern outskirts of Tallinn, which after a lengthy period of planning finally opened in 2006, also needs to be mentioned here. Furthermore, there are many examples of new school buildings and bus stations all over Estonia. Nonetheless, if we focus on the center of Tallinn, the general picture outlined above remains accurate. One of the very few noncommercial buildings to be addressed in this context is the Okupatsioonide Muuseum (Museum of the Occupations) by Indrek Peil and Siiri Vallner, completed in 2003 (figure 4.14). The rather small structure consists of an uneven concrete base and a glass-steel elevation. The entrance to the museum lies behind a small courtyard, which the visitor must enter from beneath a low gallery with a massive concrete floor; one must bend down in order to enter the building.[58] This first museum building of the post-1991 era was initiated and financed by a private institution from the United States, the Kistler-Ritso Foundation. On the one hand, it refers to an important dis-

Figure 4.14. The Museum of the Occupations, completed in 2003. Architects: Indrek Peil and Siiri Vallner. Photograph by Jörg Hackmann.

course among the Estonian population: reminders to remember their own fate as experienced under Soviet rule. On the other hand, it is connected to an international debate on the Holocaust in the Baltic during World War II. This debate arose as the Baltic states proposed joining NATO and the European Union, and it continues to this day. Because the role both issues play in the collective memory of Estonians, this small museum carries great contemporary significance.

Among the ongoing projects, the most important entails plans for reshaping the Teatri Väljak in front of the Estonia Theater and the space of the above-mentioned Sakala Keskus. The adaptation of the Sakala Keskus was the subject of an architectural competition in 2003 for a new cultural center. Plans were changed, however, in 2006, when the demolition of the interior began. Against public protest, the building was almost completely pulled down in March 2007, with a significant exception, however: The tower will be integrated into the new recreation and culture mall (figure 4.15).[59]

A last point in this overview of new architecture refers to private homes and apartment buildings. Of course, here one sees buildings of the nouveaux

Figure 4.15. The demolition of the Sakala Cultural Center in 2007. Photograph by Jörg Hackmann.

riches, but mainly outside Tallinn, on the seafront. Many of these homes are eclectic "palace" structures of a very low architectural significance. In his book, Mart Kalm presents a contrasting trend reaction in the neofunctionalist villas of the 1990s, mainly in the Nõmme garden district (figure 4.16). Kalm and others, with good reason, have interpreted these as a third wave of functionalism, opening a conscious dialogue with the modernist architecture of the interwar period, which gave rise to some remarkable functionalist dwelling houses in Nõmme.[60] These neomodernist buildings relate to the Estonian architectural discourse already outlined above.

## The Architectural and Urban Development of Post-Soviet Tallinn

Having outlined the architectural development in Tallinn after the fall of the Soviet system, some related problems need to be discussed. The first refers to the urban development of post-Soviet Tallinn. The Socialist urban master plan of 1961 and its subsequent variants through the mid-1980s,[61] as

Figure 4.16. A villa in the Nõmme garden district, 1998–2001. Architects: 3+1 Architects (Markus Kaasik, Andres Ojari, and Ilmar Valdur). Photograph courtesy of the photographer, Kaido Haagen.

well as plans of earlier decades, have had only very limited application. As argued by Karin Hallas-Murula and Mart Kalm, the plans of 1995 and 1999 that followed the Soviet era do not deserve the title "master plan," for they provide no outline for urban development. According to Hallas and Kalm, they contain a mere description of what is actually going on and do not reveal any perspectives beyond the dictates of the market.[62] In fact, urban planning in the 1990s seems to have remained behind Soviet-era planning, or, in the words of Tiit Trummal: "Things that were planned and strictly regulated in the previous system, have become self-organizing."[63] Structures like the Ühispank Building have contributed to a rather chaotic development that neglects historical structures and creates a situation in which urban planning appears simply reactionary.[64] With the Ühispank Building, the last section of Tartu Maantee was shifted toward a connection with Rävala Puiestee (Rävala Alley), where the Radisson Hotel and adjacent office buildings are situated. It now runs across a quarter once belonging to Saint John's Hospital. Archaeological relics found beneath the new street are partly presented under a triangular concrete-glass structure on the sidewalk, blocking the way for pedestrians.

Set against the powerful forces developing shopping malls,[65] urban planning appears in a similarly weak position. No only does the already-mentioned Viru Keskus Bridge over a broad street distort the facade of the Soviet-era Kaubamaja, it also influences the surrounding street fronts. In a similar manner, urban development is largely being driven by the establishment of large-scale business centers. The commercial center of the city has clearly shifted to an area between the Viru and Olympia hotels, where the main department stores, banks, office buildings, and the like are situated. As has been argued, one reason for the chaotic situation of urban planning is the fact that the city of Tallinn owns only a very small part of public ground; the largest part, however, is state property.[66] A similar analysis has been made for the former Rotermann industrial area, mentioned above. There, too, attempts to introduce a master plan were initiated *after* the architectural development of the area had begun. Such so-called plans do not provide guidelines for urban development but rather follow existing patterns of development. Several smaller projects have emerged with the given situation in that area.[67]

Other plans for Tallinn currently being discussed, such as that of "Talsinki,"[68] a combined metropolis of Helsinki and Tallinn across the Gulf of Finland, are highly speculative. Still, this one does have some basis, given the fact that most of the business activities in the proximity of the harbor area in Tallinn are connected to tourism from Northern and Western Europe.

## A National Architecture?

An important point that I would like to add here regards an issue not yet adequately discussed in Estonia: the identity of the architects active in Tallinn. A look into the various publications on contemporary architecture in Estonia[69] reveals that, until recently, architectural projects were carried out almost exclusively by Estonian architects living in Estonia,[70] although those commissioning hotels, banks, and shopping malls are usually international companies. Until 2006, the only exceptions to this have involved two ethnic Estonian architects from Canada and Sweden, and the Finnish architect Pekka Vapaavuori, who designed the KuMu Art Museum, mentioned above.[71] It also seems most of the commissioned architects were educated in Tallinn. Thus, architectural design, whether intentional or not, has largely remained in the hands of Estonian nationals in the first fifteen years after Independence.[72] One can differentiate the generations among these architects and distinguish them by the roles they played in Soviet and post-Soviet times. If a small number of architects dominated the late Soviet era (e.g., Mart Port and Raine Karp), the 1970s saw the emergence of a group of architects constituting a no less nationally motivated opposition, led by Leo Lapin, Vilen Künnapu, and Veljo Kaasik. This group, termed the "Tallinn Ten," mainly attacked what they called the "Finnish cornice architecture" of Karp; the Ten led in the development of Estonia's postmodernist architecture and followed a restorationist approach, which focused largely on the Estonian classical modernism of "white houses without roofs."[73] Apart from the Tallinn Ten, another band of the so-called prize-winning boys emerged in the 1980s.[74] They dominated most of the late Soviet architectural competitions but were not commissioned to build the projects. As indicated in this chapter, members of this group, including Ülo Peil, Raivo Puusepp, and Emil Urbel, clearly shaped the architectural development of Tallinn in the 1990s.

A discussion of Tallinn's architectural development should include the issue of the "message" of post-Soviet architecture, for several reasons. The intention to express a message was clear from the onset of the Tallinn Ten. In 1984, Lapin communicated the opinion that "Estonian architecture must be built by Estonian architects."[75] It seems this slogan not only gained support among the nationally oriented Estonian intelligentsia but, as shown in Karp's architecture discussed above, was also adopted by the dominant Soviet Estonian architects or, at least, was reflected in their works.

If Lapin's slogan was directed against Soviet-type architecture without relation to the Estonian context, the issue of Estonian architects designing typical Soviet-type architecture remains. Here it seems the Estonian architectural discourse has not excluded such Estonian architects from the Soviet period but rather included them in a national canon of architecture,[76] undoubtedly rooted in the classical modernist architecture dating to before 1940.[77] From this perspective, some of the Soviet modernism of the 1960s and 1970s could be read as a continuation of Estonian traditions. The main opposition was not so much Estonian versus non-Estonian architecture but regional traditions and projects versus Soviet influences. From that perspective, the application of folk elements following the Stalinist doctrine of "national in form, socialist in content" was less important than following international trends in the postwar period or the perception of Western architectural trends since the 1970s.[78] Thus, the late Soviet postmodernist architecture, too, was firmly integrated into a notion of national identity.

Furthermore, the development of early postmodernist tendencies in Estonia also shows that architects there were aware of international tendencies and considered themselves part of the avant-garde.[79] This issue leads to a third point: Modernist architecture (including classical modernism as well as the neomodernism of the 1990s) was interpreted in the Estonian discourse primarily as a sign of the capability of a small nation to meet the cultural state of the art. Such a message could also be read in the modernist architecture of the Soviet period, which was not least influenced by contacts with Finland starting in the 1960s.[80] Thus, even the rather closed group of Soviet Estonian architects contributed in some respect to a national concept of Estonian architecture, although there were, of course, conflicts among the above-mentioned groups of architects, arising not least from the Soviet system of privileges.

## Conclusions

To conclude, there are five salient points. First, the expression of modernity was an important feature of architectural development throughout twentieth-century Estonia. In the interwar period,[81] and again from the 1980s onward, it was closely connected to a political and social message: to show that the small Estonian nation is capable of developing ambitious contemporary architecture similar to Finland, an important model for Estonia throughout the twentieth century. Second, the restorationist approach starting in the late 1980s led to a revival of the classical modernist architecture of the 1920s and 1930s in terms of historic preservation and as emulated in the new architecture since the 1990s. Third, the quick and definite departure from the Socialist past was obviously a driving force in the architectural and urban development of Tallinn in the 1990s. However, contemporary debates are not that unambiguous about the results of this widely uncontrolled capitalism. Fourth, already since Soviet times, a tendency in

Estonian debates on architecture has been to underline elements of continuity in Estonian architecture throughout the twentieth century, including elements of the Soviet period. This neonationalist tendency has quickly developed into an openly neomodernist one, as may be noticed in the revival of an Estonian neofunctionalism, similar to the Finnish discourse on architecture.[82]

Fifth and finally, if one were to again ask the question posed at the outset —Where is Tallinn on mental maps?—Estonian architects and the Estonian public sphere would presumably not hesitate to locate the city somewhere in the North—if there is any concrete region, and not a global notion with which to identify—but certainly not in the East. And it may be assumed that the mental maps of a wider architectural audience, as well as of the international public sphere, would follow the Estonian suggestion. The architectural discourse thus disseminates a clearly international, modernist image of the nation.

## Notes

1. See the introduction to this volume.

2. Cf. Steven A. Mansbach, "Modernist Architecture and Nationalist Aspiration in the Baltic: Two Case Studies," *Journal of the Society of Architectural Historians* 65, no. 1 (2006): 92–111.

3. Jānis Krastiņš has published extensively on Riga; see, e.g., Jānis Krastiņš, *Rīga: Jugendstilmetropole* (Riga: Baltika, 1996); Art Noveau as has been a major argument for inscribing Riga to the UNESCO World heritage list; as (*severnyi*) *modern* ("Northern modernism") it has also become a fashionable feature of the architectural discourses on Saint Petersburg; see, e.g., Boris Mikhailovich Kirikov, *Arkhitektura Peterburgskogo Moderna* (Saint Petersburg: Neva, 2003); and on one of its main protagonists, Aleksei Bubyr': http://bubyr.narod.ru/index.html. Cf. also the exhibition catalogue: Jeremy Howard, ed., *Architecture 1900: Stockholm–Helsinki–Tallinn–Riga–St. Petersburg* (Tallinn: Printon, 2003).

4. We may find such a situation in cities that were hardly affected by the changes of the 1990s. For Estonia, one might discuss the cases of Narva and Paldiski in this connection.

5. The ratio of ethnic Estonians has increased slightly, from 54.2 percent in 2000 to 54.4 percent in 2004. These data were compiled from the databases of the Statistikaamet (Statistical Office of Estonia); see http://pub.stat.ee/px-web.2001/Dialog/varval.asp?ma=RV0222&ti=RAHVASTIK+SOO%2C+RAHVUSE+JA+MAAKONNA+J%C4RGI%2C+1%2E+JAANUAR&path=../Database/Rahvastik/01Rahvastikunaitajad_ja_koosseis/04Rahvaarv_ja_rahvastiku_koosseis/&lang=2 and http://www.tallinn.ee/est/linna_juhtimine/linnakantselei/struktuur/avalike_suhete_teenistus/struktuur/teabeosakond/arvud_2003/tallinn_arvudes2003_uus3.pdf.

6. On this discussion, see Priit Järve, *Ethnic Democracy and Estonia: Application of Smooha's Model,* ECMI Working Paper 7 (Flensburg: ECMI, 2000); and Aleksei Semjonov, "Ethnic Limits of Civil Society: The Case of Estonia," in *Civil Society in the Baltic Sea Region,* ed. Norbert Götz and Jörg Hackmann (Aldershot, U.K.: Ashgate, 2003), 145–57.

7. Estonian architects and scholars produced an extensive debate on this point, particularly during the late 1980s and early 1990s; see, e.g., Krista Kodres, "Rahvuslik identiteet ja selle vorm: Sada aastat otsinguid," *Akadeemia* 75, no. 6 (1995): 1136–61; and, more popularly, Liivi Künnapu, *Estonian Architecture: The Building of a Nation* (Helsinki: Finnish Building Centre, 1992).

8. John Czaplicka, "The Vernacular in Place and Time: Relocating History in Post-Soviet Cities," in *Vernacular Modernism: Heimat, Globalization and the Built Environment,* ed. Maiken Umbach and Bernd Hüppauf (Stanford, Calif.: Stanford University Press, 2005).

9. This problem already had a parallel in the interwar period, when (modern) Estonian architecture was less defined by state buildings and more so by a wide variety of public and private buildings; cf. *20 aastat ehitamist Eestis 1918–1938* (Tallinn: Teedeministeeriumi Ehitusosakond, 1938; Eesti Arhitektuurimuuseum, 2006).

10. There are many examples from the Baltic region, in particular on the architecture around 1900. This also refers to some of the Estonian publications, e.g., Karin Hallas, "Suche nach einem nationalen Stil: Architektur in Estland um die Jahrhundertwende," *Bauwelt,* no. 43 (1994): 2384–89; and Künnapu, *Estonian Architecture.*

11. For the document with the International Council on Monuments and Sites's recommendations, see http://whc.unesco.org/archive/advisory_body_evaluation/822.pdf.

12. Jüri Kivimäe and Lea Kõiv, eds., *Tallinn tules: Dokumente ja materjale Tallinna pommitamisest 9/10 Märtsil 1944* (Tallinn: Linnaarhiiv, 1997); Dmitrij V. Bruns, *Tallinn: Linnaehituslik kujunemine* (Tallinn: Valgus, 1993).

13. For more details, see the dissertation by Bradley Woodworth, "Civil Society and Nationality in the Multiethnic Russian Empire: Tallinn/Reval, 1860–1914," PhD thesis, Indiana University, 2003.

14. Igor Djomkin, *Eliel Saarinen ja "Suur-Tallinn"* (Tallinn: Kunst, 1977); cf. Saarinen's planning for Greater Helsinki, as described by Marika Hausen et al., *Eliel Saarinen: Projects 1896–1923* (Helsinki: Museum of Finnish Architecture, 1990), 200–17.

15. Hausen et al., *Eliel Saarinen,* 310; and Mart Kalm, *Eesti 20, sajandi arhitektuur—Estonian 20th Century Architecture* (Tallinn: Sild, 2002), 37–38.

16. Bruns, *Tallinn: Linnaehituslik kujunemine,* 133–36. N.B. that this refers also to the Orthodox Cathedral on Toompea; plans to replace it with an Iseseisvuse Panteon ("Pantheon of Independence") remained unrealized, cf. Leo Gens, *Karl Burman: Monograafia* (Tallinn: Eesti Entsüklopeediakirjastus, 1998), 196–97; Dmitri Bruns, *Tallinn: Linnaehitus Eesti Vabariigi aastail 1918–1940* (Tallinn: Valgus, 1998), 110–12.

17. See Ákos Moravánszky, *Competing Visions: Aesthetic Invention and Social Imagination in Central European Architecture, 1867–1918* (Cambridge, Mass.: MIT Press, 1998), esp. 216–83.

18. An interesting example provides the description of Tallinn by the Baltic German architect Ernst Kühnert; see Ernst Kühnert, *Künstlerstreifzüge durch Reval* (Reval: Kluge & Ströhm, 1909).

19. For more details, see Jörg Hackmann, "Architektur als Symbol: Nation-'Build-

ing' in Nordosteuropa—Estland und Lettland im 20, Jahrhundert," in *Riga im Prozess der Modernisierung: Studien zum Wandel einer Ostseemetropole im 19 und frühen 20 Jahrhundert,* ed. Norbert Angermann and Eduard Mühle (Marburg: Herder-Institut, 2004), 149-72.

20. I am referring here to John Czaplicka, "Geteilte Geschichte, geteilte Erbschaft: Stadtlandschaft und Kulturbild im Baltikum und in Polen," *Nordost-Archiv N.F.* 6, no. 1 (1997): 9-40.

21. Bruns, *Tallinn: Linnaehituslik kujunemine,* 125-54.

22. Cf. Ojārs Spārītis, "The Rebirth and the Restoration of Administrative, Political and Cultural Symbols in Riga's Town Hall Square," in *Composing Urban History and the Constitution of Civic Identities,* ed. John Czaplicka and Blair A. Ruble (Washington and Baltimore: Woodrow Wilson Center Press and Johns Hopkins University Press, 2003), 341-71.

23. For a photographic documentation of Tallinn's Soviet architecture, see Dmitri Bruns, Rasmus Kangropool, and Valmi Kallion, *Tallinna arhitektuur* (Tallinn: Eesti Raamat, 1987).

24. Most of the following data are taken from Karin Hallas et al., *20th Century Architecture in Tallinn: Architectural Guide* (Tallinn: Eesti Arhitektuurimuuseum, 2000); for more details, see the very instructive book by Kalm, *Eesti 20, sajandi arhitektuur.* See also Jaan Tamm, ed., *Tallinn. Entsüklopeedia,* 2 vols. (Tallinn: Eesti Entsüklopeediakirjastus, 2004).

25. There is a good interpretation by Andres Kurg, whom I would like to thank for his comments on my chapter. Andres Kurg, "Estonia: The Remarkable Afterlife of the Linnahall Concert Hall," *Architectural Design* 76, no. 3 (2006): 46-53. Since 1997 the Linnahall, now owned by the city of Tallinn, has been registered as an architectural landmark (see http://register.muinas.ee/pdetail01.asp?halu=1&nimi=checkbox&text7 =mere&radiob2=0&mo_id=8787&url=haldoman.asp), but it has remained rather out of use since the 1990s.

26. Cf. the model of Port and Sepmann from 1966 in *Istoriia Tallina s nachala 60-kh godov 19 stoletiia do 1970 goda,* ed. Raino Pullat (Tallin: Eesti Raamat, 1972); also see Bruns, *Tallinn: Linnaehituslik kujunemine,* 162, 192.

27. On his oeuvre and importance for the Estonian architecture, see Mart Kalm, "Kolm nuppu ja lint: Helsingi Pihlajamäelt Tallinna Trummi tänavale," *Maja,* nos. 1-2 (2004): 57-62. Also cf. Kalm, *Eesti 20, sajandi arhitektuur,* 302-3, 309, 423; and the photographs in *Tallinna arhitektuur,* by Bruns et al., 184-85, 226, 230-35.

28. This building was finished in 1968 (architects Mart Port and Raine Karp), and for a couple of years before the building of the Viru Hotel, it was the highest building in Tallinn; for a photograph of the original shape with a statue of Lenin in front of the building, see Bruns et al., *Tallinna arhitektuur,* 184-85.

29. Rein Einasto and Karin Hallas, *Eesti paas: Estonian Limestone* (Tallinn: Eesti Arhitektuurimuuseum, 1997).

30. Karin Hallas et al., *Tallinn im 20, Jahrhundert—Architekturführer* (Tallinn: Huma, 1994), 80.

31. Interestingly, the library and the Sakala Cultural Center are only marginally treated by Kalm, *Eesti 20, sajandi arhitektuur,* 410.

32. A major role in this restorationist approach all over the country was played by the Eesti Muinsuskaitseselts (Estonian Monuments' Protection Society), founded in 1987; for the details, see Rein Ruutsoo, "Transitional Society and Social Movements in

Estonia 1987–1991," *Eesti Teaduste Akadeemia Toimetised. Humanitaar–ja Sotsiaalteadused* 42, no. 2 (1993); and Rein Ruutsoo, *Civil Society and Nation Building in Estonia and the Baltic States* (Rovaniemi: Lapin yliopisto, 2002), chaps. 5.5, 6.2.2.

33. See the publications by Juhan Maiste, e.g., Juhan Maiste, *Tuldud teed tagasi: Retracing Steps* (Tallinn: Eesti Kunstiakadeemia, 2002).

34. For a description, see Ernst Kühnert, "Der Neubau für die Estländische Staatsversammlung im Schloß zu Reval," *Deutsche Bauzeitung* 60, no. 51 (1926): 417–24.

35. Mart Kalm and Peeter Säre, *Riigikogu Toompea Lossis: Riigikogu in Toompea Castle* (Tallinn: Riigikogu Kantselei, 2002); see also the description in "Riigikoguhoone saali restaureerimisest," *Maja*, no. 4 (1997): 8–15; a photograph of the pre-1991 situation appears in *Tallinna arhitektuur*, by Bruns et al., 113.

36. I have analyzed this in more detail in Hackmann, "Architektur," 159–64.

37. Hugo Peets, *"Estonia" Teatri- ja kontserthoone ajalugu* (Tallinn: "Estonia" Kirjastus, 1938).

38. Mart Kalm, *Arhitekt Alar Kotli: Monograafia* (Tallinn: Kunst, 1994), 146–56.

39. Kalm, *Eesti 20, sajandi arhitektuur*, 246.

40. For a description, see "Estonia kontserdisaali renoveerimine," *Maja*, no. 4 (1997): 16–23.

41. A similar case outside of Tallinn is the "Villa Tammekann" in Tartu, the only realized design by Alvar Aalto in Estonia.

42. Villem Raam, ed., *Eesti arhitektuur*, vol. 1; Tallinn (Tallinn: Valgus, 1993), 16.

43. Teddy Böckler, *Tallinna Raekoda: Uurimine ja restaureerimine 1952–2004* (Tallinn, 2004).

44. See Hanno Grossschmidt and Süri Vallnek, eds., *Vaba Eesti ehitab: 10 aastat ehitamist Eestis 1991–2001* (Tallinn: Solnessi Arhitektuurikirjastus, 2001).

45. For more details, see this DOCOMOMO publication: Mart Kalm, *Eesti funktsionalism: Reisijuht / Functionalism in Estonia. Guidebook* (Tallinn: DOCOMOMO-Eesti, 1998); for early documentation, see Mart Kalm and Krista Kodres, *Toisin: Funktionalismi ja neofunktionalismi Viron arkkitehtuurissa* (Tallinn: Eesti Arhitektuurimuuseum, 1993).

46. Cf. Leonhard Lapin, *Kaks kunsti: Valimik ettekandeid ja artikleid kunstist ning ehituskunstist 1971–1995* (Tallinn: Kunst, 1997).

47. E.g., "Docomomo special," *Ehituskunst* 15 (1996); "Eesti arhitektuur XX sajandil," *Ehituskunst*, nos. 24–26 (1999).

48. The *Tselluloosi- ja paberivabrik* (1910–1937) is a registered landmark, see http://register.muinas.ee/mkandmed.asp?text1=&text2=&radiob1=1&cb=1&lb=3& radiob2=0&nimi=checkbox&text7=tselluloosi; however, demolition has only partly been stopped, as with a glass-and-steel box placed on top of the cellulose department.

49. There are, however, plans for a reconstruction and new functions, cf. Kurg, "The Tallinn Utopia," and Margit Mutso, "Sustainable, and Not in Words Alone," *Time Out Architecture: La Biennale di Venezia 9th International Architecture Exhibition Estonia*, 2004, http://biennaal.arhliit.ee/en/timeout/mutso/.

50. Epp Lankots, "Chaos and Order in Historical Areas of Tallinn," *Estonian Art* 2 (1999), http://www.einst.ee/Ea/architecture/lankots.html.

51. For a description, see "Eesti Forekspanga panga- ja büroohoone," *Maja*, no. 4 (1997): 34–51.

52. Akademie der Künste, *Baustelle: Estland: Zehn Jahre Bauen im Wieder Unab-*

*hängigen Estland* (Berlin: Akademie der Künste, 2001); Grossschmidt and Vallmer, eds., *Vaba Eesti ehitab.*

53. Mart Kalm, "Ühispanga hoone: Eesti edu tähis," *Maja,* no. 1 (1999): 24–31 (the citation here is on 25); cf. Kalm, *Eesti 20, sajandi arhitektuur,* 458–59.

54. Kalm, *Eesti 20, sajandi arhitektuur,* 458, 466; cf. figure 4.1.

55. See Kalm, *Eesti 20, sajandi arhitektuur,* 453–54.

56. Grossschmidt and Vallmer, eds., *Vaba Eesti ehitab.*

57. This journal, which has been published since 1998, it seems to have become more important for architectural debates than *Ehituskunst,* which focuses more on the artistic features of architecture.

58. For a description, see *Maja,* no. 3 (2003): 24–29; and Indrek Peil and Siiri Vallner, "Okupatsioonimuuseum Tallinnas Toompea tn. 8," http://www.solness.ee/maja/index.php?gid=57&id=217.

59. See Panu Lehtovuori, "Uus Sakala arhitektuurivõistlus," *Maja,* no. 4 (2003): 88–91; and Karin Hallas-Murula, "Sakala JOKK," *Eesti Päevaleht,* December 18, 2006.

60. Kalm, *Eesti 20, sajandi arhitektuur,* 468–69. See also Ingrid Lillmägi: "Valgete majade kolmas tulemine," *Maja* no. 3 (2002), and Andres Kurg, "Estonia Expanding Suburbia—White Neomodernist Villas and Beyond." *Architectural Design* 76, no. 3 (2006): 62–67.

61. Bruns, *Tallinn: Linnaehituslik kujunemine,* 148–62; Kalm, *Eesti 20, sajandi arhitektuur,* 480.

62. Kalm, *Eesti 20, sajandi arhitektuur,* 480–81, quoting Karin Hallas; cf. Karin Hallas, "Deliiriumis Tallinn 'Manhattanist' Tartu Maantee Alguses," *Maja,* no. 2 (2001), http://www.arhitektuur.ee/maja/arhiiv/2001_2/eesti/deliirium.html.

63. Andres Alver, "Talking about Urban Planning and Design and Dealing with It Is Out of Context in Estonia: Conversation between Andres Alver, Veljo Kaasik, Tiit Trummal," *Maja,* no. 2 (1999), http://maja.arhitektuur.ee/arhiiv/1999_2/english/alver_eng.html.

64. Triin Ojari, "Eralinn: Avaliku Ruumi Võimalikkusest Tallinnas," *Maja,* no. 2 (2003): 16–19. Conversely, one might even argue that this kind of urbanism continues Soviet urban policy, which did not care much about historical structures.

65. Ojari, "Eralinn."

66. Ibid.

67. The criticism on this area refers also to other parts of prewar districts of Tallinn; cf. Lankots, "Chaos."

68. "Talsinki,"*Maja,* nos. 1–2 (2004): 64–73.

69. Akademie der Künste, *Baustelle: Estland;* Grossschmidt and Vallmer, eds., *Vaba Eesti ehitab;* Kalm, *Eesti 20; sajandi arhitektuur,* Hallas et al., *20th Century Architecture.*

70. N.B.: The situation was similar in the interwar period, when, e.g., Alvar Aalto was the only important foreign architect, who designed one house in Tartu and contributed to the competition for the Art Museum in Tallinn.

71. These two are Aare Saks (Tallinn Bank) and Henno Sillaste (Kawe Plaza Building).

72. E.g., compare this with the contemporary Danish discussion on "Grænseløs Arkitektur," focusing on projects of prominent foreign architects, e.g., Daniel Libeskind, Norman Foster, and Coop Himmelb(l)au in Denmark; for the details, see http://www.dac.dk.

73. See, in particular, the journal *Ehituskunst,* edited by Leo Lapin, and see also An-

dres Kurg and Mari Laanemets, eds., *Environment, Projects, Concepts: Architects of the Tallinn Schools, 1972–1985* (Tallinn: Este Architectuur Muuseum, 2008).

74. Kalm, *Eesti 20, sajandi arhitektuur,* 420–21.

75. Krista Kodres, "Sada aastat ehitamist Eestis: Ideid, probleeme ja lahendusi," *Ehituskunst,* nos. 24–26 (1999): 7–85; the quotation here is on page 10.

76. See, e.g., Kalm, *Arhitekt Alar Kotli,* and in particular the extensive description by Kalm, *Eesti 20, sajandi arhitektuur,* 240–417.

77. Cf. Lapin, *Kaks kunsti,* 118–29.

78. Cf., e.g., the interview with Villem Künnapu, in *Maja,* no. 3 (2001), http://www.arhitektuur.ee/maja/arhiiv/2001_3/eesti/kodres.html.

79. Kalm, *Eesti 20, sajandi arhitektuur,* 410.

80. E.g., see Raine Karp's first trip to Finland in 1965, as described by Kalm, "Kolm nuppu ja lint."

81. Hanno Kompus, "Eesti ehituskunsti teed," *Eesti kunsti aastaraamat* 2 (1926): 47–58; and *20 aastat ehitamist Eestis 1918–1938,* 7–31.

82. Cf. Marja-Riitta Norri, "A Century of Finnish Architecture," http://virtual.finland.fi/finfo/english/arkkit2.html: "From early on, there was an unprejudiced attitude to the making of architecture; the ideal of a modern dynamic nation was to be expressed through the formal language of new public buildings." In recent discussions among Estonian architects and architectural critics, this aspect, however, has declined in importance. Instead, global trends have seemingly arrived in Tallinn; cf. Krista Kodres, "Arhitekt: Sotsiaalse tellimuse täitja," *Maja,* no. 1 (2005), http://www.solness.ee/maja/index.php?gid=36&id=491.

# 5

# The Persuasive Power of the Odessa Myth
*Oleg Gubar and Patricia Herlihy*

The citizens of Odessa have cherished their ethnic diversity and vibrant economy since Catherine II officially founded the city in 1794 (figure 5.1).[1] She took over a remote, sparsely populated Turkish fortress and then set out to attract settlers who could defend it.[2] She sent notices throughout Europe offering emigrants land, tax exemptions, and religious freedom. In addition to a nucleus of Russian officials, Polish landlords, and Ukrainians, many non-Slavs responded to her call. Among the early settlers of Odessa were Greek and Italian merchants, Bulgarians, Albanians, Tatars, Swiss, Germans, the French, and even a few English people. Many Jews, notably from Galicia and Poland, took legal residence there.[3] Serfs were not officially invited, of course, but the local authorities, eager to build a population base, often turned a blind eye to the arrival of fugitives. Some of these settlers were eager to acquire a homestead, while others were drawn by the economic opportunities afforded by the new and growing city.

Figure 5.1. The monument to Catherine II and to the other founders of Odessa. Sculptor: Boris Eduards. The monument was erected in 1900 and destroyed in 1920. It was reconstructed by Oleg Chernoivanov and unveiled in October 2007. Photograph by Ivan Cherevatenko.

## Origins of the Myth

Early visitors from Europe, the United States, and Russia as well as early Odessits began to issue flattering reports, sparking the "myth of Odessa," a magical place where one could instantly become rich simply by setting one's foot in the city. As Menachem-Mendle puts it in a letter to his wife around the turn of the twentieth century, "I want you to know it is simply not in my power to describe the city of Odessa—how big and beautiful it is—the people here, so wonderful and good-hearted, and the terrific business one can do here" (figure 5.2).[4] In the early 1820s, N. Chizhov, a naval cadet and friend of the poet Aleksandr Pushkin, and a future Decembrist, writes lyrically of Odessa:

> Imagine that everyone gathers here [in the garden] to enjoy the cool evening and aromatic fragrance of flowers. The tall Turk offers you a

Figure 5.2. Cafe Fankoni, showing the cosmopolitan liveliness of Odessa. Postcard from the early twentieth century.

tasty Asian drink, while a pretty Italian woman sitting under the dense shade of an elm brought over from the shores of the Volga, proffers ice cream in a cut-glass tumbler. . . . A fellow citizen of the great Washington walks alongside the bearded inhabitants of Cairo and Alexandria; the ancient descendants of the Normans from the steep cliffs of Norway, the splendid Spaniard from the shores of Guadalquivir, residents of Albion, Provence, and Sicily gather, it seems, in order to represent here an abridgement of the universe. It can be said that nowhere in Russia is there another place where you might find such a spectacle.[5]

Throughout the nineteenth and early twentieth centuries, local historians, filmmakers, poets, novelists, journalists, and memoirists universally extolled Odessa as a cosmopolitan, energetic oasis of freedom and beauty and elaborated on the Odessa myth.[6]

The legend of the "golden city" was not without some foundation. In its first half century, young Odessa was the largest exporter of grain in the world, even in the years of the Continental Blockade.[7] A typical Mediterranean port in appearance and function—cosmopolitan, energetic, with an independent character—emerged improbably on the *dikoe pole* (wild field) at the border of a subdued and servile Russia (figure 5.3). Persuaded that they were indeed exceptional, Odessits embraced the image projected on them by outsiders. As a result, some might charge, that they generated in themselves superciliousness, arrogance, and an augmented self-esteem completed by a certain narcissism and infantilism. The self-image of the Odessits guaranteed them a priori a special quality, one that lent them moral dividends. The Odessit derived as much self-satisfaction from urban citizenship as from a certain perception of Odessa's historical past. The popular singer and bandleader Leonid Utesov expresses this pride in the first lines of his memoirs: "I was born in Odessa. You think I am bragging? But it's really true. Many people would like to have been born in Odessa, but not everyone manages to."[8] Or more recently, Anatolii Kazak, a cinematographer, notes that whenever one informs others that he or she was born in Odessa, they smile and mention, "Odessa humor, Odessa songs, Odessa jokes, and the characteristic Odessa speech, an Odessit is without fail merry, witty, sharp; he is never despondent, petty; he has a superior and fascinating personality.[9]

Figure 5.3. A view of Odessa Harbor. Lithograph from the middle nineteenth century.

## The Soviet Appropriation of the Myth

During the Soviet era, the authorities celebrated whatever elements of the myth that suited their ideology. For example, the new Soviet regime, hungry for heroes and national treasures, rapturously accepted the axiom of the exceptionalism of Odessa. Long before the Great Patriotic War (i.e., World War II), before the heroic defense in the summer and fall of 1941, Odessa was considered not simply golden but Soviet golden. In Odessa, "by the bluest Black Sea in the world," diggers, pilots, reindeer breeders, builders of Dneprogas and Magnitigorsk, and—"swineherdesses and shepherds"— took refuge from their heavy labors.[10] Here these vacationers met Odessits, reputedly the most hospitable, the merriest, the most fascinating, and the wittiest citizens in the world. Multinational Odessa was a miniature "new historical community—the Soviet people."

The Soviet view of Odessa and the image conveyed in the belles lettres of Pushkin, Batiushkov and Tumanskii, Babel', Paustovskii, and Il'f and Petrov were of a carefree and harmonious Odessa.[11] Yet a few "renegades" or "dissidents" looked around and noted that not all was affable, hospitable, or funny. Citizens of various ages and professions strolled around, but they were not really jovial. Even though they all had pleasant expressions on their faces and they would look at you and listen, they did not truly want to hear or understand what you were saying, but only used your remarks as a pretext to joke, pun, or banter. And that is exactly the synthesis of Odessan and Soviet ideology—an excising of the very substance of meaning, leaving only the exotic aesthetic of humor. This stereotype is the source of the never-ending masks, images of the happy heroes of film such as *Happy-Go-Lucky Guys, Two Soldiers,* and other artistic personages composed of "100 percent Odessits."

Soviet Odessa served a special function as a supplier of satire and humor, as a home for funny shows and witty punning, as a haven for outspoken Jews. Limited criticism of Soviet reality spiced up Odessan irony and was not only tolerated but also even encouraged from time to time. In a sense, Odessa was conferred the privilege of being an urban "Holy Fool," a harmless character who could speak the truth under the cover of feigned madness. This veneer of affability to a certain extent protected Odessa from being as thoroughly "Sovietized" as other cities. Simple neglect prevented massive substitutions of Soviet buildings for the older European styles. The Soviet regime needed only to be assured that there were sufficient sanatoria and camps for workers from all over the Soviet Union, but it cared little for the housing needs of the city's residents.

Odessa was content to carry out its role of reveling in its own importance and uniqueness, being able to show its readiness to doubt and disagree without openly challenging the authorities. After all, it has always shown "more color, spunk, and irreverence than other cities in the former Soviet Union."[12] The Club of the Merry and Witty (KVN) has been functioning from the mid-1960s and won the All-Soviet-Union humor championship four times. The important Odessa "Iumorina," the All-Union First of April holiday of humor with elements of carnival, has been celebrated since 1973. The Golden Duke Film Festival, the annual international jazz festival, the festival of contemporary art, the first Literary Museum in the Soviet Union, the International Club of Odessits, and other groups and activities also mark the celebratory inclinations of the natives.

Although now a part of an independent Ukraine, Odessa has largely retained its historical-cultural baggage. To be sure, Communist Party ideologues at first tried to recolor the biography of the city to fit the new stereotypes. Soon this latter-day Bolshevik zeal abated, however, as authorities in the capital Kyiv realized that Odessa's traditional image was still attractive. The designations of the "southern Palmyra" or the "capital of humor" thus remained as before. Nevertheless, the city began to reflect on its dried-up moral and material resources.

During the time of the Soviet Union, the economy of the city fell into complete decline; its housing stock became dismally dilapidated, and a large part of the municipal and cultural monuments as well as the entire urban transportation system sank into a catastrophic situation. At the collapse of the Soviet Union, the process of privatization in Odessa and the first accumulation of capital proceeded chaotically and barbarically, a far cry from democratic ideals.

When the matter arose concerning the monuments of history and culture, the responsible government department often acted the dog in the manger. Instead of leasing these buildings for a modest rent for an extended term requiring simple maintenance, officials burdened investors with the requirement of reconstruction as a condition for low rent. This policy has produced a sharp worsening of the structural condition of the buildings. Historical buildings such as the Odessa Branch of the Russian Technical Society, the Palace of Sailors, and even the Vorontsov Palace went without owners for years because of such exactions (figure 5.4). The "star of Odessa," the academic Theater of Opera and Ballet, was in the midst of restoration for many years.

Odessa's arrogance, encouraged by the high and the low, has in the end played a nasty joke on the citizenry. Odessa's delusions of its worth extended so far that that it never once during the Soviet regime turned to UNESCO

Figure 5.4. The Vorontsov Palace on Premorskii Boulevard. Architect: F. Boffo, 1826–28. Photograph by Ivan Cherevatenko.

with a list of city monuments or statues to ask for assistance with preservation. Such apparent foolishness can be explained not only by patriotic blindness but also by the isolation of the Soviet people for many years from the outside world, from the living city-legends of Europe, and from the planet. In comparison with other cities in Russia, Ukraine, and the USSR, Odessa actually is something outstanding both with regard to its society and to its architecture.[13] In this judgment, world opinion was in accord with that of Odessits. When they were finally solicited, however, the experts of UNESCO concluded that Odessa's historical-cultural monuments did not possess conspicuous cultural value.[14] Perhaps the single truly attractive feature of Odessa's urban design rests on the fact that its historic center was shaped by a single general plan as brilliant as it was simple (figures 5.5 and 5.6).

## Shaping the City

One could say that Odessa sits on a high precipice, with its legs hung over to the basin of the Bay of Odessa. François De-Voland—a colleague of one

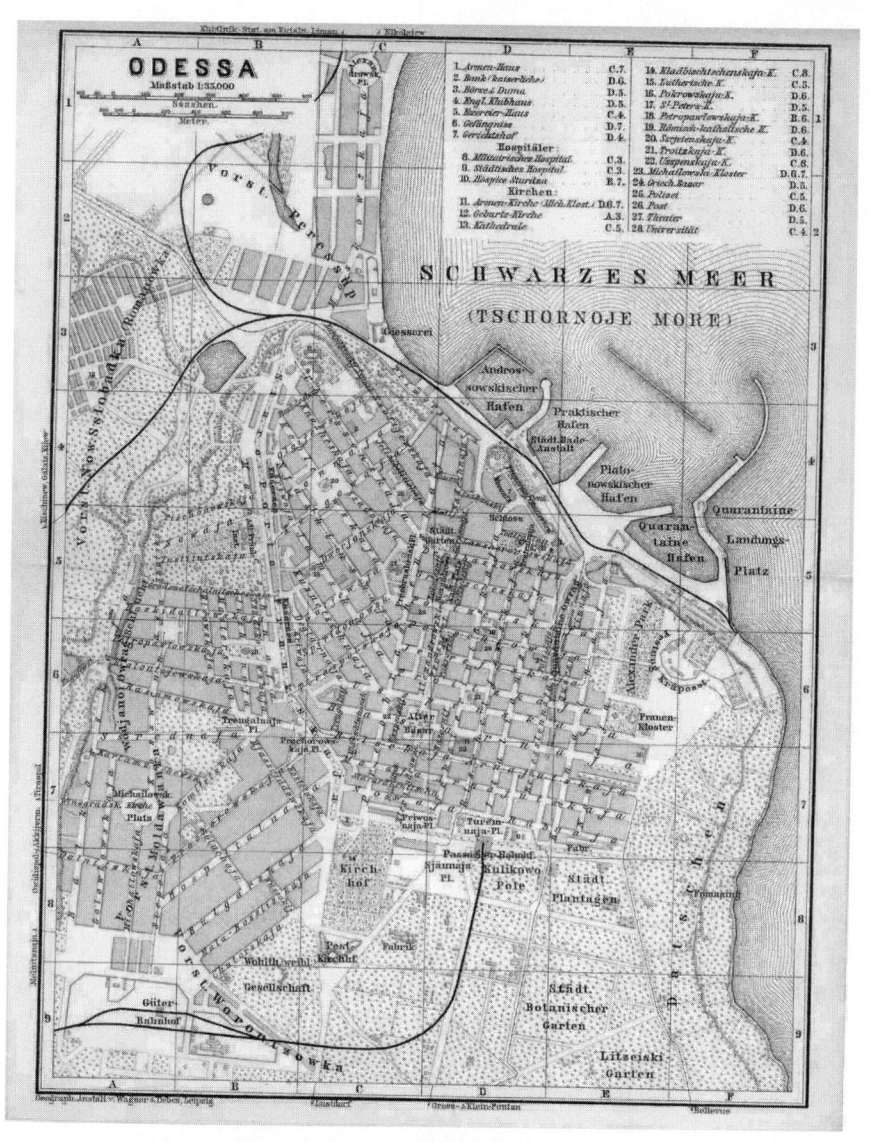

Figure 5.5. A plan of Odessa, 1892. Published in Leipzig.

Figure 5.6. Ekatererininskaia Square. Lithograph from the end of the nineteenth century.

of the main founders of Odessa, Joseph de Ribas, and a military engineer from Holland—planned the street design, having in mind above all the importance of the port for the future city.[15] Aiming to make his design conform to the natural contours of the terrain, De-Voland planned a system of straight perpendicular streets, the direction of which conformed to the orientation of the deep ravines cutting through the high Odessa plateau. The ravines served as natural steep descents to the shore and to the Quarantine and Practical harbors (figure 5.7). To the west of the rectangular streets was planned another grid of blocks, lying at a 47-degree angle in relation to the first. Every street led to the sea.

The transition from this general plan to specific details was accomplished by architects primarily of Mediterranean origin: Francesco and Giovanni Frapolli, Giordano Toricelli, Francesco Boffo, Gaetano Dall'Aqua, Giovanni Scudieri, Luigi Cambiaggio, and Francesco Morandi, whose best work coincided with the governance of Richelieu, Koble, Langeron, and Vorontsov. As a direct descendant of the ancient Greek colonies of the Northern Black

Odessa. Descente, au port de pratique.

Figure 5.7. A view of the Practical Harbor of the Odessa Port and the Vorontsov Palace. Lithograph.

Sea—mythology was embedded into the very birth of the city—Odessa replicated their design. The social centers were formed basically around three market squares: the Old Bazaar (Free Market), the Greek Bazaar (Northern or Aleksandrovskii Square), and the New Bazaar (Kherson Square) (figure 5.8).[16] These squares lying along the transportation arteries imitated the ancient agora and were bordered exclusively by buildings earmarked for trade and decorated with stone arcades and porticos. To the rear of these imposing facades were built the modest houses of the Greek commercial elite.[17]

The style of their one- and two-story houses, with deeply vaulted cellars and isolated internal courtyards to ensure privacy, confirmed the tradition of "my house is my castle." The only demand made by homeowners of the Italian architects was functionality. The natives of Southern Italy and France, South Slavic countries, and Anatolia also incorporated the essentials of their native ways of life into their new residences in Odessa. Imposing houses were relatively rare at the turn of the nineteenth century, but there were a few: the house of M. Kramarev on Preobrazhenskaia Street, of F. Deribas on Deribasovskaia Street, and of L. Lashkarev on Grecheskaia Street. Later a series of mansions appeared, among which were the palatial country house of Vorontsov, the State Stock Exchange, and various offices. Then came stone bridges, the Boulevard Staircase, and the monument to the Duc de Richelieu (figure 5.9). Even in later years of deliberate beautifica-

Figure 5.8. The Commercial Row of the New Bazaar. Architect: F. Frapolli, 1813. Photograph by Ivan Cherevatenko.

Figure 5.9. The monument to the Duc de Richelieu on Primorskii Boulevard. Postcard from the beginning of the twentieth century.

tion, functionality nonetheless always dominated Odessa's approach to urban planning. For example, the colossal storehouses of Sabanskii and Papudov played an important role during the period of the Free Port from 1819 to 1857. After the Crimean War, which was disastrous for Russia and the Odessan grain trade, the storehouses were transformed into expensive rental properties while the gigantic grain storage place of Rafalovich was reconstructed into the Russian Theater.

For almost the entire second half of the nineteenth century, the real estate market in the city experienced an enormous boom in rental property. The precipitous growth of the population, the development of stylish sea health-resorts, the building of railroads, the creation of the Russian Society of Shipping and Trade, the Voluntary Fleet, private shipping companies, the growth of export-import operations, the strengthening of the regional money market—each of these factors inflated prices for real estate and correspondingly for rents. A new army of landlords was more concerned about extracting profits than in erecting pompous outward appearances. Dozens of such monotonous buildings from that time survive to this day.

A fortunate exception is the few private residences and offices belonging to the generation of sons, that is, the descendants of the patriarchs of grain exporters and traders (Marazli, Abazy, Rodokanaki, Ralli, Mavrokordato, Papudov, and Sevastopulo), who received European educations with corresponding polish. These youths had a predilection for buildings not with the patina of antiquity, imitating the picturesque ruins of Ol'via and Pantikapea, but for buildings like those of European capitals. Even the nouveaux riches rooted in Odessa, such as Anatra, Ashkenazi, Dement'ev, Efrusi, Liban, Mendelevich, Russov, and Fal'ts-Fein, rose to the new European standard with their buildings. These moguls competed to simulate Western Europe so that the patriarchal architecture of ancient Odessa and of the Southern Palmyra gradually dissolved and Odessa metamorphosed into "Little Paris." Unlike their frugal fathers, the sons learned how to put on airs and to master pretentiousness. By about 1830, Odessa presented a unified architectural ensemble, one that was a successful mirror of an ancient city; by the middle of the nineteenth century, however, eclecticism, but to be sure of a European style, had become a dominant characteristic of the city scene. Even the scattered oriental motifs echo European predilections for the exotic, such as the arch at the entrance to Otrada on Frantsuzkaia Street, the spa on the corner of Shcheplinskaia and Preobrazhenskaia streets, and the arabesque decoration on the facade of the Vorontsov Palace.

Little by little, the porticos along the length of the thoroughfare Aleksandrovskii Prospekt were closed. Instead of facades with Ionian and Doric columns, at most there remained decorative pilasters. And the Prospekt itself lost importance. It was closed on one side by the Deribaskovskaia Street houses built by the city architect, G. I. Toricelli. And in the middle of the Greek market arose the round house of A. I. Maiorov, along with the no-less-extensive home of the beer king I. A. Ansel'm. From the 1870s, profitable houses replaced buildings of classical design. The building boom at the turn of the twentieth century led to the formation of a kind of metaphorical modern museum under the sky, while sometimes destroying the best of the classical models—for example, the house of Kramerev (now the Passage), the guardhouse (the house of Libman), and the house of Marini (the Hotel Bol'shaia Moskovskaia).

The making of the architectural fabric of the city in the late nineteenth century became completely pragmatic, with no one casting a glance at the past. Today, no one would find controversial the then-modern designs of the prominent architects Aleksandr Bernardazzi, L'ev Blodek, Eduard Mesner, Valer'ian Shmidt, Felix Fonsiorovskii, and Vil'gel'm Kabiol'skii, who worked between 1880 and 1910. Simply put, life's demands had to be met and people had to put up with it.

In later years, the Bolshevik state joyfully squeezed common workers and countless Communist Party and Soviet institutions into the spacious rental houses and into the luxurious single homes of the destroyed nobility. Sturdy as were those buildings, they could not last forever, and after seventy heroic years they were in a sorry condition. The highest achievement of the years from 1930 to 1950 was the Stalinist imperial style, a form of housing that proved its worth in building for the "radiant future." Nonetheless, later Odessits rejoiced in Khrushchev-style houses, where hundreds of people lived like worker bees in individual cells to await the soon-to-arrive fully communistic society.[18]

The inevitability of change is supremely evident, but not to the Odessit, an inveterate municipal patriot, who, furiously gesticulating, tries to convince the visitor that the local theater is the third in the world according to its beauty or that this or that house has the longest balcony in Europe, that the Potemkin Steps are the eighth wonder of the world, and so on. Odessa, it must be said, when it comes to formal art criticism, lives with its head turned backward. In resisting change, regional experts invoke memoirs, and anecdotes by regional historians or by their dilettante analogues, to support the notion of the purported harmonious architectural beauty of the past.[19]

Odessa is simultaneously seized by two mutually exclusive realities. One is an active, sometimes too frenetic attempt to inscribe the city into a new historical context. The second is a convulsive, rather hysterical, grasp for the past, one that is putatively heroic. Those who wish to justify bulldozed attacks on the old houses grope for some kind of ideological basis, although progress for itself need not be based on theory. New buildings and structures thrust through the turf suddenly as though they were mushrooms. Everything gives evidence that the city has a "primitive accumulation of capital," sufficient for massive construction projects, even making allowances for mammoth corruption. As Mikhail Gorbachev put it, "The process has started and it cannot be stopped."

## The Once and Future Myth

The peculiarities of Odessa—that is, the aspects of the Odessa myth, particularly the city's multiethnic composition—dictate policy at all levels, including that of the local administration in shaping the construction process. Investors and their shadowy protectors and comrades in arms, the officials, demonstrate constant loyalty to the idea of a multiethnic city, with stress on generously financing the building of cultural and educational centers, churches, and memorial complexes, representing various religions and ethnic groups. The construction of new buildings, not only as a battle for spheres of influence and an instrument to launder money but also as an opportunity to pay reverence to the Odessa mentality—to invoke an element of the Odessa myth insofar as this myth is profitable—serves the purpose of manipulating social consciousness, providing regional and material surrogates for bread and circuses.

The Rabelaisian model of the carnivalesque city (once inhabited by Mikhail Bakhtin) remains real. Odessits continue to pose with alacrity as mutes donning masks corresponding to their assumed identity, preferring even fake holidays to monotonous provincial vegetation. This is a struggle in which all the intellectual efforts of the municipal patriots oddly coincide with the goals of businesspeople, who pragmatically exploit the Odessa myth to extract money from it.

Despite the expressed doubts concerning the durability of the Odessa myth, the recent election of the president of Ukraine only demonstrates its lasting power. During the elections of 2004, Odessa behaved exactly as it did in 1917–18; it did not take sides. During the Civil War, the choice was between Petrograd and Kyiv, between the Petrograd Soviet and the Central Rada. In 2004, the choice was between Donetsk and L'viv. So, wrapped up in the myth of its uniqueness, Odessa as before attempted to creep by Scylla and Charybdis. Already at the time of perestroika, Odessa nurtured radical ideas of becoming a free city, or a city-state, based on a series of precedents, among which was the historical experiment of Odessa as a *porto-franco* (1819–57). At the time of Gorbachev, no one could predict to what degree the USSR would collapse, or if a free city would be permitted, resembling something like those of the Hanseatic League. This invaluable experience with the powerful myth of a free city does not register with contemporary masters of public relations. With the building, in part by German investors, of a superhighway from Odessa to Kyiv, Odessa will be tethered more tightly to its capital, thus thwarting its inclination to float by the sea as an independent entity. Ukraine has also declared its intention to use the Odessa-Brody pipeline, not to carry Russian oil, but to transfer Caspian oil to Plock and Gdańsk in Poland for further transshipment to Europe, especially to Germany.[20] Thus Odessa's name is linked, willy-nilly, with a westward thrust of Ukraine's foreign policy.

At the same time that the prestige of Odessa and the region is decaying and declining and there is no possibility of political separation, Odessa impetuously sees its golden, separate future. Believing in the Odessa myth, municipal ideologues proclaim, "We are not Russians, nor Ukrainians, nor Jews, nor Americans, nor Bushmen, nor Chinese—we are Odessits!" The centralizing power must understand, respect and, if worse come to worst, tolerate regional mentalities, perhaps even going so far as to form a federal government. Only the blind do not see the difference between Odessa and Ivano-Frankov, Donetsk and L'viv, Ternopol' and Kharkiv, and Chernivtsi and Sevastopol. Attempts at a totalitarian leveling of regional ideologies that are based on historical and cultural traditions, even the most absurd and paradoxical ones, are perceived as only leading to the strengthening of centrifugal forces. Another conundrum: The more independent Odessa becomes (and not it alone), the more it will become a Ukrainian city.

As Ukraine is being drawn closer to the orbit of European power (it is already on its way to joining NATO), it will of course take its major seaport with it, although the smug Odessa myth insists that the city, despite its Turkish roots, has been European in its architecture, in its cosmopolitan nature, and in its climate since its birth. To the extent that Western Ukraine (e.g., L'viv) can boast of its European roots in Austrian Galicia, so too Ukraine's "Window to the South" relies on its European foundational myths to assert its unique European genesis.

Odessa no longer attracts foreigners as settlers, as it did in the nineteenth century, but it harbors the notion that it is multinational by catering to the descendents of foreigners. Various ethnic and religious communities contributed to the establishment of many societies and churches. Funds from expatriates helped to rebuild Catholic and Protestant churches and to restore synagogues. In recent years, cultural institutions of various faiths and ethnic groups have either been rebuilt or created anew, namely, a series of Orthodox churches such as the Cathedral of the Transfiguration (figures 5.10 and 5.11), Gregory Bogoslov Church, the port church named for Saint Nicholas Mirlikiiskii (figure 5.12), the Alexander Church, the Archangel Michael women's monastery, the Church Sturdza Charitable Community, and the Church of Adriana and Natalie. Other confessions are also well represented, with the Armenian Apostolic Church of Saint Gregory the Teacher (figure 5.13), the main Catholic Church on Ekaterinskaia Street, the Church of Saint Gregory Prosvititel, the renovated Main Synagogue on Richelieu Street, the synagogues on Remeslennaia and Malaia Arnautskaia streets, the rectory of the Evangelical Lutheran Church on Novosel'skaia Street, the Reformed Church on Pasteur Street (Khersonskaia), the Evangelical churches on Balkovskaia and Kartamyshevskaia streets, and the Arab Cultural Center on Richelevskaia Street, built largely through the generosity of Kivan Adnan, a Muslim entrepreneur (figure 5.14). Suddenly, the city boasts Greek, Bulgarian, French, Italian, and other cultural associations, as well as a variety of Jewish cultural educational organizations and societies

Figure 5.10. Cathedral Square. Lithograph from the 1840s.

Figure 5.11. The steeple of the Cathedral of the Transfiguration of the Savior. The cathedral was built in 1837, destroyed in the mid-1930s, and restored in 2001. Photograph by Ivan Cherevatenko.

for the approximately 36,000 Jews in a city of 1.2 million. Most of these institutions either own their property within the city or in the region (oblast), or they are in the process of acquiring the property. A few Westerners do emigrate to Odessa, such as Hobart Earle, an American, who for the past dozen years has been the conductor of the Odessa Philharmonic Orchestra, which performs in an ornate early Italian Renaissance–style building that once served as the Stock Exchange.

It is telling that the creators of many of these new buildings of culture, indeed the new constructions in general, give little heed to the surrounding architecture and are not overly concerned with visual or city planning harmony. The hastily assembled contemporary architecture reminds one of the cloak of a dervish with his multicolored pieces of splendid brocade and cashmere sewn together with homespun linen and sacking. The words of a

Figure 5.12. The Church of Saint Nicolas Mirlikiiskii on the wharf at the Black Sea port, built 1993–94. Architect: Vladimir Kalinin. Photograph by Ivan Cherevatenko.

Czech journalist, observing Times Square with its vibrant coloration, likewise apply to Odessa: "The colors completely do not match one another, and as the saying goes, there is here neither rhyme nor reason, and yet this motley collection unexpectedly creates a thing of beauty."[21] In odd and inexplicable ways, the seemingly unsuitable buildings in terms of scale, chronology, style, function, and structure in the historic center of Odessa convey a sense of harmony. Whatever attempts have been made to regulate this flow of construction and to direct it into some artistic channel have, as a rule, ended in failure. The usual view of chaos clearly needs revision.

Possessing only some formal "general plans" for the development of the city, Odessa is oblivious to the direction in which it should move, or where to perch and how it should develop. It ponders, "does preservation sterilize creativity and innovation? But if there is no preservation will it not then deprive us of roots and indispensable memories needed for innovation?"[22] If Odessa chooses the direction of becoming a tourist and resort city, then it

Figure 5.13. The Armenian Apostolic Church of Saint Gregory the Teacher. Photograph by Ivan Cherevatenko.

would be expedient to reconstruct memorial buildings in the historic center in the genre of "green archaeology," removing the chief transportation lines, one by one, to the periphery, and leaving the city as "a museum under the open sky," exclusively for pedestrians and bicyclists, ice cream vendors, street musicians, beggars, and prostitutes. To live up to its glory as a strong industrial and commercial center, the city has restored historical facades and, in some cases, added on a story or two and large plate glass windows. Although the Municipality of Odessa has a city Architectural Commission, which offers advice on the city's building needs and their architectural merit, the City Council has the final determination on what is built and where.

What standards will be adopted for Odessa's revival—those of the period before the memorable prewar year 1913, or before a year such as 1894, the year of the one-hundredth anniversary of Odessa? Or should it be those before 1854, in the era when the city wore the crown as the world's leading exporter of grain? No one answers these questions because some answers

Figure 5.14. The Arab Cultural Center on Richelevskaia Street, 2002. Architect: Dmitrii Povstaniuk. Photograph by Ivan Cherevatenko.

might suggest a return to cesspools, heating by stove, kerosene lighting, hauled or rain water for drinking and household needs, and transport by carts. This is how the mythmaking of the glorious past functions in the civic consciousness of Odessits, who avoid the logical consequences of returning to the past. Though romanticizing Odessa of old, Odessits do not want anything to do with shriveled acacias or privies. Odessits have become accustomed to the fact that nothing depends on them; they take no initiative but treasure paperweight mementos and picturesque ruins.

Not a single city in Ukraine and in all probability in all the former USSR can boast of such an abundance of monuments, memorial plaques, and other "street furniture" per capita as can Odessa. Suffice to say that on one day alone, September 2, 2004, the anniversary of Odessa's 210 years, four new monuments were unveiled: the first to the romantic Polish poet, Adam Mickiewicz; the second to the former Greek city head, Grigorii Marazli; the third to the founder of the Greek independence society, Filiki Eteriia; and the fourth to the orange. This last is instructive. As the nineteenth century began, Odessan Greeks on behalf of the citizens sent oranges to Saint

Petersburg to Emperor Paul I. An orange was an exotic item in those years, especially in the winter, and all the more so in the north of Russia. The reason for the gift was that the new emperor jealously sought to destroy all the projects undertaken by his mother Catherine II, among which was her pride and joy—Odessa. Paul I had refused, therefore, to finance the budget of young southern Odessa, so the building of the city and port declined in consequence, and it was in danger of never being completed. Quick-thinking Odessits resorted to a time-proven method—the bribe. Paul took the gift and immediately became more receptive to Odessa, restoring credits and privileges. After two hundred years, the citizenry decided to honor this curious historical fact with a monument, *The Orange That Saved Odessa,* by the sculptor Aleksandr Tokarev. Literally a couple of months later, "the Orange Revolution" laid claim to the color of this monument as its own symbol. It can be no coincidence that in December 2004, the opponents of Viktor Yushchenko hurled oranges at his supporters when he was speaking at an election rally in Odessa.[23]

Memorials of literary figures in the Sculpture Garden of the Literary Museum lie a few meters from *The Orange.*[24] Outdoor monuments to the citizens' favorite writers, their literary heroes, and figures of the city's folklore have been planted in the Sculpture Garden here each year beginning in 1995, on April 1. There can be seen the personages of Il'f and Petrov, Kuprin, and Kozachinsky; the heroes of the Jewish anecdotes of Rabinovich (figure 5.15); the writer Zvanetsky, "the future Odessan genius"; the text of the song from the film *Two Soldiers;* and phrases from "Odessa Mama" embodied in bronze and marble. The *Monument to the Reader* by the Kievan sculptor Oleg Chernoivanenko took its place in the Literary Museum Sculpture Garden on April 1, 2005. It is a miniature replica of the original enormous monument in Catherine Square dedicated to Catherine II, which was torn down by the Bolsheviks. As before, the empress is surrounded by her four favorites: de Ribas, De-Voland, Potemkin, and Zubov. But in this new version, the men are holding books in their hands; one is reading Babel', another is reading I'lf and Petrov, another is perusing Zhvanetskii, and De-Voland, the city's planner, is reading a guidebook to Odessa. The empress herself studies a Russian-Ukrainian phrase book. Apparently the city has changed physically beyond the city's planner comprehension and Catherine is searching for the new basis of her Imperial power—Ukraine.

The difference in distance between *The Orange* and the Sculpture Garden is just about the same degree as that between the latter and the City Duma, where stands the prerevolutionary monument to Pushkin. Shoulder

Figure 5.15. The monument to the heroes of the Jewish anecdotes of Rabinovich in the Sculpture Garden of the Literary Museum. Photograph by Ivan Cherevatenko, 1995.

to shoulder with *The Orange* stands the old and durable Italian copy of Laocoön. Conversely, the classic Primorskii Boulevard and Ekaterinskii Square have long had monuments side by side of differing quality: the refined bronze monument of the first Odessa governor, the Duc de Richelieu (1828), is twinned with the granite block of the sailors of the battleship *Potemkin* (1965), nicknamed *The Iron* by Odessits. On the eve of the fall of the Soviet Union, it was possible for Soviets to write, "Perestroika and democratization in all spheres of life in our nation opened the broad possibility to exploit monuments to create human consciousness and humanistic ideas."[25] In Odessa, that prescription meant turning from the heroic to the humorous.

In celebration of the two-hundredth anniversary of Pushkin's birth, a new, modernized version of the poet sculpted by Aleksandr Tokarev (figure 5.16) was installed and awaits photograph opportunities a mere two blocks from the classic Pushkin monument erected in 1899. Suddenly, the revered Duc de Richelieu, clad in a toga, overlooking the grand staircase, reappears in another statue as a twenty-first-century dude in jeans. On Deribasovskaia Street have been placed monuments to Joseph de Ribas (figure 5.17); to the legendary balloonist and sportsman Sergei Utochkin, who is portrayed as about to launch a paper airplane (figure 5.18); to the founder of Soviet Jazz, Leonid Utesov; and to a bronze chair from Il'f's and Petrov's best-selling book *The Twelve Chairs*.[26]

Figure 5.16. The new monument to Aleksandr Pushkin on Pushkin Street. Sculptor: Aleksandr Tokarev. Photograph by Ivan Cherevatenko, 1999.

Figure 5.17. The monument to one of the main founders of Odessa, Joseph de Ribas, placed on Deribasovskaia Street in 1994 for the two-hundredth anniversary of the founding of the city. Sculptor: Alexander Kniazik. Photograph by Ivan Cherevatenko.

On Preobrazhenskaia Street stands an outdoor monument to the film star Vera Kholodnaia (figure 5.19), and nearby a much earlier sculpture had been placed of "Petia and Gavrik," personages in another best seller, *White Sails Gleam* by Valentin Kataev. At the sea terminal stands the controversial monument *Golden Child,* the work of Ernst Neizvestny symbolizing the city and port. And at the ninth sea station, Large Fountain, on the outskirts of the city, one finds the sculpture complex *The Rape of Europe.*

Somber recollections of the darker moments of the recent past are the monuments to the Odessan victims of Chernobyl, to the victims of the Afghanistan War, to sailors lost at sea, to a sailor's wife, to the fighter pilots of World War II, to the heroes of the U-boat fleets of both world wars, to the second Jewish Cemetery destroyed in the 1970s, to the massacre of 25,000 Jews by Romanians in 1941, and to the Jews who were annihilated after they were sent on the Road of Death to the Nazi concentration camps.[27]

What, then, does one see? One sees that the historical, literary, and folklore heroes are all abandoning the confines of museums in droves to dot

Figure 5.18. The monument to the aviator Sergei Utochkin on Deribasovkaia Street. Sculptor: Aleksandr Tokarev, 2000. Photograph by Ivan Cherevatenko.

the landscape, and in dominating the terrain, they intensify and strengthen the Odessa myth in the consciousness of Odessits as they go about their ordinary daily business. With each monument, it becomes more and more difficult to find suitable space for another. Currently, only a handful of sculptors—such as Aleksandr Tokarev, Nikolai Stepanov, Vladimir Traskov, Alexander Kniaznik, and Taisia Sud'ina—create all these monuments. Especially distinctive is the statue of the Hetman Golovatyi, one of the leaders of the Black Sea Cossack Host, which joined the Russian regular army.

Figure 5.19. The monument to film star Vera Kholodnaia on Preobrazhenskaia Street. Sculptor: Aleksandr Tokarev, 2003. Photograph by Ivan Cherevatenko.

This monument was erected to please contemporary nationalist patriots who probably do not understand that their hero was a mercenary, an active participant of the bloody conquest of the Caucasus and, it must be said, a rather curious precedent to current events.

Of course, aging Odessa maintains its pretensions and claims to originality for the way it decorates itself, for how it applies makeup to prepare for its role. The majority of the monuments of the city, whether international or European, of local significance or not, are becoming decrepit and neglected. The contrast between the old homes and the new elements of architecture and decoration is striking. As a rebellious and independent-minded city under the tsars, Odessa lost favor with the powers that could have helped maintain the city; as a Soviet spa, the city's central structures and infrastructures were neglected. Now as a city with a distinctive Russian culture serving as the major port of Ukraine, it is attempting to adjust the myth to suit new realities.

Today, Odessa has great difficulty in representing itself as a soubrette. On the contrary, it more often inspires pity and sympathy, and itself to be debased and scorned. Rejuvenation cannot, however, be done piecemeal. Steps must be taken for a makeover. First, Odessa must cease to engage in self-delusion—fasting will not be followed immediately by feasting. No noble benefactors will appear to support the carnival. Odessits themselves must lend their own time and efforts to the project of self-realization. Only under these conditions will the Odessa myth be strengthened, nourishing itself with new affirmation.

Notwithstanding the ephemeral nature of the Odessa myth, it remains and continues to be a powerful ideological factor. To be sure, the old architecture and new monuments draw attention to the past, but the shape and symbolism of new monuments and buildings force Odessits to confront their future. With earnest effort and honest direction, this Black Sea port may well have commenced creating a new legend for itself.

## Notes

1. For a general history of the city, see Patricia Herlihy, *Odessa: A History, 1794–1914* (Cambridge, Mass.: Harvard University Press, 1986).

2. Roger P. Bartlett, *Human Capital: The Settlement of Foreigners in Russia, 1762–1804* (Cambridge: Cambridge University Press, 1979), 135–42, 210–12.

3. Steven J. Zipperstein, *The Jews of Odessa: A Cultural History, 1794–1881* (Stanford, Calif.: Stanford University Press 1985); Patricia Herlihy, "Port Jews of Odessa and Trieste: A Tale of Two Cities," *Jahrbuch des Simon–Dubnow–Instituts* 2 (2003): 183–98.

4. Menachem-Mendle is Sholem Aleichem's fictional character in his *The Adventures of Menachem-Mendl* (New York: Putnam, 1979), 10.

5. N. A. Chizhov, "My vkhodim v sad," *Syn Otchestva* 2 (1823). Other Russian travelers also commented favorably: E.g., N. S. Vsevolozhskii: "Walking around the city I was happy, I delighted in the activity, concern, novelty, liveliness, which one almost always meets in merchant cities on the sea. I saw here people of all nations: Greeks, Italians, Germans, French, Jews (there are many here), Armenians and a crowd of Ukrainians, resting between oxen and their carts on the squares. The latter only come to unload their wheat. In general the various pictures of the sea, the completely European, magnificent city is astonishingly attractive." N. S. Vsevolozhskii, *Puteshestvie cherez Iuzhnuiu Rossiiu, Krym i Odessu v Konstantinopol', Maluiu Aziiu, Severnuiu Afriku* (Moscow, 1838), 42. And O. P. Pushkin: "Sometimes I think I am in a foreign land alone among foreigners, but Russian speech, Russian uniforms remind me that I am indeed in Russia and I am all the more delighted, walking and resting with the elite society under the beautiful southern sky in the evening coolness." O. P. Pushkin, *Zametki i vospominaniia russkoi puteshestvennitsy po Rossii v 1845 gody,* part 2 (Saint Petersburg, 1848), 32.

6. For a sampling of foreigners' reports before 1830, see Thomas Alcock, *Travels in Russia, Persia, Turkey, and Greece, 1829–9* (London: E. Clarke, 1831); Ignace Antoine Anthoine, *Essai historique sur le commerce et la navigation de la Mer-Noire* (Paris: H. and Ve. Agasse, 1805 and 1820); T. B. Armstrong, *Journals of Travel in the Seat of*

*War, during the Last Two Campaigns of Russia and Turkey* (London: A. Seguin, 1831); G. de Castelnau, *Essai sur l'histoire ancienne et moderne de la Nouvelle Russie,* 3 vols. (Paris: Rey et Gravier, 1820); Edward Daniel Clarke, *Travels in Russia, Tartary and Turkey,* 2 vols. (Edinburgh: William and Robert Chambers, 1839); Josiah Conder, *Modern Traveller, Russia,* vol. 10 (London: J. Duncan, 1830); Henry S. Dearborn, *A Memoir on the Commerce and Navigation of the Black Sea,* 2 vols. (Boston: Wells and Lilly, 1819); Charles B. Elliott, *Travels in the Three Great Empires of Austria, Russia and Turkey,* 2 vols. (Philadelphia: Lea and Blanchard, 1839); W. Eton, *A Concise Account of the Commerce and Navigation of the Black Sea* (London: T. Cadell and W. Davies, 1805); Piero Gamba, *Voyage dans la Russie méridionale* (Paris, 1826); Maria Guthrie, *Lettres sur la Crimée, Odessa et la Mer d'Azov* (Moscow, 1810); Ebenezer Henderson, *Biblical Researches and Travels in Russia* (London: J. Nisbet, 1826); Mary Holderness, *New Russia: Journey from Riga to the Crimea by Way of Kiev* (London: Sherwood, Jones and Co. 1823); Comte de La Garde-Chambonas, *Voyage de Moscou à Vienne, par Kow, Odessa, Constantinople, Bucharest et Hermanstadt* (Paris: Treuttel et Wuertz, 1824); Robert Lyall, *Travels in Russia, the Krimea, the Caucasus, and Georgia,* 2 vols. (London: T. Cadell and W. Blackwood, 1825); Edward Morton, *Travels in Russia and a Residence at St. Petersburg and Odessa in the Years 1827–1829* (London: Longman, Rees, Orme, Brown and Green, 1830); Robert Stevens, *An Account of Odessa* (Newport: William Simons, 1819); and James Webster, *Travels through the Crimea, Turkey and Egypt,* 2 vols. (London: H. Colburn and R. Bentley, 1830).

7. Patricia Herlihy, "Odessa, Staple Trade and Urbanization in New Russia," *Jahrbücher für Geschichte Osteuropas,* 21 (1974): 121–37.

8. Cited by Robert A. Rothstein, "How It Was Sung in Odessa: At the Intersection of Russian and Jewish Culture," *Slavic Review* 60 (Winter 2001): 788.

9. Anatolii F. Kozak, *Odessa zdes' bol'she ne zhivet* (Samara: Tarbut, 1997), 139.

10. "Bluest Black Sea" is a refrain from the popular song "He Who Was Born by the Sea," from the Khrushchev-era film *A Sailor from the Kometa;* "Swineherdesses and Shepherds" is from the Stalinist film of that name extolling the multinational composition of the Soviet Union.

11. A. S. Pushkin, 1799–1837; K. N. Batiuskov, 1787–1855; V. I. Tumanskii, 1800–60; I. E. Babel', 1894–1941; K. G. Paustovskii, 1892–1968; Ilia Il'f (I. A. Fainzilberg), 1897–1937; and Evgeny Petrov (E. P. Kataev), 1903–42.

12. See http://www.theodessaguide.com/index.htm.

13. For architecture, see Oleg Gubar, *Odessa: Pale-Roial', Illiustrirovannyi Al'bom* (Odessa: IP-Odessa, 2005); and Patricia Herlihy, "Commerce and Architecture in Odessa in Late Imperial Russia," in *Commerce in Russian Urban Culture 1861–1914,* ed. William Craft Brumfield, Boris V. Anan'ich, and Yuri A. Petrov (Washington and Baltimore: Woodrow Wilson Center Press and Johns Hopkins University Press, 2001), 180–94. For civil society, see Guido Hausmann, *Universität und städtische Gesellschaft in Odessa 1865–1817* (Stuttgart: F. Steiner, 1998).

14. "Vysotkami—po staroi Odesse," *Migdal'* 50 (August–September 2004): 14–18.

15. General François De-Voland, *The Essay of My Service in Russia, 1787–1811* (Odessa: Optimum, 1999).

16. For the connection between Odessa and the Ancient Greek colonies, see Neal Ascherson, *The Black Sea* (New York: Hill and Wang, 1995), 7–84; and Charles King, *The Black Sea: A History* (Oxford: Oxford University Press, 2004), 25–61.

17. Patricia Herlihy, "Greek Merchants in Odessa in the Nineteenth Century, *Har-*

*vard Ukrainian Studies* 3–4 (1979–80): 399–420; and Patricia Herlihy, "The Greek Community in Odessa, 1861–1917," *Journal of Modern Greek Studies* 7 (1989): 235–52.

18. Oleg Gubar, "Kamennaia letopis' Odessy," in *Odessa v novykh pamiatnikakh, memorial'nykh doskahk i zdaniiakh* (Odessa: Optimum, 2004), 8–14.

19. Oleg Gubar, "Bez ansamblia, sam," *Or sameakh* 28 (September 2004).

20. Laurence Mackin, "Poland Tapping Up Ukraine for Oil," *Warsaw Business Journal*, March 29, 2005.

21. Liudvik Ashkenazi, *Bab'e leto* (Moscow: Izdatel'stvoi inostrannoi literatury, 1958), 2.

22. Aloïs Rigl, *Le culte moderne des monuments: Son essence et son genèse* (Paris, 1984).

23. See http://webmail.east.cox.net/agent/mobmain?mobmain=1.

24. Oleg Gubar, *Odessa v novykh pamiatnikakh, memorial'nykh doskahk i zdaniiakh* (Odessa: Optimum, 2004).

25. M. A. Poliakov and E. A. Shulepov, eds. *Voprosy okhrany i ispol'zovanii pamiatnikov i kul'tury* (Moscow: Nauchno-issledovatel'skiĭ institut kul'tury, 1990), 4.

26. For a discussion of Utochkin, see Patricia Herlihy, "Odessa Memories," in *Odessa Memories,* ed. Nicholas Iljine (Seattle: University of Washington Press, 2003), 31–32; and Oleg Gubar and Alexander Rozenboim, "Daily Life in Odessa," in ibid., 98.

27. Gubar, *Odessa v novykh pamiatnikakh,* 43–55.

# 6

# Traveling Today through Sevastopol's Past: Postcommunist Continuity in a "Ukrainian" Cityscape

*Karl D. Qualls*

Walking along Soviet Street on the high central hill in Sevastopol, the visitor confronts spray-painted graffiti on the yellowed wall of a building that reads: "Sevastopol is Russia." While graffiti is a common form of self-expression in most cities, it is also a political statement in this Ukrainian port city that would likely choose the leadership of Moscow over Kyiv. The uninitiated viewer would likely also be confused by the persistence of the name "Soviet Street," which leads to a large statue of Vladimir Lenin that towers over the city. Cities throughout Eastern Europe are now Westernizing by erecting glass-and-steel skyscrapers while also destroying remnants

---

The project on which this chapter is based received generous support in the form of a J. Paul Getty Postdoctoral Fellowship in the History of Art and the Humanities and a Library of Congress Fellowship in International Studies, which is administered by the American Council of Learned Societies and funded by the Andrew W. Mellon Foundation, the Association of American Universities, and the Library of Congress. Dickinson College's Research and Development Committee provided numerous resources in time and money for the project.

of the past by tearing down buildings and statues and renaming streets and squares. Are Sevastopol's residents and city leaders stuck in the communist past, or is there another way to explain this Russian-minded enclave so many years after the fall of the Soviet Union? Why has Sevastopol changed so little and shown less of a concern with creating new local identity as part of a European community?

On the basis of interviews, a review of the press, a decade of personal observations, and previous research, this chapter seeks to explain how a predominantly Russian city within Ukraine is fighting the trend to integrate into Europe. As the 2004 Ukrainian presidential elections showed, Sevastopol, like much of Eastern and Southern Ukraine, identifies more with Moscow than Kyiv. Unlike many cities in Eastern Europe, Sevastopol has seen virtually no renaming of streets and squares to signal its status as part of an independent Ukraine. Likewise, the configuration of new sites of identification with Ukraine is rare. The obligatory statue to Ukraine's greatest literary icon—Taras Shevchenko—is the single exception. Aside from the commercialization of ground-floor storefronts on the central ring road and new dachas on the outskirts, one would notice little change in the cityscape over the last decade.

This chapter shows that this relative continuity in Sevastopol's built environment is the result of a well-defined, long-lasting local identity developed both before and after World War II. Moreover, this identity was easily adapted to the post-Soviet transformation and thus mitigated the need to redefine the city, as has been so common elsewhere. This local identity transcended the Soviet Union and continues to frustrate attempts to develop a Ukrainian identity. Because the Russian Black Sea Fleet is still based in the city and most of the sites of memory created in the twentieth century highlight the contribution of Russians, political affinities tend toward Moscow rather than Kyiv. Whereas other Eastern European cities have seen great transformation, none shared Sevastopol's demographic makeup or maintained as strong a connection to their pre-Soviet roots throughout the twentieth century.

## The Importance and Persistence of the Past in Sevastopol

Any political entity bent on reshaping the identity of Sevastopol over the short term has a Herculean task ahead. For over two hundred years, Sevastopol has been first and foremost a Russian naval city. However, when

Catherine the Great founded the city in 1784 as an outpost against the Turks, she built upon the foundation of earlier inhabitants. The ancient Greeks founded the city of Chersonesus (Khersones to Slavs) 2,500 years ago on land that is now part of greater Sevastopol. Whether Greeks, Turks, or East Slavs, all the powers who held sway in the city realized the commercial and military potential of this spot at the southern tip of the Crimean Peninsula with its deep and numerous bays and heights at the perimeter of the city. Sevastopol and its surroundings played a vital role in defending Russia in the Turkish Wars, in the Crimean War, and in World War II.

One site of memory—the Monument to Scuttled Ships—stands at the center of Sevastopol's identity as a naval bastion. Because of the difficulty of attacking from land, British and French forces during the Crimean War tried to move into the bays, which would have put the city center within range of their guns. To prevent what would have resulted in immediate capitulation, the Russian Navy chose to sink some of its own ships at the mouth of the bay to prevent the enemy from entering. This sacrificial act became a defining event for the city; and in World War II soldiers, sailors, and citizens threw themselves under tanks, charged machine gun nests, and threw bombs off burning ships in emulation of the previous century's sacrifice.[1]

Despite the "two great defenses" (as the Crimean War and World War II are known in Sevastopol), much of the city's projected character and identity have been derived from its first monument, which honors the brig *Mercury* and its commander, Aleksandr Kazarskii. In May 1829, Kazarskii and his crew on the *Mercury* found themselves facing Turkish ships with ten times the number of guns. Rather than flee, Kazarskii skillfully maneuvered his lone ship and harassed the Turkish fleet into retreat. The first of Sevastopol's over two thousand monuments honored this courageous and creative victory. The inscription on the pedestal has become a mantra for the city: "An Example for Posterity." Kazarskii's victory against all odds inspired the Russian forces facing the British, French, Turks, and Sardinians in the Crimean War. Likewise, in World War II, German, Rumanian, and Italian forces initially had a greater quantity and quality of troops and technology in their successful assault on the city. For two years, the residents who were unable to flee the city lived under Nazi occupation. However, an underground movement immediately developed and helped the Red Army recapture the city in May 1944. For over a century, the city's life was devoted to war, to preparations for war, or to reconstruction after destruction, often against great odds.

Although Soviet officials wanted to highlight the city's revolutionary history, post–World War II narratives of the city clearly placed the revolutions and Civil War behind the importance of the "two great defenses."[2] Since the end of World War II, residents and nonresidents alike have been bombarded with a set of images that help to define the city's identity and role in Russian and Soviet history, often in conflict with Europe. Even as World War II raged, newspapers carried stories of the new heroes and linked them to the heroes of a century earlier. Newspapers today continue the tradition of recalling the "two great defenses" for audiences far removed from the events.[3]

Reminders of the Russian naval past are inescapable for residents and visitors. Before World War II, Sevastopol had already started to become an open-air museum of monuments, memorials, and plaques, and the war catalyzed a resurgence of mythmaking during the second half of the twentieth century, which has led to roughly 2,015 monuments today. Though Moscow-based planners wanted to turn the city into a museum to Soviet power and the victory in World War II, local officials diverged from these plans to encompass the city's larger heritage. When the local architectural team rebuilt the city, which had been 97 percent destroyed, they emphasized its naval heritage and especially its role in the Crimean War. For example, the Moscow planners had proposed relocating the beautiful but destroyed panorama and museum to the Crimean War off of Historical Boulevard to highlight the most recent victory. Local planners successfully argued that the Crimean War should not be marginalized, but rather it should remain figuratively and geographically at the heart of the city as a key facet of its identity and landscape.[4]

After World War II, renamed streets, parks, and squares highlighted Sevastopol's nineteenth-century legacy and lent continuity to its identity.[5] Wherever one turned, residents and visitors were reminded of the city's ongoing struggle against European attacks. The city's place in Russian and Soviet history, its relationship to the ruling Soviet ideology, and the place of ethnic minorities all found expression in the changing urban fabric. In some cases, the Soviet present came to the fore, as when city officials renamed Catherine the Great Street in favor of Lenin Street following the Revolution. Although many post-Soviet cities have removed all traces of the Bolsheviks, Sevastopol retains Sovietized street names and Lenin's statue still looks down over the city from the central hill. In fact, Sevastopol's central district is still called "Leninskii."

The postrevolutionary period also saw the creation of Karl Marx and Mikhail Frunze streets as the other two main conduits around the central hill. Thus, the father of the Revolution (Lenin), the creator of its ideology

(Marx), and the liberator of Crimea during the Civil War (Frunze) all became a part of one's daily life walking about the city center. However, unlike Lenin Street, Marx Street and Frunze Street disappeared as toponyms in the years after World War II. In reverting to the prerevolutionary names Bol'shaia Morskaia (Big Naval) Street and Admiral Nakhimov Prospect, urban planners indicated a preference for historical figures related to local, rather than Soviet, identity. These figures provide residents points of historical reference for developing national and local pride not related to the propagation of Socialist values. Marx had no direct link to Sevastopol, and few considered Frunze a "local" hero despite his role in "liberating" Sevastopol from the Germans in the early 1920s. In contrast, Admiral P. S. Nakhimov was first among the local heroes of the Crimean War, and Bol'shaia Morskaia could express the city's character as a naval port, unlike Marx or Lenin.

For similar reasons, after World War II planners gave new names to the squares marking the intersections of Sevastopol's chief ring roads. The Square of the Third International became first Parade Square and then Nakhimov Square. Novoselskaia became Commune Square after the Revolution but took the name of Admiral Ushakov during reconstruction. Even Revolutionary Square disappeared in favor of the eighteenth-century commander of the fleet, M. P. Lazarev. The preeminent role of the navy, the presence of naval representatives on review boards, and a cooperative civilian leadership conspired to make Sevastopol a city steeped in its prerevolutionary naval tradition.[6] By linking this history to the events of World War II Sevastopol's citizens and sailors could claim a long and glorious tradition of defending the Motherland. One could view these name changes as an abandonment of Socialist goals, but like the refashioning of local histories and aesthetics in Eastern Europe today, it was more important to the city's stability and rapid reconstruction to resurrect a unique local character to which residents could attach their ideals and aspirations. Moreover, the virtues associated with the defense of the city during the Crimean War seemed to be mirrored in the Soviet values of duty, sacrifice, and fighting against all odds for the Motherland. Therefore, such an emphasis on local identity did not necessarily undermine the patriotic facets of a Soviet identity, but in fact complemented them. Because architects and planners had created the city as specifically Soviet after World War II but rather also relied on its prerevolutionary Russian heritage, its transformation after 1991 was less traumatic and dramatic than in those cities that had had their pre-Soviet history expunged during the twentieth century. Postwar urban planners had already placed the city's nineteenth-century heritage ahead of the Soviet revolutionary tradition. Therefore, with the collapse of the USSR, Sevastopol could easily revert to its Russian orientation, although the definition of "Motherland" would now be open to interpretation.

Toponyms amid the rubble of the city marked it as an ethnically and culturally homogenous Russian/Slavic city and ignored its more heterogeneous past. The architectural footprint left by the two non-Slavic, non-European groups in the city disappeared in the war and its aftermath. The Soviet regime deported Crimean Tatars en masse for alleged collaboration with the Nazis, and Crimean Karaite Jews suffered like most European Jews under Hitler.[7] With the decimation of these populations came the destruction of their places of worship. The postwar planners ignored this multiethnic heritage in reconstructing the city and in refashioning its image. Eliminating the remnants of "collaborators" and "anti-Soviet cosmopolitans" (the catchphrase for Jews) became paramount in an era marked by further paranoia about "enemies" and growing anti-Semitism after the establishment of Israel.[8] The Kenasa, a Karaite prayer hall on Bol'shaia Morskaia, became the Spartak Sports Club; the Tatar mosque just two streets off the ring road became the naval archive after workers removed the minarets and "erased" Koranic inscriptions on the building's facade.[9]

In that city purged of its cultural diversity, designers also set about unifying the architectural style that had been an eclectic blend of nineteenth-century neoclassical, constructivist, and early Stalinist functionalist buildings. Late Stalinist architecture, marked in most people's minds by "wedding cake" buildings with highly decorative facades, found no place in Sevastopol. Instead, designers turned to an aspect of Sevastopol's architectural heritage, the partially preserved Greek ruins of the Khersones Archaeological Preserve. Recognizing these architectural remains as a local prototype allowed architects to preserve and restore some of the city's best neoclassical (and often religious) architecture, such as the 1844 Parthenon-like Saints Peter and Paul Cathedral, which otherwise might have fallen victim to the official policy of promoting atheism.[10]

In addition to the neoclassical style, architects included balconies and loggias on nearly all their buildings to take advantage of the seaside character of the city. Likewise, most buildings were finished with stucco and painted ochre to contrast with the blue-black sea and to take advantage of the bright sunlight. Doric, Ionic, and Corinthian columns, massive pediments, and geometric precision defined new buildings after the war. But unlike Moscow, where architects applied historic styles to tall high-rises, all new construction in the historic center of Sevastopol was limited to three to five stories. Architects argued for this limitation on aesthetic grounds, but the great 1948 earthquake in Ashkhabad/Ashgabat, Turkmenistan, revealed that Sevastopol's seismic activity would not permit greater vertical construction.[11] The elimination of culturally diverse elements, the accommodation to the climatic and topographical peculiarities of the site, the choice of a local architectural prototype, and a limitation on the height of construction lent the city a unique and homogenous character.

The consistent Russian character of the city would seem to be projected through neoclassical facades that recalled the 2,500-year-old ruins of the ancient Greek city at nearby Khersones. This historical appropriation of an architectural style is symptomatic of the local invention of tradition and the promulgation of a selective history. Planners designed Sevastopol envisioning its role within the Soviet Union, lending it a unified appearance that helped project a unified history.

## Post-Soviet Ukrainianization and Resulting Tensions

After the demise of the Soviet Union and the emergence of an independent Ukraine, the overwhelmingly Russian-speaking population of Sevastopol wondered what would become of them, of the city's "Russianness," and of its privileged position vis-à-vis the state of which it had been a part. Sevastopol also had enjoyed a special status as a "city of republic subordination."[12] Simply put, the city had much more autonomy and a direct relationship with the Soviet capital that often bypassed the regional governments. Because of its military importance, it was better provisioned than other Crimean cities and most other Ukrainian cities as well. Many wondered if an independent Ukraine would continue to support Sevastopol in the same manner as the Soviet Union. Moreover, as Ukraine started dialogue with NATO and the European Union, Russian naval personnel and the pro-Russian population that shared Moscow's disdain for these links to Europe saw their worldview challenged. This situation played itself out in national, regional, and local politics.

When Iurii Meshkov won the presidency of the Crimean Autonomous Republic in January 1994 and came into office with a proseparatist Parliament, he tried to make good on his promises to reunite the nation with Russia, and Sevastopol's City Council supported this by declaring the city Russian territory.[13] But when Meshkov pulled back from preelection promises to appoint pro-Moscow Crimeans to key posts and instead appointed Muscovites, Parliament voted to curb his powers, which in turn led him to disband Parliament. With a Parliament-appointed prime minister, Crimea in essence had two governments, neither of which functioned. On March 17, 1995, the Ukrainian Parliament, backed by President Leonid Kuchma, eliminated the presidency of Crimea and revoked its Constitution. Thus, Meshkov was left without power or a position. Kuchma sent Interior Ministry troops into the Crimean capital of Simferopol, and they disarmed Meshkov's entourage. Russia, which immediately after the Soviet collapse protested that Sevastopol was still Russian territory, could undertake little while still waging war with secessionists in Chechnya.[14]

Two years later, President Kuchma demanded that Crimea change to the same time zone as Kiev, not Moscow.[15] With the signing of the Treaty of Friendship and Cooperation between Russia and Ukraine in 1997, Russia agreed to recognize Ukraine's territorial boundaries, including Crimea. Thus Crimea and Sevastopol lost their special status even while an internal battle in the Crimean government continued concerning the relationship to Russia and Ukraine.[16]

The most important aspect of this conflict for Sevastopol was the question about the disposition of the Soviet Black Sea Fleet. When in 1995 Russian president Boris Yeltsin and Ukrainian president Kuchma divided the former Soviet fleet, it seemed to promise an end to one of the most persistent and potentially violent disputes between the two countries.[17] Since 1991, the former Soviet fleet had flown the flags of both countries, but commanders usually followed orders from Moscow, which, after all, paid most salaries. As the Crimean government fought to secede from Ukraine, the issue of the fleet became a powder keg. Bloody fights between Ukrainian and Russian sailors ensued and only declined in number after 1995 when Russia received 82 percent of the fleet and agreed to lease Sevastopol's naval facilities.[18] Furthermore, NATO exercises in the Black Sea enraged many Russians, who saw it as a provocation and an attempt to woo Ukraine away from its Slavic brother.

For four years, the sailors of the two fleets had looked at each other with contempt, suspicion, and animosity. They blamed each other's governments for poor maintenance and inadequate funding and for harboring nationalist pretensions.[19] In one famous incident, Ukrainian commandos stormed a Russian naval base in Odessa and arrested three officers; the Russian authorities claimed that even the officers' children were beaten. Ukraine claimed it was retaliating for the theft of $10 million in navigation equipment aboard the Sevastopol-based ship *Chekelen*. When two Ukrainian ships tried to intercept the *Chekelen,* the Russian Navy sent an attack group from Sevastopol that chased the Ukrainian ships away. Ensuing Ukrainian seizures of former Soviet bases led Moscow to place its warships on full alert.[20]

When the number of Russian sailors quickly increased in the 1990s, the navy started appropriating parts of the city near the port for dacha-style housing, thus establishing a "home" for the navy and not merely a military posting.[21] This heightened animosity with Ukraine. In 1997 Moscow mayor Iurii Luzhkov increased tensions by financing and building an apartment building for Russian sailors in Sevastopol, something that met with the approval of the local Russian population. One resident noted that "Luzhkov is right. Sevastopol is a historic military city of Russia. All its major events and achievements are important chapters in Russian history."[22] One and a half years later, the mayor of Moscow continued to insist that "Crimea must be returned to Russia."[23] Rear Admiral Vadim Vasyukov appeared on a Moscow television program and noted that it is "hard to overestimate the contribution of the Moscow municipal government and Iurii Mikhailovich Luzhkov personally" to the work of the Black Sea Fleet.[24] Luzhkov fortified the Russian presence in the city by signing an agreement to aid Sevastopol in economic, cultural, and technical matters through 2005.[25] The strong Russian presence that still prevails both demographically and politically has worked toward keeping the physical character of the city relatively unchanged. Sevastopol's close identification with Russia has led it to turn away from Europe even as Ukraine tries to position itself for NATO and European Union membership against the wishes of Russia.

This raises the question about whether or not Kyiv will try to "Ukrainianize" post-Soviet Sevastopol, just as local Soviet officials had "Russianized" it after World War II. At the beginning of the new millennium, with the Crimean Parliament under their control and the questions of boundaries and the fleet resolved, Ukrainian authorities erected a statue to the Ukrainian literary hero Taras Shevchenko in front of the Gagarin regional administration building. Local citizens, the overwhelming majority of whom do not speak Ukrainian, did not appreciate a monument dedicated to the Ukrainian national poet, who had no connection to the city. When asked, some residents of the city explained that this lack of appreciation did not derive from Russophilia or Ukrainophobia. After all, they fully accepted monuments to Ukrainians, Armenians, Georgians, and any other non-Russians who had fought and often died defending the city. What they resent, they say, is seeing local military heroes standing alongside the revered Ukrainian artist meant to symbolize the claims of the Ukrainian nation.[26]

The Shevchenko statue remains the only clear symbol of the Ukrainianization in the city, although Ukrainian place names are not uncommon. For example, in 2004 twenty streets carried a distinctly Ukrainian surname. Of those twenty, nine were named for heroes of World War II, four for participants in the Civil War, and two each for the Crimean War and the 1905 uprising in the city. In short, seventeen of the twenty street names honored service to the city and country, not nationality. All twenty streets were named up to the mid-1960s, except one—Taras Shevchenko Street (1987). Sevastopol's *Encyclopedia* discusses each of the namesakes of these streets, and Taras Shevchenko's entry is clearly the briefest at seven lines; Ignatii Shevchenko (a prominent figure from the Crimean War) earned thirty-seven! In fact, the *Encyclopedia*'s biography of Taras Shevchenko—"(1814–1861) great Ukrainian poet, artist, thinker, revolutionary democrat"—is shorter than its description of the street's location.[27] No renaming of streets occurred after Ukrainian Independence.

Much like the patterns of name giving, the patterns of historic preservation in Sevastopol suggest a deeper connection to Russia while eschewing at least part of the Soviet past. As in other cities around the Soviet Union during the 1920s and 1930s, places of worship in Sevastopol were torn down or given new functions. The end of the Soviet Union opened the possibility of national revival through religious revival. In the years since the Soviet collapse, the Municipality of Sevastopol has started to restore part of this Orthodox heritage. Four key churches dot Sevastopol's landscape and help to define the city in different ways. The Pokrovskii Cathedral (1905; architect, V. A. Fel'dman) on Bol'shaia Morskaia suffered severe damage in World War II, but was restored by 1950. For the next nine years, it hosted services, but from 1959 to 1969 it housed a sports hall and the city archive. From 1969 to 1994, the municipal archive took possession of the entire complex. Since 1994, the church has been reopened for religious services, despite ongoing restoration. With its Byzantine style and setting among trendy shops and restaurants at the very heart of the city, this Russian Orthodox church presents one clear token of the religious revival.

Sevastopol also has retained its two Saint Vladimir cathedrals. One sits atop the central hill, and the other stands in the Khersones Archaeological Preserve, where it marks the supposed spot of Vladimir the Great's baptism in 988. Designed in 1842 and initially intended for Khersones, Saint Vladimir Cathedral was instead constructed on the central hill (1848–88) because the fleet commander demanded that the church be built close to naval headquarters. Behind the imposing facade of this edifice lie the tombs of the admirals Lazarev, Nakhimov, Kornilov, and Istomin, and thirteen other heroes of the Crimean War. During the Nazi siege of the city, the cathedral suffered heavy damage. Only in 1966, after residents bitterly contested plans to raze the building and move the crypts of the naval heroes, were the authorities moved to restore the cathedral.[28] I. L. Shmulsom began the restoration of the Russian Imperial–style facade the next year, and by 1971 the exterior was largely restored. In 1972 the building housed the Museum of the Heroic Defense and Liberation of Sevastopol, but in October 1991 it was again returned to the church. Restoration work continues. This church symbolizes more than the revival of religion; it embodies the sacrifice of war. Large plaques on its facade remind visitors of the Crimean War heroes, and the remaining shell damage recalls World War II, thus allowing the building to commemorate both wars.

Saint Vladimir Cathedral at Khersones, rededicated in 2001 with the Russian and Ukrainian presidents Vladimir Putin and Leonid Kuchma in attendance, once again dominates the skyline of the architectural preserve.[29] Erected in 1891 by D. I. Grimm on the spot where Vladimir the Great is said to have adopted the Byzantine faith and thus brought Christianity to the Kievan Rus', the cathedral functioned for only twenty-three years before the Soviet government closed it. Nazi bombing and local looting of stone rubble for housing left the structure in ruins after World War II. In 1992 the church reclaimed the building, and in 2004 Sevastopol's mayor handed this magnificent structure to the Moscow Patriarchate because it is the "largest confession in the region."[30] The presence of Putin and Kuchma signaled the importance of the common heritage of the two states, but the control of the site by Moscow suggests that Vladimir the Great and his capital at Kyiv are more a part of Russian history than Ukrainian. This would be consistent with most Russian historiography, which traces the beginnings of the Russian state to Kyiv.

Another cathedral dedicated to Saints Peter and Paul (1839–43; architect, V. A. Rulev) stands on the previous site of a Greek church. It was destroyed during the Crimean War and rebuilt by two merchants in 1889. From the Revolution to World War II, it served as the city's archive. In 1946 the city restored it as the Lunacharsky Drama Theater, until it became the House of Culture in 1957. Only recently has the building been returned to the church, but no evidence of construction could be seen in 2004. Saints Peter and Paul Cathedral's facade is clearly reminiscent of the Parthenon; again the point of both local and limited European reference is ancient Greece.

The rebuilding of all the churches signals a return to "Russianness" both in the revival of architectural styles associated with Russia and in the revival of the institution most closely associated with a traditional Russian identity: the Russian Orthodox Church. Sevastopol is unlike other former Soviet cities such as Riga or Vilnius that have a Roman Catholic or Protestant heritage that allows them to link their local heritage and to the broader religious heritage of Western Europe. As Patriarch Alexy II of the Russian Orthodox Church has clearly stated, those other forms of Christianity are not part of the Russian religious heritage. His consistent refusal to allow Pope John Paul II to visit Moscow set a clear divide between Russia and Europe. The Russian state agreed in 1997 when it decreed that the Russian Orthodox Church was the only traditional Christian religion of Russia.

Just as religious revivalism serves as a vehicle to overcome divisions between state and society by defining a common cultural space, war remembrance added an opportunity to bring Sevastopol and Ukraine together in a common history. In 2004 Sevastopol celebrated the two-hundred-twentieth anniversary of its founding, the one-hundred-fiftieth anniversary of the Crimean War, and the sixtieth anniversary of the liberation of Sevastopol (May) and Ukraine (October). Tourists, including Prince Phillip of the United Kingdom, flocked to the city to commemorate various events. Buses and trams carried signs that read "Sevastopol—220 years" and "Hero-City Sevastopol," and banners announcing the sixtieth anniversary of the "liberation of Ukraine from the German-fascist invaders" adorned utility lines. Newspapers from the communist *Sevastopolskaia pravda* to the more mainstream *Slava Sevastopolia* and popular *Sevastopolskaia gazeta* carried historical articles about the two midcentury defenses and remembrances from veterans of the latter one.[31] Television stations also aired brief documentaries and reports on the various celebrations. Posters lined store windows, and publications on the Crimean War and World War II filled bookstore shelves. The interested buyer could even buy multilingual postcards celebrating the one-hundred-fiftieth anniversary of the Crimean War. The foldout cards had historical images adjacent to the same scene from the present.[32] Thus, the education of the traveler about Sevastopol's past continues. Whereas the celebration of the Crimean War and World War II were common, only recently has Sevastopol celebrated the anniversary of Ukraine's liberation from the Nazis in any meaningful way. In doing so, it is beginning to blend the image of Sevastopol's liberation with the narrative of Ukraine's struggle.

Although tourism and celebrations have started to relate Sevastopol's history more closely with the history of Ukraine and bring Europeans and other foreigners to the city, the local history of the city's defense against Europeans still dominates. Tourism centered on war remembrance understandably increases in anniversary years, and even children are frequent visitors. For example, in the fifteenth season of what is described as "intellectual games," forty-two teams of students matched wits about ancient and medieval Khersones, the Crimean War, and the region's natural resources.[33] More than seven hundred young students from the Donets Oblast (region) "visited historical and memorial places, [and] placed flowers at the Memorial of hero defenders of Sevastopol in 1941–1942."[34] The naval news program *Reflection* also reported on the visit of a school group from Saint Petersburg studying the city as a Russian naval outpost and as the birthplace of Orthodox Christianity for the East Slavs.[35] Although the city is part of Ukraine, it is not yet a site of "Ukrainian" tourism, and in these examples students are learning what makes Sevastopol unique and how it is connected to Russian history and traditions.

## The Commercialization of Post-Soviet Space

Although ritual space and sites of memory have remained relatively unchanged since the end of the Soviet Union, newly commercialized space has created a drastic juxtaposition between old and new. There is nothing clearly "Ukrainian" in this development, but it does seem "European." The twenty-first century has brought commercial storefronts to the ground floors of buildings along the central ring road. Unlike the mid-1990s, Sevastopol today boasts several fashionable restaurants (and unfashionable ones, like McDonald's), jewelers, clothing stores, and more. Many stores promote foreign products with foreign advertising, but even stores for local Russian and Ukrainian products have transformed the aesthetic of the urban environment. The contrast between old and new is clear to any observer. Though many ground-floor shops sport modern glass display windows and steel entryways with newly painted plaster facades, the upper residential floors show the wear of the years since the buildings rose out of the rubble of World War II. On the upper floors, which are primarily residential, yellowed and grayed plaster remains and ferro-concrete balconies and loggias crumble. Though residents live in the old Sevastopol, tourists and wealthy residents shop in the new.

Two stores on Bol'shaia Morskaia Street, today the most fashionable shopping area of the city, show the contrast between the traditional Soviet use of built space and the new commercialization of post-Soviet space. Megasport is the largest sporting goods store in the city center. The large, heavy, Soviet-era wooden doors greet visitors as they walk beneath the English-language store sign. Brightly colored placards (also in Latin characters) promoting Reebok, Nike, Speedo, and Adidas flank the entryway down the length of the sidewalk. Two large color posters of male athletes hang on either side of the doorway with text in Ukrainian and store hours in Russian. Thus, we have a multilingual storefront promoting an all-foreign line of sporting goods. Moreover, the plaster wall facades have been painted a bright white, offsetting the color of the promotional material. Juxtaposed with the bright, colorful lower floor are the essentially untouched upper two floors. The plaster walls have grayed, and the faux balustrade immediately above the store looks particularly shabby when set off against the new white paint (figure 6.1).

Figure 6.1. The Megasport sporting goods store in 2004. Photograph by Karl D. Qualls.

On the opposite side of the street, the new women's clothing store Fete and its neighboring casino shows an even greater juxtaposition between old and new. A new arched doorway cut in the stone facade was reinforced with highly polished steel. The glass door and display window were topped by a similar glass arch. Clean, modern lines dominate the interior and exterior, but the balcony and the Doric-style balustrade that serves as a railing on the floor above are disintegrating. In one section of six balusters, five are missing. Much like Megasport, the newly painted facade sets off the new commercial floor from the older dilapidated residential floors above (figure 6.2). The casino, something strictly forbidden in the Soviet period, beckons a new generation of residents with disposable income and/or in desperate hope for a better future.

This juxtaposition of wealth and poverty is also visible in other places along this stretch of street. A wide consumer products store with a painted white facade shines below a second-floor balcony that has rotted and shows clear signs of patchwork repair. Directly above this dangerous balcony is a loggia also painted stark white, including its Ionic columns, which contrasts starkly with the neighboring apartment's unpainted and enclosed loggia (figure 6.3). Sevastopol's commercial development has created a wealth gap that has led to an uneven urban transformation and changed the original uses and appearances of buildings.

Only one building in Sevastopol's center stands out as unabashedly "Western" in every way. Situated on Lazarev Square nearly equidistant from the city's main theater and cinema, McDonald's, though small, looks like a McDonald's anywhere in the world, save for its Russian-language menu. The color, decor, food, and service are completely out of place in Sevastopol. A life-size Ronald McDonald stands outside and beckons to the passing crowd. Whereas Fete and Megasport send mixed messages, McDonald's leaves no doubt that it is *the* symbol of Westernization. The "otherness" of these new modern structures and businesses equate Europe and the West with modernity and affluence, but they also create and represent economic inequality.

However, some commercial interests in the city are embracing the past. The most well-known restaurant in the city, Traktir, is named for the 1855 Crimean War battle that attempted to remove the French from the city, and its interior is covered with paintings on nautical and military themes. All the servers, although they are women, dress as Imperial Russian sailors. Ironically, the restaurant is known for the best and most authentic Russian cuisine in the city, but its borsch is Ukrainian. This does not seem to matter to

Figure 6.2. The Fete store in 2004. Photograph by Karl D. Qualls.

Figure 6.3. A store and apartments on Bol'shaia Morskaia in 2004. Photograph by Karl D. Qualls.

the Russian marines and sailors, tourists from Europe and North America, and civilian residents who frequent the restaurant. Visitors and city residents are transported into Sevastopol's heroic past (although very superficially) during their meal.

Advertisers have also learned to target local consumers by associating their products with the city's past. The meat products firm KAMO has placed billboards around the city stating that "There are Sausages. And there are KAMO Sausages" (figure 6.4). The background to this unimaginative slogan is the Monument to Scuttled Ships, the most beloved monument in the entire city. In short, such advertisers draw not only on the city's Russian past but also on residents' sense of local patriotism and identity. The intent is to associate KAMO with the city and create modern brand loyalty.

## Ethnicity, Tourism, and the Redefinition of Space

Much of Sevastopol's commercial and economic expansion no doubt comes from the renewed tourism in part stimulated by the return of Tatars to Crimea.

Figure 6.4. An advertisement for КАМО sausages. Photograph by Karl D. Qualls.

Tatars are the largest non-Slavic national minority in Crimea and are transforming the peninsula and to a lesser degree Sevastopol. During the 1990s, many Crimean Tatars repatriated themselves to Crimea after nearly fifty years of forced exile and began to assert their rights to ancestral lands.[36] After a harsh decade of dramatic economic decline, some entrepreneurs in Sevastopol and Crimea realized that there was money to be made in tourism, and more specifically in ethnotourism.

The return of the Tartars has not left much of a mark on Sevastopol except for the appearance of women in traditional Muslim dress on the streets and the newly reconstructed minaret of the mosque. The greatest change has come in tourist packages that include Sevastopol and Bakhchisarai, the former capital of the Crimean Khanate, which in a sense stretches the perceived boundaries of the city. The city's military heritage is still the central theme of most Sevastopol tours, but packaging it with ethnotourism has become increasingly popular.[37] One- to five-day tour packages always include a walking trip around the central ring road and its monuments, the Crimean War panorama and museum on Historical Boulevard, and, for some, a trip to the diorama museum of World War II at Sapun Gora. This allows the visitor to quickly "experience" the city's military and naval past. For those who can spend more than one day, packages usually include a discussion of the city's Greek heritage at the Khersones Archaeological Preserve.

Many longer tours also now include side trips to Bakhchisarai and Chufut-Kale. Located about one hour outside the city center, these two sites highlight the region's Tatar and Karaite heritage, respectively. Sandwiched between the two sites is the Russian Orthodox Uspenskii Monastery, which is built into a cave. Whereas Khersones takes tourists back 2,500 years, Bakhchisarai and Chufut-Kale illustrate the close relationship between Tatars and Karaites since the Middle Ages. The additional attention paid to Orthodox sites like the Uspenskii Monastery, the site of Vladimir the Great's baptism at Khersones, and the various cave monasteries surrounding the city brings a new dimension to Sevastopol tourism that one could not experience in the Soviet era. Highlighting the Russian Church, Tatars, and Karaites illuminates the centrality of Crimea to all these groups and separates the peninsula demographically and religiously from Europe. The projected uniqueness of the city and region further places Sevastopol outside a Europe toward which much of the former Soviet bloc gravitates. An October 2004 survey in one of Sevastopol's local newspapers asked people what the first priority of a new Ukrainian president should be, and "closer relations with the European Union" and "entrance into NATO" were nonissues for respondents.[38]

Other influences appear on Sevastopol's streets. Tourists who crave trinkets, souvenirs, and kitsch will find a curious array on Primorskii Boulevard in the city center (figure 6.5). Alongside the magnificent outdoor art market, dozens of vendors sell traditional knickknacks that represent Sevastopol: sea shells, ceramic dolphins, T-shirts, and more. However, the twenty-first-century mix includes a tremendous number of Buddha statues, pyramids, incense sticks and mystical signs, symbols, and jewelry. There are several possible explanations for what appears to be an odd turn to Eastern mysticism. Market forces may be driving the supply of these goods at the tourist markets because visitors perceive Sevastopol/Crimea as "the East." But this begs the question as to what formed this perception. Perhaps the tour packages to Bakhchisarai and other places have started to create a "non-Western" image for the region that tourists find appealing. Vendors might also be consciously orienting themselves toward the East. The latter explanation seems more problematic because political and cultural orientations trend toward Russia, but Sevastopol also could be in the throes of yet another attempt to rediscover and promote its "Asiatic" nature, à la Sergey

N↑

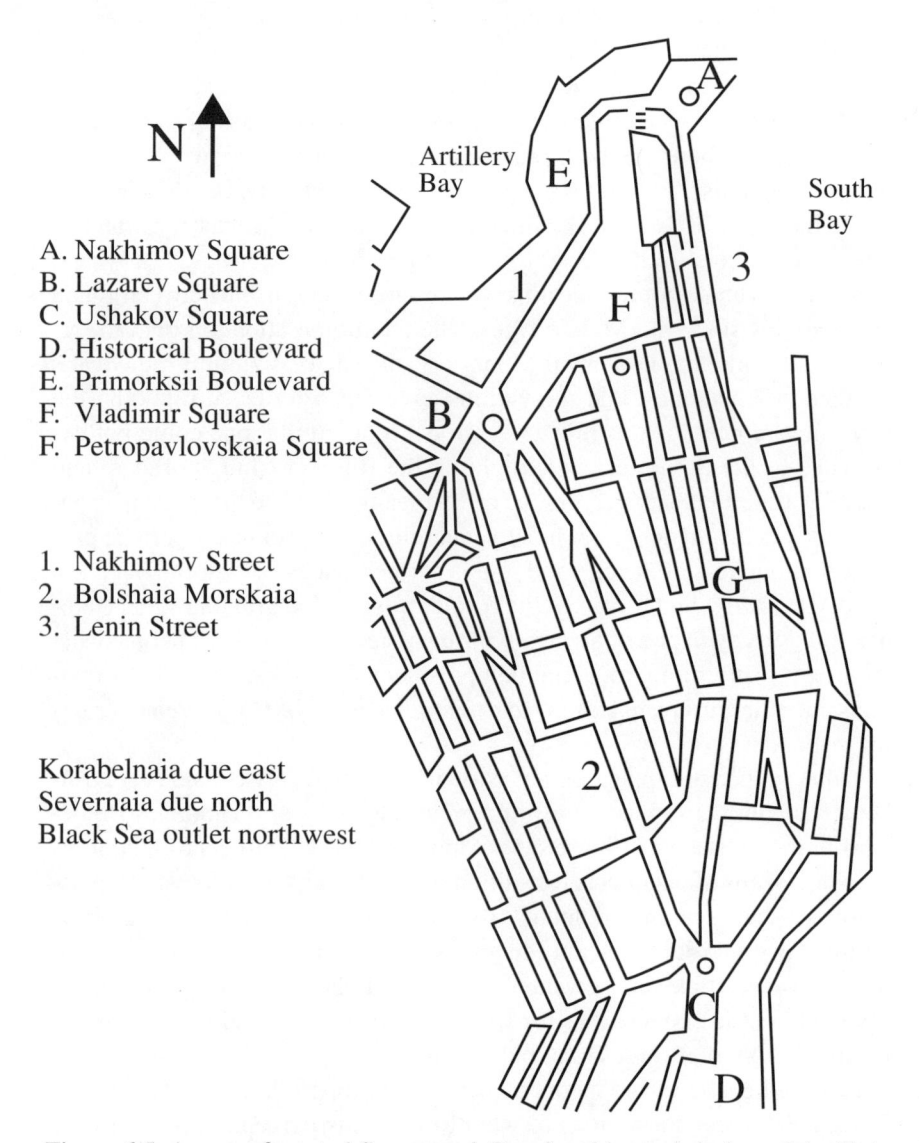

A. Nakhimov Square
B. Lazarev Square
C. Ushakov Square
D. Historical Boulevard
E. Primorksii Boulevard
F. Vladimir Square
F. Petropavlovskaia Square

1. Nakhimov Street
2. Bolshaia Morskaia
3. Lenin Street

Korabelnaia due east
Severnaia due north
Black Sea outlet northwest

Figure 6.5. A map of central Sevastopol. Reprinted by permission of the University of Pittsburgh Press, © 2001, from "Local-Outsider Negotiations in Postwar Sevastopol's Reconstruction, 1944–53," by Karl D. Qualls, in *Provincial Landscapes: Local Dimensions of Soviet Power, 1917–1953,* edited by Donald J. Raleigh (Pittsburgh: University of Pittsburgh Press, 2001).

Diaghilev's Ballet Russe a century earlier. Though its marketplace might sometimes seem torn between Western consumerism and Eastern mysticism, the monuments to the Crimean War and World War II remain the most important loci of identity and dominate public space.

## Politicized Space in Sevastopol's 2004 Presidential Campaign

The 2004 presidential election campaign highlighted the juxtaposition of old and new, Russia and Europe in Sevastopol. Traditionally, Nakhimov Square, one of the oldest parts of the city, has been the site of demonstrations and parades. Sevastopol celebrated all major holidays with parades and marches around the ring road that started and ended at Nakhimov Square.[39] It is not surprising that the Communist and Socialist parties in the 2004 presidential campaign used this area for their demonstrations with speakers, megaphones, songs, and marches. One of the communist parties held a nearly daily vigil at the entrance of Primorskii Boulevard, the city's traditional and still most popular leisure area, into Nakhimov Square. Along the wrought iron garden fence the communists placed placards, all in Russian, decrying capitalism, nationalism, and Ukrainian participation in the occupation of Iraq. This older geographic space became the location for the older residents' political stand.

Viktor Yushchenko's younger and distinctly Ukrainian "Orange Revolution" was not well received in overwhelmingly Russian Sevastopol.[40] His supporters chose a location that could not be more different from the communists' choice. A lone Yushchenko information tent stood along the central ring road directly in front of McDonald's. In talking to the twentysomethings working for Yushchenko's campaign, none knew if the location was selected for a particular reason. Situated on the ring road, there is a great deal of foot traffic in the area, both by residents and tourists. Moreover, McDonald's, as in many countries, serves as a meeting place for the city's youth. Because the Yushchenko campaign targeted youth in particular in Eastern and Southern Ukraine, McDonald's seemed to be a perfect location to bring his message to the youngest voters in the city. It is likely that the symbolism of this location was intentional. Closer ties to Europe and greater economic integration and development formed the base of Yushchenko's campaign; therefore, an information tent in front of one of the largest global corporations based in the West would link Yushchenko with economic vitality and modernization. Contact with the European Union and

NATO stood near the top of his international agenda, but the local press decried Yushchenko's plans to prepare Ukraine for entry into the EU as the harbinger of "national catastrophe" that would create conflict with Russia, as happened in Georgia after its revolution.[41] Questions of illegal campaign contributions and U.S. interference on his behalf were also common.[42] When juxtaposed with the communist-defined space on Nakhimov Square and its statue to the Crimean War admiral P. S. Nakhimov, the contrast between old and new could not have been clearer.

The campaign of Yushchenko's opponent, Viktor Yanukovich, moved unhindered throughout Sevastopol's built space, unlike Yushchenko, who rarely ventured past Simferopol's airport, about 100 kilometers from Sevastopol. Yanukovich's overwhelming popularity among the largely Russophile residents allowed him and his supporters to roam freely throughout the city. His placards and information kiosks dotted the urban landscape. The most persistent location for Yanukovich's presence was at the newspaper kiosk. In addition to large posters of a smiling Yanukovich in the kiosk windows, local newspapers consistently carried pro-Yanukovich articles and carried scathing exposes of Yushchenko and his policies. Journalists portrayed Yanukovich as the champion of the poor and downtrodden and Yushchenko (especially during his time as prime minister) as taking money from invalids and families with children.[43] In both cases, Yanukovich was careful to play on Sevastopol's existing identity and pledged to support it. He made appearances at war memorials to praise the city and its heroes and promised 10 million hryven from the central Ukrainian budget for a new war memorial and museum.[44] With Yanukovich's defeat, the fate of the new project and Kyiv's financial support for the city are in question.

The political campaigns used the traditions and innovations inscribed in the urban fabric for their purposes. As long as the boundaries of tradition were maintained, the electoral campaign remained civil. Even though communists were a distinct minority, they played a role familiar to the city's past in an area long used for demonstrations. Yushchenko's nationalist, pro-Western campaign, however, violated Sevastopol's traditional identity as a protector of Mother Russia and thus had less access to the public spaces of the city. Although this researcher saw no physical violence toward Yushchenko's supporters in the city, verbal abuse was commonplace in public and in private. The abuse of Yushchenko's supporters ranged from old women screaming about how a Yushchenko victory would undo all their sacrifices in World War II to the scolding of young men and women trying to distribute campaign literature. One clever middle-aged man commented that the life-sized Ronald McDonald statue directly behind the campaign tent would be a better president than Yushchenko and also wondered if it was a statue of Yushchenko's American wife. Had the Yushchenko campaign tried to organize at Russian military sites of memory, the local response might have been more violent. By staying in the most commercialized region of the ring road, the campaign aligned Yushchenko with economic progress, although one could clearly also read McDonald's as a symbol of the destruction of the past. Communists remained true to the past both in the language and location of their political campaign. Yanukovich, who was portrayed as a protector or savior for the city and its residents, roamed freely throughout the city, crossing the boundaries of old and new, poor and rich, military and civilian.

## Conclusion

Since at least World War II, Sevastopol's residents and visitors have been bombarded with images propagating the city's role in defending the Russian Motherland against European invaders. The constant repetition of these ideas in school, tourism, the media, and obligatory visits to sites of memory has reinforced a belief in the city's "Russianness." Despite recent changes that have introduced the Ukrainian language and history into public schools, Sevastopol's pro-Russian orientation will likely continue as long as the Russian Fleet and its economic and military presence remain. This will also help to bolster Russian as the chief language of the city. The City Council seems hesitant to change street names en masse or to introduce new Ukrainian monuments unconnected to military themes. When Russia's lease of Sevastopol's ports ends, the World War II generation will have passed away and the direct connection to the last great defense of the city will have been severed. A younger generation of ethnically Russian children will have completed their education, including mandatory Ukrainian history and language. At that point, there may be an opportunity to inject a Ukrainian element into Sevastopol's local identity and lend it a more European orientation. However, this seems implausible, because memories of the Crimean War and of World War II are allied so closely with the history of Russia and the Soviet Union. Unless another catastrophe levels the city and provides a tabula rasa for Ukrainian interventions, Sevastopol likely will remain in large part a Russian city, even if only in its residents' historical imagination. And as long as the Russian Federation continues to see itself as separate from Europe, Sevastopol will likely do the same.

Unlike the streets of Tirana, Albania, where in 1991 residents tore down street signs and the government has not yet agreed on new names,[45] Sevastopol has seen little change in its toponyms since the end of the Soviet Union. Because Sevastopol after World War II returned to its pre-Soviet past as a vital outpost of the Russian Empire, there has been little need to radically construct a new identity as is common in many former Soviet bloc cities. No monuments have been torn down, street names remain the same, some Russian Orthodox churches have been reconsecrated, and, most important, the Russian Fleet remains at home in this Ukrainian port city. The fleet keeps Sevastopol's demographic composition overwhelmingly Russian and makes Ukrainianization and Europeanization more difficult.[46]

## Notes

1. *The Heroic Defence of Sevastopol* (Moscow: Foreign Languages Publishing House, 1942); *Sevastopol: November, 1941–July, 1942: Articles, Stories and Eye-Witness Accounts by Soviet War Correspondents* (London: Hutchinson, 1943); Karl Qualls, "Imagining Sevastopol: History and Postwar Community Construction, 1942–1953," *National Identities* ( July 2003): 123–39.

2. Travel guidebooks were one of the chief sources for official narratives. See, e.g., Zakhar Chebaniuk, *Sevastopol: istoricheskie mesta i pamiatniki* (Simferopol: Krymizdat, 1957); Emiliia Doronina and T. I. Iakovleva, *Pamiatniki Sevastopolia: spravochnik* (Simferopol: Tavriia, 1987); and Boris Rosseikin and Georgii Semin, *Sevastopol: putevoditel-spravochnik* (Simferopol: Krymizdat, 1961).

3. E.g., see "9 maia: Den' Pobedy!" *Slava Sevastopolia,* May 8, 2003; "Znatoki istorii," *Slava Sevastopolia,* September 9, 2004; Elizaveta Iurzditskaia, "150 let: Voina i mir, Sevastopol'skaia strada," *Slava Sevastopolia,* September 9, 2004; and Vladimir Shalamaev, "Vo imia pavshikh i zhivykh," *Slava Sevastopolia,* May 7, 2004.

4. On local initiatives in planning, see Karl D. Qualls, "Local-Outsider Negotiations in Sevastopol's Postwar Reconstruction, 1944–53," in *Provincial Landscapes: The Local Dimensions of Soviet Power,* ed. Donald J. Raleigh (Pittsburgh: University of Pittsburgh Press, 2001), 276–98.

5. For an overview of Soviet name changes, see John Murray, *Politics and Place-Names: Changing Names in the Late Soviet Period* (Birmingham: Birmingham Slavonic Monographs, 2000).

6. For more on the role of the Navy, see Qualls, "Imagining Sevastopol."

7. Crimean Karaites (Karaim) differ from the other Karaite Jews because the former developed from a Turkic language community rather than Hebrew, Aramaic, or Arabic. This further separates Crimean Karaites from other Jews in general and other Karaites in particular. This chapter uses "Karaite" to refer to the Crimean community.

8. For a brief introduction to postwar anti-Semitism in the Soviet Union, see Shimon Redlich, *Propaganda and Nationalism in Wartime Russia: The Jewish Antifascist Committee in the USSR, 1941–1948,* (Boulder, Colo.: East European Quarterly, 1982); Joshua Gilboa, *The Black Years of Soviet Jewry, 1939–1953* (Boston: Little, Brown, 1971); and G. V. Kostyrchenko, *V plenu u krasnogo faraona: Politicheskie presledovaniia evreev v SSSR v poslednee stalinskoe desiatiletie: Dokumental'noe issledovanie* (Moscow: Mezhdunar Otnosheniia, 1994).

9. State Archive of the City of Sevastopol (hereafter GAGS), f. R-79, op. 2, d. 131, l. 88.

10. E. V. Venikeev, *Arkhitektura Sevastopolia: Putevoditel* (Simferopol: Tavriia, 1983), 67–70.

11. The Soviet Union denied the 1948 earthquake until the 1990s. According to the U.S. Geological Survey, it was a magnitude 7.3 with over 100,000 killed, which makes it one of the deadliest on record. See http://neic.usgs.gov/neis/eqlists/eqsmosde.html. The Directorate for the Reconstruction of Sevastopol discussed the issue in 1949. See Russian State Archive of the Economy (hereafter RGAE), f. 9432, op. 1, d. 387, ll. 330–35.

12. In 1948 the Council of Ministers ordered that Sevastopol be completed in "3–4 years." To facilitate this, it raised Sevastopol to a "city of republic subordination," which meant, among other things, that its budget and orders came directly from the Russian Federation, not the Crimean Soviet Socialist Autonomous Republic. See GAGS, f. R-79, op. 2, d. 103, l. 221.

13. "Crimea: Who's in Charge Today?" *The Economist,* September 17, 1994, 56–57.

14. For more on the separatist movement and the fall of Meshkov, see Vyacheslav Savchenko, "Crimea Is Shaken by President-Parliament Clash," *Current Digest of the Soviet Press* 46, no. 37 (October 12, 1994): 5; "Ukraine: Time to Scratch," *The Economist,* March 25, 1995, 58; and "Crimea: Guess Who Won," *The Economist,* July 15, 1995, 33.

15. Tony Barber, "Kiev Tries to Drag Crimea Back in Time," *The Independent,* 28 March 1997, 15.

16. David R. Marples, "Insight Into the News: Kyiv and the Power Struggle in Crimea," *Ukrainian Weekly,* August 6, 2000, 2.

17. For an overview of the conflict and treaty, see Steven Erlanger, "Russia and Ukraine Settle Dispute over Black Sea Fleet," *New York Times,* June 10, 1995.

18. The author personally witnessed two Russian sailors bloodying a Ukrainian sailor in 1997. Russian hegemony was also apparent during the military parade celebrating the city's liberation from Nazi Germany, when most onlookers left the sidewalks after the Russian forces marched by, leaving near empty streets for the Ukrainian fleet.

19. Richard Boudreaux, "Russia and Ukraine Seek Sea Change in Sevastopol Politics: Control over City that is Port to Black Sea Fleet, and Kiev's Navy is a Sticking Point Between Two Nations," *Los Angeles Times,* April 23, 1995.

20. Julian Borger, "Moscow Puts Warships on Full Alert," *The Guardian,* April 15, 1994; Lee Hockstader, "Ukraine Detains Officers after Russia Grabs Ship, as Fleet Conflict Escalates," *Washington Post,* April 12, 1994.

21. Mary Mycio, "Regional Outlook a Dacha Duel in Crimea Between Russia, Ukraine: Under Cover of Political Chaos, a Land Grab Rages in Sevastopol, Home of the Black Sea Fleet," *Los Angeles Times,* May 24, 1994.

22. Carol J. Williams, "Ribbon Cut on a New Crimean War: An Apartment House,

Built by Moscow's Mayor, Opens in Sevastopol; and as Russians Move in, So Enters a New Jab at Black Sea Fleet Deal," *Los Angeles Times,* October 5, 1997.

23. Lev Ryabchikov, "Moscow Mayor Insists that Crimea be Returned to Russia," *ITAR-TASS Newswire,* March 19, 1999.

24. "Russian Black Sea Fleet's Flagship Back in Service Thanks to Moscow Mayor," *BBC Monitoring,* April 9, 2000.

25. "Moscow Mayor Signs Cooperation Agreement with Ukrainian Sevastopol," *BBC Monitoring,* March 21, 2002.

26. Interviews in Sevastopol with Lika Drozdova, October 17, 2004; Iurii Fefer, October 23, 2004; and Vladimir Semenov, October 23, 2004. Their sentiments were echoed in the author's casual conversations with commuters at the bus stop in front of the monument.

27. M. P. Aposhanskaia, comp. and ed., *Sevastopol: Entsiklopedicheskii spravochnik* (Sevastopol: Muzei geroicheskoi oborony i osvobozhdeniia Sevastopolia, 2000), 592.

28. In 1952, Sevastopol's Executive Committee and the Military Council of the Black Sea Fleet agreed to petition the Russian Federation to restore the cathedral as a "historical memorial" to the four admirals rather than pulling it down and constructing a mausoleum. See GAGS, f. R-79, op. 2, d. 340, l. 286.

29. In addition to the Sevastopol encyclopedia entries for these sites, see Venikeev, *Arkhitektura Sevastopolia;* and E. V. Venikeev, *Sevastopol i ego okrestnosti* (Moscow: Iskusstvo, 1986). *Putevoditel': Sevastopol'* (Simferopol: Svit, 2004), 5, suggests that the reopening of the cathedral is central to the city's plan to remake its image by 2010 into a tourist center.

30. "Vladimirskoi sobor peredan tserkvi," *Sevastopol'skaia gazeta,* November 5, 2004.

31. E.g., see "Chto sluchilos' 150 let nazad?" *Sevastopol'skaia gazeta,* November 3, 2004; "K 60-letiiu osvobozhdeniia ukraina," *Sevastopolskaia pravda,* October 18–24, 2004; "Vse, chto nuzhno znat' o Krymskoi voine," *Sevastopol'skaia gazeta,* September 2, 2004; and Mariia Gridasova, "Den' Pobedy: dve sud'by," *Sevastopol'skaia gazeta,* May 6, 2004. Also see note 3 above.

32. "Sevastopol: 150-letiiu Krymskoi (Vostochnoi) voiny," n.d.

33. "Nachinaiutsia turniry znatokov-kraevedov," *Slava Sevastopolia,* October 23, 2004.

34. "Spetspoezd s donetskimi det'mi," *Sevastopol'skaia gazeta,* October 28, 2004.

35. "Otrazhenie," NTS (Independent Television of Sevastopol), October 22, 2004.

36. Edward Allworth, ed., *The Tatars of Crimea: Return to the Homeland,* Studies and Documents 2 (Durham, N.C.: Duke University Press, 1998); Greta Uehling, "Squatting, Self-Immolation, and the Repatriation of Crimean Tatars," *Nationality Papers* 28, no. 2 (June 2000): 317–42; Brian G. Williams, *The Crimea Tatars: The Diaspora Experience and the Forging of a Nation* (Leiden: Brill, 2001).

37. For a sampling of sites (whose content was available as of December 2004), see http://www.tourism.crimea.ua (the official site of the Ministry of Resorts and Tourism of Crimea); http://sevtour.by.ru; http://www.dreamland.crimea.ua/; and http://rest.crimea.ua/; http://www.tour-ethno.com.

38. Elena Gracheva, "Chto zhe budet posle vyborov," *Slava Sevastopolia,* October 20, 2004.

39. Many specialists reviewing the initial reconstruction plans after World War II noted that all redesigning of the square had to account for its central function as an agitational space. See RGAE, f. 9432, 1, d. 243, l. 13.

40. In the first round, he garnered only 5.98 percent of the vote in Sevastopol. "Predvaritel'nye rezultaty vyborov," *Sevastopol'skaia gazeta,* November 4, 2004.

41. A. Tikhii, "Gruzinskoe ruslo ukrainskoi evrointegratsii," *Slava Sevastopolia,* October 22, 2004.

42. A. Artemenko, "Kriminal'nye avtoritety sobiraiut den'gi na prezidentskuiu kampaniiu 'messii?'" *Slava Sevastopolia,* May 27, 2004; P. Ivanits, "Posol SShA Dzhon Kherbst kak agitator kandidata v prezidenty Viktora Iushchenko," *Slava Sevastopolia,* July 21, 2004.

43. Ia. Stetsenko, "Bor'ba s bednost'iu—glavnaia zadacha Viktora Ianukovicha," *Slava Sevastopolia,* October 22, 2004.

44. "Blagodaren sevastopoltsam za to, chto segodnia veriat vlasti," *Slava Sevastopolia,* October 29, 2004.

45. "From Our Own Correspondent," *BBC Radio,* December 15, 2004.

46. As of 2001, 74 percent of Sevastopol's population was Russian, 21 percent was Ukrainian, and 5 percent was Belarusans, Crimean Tatars, Jews, Armenians, Greeks, Germans, Moldovans, Poles, and more. Aleksandr Dobry and Irina Borisova, *Welcome to Sevastopol* (Simferopol: Tavriia, 2001), 5.

# 7

# Locating Kaliningrad/Königsberg on the Map of Europe: "A Russia in Europe" or "a Europe in Russia"?

*Olga Sezneva*

A common trend in the development of cities in Eastern Europe since the end of the Cold War has been the search for a lost past. Elements of this search can be seen in the reconstruction of cities' landmarks, such as royal palaces and medieval castles; the renovation and adaptation of cities' remaining historic architecture as prime residential or commercial real estate; and the revival of cities' old ethnic neighborhoods—followed by the celebration of these places' multicultural and cosmopolitan character. The developments represent a shift from the future-oriented urbanism of Socialist modernity to the history-attentive urban development of postcommunism. By no means should this phenomenon be viewed as unique to postcommunism. Throughout the former Communist bloc, urban centers have undergone a historical revival that in many aspects corresponds to the current imperative elsewhere for localities to reclaim their histories. One can convincingly argue that, as cities are transformed by the pressure of economic restructuring into major loci of capital accumulation and capital flows, their spacial layouts and architecture turn into assets and attractions.[1] Given the nature of the post-1991 transformations—toward the introduction of free markets and openness to capital investment—it is not surprising that similar imperatives govern urban development in former socialist cities as well.

However, the structural economic similarity between the postsocialist cities and their counterparts in the developed capitalist world should not obscure features particular to them, which are responses to their historically specific local political and cultural processes. There are two ways in which socialism is relevant to contemporary urban development: as a path-dependency, something that operates as a structural context in which changes take place; and as a period that produced particular historical "truths" and represented local histories of place so as to fit a master narrrative of the Soviet state. Throughout the late Socialist period, to have a local history was a claim imbued with moral value. A number of studies elucidate this connection between cities' histories and politics.[2] In the first years of the post-1989 postcommunist transformations, private memories provided bases for interpretations of the old regime's actions that were alternatives to the dominant narratives of power during the Socialist period, and that as loci of resistance were later deployed to signify a symbolic break from the old regime by the newly elected governments during the transformations. Alternative memories and countermemories of communism, similar to other situations of regime change and transitional justice, played an important role in social therapy—for example, in the former East Germany. They allowed the victims to be heard and the villains to be persecuted. During Perestroika and immediately after, celebrating the local past, Svetlana Boym observed, was the first public gesture toward the newly imagined future.[3] As a result, the appeal of the historical past to residents of Eastern European cities is an admixture of two forces: the economic force of capital and the force of anti-communist national and moral sentiment. The first creates a particular regime of distribution in which localities compete for the attraction of investments and economic growth; and the second provides a set of meanings that turn historical architecture into a valued heritage.

How the history of a place should be constructed and what architectural preservation would be adequate, however, are contentious questions, not least because imperial histories of the Eastern European region provide diverse possibilities for historical recovery. Thus, in the cities of Central and Eastern Europe during the last decade of the twentieth century, choices of contemporary architecture and design related to the development of distinct national and regional architectural styles, and to issues of historic preservation, which tightly interwove aesthetics with the politics of history and, in the latter case, with national identity in formation. Following a certain nationalist logic, postsocialist nation building would seem to require the creation of an exclusive narrative of ethnocultural development and cultural homogeneity for a titular ethnicity or national group. But what we see instead are the offspring of Lithuanian, Estonian, and Latvian peasants uncovering historical affinities with their former Polish, Swedish, or German landlords. The cities of independent Ukraine—the two parts of which, eastern and western, cannot settle on the issue of pro-Russian or pro-European Union politics—envision their histories as composed of multiple ethnicities in a way they did not before. Jewish and Polish traces are being carefully restored in L'viv, and the return of Crimean Tatars is being officially celebrated in Sevastopol. The engineers of public history acknowledge the fragmented, polyvalent, and incomplete character of their historical material; yet the fact that they are creating historical cohesion by engaging with "foreign" pasts does not seem to contradict the goal of nation building—and also does not seem to cause a schism between urban and national identity.

Neither the perspective of political economy nor that of political resistance alone will enable us to understand this phenomenon. While viewing historical revival in architecture through the lens of political resistance and political restructuring helps to explain the emotional component of identity formation, it does not explain why local, and not state-level, politics is preferred. Why do cities matter in something that seems to affect nations and nation states? A third explanation is needed—one that is sensitive to the multiplicity of scales at which identity is articulated and that recognizes the power of culture to organize material processes. What enables one to construct an imaginary urban geography in a way that does not conflict with a new national identity, I argue, is to interject the "politics of location"[4]—an actual spatial as well as symbolic reterritorialization of the cities in the Central and Eastern European region to occupy the "European" space (as opposed to that of Russia or of Russia's former domain). Europeanization is a vision and a process distinct from the European Union itself; it applies to places that technically are not included in the administrative complex of the European Union.[5] Claiming identities and matching them with localities' material foundations, architecture, and spatial layout are the means of altering the "hard" facts of geography and international border regimes, or at least "softening" them.

In this chapter, I discuss one such construction of a "European city" in a Russian exclave territory: Kaliningrad. This city is one of the most radical cases of historical disruption—the city of Königsberg was annexed by the USSR in 1945 from Germany, and it then was resettled with Russian speakers. The city's new residents carried strong hatred against Germany, their wartime enemy, and the official Soviet regime imposed an ideological prohibition on the public commemoration of the city's German history. In the summer of 2005, Kaliningrad celebrated the seven-hundred-fiftieth anniversary of its founding. A number of German landmarks were restored to their original look and became symbols of official celebrations attended by three presidents—of Russia, Germany, and France. At the same time, to counterbalance the highlighted German-period architecture, a voluminous Orthodox cathedral was built in the city's center, and the surrounding area was refurbished to echo Moscow's Kremlin. The new official policy in Kaliningrad is to carefully balance its "German architecture," a category that encompasses all its prewar structures, and its "Russian architecture," a similarly undifferentiated and indiscriminate term.

This chapter examines the "politics of location" that affected Kaliningrad since the collapse of the Soviet Union, by discussing the meaning and the uses of the construct the "European City." It provides an analysis of how different social actors envision the development of Kaliningrad, and whether or how they conceive it to be a "European City." The chapter first offers a brief review of Kaliningrad's history and how this Russian territory became an exclave amidst the European Union. Second, it describes how the current status of the region affected the ways in which its residents identify themselves. In this description I pay particular attention to the categorical identities "European" and "Russian," and the role that architecture plays in altering the contents of these identifications. The latter focus grounds my discussion of two urban development projects, The Fish Village and Luisenwhal. Luisenwhal developed as a local initiative aimed at launching a public debate and extending local public participation to an issue of city building. The Fish Village was commissioned and financed by a large Moscow-based financial group looking for profits from the city's burgeoning real estate market. Both projects are intended to "map" Europe onto the space of Kaliningrad. The different intellectual underpinnings and architectural solutions of the two projects, however, indicate diverging imageries of how Kaliningrad can be integrated into the space of Europe. If the first project takes as its core a reconstructive approach tracing a "genealogy" of place, the second inserts "Europe" into Kaliningrad.[6]

## Violent Geography

The Kaliningrad region is the border zone of Russia squeezed between Poland and Lithuania on the fringe of the Baltic Sea. There reside nearly

1 million Russian speakers. Population replacement and military conflicts have not been unfamiliar in the region, for it has been the site of many struggles among diverse powers. In more distant, less-documented times, the indigenous Prussian tribes (Pruzzi or Prusai, in various records) were fought, colonized, and baptized by the Teutonic Order of German Knights in the early thirteenth century. By the fifteenth century, these people had only left their name, Prussia, to the territory. Later, successive conflicts involved disputes with the Kingdom of Poland and Lithuania, Sweden, Napoleon's France, Tsarist Russia, and most recently Soviet Russia. In 1945, the Soviet Union annexed the East Prussian and Memel lands, expanding its territory to the Baltic Sea. Königsberg became a Russian city, forming with its adjacent area the smallest (21,000 square kilometers) and the westernmost region of Russia.[7] In 1946, Königsberg was renamed "Kaliningrad." Most of its German residents fled; the 120,000 who remained were forcefully evicted. The Soviet integration of the new territory and its largest city into the space of the Soviet Union was interlinked with the partitioning of its history into "pre-" and "post-" periods. The place's temporality was dissected, and its German period was excluded from the official historiography.

The losses of the city's architecture to the war, the British aviation bombings in August 1944, and the Soviet storming in April 1945 were tremendous. By some estimates, only about 12 percent of the city's structures remained standing in 1950 when the local administration was preparing itself to undertake postwar reconstruction.[8] Discussions of the status of German architecture among Kaliningrad's architects and planners did not signal the competing interests of different political actors so much as the uncertainty of the moment. No definitive policy guidance was issued from the central state. One architect, for example, proposed to develop a new city center in the area of relatively intact vernacular architecture. He did so because he believed that planning a new spatial configuration of the city would require unnecessary spending.[9] Other city architects of the time advanced different views: They proposed "to change the face of the city, Prussian in all its details" and "to create new perspectives that are open, bright and emotionally appealing."[10] The latter view won, and Kaliningrad was transformed to replicate other provincial Soviet cities. Unique to Kaliningrad, however, a campaign against the Prussian-German legacy in architecture continued, through the Communist Party's directives to demolish buildings (as in the case of the blown-up Castle of Prussian Kings) or through mere neglect, as in the case of countless buildings left to decay.

The end of the twentieth century, with the disintegration of the Communist bloc, saw the Kaliningrad region transformed into an enclave engulfed by other states. This happened twice during the century. First, under German sovereignty after the Treaty of Versailles, in an effort to connect isolated East Prussia to the reduced Germany, Königsberg produced the infamous "Danzig Corridor" crossing the territory of Poland. And second, after the Baltic states' declaration of independence in 1991, the region became an island of Russian sovereignty and Russian speakers within the European Union. These territorial changes presented a material challenge—being cut off from direct access to the rest of Russia, among other things, severed transportation connections, raised the costs of non–locally produced goods, and undermined the military effectiveness of the city's large navy base.

## "Kaliningradnik": Revising Identity

The people of the Kaliningrad region are struggling to make sense of their situation—the prolonged train rides to other cities of Russia; the confusions with passport control on the recently materialized and still "hardening" borders; the overflow of German, Polish, and Lithuanian consumer goods and the thinning supply of locally made products. How much longer, some Kaliningraders wonder, will the territory remain Russian? How is the fact of the city's German origins going to affect its future? How, if at all, can the city's non-Russian history be of benefit for its Russian residents?

People derive their understanding of the situation and project their future based on the historical facts of which they are aware, or the experiences that have been transmitted to them as "historical memory." For example, Kaliningrad's older Russian residents rely on the preexisting models of nation-states—and implicitly on historical precedents of territorial transfers. As a result, they fear restitution, in which case, they do not doubt, they will be expelled: "[The Germans] will push us out of here within twenty-four hours." This position rests on the belief that "this is what states do, this is what we did to them, so why should they be different?"[11] Younger people, however, operate within an interpretive frame that instead relies on current discourses about human rights. They cite instances of international intervention in domestic situations as proof that the mass deportations of the twentieth century will not be repeated. Patriotically oriented youth call for opposition to what they see as the "quiet" "market" colonization of Kaliningrad by "the West." Such discourses about the future of Kaliningrad's belonging to Russia—no matter how contradictory or disparaged—are a means of responding to the current state of contingency, amplified to uncertainty.

Kaliningrad's territorial isolation engenders a sense of boundedness, providing social actors with the means of treating groups, culture, and place as isomorphic. An excerpt from a focus group discussion illustrates the point:

> Participant 1: We have no common border with Germany, hence we will not become German. We have no common border with Russia, hence we will never be completely Russian here.
> Participant 2: This is neither Russian nor German land, but ours.
> Participant 3: We are cosmopolitans here. We live without homeland, without Russia. We're different here, non-Russians. We are the hybrid of Russians and someone else.
> Participant 1: We have no roots.
> Participant 4: We all came from different places; my father is from the city of Saratov, my mother is also from some Russian hinterland. We are some kind of America here—we are born here, for sure, but still are somehow not from here.[12]

This excerpt demonstrates how Kaliningraders imagine their identity in spatial as well as historical terms. First, it is through spatialized "borders," which operate as "hard" geographic facts that provide a "condition of impossibility" to be "completely" Russian or German. Geographic borders translate into social boundaries. The choice of Kaliningraders from whom to distinguish themselves, Germans or Russians, combines together two temporalities. Being "German" is an option provided by the past. Being "Russian" is determined by the present. This is an instance of the "presentist" understanding of historical memory—its relevance in its capacity to determine the present states of meaning and influence future-oriented action. The combination of historical memory and geography constitutes a distinct kind of community in Kaliningrad. Another instance of this incipient sense of bounded collectivity and autonomy of identification is the 2000 governor's election campaign. At that time, a slogan was popular among Kaliningraders that eventually brought victory to Admiral Vladimir Egorov: "For us, Russia begins here, in Europe." Three distinctions that this slogan evoked can be summarized as follows: that Kaliningraders ("us") are somehow different from other Russians (Rossiyane); that Russia is a geographic space somehow distinct from Europe (although the clarity of this delineation is a subject for debates); and that notwithstanding the delineation and difference, there is a progression from one to the other. But in what sense is Europe "here" and does Russia "begin"? Who are the "us"? How is this "us" different from other Russians?

Since the late 1980s, Kaliningraders' cultural self-understanding has been structured around a notion of quasi-ethnicity primarily based on the region's geographic isolation and foreign history.[13] The historical past plays a double role. The Soviet history of Kaliningrad—a directly shared experience of repopulation and building a new city—serves as one important criterion of intragroup solidarity. The prewar German history, which is not collectively shared but appropriated, is a locus of Kaliningraders' constructed difference from other Russians. Regional categories function like national categories, relativizing national ones, and stereotypical knowledge about "those" Russians, as well as Europeans, may come to devalue national and valorize transregional subcategories, in this case being "European." Consider this excerpt from another group discussion:

> When someone asks me what is European here compared to the rest of Russia, I say that it is in the relationships among people. People in Kaliningrad are nonaggressive to a rare degree. In this sense, they are more European. I was touched once when a bum crawled out of the trash collector and asked, politely, "Would you spare a cigarette, please?" In Russia, this is unimaginable. There once, on a bus, I asked "Could you be so kind as to pass me a ticket," and the whole crowd turned their heads to me. They are so not used to a civilized talk![14]

The putative difference between ethnic Russians in "mainland" Russia and ethnically Russian Kaliningraders (who today make up 78 percent of the city) is often cast in civilizational terms, as in the quotation above. The current state of Kaliningrad is often contrasted by the memories of how it was before (these counterimages often come from "postmemories," ideas about the events of objects of the past circulating among the second generation, which did not witness them directly). Ekaterina Romanovna, who is sixty today, recalls:

> When we came [to Kaliningrad] forty years ago, everything was in ruins, but even the ruins were clean and organized. The German culture was felt here, and people tried to live up to that. You go down the street, there are all in parts and pieces, but sidewalks are swept anyway. No garbage in the streets. Clean, healthy air; no bad odors. That's what we should've kept—

a culture of cleanness. We, Russians, lost it. Maybe, it is still better here than in Russia, but compared with how it once was and how it is now.

Politeness and cleanliness are expressly linked to different stages of cultural development. Regional identity is associated with a more advanced state of civilization. It relativizes national identity—and even stigmatizes it. The following excerpt is a good example of a complex, situated use of categories such as "European," "Russian," "Soviet" in conjunction with civilizational terms. The reader should note the use of the city's architecture in the relational positioning of selves that the speakers perform:

> Moderator: What does make you say that Kaliningrad is your city, that you belong here?
> Participant 3: This is not ours, not the Russian land, that's for sure.
> Moderator: Why?
> Participant 3: It takes to see around the countryside, to see what we've done to German houses, to everything that was built in the many years before us. Such things cannot be done to one's own land. I served in the army in the [Kurily Islands]; there were things left after the Japanese. And I saw what our people did to them—very similar to what I found here. Same story.
> Participant 7: Yeah, you feel it there—there were the Japanese.
> Participant 3: Many good tings were built there. Well, they were built by war prisoners, but this is not the point. The quality was good. And now, everything is in decay.
> Moderator, to Participant 2: You disagree?
> Participant 2: This land after the war became Russian. Because we all Russians here, the land is also Russian, and the treatment of it is purely Russian.
> Participant 1: [Expletive] purely Russian treatment! We ruined all, disheveled, nothing German was left. The pure Russian-style. Same way we built the BAM [Baikal-Amour Railroad], in the Russian style. We killed the tundra and left industrial trash behind, and now it all lies there.
> [Pause: 7 seconds.]
> Participant 3: Mismanagement [*beskhozyaistvennost'*].[15]
> Participant 2: Look, a beautiful tower is still standing along the expressway. Or what has left of it. It's been simply taken apart, brick by brick. But it is such a pretty structure.

Participant 3: It is centuries old!
Participant 2: It will be looted, taken apart brick by brick. Where they cannot take just one brick, they break off whole parts, and leave behind rubble. I believe that this is a purely Russian treatment.
Participant 1: Not Russian—Soviet.
[Silent nodding of heads around the table.]

A remarkable feature of this discussion is the use of pronouns—the indexical expressions that denote these social actors' self-understanding as a collectivity. The meaning of these pronouns depends on the context. The first speaker establishes the initial referential meaning; "ours" stands for the Russian. He does not view Kaliningrad as the "Russia land," pointing to the signs of neglect and disrepair, and even to evidence of assaults on the local architecture. He claims that the causes of this decay should be found in the absence of a relationship between the current residents and the land and place. What he points to is estrangement—the absence of the unity of the territory and the community, the fact that the relations between the people and the territory are not naturalized as "one's own."

The treatment of German period architecture makes this estrangement evident. The outcome of this severed relationship is mismanagement; the cause is the lack of a sense of ownership. The pronoun "we" indexes Russians as a nation; it/we "acts" in the same fashion, from the westernmost place, Kaliningrad, to the easternmost region, Kurily. Participant 2 introduces further relativization: "Where *they* cannot take just one brick, they break off whole parts. . . ." Here, "they" has nothing to do with the ethnicity of being "Russian"; rather, it is an operator that accommodates the distancing of the speaker from the object of the speech to be condemned. The discussion ends with a new descriptor—"Soviet"—that denotes an identity different from being Russian.

The city's former identity as Königsberg looms large in these conversations, and it is hardly a surprise that in the year preceding the 2005 celebrations of the seven-hundred-fiftieth founding anniversary of the city, a number of German landmarks were restored to their original look. The investment into these restorations measures the extent of change in the perception of the German past. But the restorations have also instigated public conversations about historicity and historical ascendancy between Königsberg and Kaliningrad. Designs that involve German historical landmarks build quite literally two different future possibilities for the region. It is from this perspective that I introduce the reader to two architectural development projects in Kaliningrad.

## The Politics of Location

One Kaliningrad writer and public intellectual, Alexander Popadin, wrote in 2001:

> In the consciousness of Kaliningraders, Königsberg has been pushed into an inarticulate function of the subconscious, and they, after having overcome historical prohibition, throw themselves into the embrace of Königsberg. The television fiction-mystery of Mr. Trifonov is a vivid illustration of a casual exploitation of these subconscious impulses: the old city is expected to give away a riddle, a secret, a horror, to titillate the atrophic nerves of its dwellers. This is a layperson's attitude toward Königsberg. The rational thinking of a city builder, however, requires something different: historical inquiry, cataloging, analysis, synthesis— all in order to materialize the dissolving spectrum of Königsberg. From there the steps toward defining the orientation marks, the direction signs of city planning and of its fabric, can be taken.[16]

Two urban development projects precisely engage with this reality—one named by its designers "the Fish Village," and the other "Luisenwhal." These projects express two kinds of geographic metaphors, both of which are instances of the politics of location—the imaginary geography that takes its meaning from politics. One project's metaphor positions Kaliningrad at the westernmost edge of Russia; the other's positions it at the easternmost frontier of Europe. From this contestation, two ploys emerge. One is for Kaliningrad to become an island of Russia in Europe; and the other is for it to become a "sample" of Europe in Russia. Despite the fact that behind each vision lie different social forces, both projects face the challenge of how to interpret the relationship between the Russian present and the German past. A tradition has to be found or invented. Russians need to put on Prussian shoes, but without becoming German. This need meets a particular challenge for Kaliningrad's architects: an absence of knowledge about the vernacular building traditions and an explicit tension between the Russian and Prussian cultures. Both the projects considered here developed within this general rubric of historical revival. But each treats the issues of authenticity and the meaning of history in a different way.

## The Fish Village / Lomse Project: A Europe in Russia

Historically, the territory designated the "Fish Village" in the first project was part of the town of Lomse, whose Prussian name meant "Swamp," and which was separated from the town of Kneiphof by one of the two branches of the Pregel River. The Teutonic Order, which controlled this territory, ceded the land to a settlement called Altstadt, and a wharf, piers, and warehouses were built. During the sixteenth century, encircled by the water, Kneiphof's population grew, so by 1613 citizens began to cross the river from Kneiphof Island to settle in Lomse, which grew to have its own population and residential quarters. As three settlements—Altstadt, Kneiphof, and adjacent Löbenicht—were unified into Königsberg at the end of eighteenth century, the populating and settling in Lomse took on a planned and systematic character. But industries, being limited in their growth by swamps and the river, began to leave Lomse in the late nineteenth century, and the newly vacated land was then converted to residential use.

Although the few plans and photographic prints that could be found in private archives as well as contained at the Kaliningrad Regional Archive do not provide much information, they do show the ordinary architecture of the old village of Lomse: low-rise residential buildings and warehouses. Significant parts of the village were destroyed during the war, and the postwar Soviet rebuilding did not benefit its resurrection. Apart from a few random buildings, only some of the engineering structures, such as embankments and bridge supports, still remain today in the village. At the end of the Socialist period, the village was subjected to a centralized planning principle oriented toward *microrayon* (miniblocks). An unfinished mass of standardized housing dating from this time now encircles and restricts the remaining small, empty territory that has been chosen for the project called "Fish Village."

A project to develop the Lomse area originated in 2001 as a compromise between the needs of local businesses and commerce and those of international tourism—two strategic orientations in Kaliningrad's overall development. The designers turned to such analogous models as the German quarters in Bergen and the Old Place in Gdańsk, to cite just a few. The main developer of the Fish Village project is a large financial group, which incorporated Kaliningrad- and Moscow-based capital with management, as some evidence indicates, connected to officials in the Russian federal government. These connections and the volume of capital involved made the ambitions of the developers and architects possible, but at the same time forced them to follow the aesthetic preferences and design ideas of the Moscow-based investor.

### *"Theater of Architecture"*

The terrain of the Fish Village/Lomse was conceived by the groups of Kaliningrad architects hired to design the project to take as its core the principle of an "ethnographic village," in which are represented the craftsmanship of the Pruzi (Prussians), Lithuanians, Poles, and the other ethnic groups that populated the territory, including Russians. In addition, tourist agencies, hotels, financial services, and retail stores would be offered to visitors. Restaurants with European cuisine would complete the picture.

Driven by the idea of imitating the architectural style of Prussian Königsberg in the new project's design, the architects worked out the idea of "a script" to guide their architectural and planning decisions. This script is defined as "professional" architectural "recollections" in the form of style citations, as well as ascribed semantic meanings, through the means of exterior and interior design. These meanings refer to associations of particular urban sites or buildings with historical events and figures. Through them, Königsberg would reemerge as a "historical European city."

Within this paradigm, for example, the architects decided to reconstruct the planning principle that was dominant in all three townships of Königsberg—Kneiphof, Löbenicht, and Altstadt: the principle of a historical block, small in scale and densely built. Such a block would contrast the modernist unit of the *microrayon*. The orientation of the Fish Village would be to stand on the opposite side of the Pregel River from Königsberg Cathedral, the philosopher Immanuel Kant's grave, and the preserved original Honey Bridge. Imaginatively included in this orientation are the no-longer-existing Albertina (Königsberg) University in Kneiphof and the Fish Market of the destroyed Altstadt. Three structural elements were chosen to constitute the Fish Village: a semi-enclosed city square, a commercial street, and a square enclosed with arched passageways, columns, and balconies. All three elements have their historical prototypes: The first is a particular square, Lastadi, which was part of Lomse and was open on one side to the Pregel

River; the second is a generalized image of a merchant street from medieval Königsberg; and the third is a generic public space that can be found in many Central European cities. The architects' underlining intention for the Fish Village is to reproduce a historical and cultural landscape perceived as a generic "European city."

Although much attention has been devoted to reconstituting a "European city" on the small scale of a neighborhood, all of the "reconstruction" is meant to be a stylistic quoting without actually referencing specific sites. It is intentional that neither the overall layout of the Fish Village nor that of its individual buildings replicates any that existed historically. What is being achieved by such a decisive stance on this veneer?

The reader will recognize in the following descriptions of the Fish Village plan's different elements a desire to represent a particular kind of genealogy, and not a place itself, that organizes a relationship between Königsberg and Kaliningrad—that is, an expansive history of Russian-Prussian and German relationships. To emphasize the overall purpose of the Fish Village as a "theme" park—a kind of historical Disneyland—single buildings or architectural ensembles are assigned particular "scripts"—staged events that link these sites to historical and mythological events and figures. Rather than limiting themselves to stylistic quotations from Königsberg to create a "theater of architecture," the architects have chosen to name specific buildings after Prussian, as well as Russian, historical figures or to reenact scenes from Baltic folklore in ensembles.

One example of this architectural spectacle through the ascription of a historical character to a building is an architectural complex in the form of a quarter, titled "Albert" (a variation on the name "Albrecht"), after Herzog Albrecht von Brandenburg-Ansbach, the founder in 1544 of Königsberg University, also nicknamed Albertina. Its main facade is designed in the Baroque style, and its back imitates the facades of the warehouses that originally lined the banks of the Pregel River. A similar example of a historical quotation is Caroline's Court, named after the historical figure Caroline-Amalia Kayserling, a salon hostess and a supporter of local arts and sciences in the time of Kant. Her Prussian husband served in the Russian Court that was stationed in Königsberg during the Seven Years' War. Her salon was visited by Kant himself, as well as other representatives of Russian nobility. Curious in this regard is the amplified significance of the connection between the Russian and Königsberger high societies, a tie that suggests if not a tradition then at least a moment in history when mutual respect was the norm. On one of the walls of the inner courtyard of the original Kayserling house was a mural titled *The Prussian Roots of the Russian Tree,* representing the interconnections between the Prussian and Russian dynasties. Creating a replica of this mural is one of the ideas for the future design of the newly built Caroline's Court.

Another example of a historical figure ascribed to a site is the Hotel Suvorov, named after the legendary and victorious Russian general. It is to be located on Fish Square and oriented toward the reconstructed Königsberg Cathedral, the newly built Keiserbrucke, and the renovated Honigbrucke. Conveying a sense of the Russian military might associated with General Suvorov, the hotel is designed in the style of a fortress, characteristic of Königsberg, and also contains a stylized armory. The Hotel Suvorov lines up the southern side of Fish Square. It is balanced in size and scale by Fish Passage, a voluminous barn, serving as a market for seafood and international foods. It is an example of architectural modernism roughly attributed to the early 1920s and 1930s. Modernism is also represented by the Bessel Cupola Building, which complements the Lomse Tower. The overall low-rise (typically four to five stories) buildings of the Fish Village are overaccentuated by the Bessel Cupola and the Sentry Tower, which visually halt the movement along the main avenue toward the river.

Because the Fish Village project has been financed and controlled by the capital, Moscow, in the eyes of its creators it expresses the desire of Russian elites to see Kaliningrad as a fragment of Europe in Russia. The overt sampling of different styles of historical architecture, from the North Gothic to Bauhaus, firmly locates the Fish Village among postmodern reconstructions. This makes the Fish Village what David Harvey called "urban spectacle and display"—the use of an architecture of festivals to produce a sense of the transitory and ephemeral but "participatory pleasure."[17] "The mobilization of the spectacle" in the Fish Village project has a political and ideologically defined goal: to represent and historicize Russia's interest in the territory. For this reason, the Fish Village is best viewed as a diffuse cultural image, in which urban history is consumed as an urban form writ as a sign. Königsberg's past is a conglomerate of images, fragments, and spectacles organized around one point of view: Russian.

### *The Luisenwahl Project: A European City*

The Luisenwhal project—which is being developed under the auspices of the Kaliningrad Municipal Administration and the Municipal Department of Architecture and City Planning—represents a completely different conception of historicism. This project takes as its core a partially preserved area of the old district named Amalienau, currently the district called Tsentral'nyi, and incorporates it into a plan for the area's urban renewal.

The origins of the settlement in this once rural area outside the walls of Königsberg go back to the early nineteenth century, to the private estate of a citizen named Busolt Garden, which was occupied during the summer by Queen Louise of Prussia and her children (during the winter, the family lived in the castle). A legend suggests that in 1807 Queen Louise saved Königsberg from looting by the occupying French army by giving romantic favors to Emperor Napoleon as he marched through the city. This act endeared her memory to the city's citizens. In 1874, as a token remembrance of her generous action, a modest memorial was erected in her honor and topped with her bust by Christian Daniel Rauch. The memorial included a bench and a semicircular low wall decorated with vases.

At the end of the nineteenth century, a colony of private villas expanded into the area. The area received the name "Amalienau," and the architect Friedrich Heitmann (1853–1921) was appointed to supervise and direct its development, assuring its planned character. It was Heitmann who pioneered the idea of a more monumental memorial to Queen Louise at the very end of the 1890s: the building of a memorial church and a vicarage. The church, Luise-Gedächtinskirche (Memorial Church of Queen Louise), was designed and built in 1899–1901 by Heitmann himself. Moreover, the entire area was built up with villas in the then-dominant style of historicism; Romanticism was deemed a more appropriate representation of the historical period in which Queen Louise had lived, and thus as more expressive of the commemorative purpose of the Luise-Gedächtinskirche.

During World War II, the Luise-Gedächtinskirche suffered significant destruction, but its external walls, part of its tower, and most of its vaults survived. In 1954, the first postwar Soviet city department store, Sputnik, incorporated the foundation and the bearing walls of an older German building, and added to them elements of Stalinist architecture. Later, in the 1960s, new prefabricated concrete panel buildings were added, contrasting in their appearance with the prewar architecture of the bourgeois villas. Louise Kirche, as the church was now known, was slated for demolition in the 1960s but was then salvaged by a proposal to be converted into a puppet theater. Though the interior was completely revamped during this 1971 renovation, the restoration of the exterior closely followed the German original.

Busolt Garden lost its bridge and waterfall, and because its drainage system had become clogged, springs had turned into swamps and the original cultured "wilderness" had grown into a desolate wood. Years of proliferating, uncontrolled small-scale commerce had transformed the Louise Platz into a market square central to the life of Kaliningraders. As the real estate market developed in the 1990s in Kaliningrad, this quarter, consisting mainly of German-style architecture, became popular and housing prices skyrocketed. History is an attraction for the new moneyed elite, and it gives added value to a house.

## The Concept for Reconstruction: A Genealogy of Place

A group of two architects and a cultural historian saw an opportunity in developing a methodology by addressing issues of urban development in the area of Louise Kirche. In their public statement, these designers wrote:

> One formula dominated city planners' minds in the past decades when it came to the relationship between the city before 1945 (K1) and the city after 1945 (K2): $K = K2 - K1$. Today, it had been replaced by the formula $K = K2 + K1$. The result is a protectionist approach: Kaliningrad subdues Königsberg by producing "historical conservatories," freezing the existing forms and "storing away" the protected zones labeled "the past." In another paradigm, history exists as a citation in the postmodernist play of styles. Elements of style do not require an internal agreement, an engagement with the historic legacy. It is a veneer, in this case, a blend of turrets, gabled roofs, and red tile.[18]

Although both preservation and a stylistic play are legitimate ways of dealing with urban space, in the view of these designers, neither of them is a cultural-historical reproduction in the true sense of the word. The best inspiration for forming the city's fabric should come from a genealogical approach—a version of "critical reconstruction" developed by Berlin-based architects and applied to Kaliningrad, this city of disrupted development, where national traditions of building have changed dramatically.

The architects (one of whom also partook in the design of the Fish Village) argued that a genealogical integration of the environment of a "European historical city" with a modern Russian style would bring together the ethoses of two cultures. This paradigm would express not an opposition but a homology—first, between Russian and European architectures; and second, between "Russian" and "European" cultural identities. One city would not be colonized by another; nor would there be a mere adding of discrete elements.

The first task that the team defined was to design the urban fabric rather than to fill the urban space with single buildings. This implied that distinct characters of different sites within the area need to be examined in their sociological, cultural, and historical contexts, with respect to their meaning and significance, and viewed as grounds for the development of specific social activities. On the basis of these activities, the team identified places in terms of the different social types identified by their "typical" activities—for example, orientation toward the stroller, or the urban flaneur, would require the inclusion of pedestrian zones, an emphasis on ground floors and activities. A user-friendly space may not be a new idea for American urban dwellers, but it is a novelty for the residents of a Soviet-era settlement.

The Louise Kirche was designated as a symbolic center and as the project's organizing principle. It was to be preserved in its 1970 reconstructed look and augmented with the replica of the Queen Louise Memorial. The kirche was to be balanced in the plan by a newly constructed building, Kashtan (Chestnut)—a homage to the trees in the area planted at the time of Frederick Heitmann.

The designers' interpretation of Soviet architecture allowed the department store Sputnik to play a strong role, punctuating the otherwise pastoral character of the area with a geometrical, modernist form. The challenge, however, arrived from four houses alongside Sputnik. Their prefabricated gray concrete panels were discordant with the stucco facades of the old villas and the natural stone facade of the church. Rather than demolish these buildings, it was decided to build a new single "faux facade" that would connect all four buildings using arcades. The arches would emulate those of the Louise Kirche, and the church's contours would be reflected in the new glass facade. Such an almost environmentalist orientation (such trends arrived with delay to Kaliningrad) would make the buildings fit in, while also closing off the western side of the project area. Finally, an undeniably appealing aspect of this project is the space that it reserves for florists, most of whom are not licensed and are often residents of nearby homes. This trade, which has been located here for more than thirty years, put a final accent on the narrative of Luisenwhal. The project was presented to the public in January 2003. Yet because the sizable investment that the project requires has not been forthcoming, it has not been realized.

## The Future of the Past: Play of Citations or Genealogy?

The two plans for the reconstruction of Kaliningrad presented here have a single intent: to make Kaliningrad a Russian city with a historic European character. Driven by a sense of loss and of history's irreversibility, the designers of both projects have struggled to revive a sense of history, of its continuous temporality and culture. It is as if, cultivated within, history would give license to the entire city to rejoin the celebrated European history and culture.

These two projects represent two different ways of incorporating historicity, and both fall into more general patterns defining urban development around the world. In this sense, Kaliningrad is by no means separate from global developments. The Fish Village is a recognizable postmodernist project that focuses on veneer and surface—a Disneyland composed of samples from Königsberg's period architecture. As an example of complex planning, it inserts itself into the space, and it orients itself toward the (outsider) tourist. One may look in vain for a sign of irony, a tongue-in-cheek attitude. Instead, there is a seriousness about representing traces of the Russian presence through numerous associations with selected personalities, both Russian and Prussian—the mural *The Prussian Roots of the Russian Tree* is one candidate for reproduction. Russian military might is blended with the German genius of Kant and the subtle charms of aristocracy. The project creates a dreamworld of noble history and erases all traces of the twentieth-century catastrophe. Supported by nonlocal money, the Fish Village aspires to become a playground for tourists by representing a fragment of Europe on Russian land.

In Luisenwahl, the past seems to be respected. The design seeks to preserve not merely the physicality but also the sociality of the site. It is oriented toward a critical regionalism that seeks the organic, the local, and the embedded. It strives for a future that can be accounted for—by tentatively bridging gaps and breaches in the historical fabric, Kaliningraders may acquire a healthier sense of self. The project reaches out beyond mere spectacle and grounds itself in the immediate life of the city's residents. However, what work of memory does this project offer to the urbanites passing trough the romantic, well-balanced, and purified routes of the park of a queen? What kind of nostalgia does it invite or incite? Why is the loss of the past no longer a loss there?

Indeed, adaptive reuse contains many good qualities, one of which is the reinsertion of a structure back into the circuit of social life. Rooting the meaning of the area in a single historical instance and personality—Queen Louise—may be understandable, as Kaliningraders tired of the chaos of postsocialist transitions and the liberalizing economy look for the positive and comfortable symbols of their life. However, a responsible treatment of history should not ignore the burden of uneasy facts and construct a fantasy escape. The challenge of the Luisenwahl project (the Fish Village simply makes no effort to seriously deal with history) is how it glosses over the unwanted episodes in the area's history—the class nature of the area's development under Heitmann, its tragic destruction during the war, its reconstruction in the Soviet period, and the current wave of gentrification pushing out lower-income families—to which the realization of this urban renewal project will undoubtedly contribute.

## Notes

1. See David Harvey, *The Urbanization of Capital* (Oxford: Basil Blackwell, 1985); David Harvey, *Spaces of Capital: Toward a Critical Geography* (New York, Routledge, 2001); Gregory Andrusz, Michael Halroe, and Ivan Szelenyi, eds., *Cities after Socialism: Urban and Regional Change and Conflict in Post-Socialist Societies* (Cambridge, Mass.: Blackwell, 1996); Neil Brenner and Nick Theodore, eds., *Spaces of Neo-Liberalism: Urban Restructuring in North America and Western Europe* (Malden, Mass.: Blackwell, 2002); and Richard LeGates and Frederic Stout, eds., *The City Reader* (London: Routledge, 2001).

2. Rubie Watson, ed. *Memory, History and Opposition under State Socialism* (Santa Fe: School of American Research Press, 1994); Svetlaa Boym, *The Future of Nostalgia* (New York: Basic Books, 2001); Denis Kozlov, "The Historical Turn in Late Soviet Culture: Retrospectivism, Factography, Doubt, 1953–91," *Kritika* 2, no. 3, special issue (2001): 577–600; Brian Ladd, *The Ghosts of Berlin* (Chicago: University of Chicago Press, 1997); Andreas Huyssen, *Present Pasts: Urban Palimpsests and the Politics of Memory* (Stanford, Calif.: Stanford University Press, 2003).

3. Boym, *Future of Nostalgia*.

4. Michael Keith and Steve Pile, eds., *Place and the Politics of Identity* (London: Routledge. 1993).

5. John Borneman and Nick Fowler, "Europeanization," *Annual Review of Anthropology* 26 (1997): 487–514.

6. See Jean Baudrillard, *Simulations* (New York: Semiotexte, 1983). Also see Mike Featherstone, "City Cultures and Post-Modern Lifestyles," in *Post-Fordism: A Reader,* ed. Ash Amin (Oxford: Blackwell, 1994), 387–408; and Xuefei Ren, "Forward to the Past: Historical Preservation and Globalizing Shanghai," *City & Community* 7, no. 1 (March 2008): 23–42.

7. Memel, renamed Klaipeda, was transferred to a newly formed Soviet Republic of Lithuania.

8. Alexei Gubin and Venzel Salkhov, "Kaliningrad: Vosstanovlenie i Stroitel'stvo," *Zapad Rossii* 1, no. 15 (1996): 180–92.

9. Ibid., 183.

10. Ibid., 191.

11. This is from a conversation I recorded standing in a shop line in the summer of 2001. By now, I was not surprised by the logic of the speaker, because I had heard it many times before and even read it in the letters section and editorials of the main local newspaper *Kaliningradskaya Pravda*.

12. This is from a September 2001 focus group conducted with eleven participants—who were born in Kaliningrad and were residents between thirty-five and forty-five years of age.

13. My discussion of the categories of identification in this section is informed by the theoretically sophisticated and thoroughly researched study by Rogers Brubaker, Margit Feischmidt, Jon Fox, and Liana Grancea, *Nationalist Politics and Everyday Ethnicity in a Transylvanian Town* (Princeton, N.J.: Princeton University Press, 2007).

14. This is from a male age forty-four years who has lived in Kaliningrad for sixteen years.

15. Another meaning of the word *beskhozyaistvennost*, as well as a possible translation of it, is "a state of ownerlessness." This neglect that occurs in the absence of an owner, *khozyain*, results in a state of chaos, loose affairs, and a lack of accountability.

16. Alexander Popadin, Alexei Arkhipenko, and Oleg Vasyutin, *Luisenwahl: Projekt Ansamblja Gorodskoi Sredy / Luisenwahl: A Project of an Urban Ensemble*, Publicity Document (Kaliningrad: Architectural Studio 4+, 2001), part I: "Preconditions."

17. David Harvey, "Flexible Accumulation through Urbanization: Reflections on 'Post-Modernism' in the American City," in *Post-Fordism*, ed. Amin, 361–86; the quotation is on 376.

18. Alexander Popadin, Alexei Arkhipenko, and Oleg Vasyutin, *Luisenwahl: An Explanation and Commentary to the Project* (Kaliningrad: Architectural Studio 4+, 2001), section 1.

# Part III

# Cities at a New East-West Border

# 8

# Kharkiv: A Borderland City

*Volodymyr Kravchenko*

Kharkiv (Kharkov in Russian) is Ukraine's second-largest city (1,470,000 citizens in 2001) and the capital of the Kharkiv Oblast (region). It was the capital of Soviet Ukraine (1920–34) and the capital of the historical region Sloboda Ukraine (Slobids'ka Ukraina in Ukrainian).[1] Last but not least, it was the center of the Kharkiv Cossack *polk* (military-administrative units or regimental districts). From its beginnings, the Kharkiv *polk,* as well as other Cossack *polky,* had semiautonomous status under the aegis of the Russian government. The Kharkiv *polk*—located on the great steppe frontier between Russia, the Crimean Khanate, the Cossack state known as the Hetmanate, and the Polish-Lithuanian Commonwealth—became an element in the system of Orthodox Cossackdom that stretched along transparent and changing borders. Besides Sloboda Ukraine, this system included the semiautonomous Cossack regions of Zaporizha and Don. Together, these Cossack regions secured a large frontier zone that included the vast neighboring lands of contemporary Russia and Ukraine.[2]

Although all the Cossack *polky* in Sloboda Ukraine ceased to exist in

1765, in the course of the Russian Empire's large-scale administrative reform, Kharkiv experienced no negative consequences—quite the opposite. The city became an important trade, educational, and industrial center of the Russian Empire and later the USSR. The first university in Russian-ruled Ukrainian territory was established in Kharkiv in 1805. The city has contributed immensely to both modern Ukrainian and Soviet national culture and mythology. Today, Kharkiv, situated within Ukrainian-Russian contact zone, is a place of contested national narratives, historical mythologies, and political projects.

## Beginnings

The city of Kharkiv traces its origins to a military fortress built in the middle of the 1650s. The fortress site that, over time, became transformed into the city of Kharkiv was originally populated by Ukrainian deserters exhausted by war and refugees fleeing the devastation of Right-Bank Ukraine during the Khmelnytsky Revolution in the middle of the seventeenth century.[3] These Sloboda settlers (Slobozhany in Ukrainian) were free people who saw no future in the state of Bohdan Khmelnytsky, or the Polish Commonwealth, and who took advantage of their right to move from one state to another and to freely possess land. Tsarist patents granted them rights and privileges, which distinguished them from the neighboring Russian population and Cossack regions. This legal status, along with their pro-Russia political orientation, would provide the basis for the formation of a distinct local identity.[4]

From the beginning of its existence, Kharkiv would have different meanings in the Russian and the Ukrainian political contexts. For Russia, the city represented a key military-strategic point on the way from Moscow to the Crimea, an outpost of the Russian expansion toward the Black Sea. In the Russian historical tradition, Kharkiv acquired the enduring image of a stronghold in the "Wild Steppe," of a fortress-protector of the "Motherland" and the Orthodox Church against their eternal enemies: nomads, Cossack "traitors," "infidels," and others.

At the same time, from the point of view of the Cossack Hetmanate, Kharkiv represented a permanent threat; it was the center for the concentration of "traitors," political dissidents, and deserters, whose claims to be Cossacks could be doubted. Different Cossacks' hetmans, starting with Bohdan Khmelnyts'ky, regardless of their foreign political orientation, aimed to liquidate the Sloboda settlements or at least put them under their control. Each time, these attempts failed. Elements of this negative image of Kharkiv and the whole region of Sloboda Ukraine proved unchanging and even left their traces in Ukraine's grand historical narrative.

It is no wonder, then, that Kharkiv's inhabitants sought to distance themselves from all political centers and from the struggle for power in the Ukrainian heartland, the Hetmanate. In the political life of Kharkiv, there were no outstanding political leaders or remarkable, shocking events. Kharkiv stood for common sense and a middle way. It was never a city of extremes. It had no military heroes or common social enthusiasms, although among its residents there always existed a logical consistency of interests.

The pragmatism of Kharkiv's founders, which sometimes bordered on cynicism, expressed itself in their political indifference and the primacy of local interests. Geopolitically, the city always seemed to locate itself within a matrix composed of historical influences on local identity and contemporary interests, whose surprisingly persistent points of gravitation are Ukraine, Russia, and the Sloboda region itself. In periods of political crisis or governmental transformation, this nexus of identities, interests, and orientations has repeatedly manifested itself—each time in different ways.

## Toward the Russian Empire

In the second half of the eighteenth century and at the beginning of the nineteenth century, after the Crimean Khanate, the Cossack Hetmanate, and the Polish Commonwealth ceased to exist, the geopolitical configuration of the region changed. Kharkiv's strategic significance was increased greatly by its economically and politically advantageous location on the crossroads of trading routes from Moscow to the southern borders of the Russian Empire. This resulted in the stable, progressive growth of the town, whereby it gradually changed from a border fortress into an important economic and cultural center. Its military functions were superseded, first by the tasks of socially and culturally integrating the newly colonized lands into the Russian Empire and second by the necessity of modernizing the country. So, if somewhat unexpectedly for contemporaries, in 1805 Kharkiv became a university city and the administrative center of an enormous educational district, which included the neighboring territories of Russia, the former Cossack areas, the Black Sea region, and even the Caucasus.[5] During its ascendancy to the status of university center, Kharkiv managed to surpass all its main rivals—Sumy, Katerynoslav, Chernihiv, Poltava, and Kyiv.

These transformations contributed to the idea of a new imagined region, which had Kharkiv at its center and bore the semiofficial title of "South Russia." The originator of the idea to reconceive Kharkiv's role and place in the Russian Empire was Vasilij Karazin, an outstanding intellectual and local public figure.[6] Being a patriot of both Sloboda Ukraine and the Russian Empire, Karazin dreamt about the time when the image of Kharkiv as a remote, provincial town would be forgotten. His dreams came true when the Sloboda Ukraine *gubernia* became the Kharkiv *gubernia* in 1835. Some of his contemporaries with similar views attributed the city's prosperity to its integration into the Russian Empire.

The university fostered a new intellectual environment that complemented Kharkiv's new image and linked it to Western European culture. The new Kharkiv educational district bordered not only the former Cossack and Turkish-Tatar lands to the South but also the Polish Wilno educational district to the West. Polish as well as Russian intellectual culture influenced the new university, whose existence lent powerful impetus to the development of local literature, journalism, and theater as well as to the study of local folklore and ethnology. The presence of the university also contributed enormously to the development of a regional identity. As a new center of science, education, and modern culture, Kharkiv was often compared with Athens and Florence (though mostly by local patriots). In the minds of foreigners or the inhabitants of major Russian cities, Kharkiv was still associated with Cossacks or the Ukrainian heartland—"Little Russia" and the Hetmanate.

In the second half of the eighteenth century and at the beginning of the nineteenth, Kharkiv started changing rapidly from a fortress town into a city in the modern sense of the word. New administrative, commercial, and residential buildings and churches typical of Russian *gubernial* centers were built according to Imperial standards for urban architecture.[7] In the first half of the nineteenth century, Kharkiv presented the picture of an exceptionally dynamic city undergoing rapid cultural and economic growth. Not only was this image cultivated in the works of local Ukrainian writers such as Hryhory Kvitka-Osnovianenko;[8] it also found a place in the works of famous Russian writers such as the literary critic Vissarion Belinsky, who called Kharkiv "the capital of Ukrainian literature." In the literature of other contemporaries, Odessa became the point of comparison as "Kharkiv" became synonymous with a certain pattern of modern and innovative urban development. This development would receive further impetus during the second half of the nineteenth century and at the beginning of the twentieth.

In the middle of the nineteenth century, Kharkiv began a rapid transformation into the largest industrial, financial, and cultural center of "South Russia" and became one of the most densely populated cities in the Russian Empire. Driving this transformation was the establishment and intensive development of the Donetsk–Kryvyi Rih region as a source of raw materials and an industrial base (the Donets Coal Basin, the Donbass or Donets region), which supplied brown coal and metal ore to the rapidly developing industries in the city.[9] As the city industrialized, it began to function as a center for engineering, administration, and investment as well as a rail hub. It also served as a staging ground for the armies of workers employed in Donbass enterprises. The rapid development of this urban industrial center led to comparisons with Chicago in its rate of economic growth for a modern capitalist city.

During this Golden Age of Kharkiv's history and the heyday of its progressive development, its historic center took shape, and new industrial complexes and residential areas were built for its urban aristocracy. Many of these areas are still preserved and continue to project the image of the merchants, nobility, university professors, and students who once populated the city. Even now, these remnant structures lend the city an air of historical significance, often lacking in the other industrial centers of Eastern Ukraine. The architectural ensemble in the core of the city reminds us of the Golden Age of its history (figure 8.1).

In considering the national identity of the city's residents during its Golden Age, one notes that the process of forming a Ukrainian national identity was far from completion within the realm of Pax Slavia Orthodoxa at the end of the nineteenth century and the beginning of the twentieth.[10] Moreover, along the Ukrainian/Russian border, this process appeared to be extremely complicated in its geographical or intellectual aspects. The national identity of Kharkiv's mixed Ukrainian-Russian population usually acquired a hybrid, complex, inclusive, and multifaceted quality, where premodern and modern components of identity were intertwined.[11]

Undoubtedly, Kharkiv's population was predominantly Russian speaking at the end of the nineteenth century. No more than a quarter of the city's residents considered Ukrainian their native language. Russian culture had flourished and spread among the masses. That is why some outstanding Ukrainian intellectuals perceived Kharkiv to be a deeply Russified city and bitterly deplored the decline of the Ukrainian language and culture there.[12]

Figure 8.1. Banks' offices, erected in the center of Kharkiv at the end of nineteenth and the beginning of the twentieth centuries. Photograph by Volodymyr Kravchenko.

The spread of Russian culture was exemplified in the large-scale campaign by the local municipality to rename the city's streets in 1894.[13] The new map of Kharkiv displayed the names of representatives of the local Imperial bureaucracy (e.g., Count Shcherbinin, the region's first *namestnik*,[14] and the grave digger of its semiautonomy), along with figures associated with Russian national culture, such as Pushkin, Lermontov, Tchaikovsky, and Derzhavin. The monument to Pushkin installed during this period is considered to be the first one erected in the public space of Kharkiv. It set a precedent that infuriated young Ukrainian nationalists to such a degree that some even attempted (unsuccessfully) to destroy it.

At the same time, the emerging historical topography of Kharkiv referred not only to Russian cultural figures but also to ones associated with local historical traditions. Among the renamed streets were those honoring the Cossack Karkach, considered to be the plausible founder of the city, after the renowned philosopher Hryhorii Skovoroda,[15] the historian Mykola

Kostomarov,[16] and the local enlightener Karazin. A monument to Karazin was set up in the center of the city in 1907, through the efforts of the liberal community of local intellectuals. It was inscribed with Karazin's declarations of love for "Ukraine," his birthplace. The erection of this monument provoked local Russian nationalists, although they made no attempts to destroy it. It is worth noting that, in this case, the exclusively local historical tradition served the Ukrainian national project. On the eve of World War I, some pan-Ukrainian historical figures gave their names to certain streets and sites in the city, among them Cossack, *haydamak,*[17] and Taras Shevchenko.[18] However, because of the war, the local Ukrainian community found itself unable to build a memorial to the national Ukrainian poet in Kharkiv.

The political, economic, and cultural achievements of Kharkiv provided a solid basis for its own grand historical narrative by the end of the nineteenth century. The narrative and its legendary aspects were first compiled in a fundamental two-volume history, *Kharkiv's History in 250 Years since Its Foundation,* and in a series of publications on the history of Vasilij Nazarevic Karazin National University (also known as Kharkiv University) that marked its centennial. Among these commemorative publications are local biographies and an appreciation of Skovoroda's work, as well as numerous historical and folkloric studies. They were predominantly written by local Ukrainian historians, with Dmytro Bahaliy (1857–1932), a professor at the university, the most prominent among them.

Bahaliy's Kharkiv writings integrate both the Russian (democratic) and the Ukrainian national (populist) historical narratives. In Russian historiography, the city's development exemplifies the successful and fruitful cooperation between the state, society, and "nation"—in other words, between various strata of society regardless of their social and ethnic origin. The city is portrayed as result of cooperation based on a common respect for culture, science, and the idea of progress. Yet, because Kharkiv as a city represented no particular nation, its image in Russian public opinion lacked originality or distinction; Kharkiv was portrayed as a vague, indefinite city—a city imitator.[19] And the city's eclectic architectural style seemed to uphold this image.

By contrast, the Ukrainian national mythology presents Kharkiv as a progeny of Cossack glory, as the cradle of the Ukrainian cultural Renaissance, and as a modern intellectual center—where the first Ukrainian university was founded and where Ukrainian journalism, artistic prose, and literary criticism were first established. Kharkiv contributed to a new Ukrainian pantheon of national heroes, including the philosopher Skovoroda, the enlightenment thinker Karazin, the philologists Izmail Sreznevskii[20] and Oleksandr Potebnia,[21] the writers Kvitka-Osnovianenko and Petro Hulak-Artemovsky,[22] and the historian Mykola Kostomarov.

## Toward the Soviet Empire

During the turbulent years of the national democratic revolution and the Civil War of 1917–20, Kharkiv became the epicenter of the struggle between the old Imperial and the new Democratic Russia as well as Communist Russia, and the new Soviet Ukraine. The Russian Provisional Government, arguing on the basis of the political preferences of Kharkiv's citizens, refused to treat this region as Ukrainian or to put it under Kyiv's control. The Central Rada in Kyiv, for its part, argued on the basis of history, folklore, and the vernacular of the majority of the population (which was Ukrainian) of the former Sloboda region. Hence, Kharkiv became a battlefield of political projects as well as competing identities.

In December 1917, the Bolsheviks proclaimed Kharkiv the capital of the new Soviet Ukraine, while Kyiv was counterposed as the capital of the Ukrainian People's Republic. Only two months later, at the beginning of 1918, a group of local Communist leaders proclaimed Kharkiv the capital of the new Donetsko-Krivorozhskaya Republic. At the time of the empire's collapse, Kharkiv was not the only city that aspired to become a national or regional capital; it joined such other cities as L'viv, Odessa, Simferopol, and even the quite provincial Kamjanets'-Podils'ky in this ambition. All these cities sought to become the capital cities of contested "republics" in the politically fragmented region. Yet in the end, all these cities were forced to yield to Kharkiv.

From 1920 to 1934, Kharkiv was the official capital of Soviet Ukraine. Just as it had been since the university was founded in 1805, during this period Kharkiv became the main center of innovation and modernization for all Ukraine. The new capital of the Ukrainian proletarian state, with its machine-age Socialist utopianism embodied in constructivist architecture, gave birth to a new generation of Ukrainian intellectuals, who tried to adapt national ideas to the challenges of the Communist epoch. Most of them were repressed, especially during Stalin's Great Terror in 1930s.

The historic center of Kharkiv survived this period of rapid construction. A distinct new center was built parallel to the historic core. It was a large, open urban space surrounded by a complex of government office buildings, later known as Dzerzhinskaya. The government complex was indeed gigantic—it was advertised as the largest open space in Europe—and it represented the major Ukrainian planning and construction effort of the late 1920s and early 1930s.

With the avant-garde style of the new buildings, the designers were able to create a geometrically powerful ensemble, conceived for utility and efficient production, and programmed to shape "the New Man of the socialist society"[23] (figure 8.2). Unique architectural structures in the constructivist style augmented the cultural landscape of the city, which gained a new symbol in the Derzhprom Building (in Ukrainian; in Russian, the Gosprom Building; in English, the State Industry Building)—"the Soviet skyscraper" (figure 8.3).

Together with the new center, the new city exhibited an outstanding example of Socialist utopianism in the residential blocks for industrial workers and their families built on its southeastern outskirts. Finally, the monument to Taras Shevchenko, representing the populist-Communist interpretation of Ukrainian history, became one of the most vivid symbols of the Ukrainian metropolis that took shape in the 1920s and the beginning of the 1930s—that is, the national-Communist epoch (figure 8.4).

Kharkiv's streets and squares were renamed after great French revolutionaries and the theorists and practical workers of the international communist movement. Such names became immensely popular in the 1920s, whereas the names of Soviet leaders were used more often in the 1930s. The first set of names have been maintained throughout, but the second set changed with each shift in party policy. More than 480 streets were renamed in 1936 following a government decree. About one-third of these names reflecting the process of the industrialization, militarization, and ideologization of society remain.[24]

Although Kharkiv lost its metropolitan status to Kyiv at the beginning of the 1930s,[25] it still remained one of the largest industrial, scientific, and cultural centers in the Soviet Union, and it was widely considered the country's third city, after Moscow and Leningrad. In its turn, Kharkiv promoted the transformation of the urban cultural area and its image in Soviet culture. A new historical narrative interpreted the city's past within the framework of the Soviet historical paradigm, incorporating the features of Russian Imperial nationalism, populism, and Marxism. A new urban toponymy commemorated the mythology of the Soviet Revolution, the Civil War, and Communist construction. Unlike Kyiv or Odessa, Kharkiv never attained the status of an official World War II "hero city," but nevertheless its urban

Figure 8.2. The administrative building of the "Donugol" Trust, erected in 1925 and decorated with statues of Soviet Donbass miners. Photograph by Volodymyr Kravchenko.

Figure 8.3. The Derzhprom Building, the first Soviet skyscraper in Kharkiv, erected in 1925–29. Photograph by Volodymyr Kravchenko.

cultural area greatly reflected the Soviet historical myth about the Great Patriotic War (i.e., World War II), which was embodied in little architectural forms, toponymics, and monuments. After World War II, two new monuments were added to the cityscape: A gigantic monument to Vladimir Lenin was erected in the middle of Dzerzhinskaya (figure 8.5), and a huge monument to revolutionaries was erected in the city's historic core (figure 8.6).

The comprehensive and deep Sovietization of Kharkiv joined hand in hand with Russification in the process of cleansing the local historical memory of all elements related to Ukrainian national mythology, including those linked to the 1920s. To conform to the Soviet interpretation of history, Ukrainian national elements were replaced by "Little Russia" protonational symbolism supporting the official doctrine of Russian-Ukrainian friendship. This friendship was embodied in a sculptural composition evoking "indissoluble fraternal unity," as well as by naming one of the city's streets after Bohdan Khmel'nyts'ky. In the official mythology of the Soviet Union, Kharkiv acquired the image of the first capital of Soviet, proletarian, and

Figure 8.4. A monument to Taras Shevchenko, erected in 1934. Photograph by Volodymyr Kravchenko.

Figure 8.5. A monument to Vladimir Lenin in the center of Dzerzhinskaya (now Liberty Plaza), erected in 1963. Photograph by Volodymyr Kravchenko.

Communist Ukraine, deemed the city-toiler and city-scientist, and made glorious through its own achievements. The informal image of Kharkiv in the post–World War II Soviet period was linked with commerce, the black market, and economic criminality, as well as with the informal activity of a few dissident intellectuals, mostly Jewish and some Ukrainian. However, these "achievements," as should be expected, left no traces in the official urban symbolism.

## Toward Borderland Status?

From the end of the twentieth century into the beginning of the twenty-first, drastic changes occurred in the life of Kharkiv caused by Ukraine's Independence and the "quadruple" postcommunist transition: democratization, marketization, state building, and nation building.[26] Kharkiv again, as it had often in its history, returned to its role as a borderland city, this time on the

Figure 8.6. A monument to the Soviet fighters of 1917, erected in 1975. Photograph by Volodymyr Kravchenko.

border of the independent states of Russia and Ukraine. This sharply limited its possibilities as a transportation center and, as a result, the city's military-industrial complex suffered a decline during this period. Kharkiv's economic and especially financial potential as an "industrial core" declined in comparison with the neighboring Donetsk–Kryvyi Rih region, with its raw-material-oriented economy that Kharkiv's industries had once dominated. The economic crisis caused Kharkiv to lose its position as a regional leader, which in turn led to a decline of its political significance in an independent Ukraine.

Commercialization and privatization caused even deeper changes in the social life of the city. Initially, the ubiquitous bazaars and markets established in every district of the city seemed to embody its social and creative potential. A few years ago, a market called (in popular language) "Barabashovka" that was much larger than the others was established, and today it is considered the largest in all Ukraine. Now, Western-style supermarkets are taking the place of the bazaars, but one can be sure that the bazaar will remain a feature of the city (figure 8.7).

For the past several years, Kharkiv has been experiencing a housing boom that has the potential to greatly influence its landscape. The pattern of such transformation becomes clear along one of the city's central highways—Moskovsky Avenue—where the now-defunct industrial enterprises of the Soviet period are being reconstructed as stores, malls, wholesale centers, and service stations. A similar sort of transformation is taking place along another central arterial city road—Klotchkivs'ka Street—which had

Figure 8.7. A bazaar in the center of Kharkiv, on Liberty Plaza, between the monuments to Vladimir Lenin and the Derzhprom Building. Photograph by Volodymyr Kravchenko.

Figure 8.8. A view along Klotchkivs'ka Street. Photograph by Yaroslava Kravchenko.

become a depressed area after the demise of the Soviet Union (figure 8.8). The most active modernization is taking place in the city's historic center. There, old buildings have been restored and new ones have been constructed. The new buildings generally house shops, banks, and restaurants, as well as offices and luxury apartments (figure 8.9).

The architecture and public places reflecting the ideology of Soviet times are the most difficult to change. Among these are the Kharkiv district administrative centers, which resemble the Kremlin and the Lenin mausoleum in Moscow; the large-scale 1930s constructions of the Socialist city; and the so-called *spal'nyje rajony* (dormitory outskirts), comprising five-story buildings constructed in 1960s when Nikita Khrushchev carried out his massive housing program. In these closed and uniform complexes, there is little or no space for a small business, let alone for the ubiquitous bazaar.

The cultural and symbolic environment of Kharkiv has also been actively reorganized. The demise of the Soviet Union, the declaration of Ukrainian Independence, and the new regional configuration all advanced the painful process of the dissolution of the "old" Soviet nation as well as the forma-

Figure 8.9. A new luxury apartment building in the center of Kharkiv. Photograph by Volodymyr Kravchenko.

tion of new nations along ethnoterritorial lines, and also began the process of reintegration of the basic aspects of the Soviet identity on all levels—from nation-state to individual.[27] On the one hand, this process was followed by the regionalization of public, political, and cultural life in Ukraine; on the other hand, it was characterized by appeals to history, with claims to "resurrection" and the disclosure of "historical truth." These two tendencies were reflected in Kharkiv's public life in the post-Soviet period.

The reinvention of an old/new historical tradition was followed by the rejection of the Soviet legacy and an appeal to the symbols and values of a former historical epoch. This resulted in intellectual debates over new interpretations of Kharkiv's history—in other words, over a new version of its identity. However, along the road going "back to the future," the first stop (after departing from the Soviet regional capital version of Kharkiv) would be Kharkiv as the capital of Soviet Ukraine. Going back further, one hits on the historical period when Kharkiv was a regional capital of the Russian Empire. And after covering even more historical distance, one reaches the period of Kharkiv as the "Cossack capital of Sloboda Ukraine." Of all these cases, only the final one seems to be an appropriate model for the city in an independent Ukraine.

The de-Sovietization of Kharkiv began in the years of perestroika, with slogans demanding the disclosure of Stalinist crimes. This first wave of public awakening led to the first renamings of city streets and squares.[28] Kharkiv's main square lost its original name, Dzerzhinskaya, to become Liberty Plaza. The name of Felix Dzerzhinsky, the founder of the Soviet secret police, was no longer used to denote the related Metro station and side street in the center of the city but was preserved in the name of the central Kharkiv administrative district. Nevertheless, the bas-relief dedicated to him remained untouched on the wall of the former Regional KGB Residence (now called the Security Service of Ukraine).

Other Kharkiv landmarks of Soviet times were renamed. The quay named in honor of Andrei Zhdanov was renamed Kharkiv Quay, and the Eighth Congress of Soviets street signs were replaced by ones bearing the name of Boris Chichibabin, a Russian Soviet-era poet-dissident and a Kharkiv citizen. Curiously, the Russian democrat Alexander Herzen ended up on the removal list, and the street named in his honor became Bondarenko Street, in honor of a local cosmonaut who died during space flight training.[29] In these cases, the renamings strengthened local cultural representation in the toponymics of the city.

The perestroika tradition continues to reform the Soviet canon and inform the new monumental architecture of the city, if one considers the memorials erected after 1991 on the initiative of local community. Among them are memorials to the victims of the Chernobyl catastrophe[30] and the Soviet war in Afghanistan.[31] Democratic openness has spawned new veins of commemorations that are evident in the memorial to Holocaust victims in the Drobyts'ky Yar (Drobitsky Ravine),[32] as well as a commemorative site dedicated to the Polish prisoners of war who were executed by the Soviets at the beginning of World War II.[33]

In the first half of the 1990s, an attempt was made to have Kharkiv's cultural space conform to the Ukrainian national narrative. The local government and a few Ukrainian public organizations established in the years of perestroika took the main initiative in this venture. Historical monuments that reflected the Ukrainian national historical myth were valued, including those referring to Cossack fame, national resurrection, and the victims and hardships of Soviet times. All-Ukrainian and local national symbols were used as well.

At first, a sculpture of a Cossack on horseback escaping from pursuit was placed in the central city park. Then the victims of the 1931–33 Great Famine were commemorated. And then monuments were erected in the city's historic core to the philosopher Skovoroda, the writer Kvitka-Osnovianenko, and the local patron and banker Oleksii Alchevs'ky; and memorial plaques were erected to honor Mykola Mihnovs'ky, an early ideologist of Ukrainian nationalism, and the local historian Dmytro Bahaliy.

The process of the de-Russification and de-Sovietization of Kharkiv's historical topography was especially marked by the metaphor of the Ukrainian "Executed Renaissance," linked to the city's role as a historic capital of Ukraine. This found expression in various commemorative sites: in the erection of the monument to Ukrainian *kobzars,* who had been executed in Kharkiv in the years of the Great Terror; in a cross raised to the victims of the Great Famine of 1932–33; and in memorial plaques to Ukrainian intellectuals of the 1920s such as Vasyl' Ellan-Blakytny, Les' Kurbas, Mykola Hvylovy, and Mar'an Krushel'nyts'ky, as well as to the victims of the trial of the Spilka vyzvolennia Ukrainy (Union for the Liberation of Ukraine).[34]

The public demonstration of Kharkiv's Ukrainianness through monumental architecture reached a high point during the celebrations surrounding the tenth anniversary of Ukrainian Independence. The local government initiated the reconstruction of one of the city's oldest historic squares, the former Trade Square, which was called Roza Luxemburg Square in Soviet times. In 2001, it became Sobornist' Square (denoting the unification of all ethnic Ukrainian regions under the "one and indivisible" Ukraine). At the center of this square is a new monumental ensemble, the Pillar of Independence, composed of a pillar with an eagle in the form of a trident (the Ukrainian National Emblem) and a ten-year-old girl symbolizing the youth of Ukrainian Independence. Recent Ukrainian history is also reflected in the name of the second-largest square in Kharkiv's historic center, Constitution Square (previously, Soviet Square). One of the oldest urban highways has regained its previous name, Poltavs'ky Shlah Street (the Soviet Sverdlova Street). A Metro station now called Kholodna Hora (Cold Mountain) was previously known as Sverdlova Station. And one of the central avenues of the city now recalls the writer Oles' Honchar and no longer refers to the newspaper *Pravda*.

In general, the historic center of old Kharkiv bears more characteristics of Ukrainian national symbolism than its modern counterpart—Liberty Plaza. It is Liberty Plaza that should be filled with symbols of Ukrainian history and statehood. But the granite stone erected at the beginning of 1990s with the solemn inscription "Here will be set a monument in honor of Ukrainian Independence" has already been there for eighteen years and is cracked at the edges (figure 8.10). It now lies forgotten with an almost undecipherable inscription, next to commercial restaurants and a police station. Other historical symbols of Ukrainian Kharkiv have suffered a similar fate. The monument to the local writer Kvitka-Osnovianenko, hastily erected in the mid-1990s, is practically a ruin, and the obscure image of a Cossack on a horse escaping the chase has simply disappeared and been replaced by another symbol: the image of the Archangel Michael. As for the Pillar of Independence, it is surrounded by a well-trafficked road, which prevents city residents from approaching it and makes the area around it largely deserted during the day. None of the new Ukrainian monuments and symbolic spaces can compete with the old monument to Taras Shevchenko, set up in 1934. This monument remains one of the city's most popular and recognizable symbols connected with its Ukrainian history.

The constellation of symbols in Kharkiv has been greatly influenced by an emerging local identity that derives from the city's progressive marginalization and its return to a borderland status. Since the end of the 1980s, its local identity has become ever more important in its cultural, social, and political life. Public organizations as well as a powerful local elite on all levels have been increasingly involved in its formation. This can be seen in the design for the city's new emblem and flag as well as in the widespread "Sloboda" semantics, employed in the names of newspapers, popular trademarks, new office buildings, and enterprises. Kharkiv is again positioning itself to be the capital of the huge former Sloboda region. Due to this process,

Figure 8.10. A granite stone in honor of Ukrainian Independence, erected in 1990. Photograph by Volodymyr Kravchenko.

the literature of local history has become extremely popular. And it came to be even more used when local history was made an obligatory subject in school curricula. Kharkiv's political elite began forging a new pantheon of heroes, offering local prizes and even handing out local orders.

Today, local patriotism finds avid public expression in the compensatory discourse about the "first capital,"[35] an idea that has lent a name to a Kharkiv television station, newspaper, and trademark. The newspaper's epigraph reads: "Love Kharkiv, or leave it." One of the founders and popularizers of the myth of Kharkiv as the first capital of Ukraine, the journalist Konstantin Kevorkyan, has made a career in business and politics by propagating this idea. He has written a magnum opus titled *The First Capital,* generously proposing its use as a textbook of local history. Under his guidance, the television channel First Capital airs a new variant of Kharkiv's history that emphasizes its achievements in the Imperial and Soviet epochs.

Kevorkyan initiated plans for the construction of a monument at the Central Station dedicated to Father Fedor, a literary character in one of the most popular Soviet adventure novels, *The Twelve Chairs.* This character, created by Il'f and Petrov in the 1920s, was a clergyman traveling throughout the whole Soviet Union who passed through Kharkiv—then the first capital of Soviet Ukraine. The monument seems to be deprived of ideology at first glance. However, its symbolism can be appreciated if one remembers that the book by Il'f and Petrov provided practical guidance for the upbringing of Soviet youth, and its aphorisms penetrated the language of colloquial Soviet culture no less than the songs of Vladimir Vysotskiy.[36] In this framework, the monument supports an informal and popular conception of the Soviet-Russian Kharkiv, one opposed not only to the "revolutionary" Soviet but also to the "national" Ukrainian paradigms of the city.

It is quite evident that the "First Capital" slogan exaggerates local patriotism and actually touches on the very pedigree of the modern Ukrainian state. In the official historical narrative of Ukraine, the first capital refers to Kyiv, and the first national government refers to the Central Rada and to the national democratic state established under its aegis in 1917. In the official Soviet interpretation, not Kyiv but Kharkiv became the first "genuine" capital of a Soviet state—of the "genuine" Ukrainian state founded after the Bolshevik coup in October 1917.

Although such projects are defined by signs of épatage and challenges to the assumptions of professional historiography, the local political and business elite liked and fully supported the myth of Kharkiv as the "first capital," as opposed to official Kyiv. For instance, on the Kharkiv administration's official Web site and in the speeches of officials, Kharkiv is called "the first capital"—without quotation marks. It can be assumed that "Sovietism" forms a bond with the intellectual community and the new Kharkiv elite. In this regard, we should remember that Leonid Kuchma's political regime sought legitimization by appealing to the old Soviet state system in Ukraine, not by building a new national democracy. The name of Vladimir Scherbitskiy— the leader of the Ukrainian Communist Party (the regional branch of the Communist Party of the Soviet Union)—was highly honored in commemorative practice because the years of his administration coincided with the formative years of present-day Ukrainian politicians and authorities.[37]

Alexander Masel'skiy, a long-term leader of the Kharkiv region until his death in 1996, can be considered Scherbitskiy's local prototype. He has been commemorated with a memorial plaque on the wall of the contemporary residence of the regional government, by giving his name to the Metro station (formerly called "Industrial"), and with a scholarship established in his honor. Another Metro station was named in honor of Grigoriy Vashchenko—a representative of the Soviet Nomenklatura and the former secretary of the Kharkiv Regional Committee of the Communist Party of the Soviet Union. Lately, the city has seen the installation of a great number of memorial plaques, dedicated to other representatives of the Soviet political, artistic, and administrative elites whose biographies to some extent were linked with Kharkiv.

The directors of large local enterprises and public offices have actively participated in the formation of Kharkiv's new monumental image. They appear eager to create personal symbols of bureaucratic or professional identity. Thus, the monuments to police officers, railway workers, and teachers have been installed by the corresponding organizations in Kharkiv. One of the leading educational establishments in Kharkiv and in all Ukraine, the National Law Academy, has set up a monument to Yaroslav Mudry (Yaroslav the Wise), the Old Rus' prince and lawmaker. Vasilij Nazarevic Karazin National University, which is of course named after Vasilij Karazin, has moved the monument to Karazin from its previous place in the local park to the central entrance of the university. Other remappings in the commemorative landscape worth mentioning include the monuments erected by the Russian Orthodox Church of the Moscow Patriarchate to mark the two-thousandth anniversary of Christ's birth and to celebrate Alexander Nevsky, the canonized Rus' prince of Novgorod.

To observe how Kharkiv's local identity is being reconfigured in the constellation of local monuments is to recognize how it is guided, on the one hand, by the Soviet tradition and, on the other hand, by the Russian Orthodox Imperial tradition. Along with the Orthodox Church of the Moscow Patriarchate and the newly fashioned Imperial emblems, the recently erected memorials to Nevsky and Mikhail Lomonosov (a renowned eighteenth-century Russian scholar) might well be seen as cultivating a Russian tradition. In the same vein, a bust to the first Imperial governor general of Sloboda Ukraine, Count Shcherbinin, was mounted at the entrance to the regional state administration building. These monuments demonstrate the intensified pro-Russian orientation of the Ukrainian government within the last years of President Kuchma's rule.

Today, this pro-Russian policy is being vigorously implemented by the City Council, which is controlled by the Party of Regions through Mikhail Dobkin, the city's elected mayor. The policy is reflected most vividly in the intensive program to build Russian Orthodox churches. For example, one of the most popular recreation places in the center of the city looks like a territory of contested Soviet and Ukrainian "narratives" (figure 8.11): There is a granite stone dedicated to the Ukrainian students who were killed in

Figure 8.11. A granite stone in honor of Ukrainian students, defenders of the Ukrainian state, who were killed in action against the Bolsheviks at the beginning of 1918. This stone was erected in recent years along the walk devoted to the Soviet heroes who belonged to Komsomol. An Orthodox church is going to be built at the end of this walk, in place of the stele decorated with the Soviet Komsomol orders. Photograph by Volodymyr Kravchenko.

1918 near Kruty village in action against the Communists along a walk devoted to the heroes who belonged to Komsomol (the Communist youth organization), and at the end of this walk is a plot with a Soviet-era stele where the Orthodox church will be built. Another nearby plot is allotted to a chapel devoted to Saint Eugenie, a Russian private killed in action during the last Russian-Chechen war who was made a saint by the Russian Orthodox Church.

The fragmentation of the Soviet political environment has only slightly affected Kharkiv's basic cultural structures. Indeed, they have been retained in the majority of former Soviet Republics, and some monuments have not only survived but have also seen their cultural significance reassessed and confirmed, making it seem as though the objects have a capacity for regeneration.[38] Kharkiv proves this observation, because commercialization,

Ukrainization, and regionalization have all failed to fundamentally reform the city's Soviet symbolic environment. Soviet symbolism is everywhere in the city: in its memorials to Soviet officials of all epochs and different branches; anchored by the huge statue of Lenin in its new Soviet center; and, with small variances on the same theme, in its administrative districts. In the city's historic center, on Constitution Square, the monument to Soviet Ukraine has been well preserved as the "Soviet" Metro Station, which runs beneath the square. In this manner, the contemporary political and business elite romanticizes its Komsomol past. In 2004, a memorable symbol in honor of the Ukrainian Komsomol appeared in Kharkiv near one of the residential blocks on an avenue named after the fiftieth anniversary of the USSR.

Many places in Kharkiv are named after Communist leaders; after the titles of various events, celebrations, and professions; and after symbolic figures of not only the Brezhnev and Khrushchev eras but also Stalin's and even Lenin's epochs of Soviet history. The names of all the city's administrative districts have not been changed; Dzerzhinskiy, Leninskiy, Ordzhonikidzevskiy, Kominternovskiy, and Moskovskiy have all been carried over from the Soviet era. In particular, a large part of the city's material culture is dedicated to conserving and even cultivating the Soviet-era historical and cultural heritage, particularly the Soviet mythology surrounding the Great Patriotic War.[39] The city's streets and squares are literally saturated with memorials and memorable symbols to the USSR, as well as the names of Soviet-era heroes, military leaders, participants in underground groups, soldiers-internationalists, and separate military formations connected with fights for the city. In recent years, they have been joined by the memorial to student-volunteers, erected next to the main building of the city's V. N. Karazin National University, as well as a new memorial on its outskirts, which was called Konev's Height, in honor of a Soviet marshal. Both memorials corresponded to a Socialist realism, which contrast with an Orthodox chapel of the Moscow Patriarchate that was already present in the complex of Konev's Height.

This tendency is also evident in the choice of new place names. In 1993, the local authorities arrived at a decision to honor the memory of four Soviet generals by naming streets after them,[40] as well as a new Metro station, "The 23rd of August," in memory of Kharkiv's day of liberation from Nazi Germany in 1943. In this case, what was once considered Soviet heritage has been resurrected as valuable due to a connection to the Great Patriotic War myth surrounding World War II, which has also recently been cultivated in Russia.[41]

"Sovietness" in the cultural politics of Kharkiv also manifests itself in the language of the current authorities, who employ the slogan "Friendship of Peoples" to propose an *internationalism* in opposition to *nationalism*.[42] Thus, two projected stations of Kharkiv's Metro will be called "Of the Friendship of Peoples" and "International." Here it is important to note how the old Soviet rhetoric about international friendship is openly or implicitly employed to resist the Ukrainian rhetoric of the newly independent nation.

Unlike the widespread public use of national symbols, both past and present, the symbolism of "Europe" is generally confined to the sphere of business and policy. The European orientation of Kharkiv residents is most evident at the level of everyday life. The names and facades of new buildings and enterprises serve as synonyms for "Europeanness." This orientation is transported into the elite consumer goods offered in retail stores; projected as the promise of skilled repair (as in "European maintenance"); or used to elevate the cuisine of a shabby barbecue bar.[43] In Kharkiv, wherever "European" appears in the public space, it signifies "of the best quality," whether referring to goods or services. Primarily, it refers to European standards of life, lifestyles, and fashion, and only secondarily does it signify standards of democracy, civil society, or professional culture. In the political rhetoric of the local elite, Kharkiv is positioned as a European city, a bearer of high spiritual values. Active contact with European regions made Kharkiv the only city in Ukraine honored by the European certificate and the flag of the Council of Europe. It has also been considered a candidate to become a cultural capital of Europe.

A few monuments that have been erected in Kharkiv in recent years seem to lack any clear ideological context, and so they might be placed in the semantic field of modern European culture. Among them is the figure of a violinist modeled after the world-renowned violinist Iurii Bashmet, which appeared in an unexpected place: on the roof of a tall building in the historic downtown (figure 8.12). Another example is a modernist sculptural group portraying two people in love (figure 8.13). In the city's central park, one can find a marker for the path of the 50th parallel that passes through downtown.

Changes in the cultural landscape and the historic topography of modern Kharkiv are directly linked with the constantly changing political environment. A vivid example of this interdependence is the double jubilee that was celebrated in 2004. That year marked both the three-hundred-fiftieth anniversary of Kharkiv and the two-hundredth anniversary of Kharkiv University, but it was also accompanied by the presidential elections in Ukraine. It is symptomatic that the anniversary of Kharkiv's founding was rolled into

Figure 8.12. A statue of a violinist. Photograph by Volodymyr Kravchenko.

a holiday marathon that united all three events: the Day of Kharkiv's Liberation from the Fascists, the Day of the City, and the Day of the Independence of Ukraine. Each "day" had its own semantics and symbolic context. The Day of Liberation was celebrated with festivities on the memorial Konev's Height and by the dedication of new Metro stations, including the one named "The 23rd of August" and a series of dedications of several me-

Figure 8.13. A modernist sculpture of a loving couple. Photograph by Gelinada Grinchenko.

morial plaques. The Soviet style of these events was accompanied by officious rhetoric drawing on an old-fashioned, distinctly Russian-Soviet myth of Kharkiv as a city-toiler and a city-protector, whose inhabitants, in the words of the former mayor of Kharkiv, are part of a "peaceful, freedom-loving, [and] talented nation."

The celebration of Kharkiv's jubilee, to which the state contributed a commemorative coin and the presence of the former president of Ukraine, Kuchma, was accompanied by the appearance of the first equestrian statue in the city, one portraying its legendary founder, the Cossack Kharko. The Russian sculptor Zurab Tsereteli designed the Cossack, who was brought to Kharkiv from Russia. It is symbolic that the statue is located not far from the modern center of Kharkiv, at the beginning of Lenin Avenue. At the opposite end of the avenue, one can see a newly constructed Orthodox church of the Moscow Patriarchate. Whether by accident or not, the whole complex arose in the northern part of the city, in the area closest to the Russian border, although, as is well known, Kharkiv's founders came from its opposite, western side.

In the last years of his regime, President Kuchma reoriented Ukraine's foreign policy toward Russia. Perhaps that was the influential factor behind the appearance of a memorial to Russian prince Alexander Nevsky next to the psychiatric hospital on Independence Day. In addition, the Day of Independence was commemorated by a memorial to the first Russian *namestnik* of Sloboda Ukraine, Count Shcherbinin, next to the governor's residence. Shcherbinin was known for doing away with local autonomy and was responsible for the absorption of Cossack land by Russia. As a result, Kharkiv's jubilee sent a definite political message, correctly perceived in Russia as one phrased in the spirit of a long-awaited "reunification" of Ukraine with Russia.

The public celebration of the two-hundredth anniversary of Kharkiv University also illustrates this tendency in the social and cultural life of modern Kharkiv. The question of the very beginning of Kharkiv University arose. Some academicians tried to break with the centennial tradition and to proclaim the university's founding year as not 1805 but 1804. The first year is connected with the beginning of the university's activity, and the second with the emperor's brevet confirming the statute of the university. It is ironic that, in fact, the brevet ended the project of developing a regional university, which had been initiated by Karazin and supported by local noble society.

The pro-Russian tendencies and simultaneously regionalist orientation of Kharkiv's political elite were clearly challenged by the so-called Orange

Figure 8.14. The Orange Revolution in Kharkiv, November 2004. Photograph by Volodymyr Kravchenko.

Revolution (figure 8.14). For the first time in its history, Kharkiv's inhabitants—who are primarily Russian speaking—picketed the Russian Consulate General in Kharkiv and protested against the interference of Russia in Ukrainian affairs as well as misrepresentation of the Ukrainian Revolution in the Russian media. When the former Kharkiv governor, Evgeniy Kushnarev, came forward under the slogans of opposition of Kharkiv to Kyiv and L'viv, Kharkiv's inhabitants came forward to oppose the political project of the so-called South Eastern Ukrainian Autonomous Republic under the aegis of Donbass-based politicians. It can be assumed that a European or, taking broader view, a pro-Western consciousness in modern Ukraine turned out to be the brake that kept Kharkiv from slipping into a new regional federation. At the same time, it may have been a particular type of local patriotism that allowed a part of Kharkiv's elite to refuse the leadership of Donetsk.

## Conclusions

On the whole, post-Soviet Kharkiv still demonstrates its cultural and political eclecticism. This eclecticism is embodied, for example, in the largest plaza in Kharkiv, which was created during the years of Soviet rule to emphasize the Soviet city's metropolitan status—and was first named after Felix Dzerzhinsky but since 1991 has been called Liberty Plaza. Currently, it houses all the main events related to the city's social, political, and cultural life. Thus it rarely stays empty. It is often filled with commercial tents or political meetings. The architectural ensemble surrounding the plaza comprises buildings from the constructivist period, complemented after World War II by buildings in the style of Stalinist monumentalism. Recently, new memorials have been added to complete the plaza's composition, including one to Karazin in a late classicist style (this was moved to the main university's building in 2004); one to the Cossack Kharko, whose effigy reminds one of the statues of the Russian generals from the times of the Russian-Turkish wars; and a bust of Count Shcherbinin, which is similar to the busts of the heroes of the Soviet Union. Whereas the monument to Karazin is situated near a building constructed in the Soviet constructivist style of the 1920s, the Cossack Kharko, legendary Kharkiv's founding father, looms above Lenin Avenue, and Count Shcherbinin stands next to the building that formerly housed the Regional Committee of the Communist Party and is now occupied by the Kharkiv governor. The space between Liberty Plaza and the monument to Taras Shevchenko erected after the Great Famine in Ukraine in 1932–33 is filled with restaurants, entertainment venues, and other establishments.

The whole space of Liberty Plaza, which is hailed as the "biggest in Europe," serves as a battlefield between political forces and opposed identities, mostly of neo-Soviet (intertwined with Russian Orthodox) and Ukrainian character. It is still difficult to say anything more certain about the Kharkiv (or Sloboda) local identity, although recent research has highlighted features of local politics and understandings of the Ukrainian past and future.[44] Although the local identity of the city's residents has appeared to resist close association with the process of building the Ukrainian nation-state (at least in its recent forms and methods), one can be sure that most Kharkivians would keep a distance from any other nation-building project in its strictly defined or exclusive forms. In everyday life, one can see the desire of the city's residents to "have it both ways," allowing the presence of not only Ukrainian and Russian identities but also any other identities inherent in the Ukrainian-Russian contact zone.[45]

Today, it is as yet rather difficult to answer the question: What time is Kharkiv? The Soviet style of life, deeply rooted in Byzantine-Russian ground, has had a far-reaching influence on Ukraine's development at its starting point as an independent state. There has been neither a radical break with the past nor a reconciliation with it. The contemporary period has yet to form a new, stable image of Kharkiv that could stand next up to its competing or hybrid identities. But it is too early to say how long Kharkiv will be in the process of finding its niche in the context of building the Ukrainian nation-state.

## Notes

1. "Sloboda" means "free settlement established by newcomers from Ukraine." From these, the whole region derived its original name, Sloboda Ukraine (in Ukrainian, Slobids'ka Ukraina). The region consisted of five Cossack *polky* (i.e., military-administrative units or regimental districts), namely, Kharkivs'ky, Sums'ky, Ostrohozhs'ky, Okhtyrs'ky, and Iziums'ky. For the best synthesis of the history of the region, see D. I. Bahalii, *Istoria Slobids'koi Ukrainy* (Kharkiv: Osnova, 1990; orig. pub. 1918).

2. On the history of the region from a geopolitical perspective, see Terry Martin, "The Empire's New Frontiers: New Russia's Path from Frontier to Okraina 1774–1920," *Russian History* 19, nos.1–4 (1992): 181–201; and Andreas Kappeler, "The Russian Southern and Eastern Frontiers from the 15th to the 18th Centuries," *Ab Imperio* 2 (June 2003) (published in Russian translation with a summary in English).

3. The Cossack uprising under the leadership of Bohdan Khmelnyts'ky in 1648 against the Polish Commonwealth is considered to be the Ukrainian Revolution, which began a process that was to result in establishing a Cossack semi-independent state (Hetmanate), further acquisition by the Russian half of Ukrainian territory from Poland, and the decline of the Polish-Lithuanian Commonwealth.

4. See V. V. Kravchenko, "Rehional'na identychnist' Slobozhanshchyny v istorytchnij perspektyvi XVIII—potchatku XX st." (The regional identity of the Sloboda Region in historical perspective from the 18th to the start of the 20th centuries), in *Ukrains'ko-rosijs'ke porubizhzha: Formuvannia sotcial'noho ta kul'turnoho prostoru v istorii ta sutchasnij politytci—Zbirnyk materialiv seminaru Kyivs'koho proektu Instytutu Kennana ta filosofs'koho fakul'tetu Kharkivs'koho natcional'noho universytetu imeni V. N. Karazina, 11 kvitnia 2003 roku* (Ukrainian-Russian borderland: The molding of the social and cultural space in history and contemporary politics—The collected works of the seminar organized by the Kennan Institute's Kyiv Project and the Philosophy Department of Karazin National University in Kharkiv, 11 April 2003) (Kyiv: Stylos, 2003), 44–48.

5. V. V. Kravchenko, "Kharkivs'kyj universytet u pershij polovyni XIX stolittia" (Kharkiv University in the first half of the 19th century), in *Kharkivs'kyj natcional'nyj universytet imeni V. N. Karazina za 200 rokiv* (V. N. Karazin Kharkiv National University during 200 years of its history) (Kharkiv: Folio, 2004), 6–124; V. V. Kravchenko, "Universytet dlia Ukrainy" (University for Ukraine), *Skhid-Zakhid* 7 (2005): 120–66.

6. See James T. Flynn, "V. N. Karazin, the Gentry and Kharkov University," *Slavic Review* 28, no. 2 (1969): 212. Also see Ivan Lysiak-Rudnyts'kyj, *Ivan Lysiak-Rudnyts'kyj, istorychni ese 2* (Ivan Lysiak-Rudnyts'kyj, historical essays 2) (Kyiv: Osnovy, 1994), 203–20.

7. Alexandr Leibfreid and Yuliana Poliakova, *Khar'kov: Ot kreposti k stolitce—Zametki o starom horode* (Kharkov: From the fortress to the capital—Some notes about downtown) (Kharkiv: Folio, 2004).

8. Hryhory Kvitka-Osnovianenko (1778–1843), a Ukrainian writer, cultural, and civic figure, is considered "the father of modern Ukrainian prose."

9. See H. Kuromija, *Freedom and Terror in the Donbass: A Ukrainian-Russian Borderland, 1870s–1990* (Cambridge: Cambridge University Press, 1998).

10. R. Szporluk, *Russia, Ukraine, and the Breakup of the Soviet Union* (Stanford, Calif.: Hoover Institution Press, 2000), 361–95.

11. P.-R. Magocsi, "The Ukrainian National Revival: A New Analytical Framework," *Canadian Review of Studies in Nationalism* 16, nos. 1–2 (1989): 45–62; P.-R. Magocsi, *A History of Ukraine* (Toronto: University of Toronto Press, 1998), 351–65.

12. V. V. Kravchenko, "Ukrains'kyj natcional'nyj rukh u Kharkovi XIX—potchatku XX stolittia" (Ukrainian national movement in Kharkiv, 19th–early 20th centuries), *Slovo i Tchas* 10 (1993): 14–20.

13. S. V. Zhuravliova, "K voprosu o toponimitcheskoi politike Khar'kovskoj dumy v kontce XIX veka" (About the problem of the toponymic policy of the Kharkiv municipality at the end of the 19th century), *Aktual'ni problemy vitchyznianoi ta vsesvitnioi istorii* 3 (1998): 75–79.

14. A *namestnik* is a head of Namestnichestvo—i.e., the basic Imperial province—created in the course of the administrative restructuring of the Russian Empire in 1775.

15. Hryhorii Savych Skovoroda (1722–94), an outstanding Ukrainian philosopher, known as the "Ukrainian Socrates" and the "wandering scholar." Most of his lyrical po-

ems and philosophical writings were created in Sloboda Ukraine from 1769 until his death.

16. Mykola Ivanovych Kostomarov (1817–85), a Ukrainian and Russian prominent historian, publicist, and writer, graduated from Kharkiv University. He was one of the leading figures of Ukrainian national renaissance.

17. A *haydamak* was a participant in popular uprisings against the Polish regime in right-bank Ukraine in the eighteenth century.

18. O. V. Khoroshkovatyj, "Lokal'na (mistceva) toponimica: Sposib tvorennia, zminy, jikh kharakter" (Local toponymy: The way of creation, changes, and their character), in *VIII Vseukrains'ka naukova konferentcia "Istorychne kraeznavstvo i kul'tura," Naukovi dopovidi 2* (Proceedings from the VIIIth Whole-Ukrainian science conference, "Historical lore studies and culture" 2) (Kyiv-Kharkiv: Ridnyj kraj, 1997): 342–46.

19. V. V. Kravchenko, M. V. Chouhuenko, and A. V. Shmal'ko, "Misto Kharkiv: Shliakh do slavy" (Kharkiv city: The road to glory), in *500 vlijatel'nykh lichnostej: Kharkovu—350* (500 important persons: 350 years of Kharkiv), ed. Albert Serebriakov (Kharkiv: Skhidno-Ukrains'kyj biohrafichnyj Instytut, 2004), 10–26.

20. Izmail Ivanovich Sreznevsky (1812–80), a famous Russian philologist, graduated from Kharkiv University, where he created one of the first intellectual centers of Ukrainian cultural activity at the end of 1820s.

21. Oleksandr Potebnia (1835–91), a prominent linguist, was a professor at Kharkiv University.

22. Petro Hulak-Artemovs'ky (1790–1865), a famous Ukrainian poet, fabulist, and translator, served as the professor and rector of Kharkiv University.

23. Tótus D. Hewryk, "Planning of the Capital in Kharkiv," *Harvard Ukrainian Studies* 16, nos. 3–4 (December 1992): 331.

24. Taranenko Yu., "Chto, gorod, v imeni tvoem?" (What is in your name, the city?) *Gorodskaja gazeta*, no. 26, 1997.

25. S. Yekelchyk, "The Making of 'Proletarian Capital': Patterns of Stalinist Social Policy in Kiev in the Mid-1930s," *Europe-Asia Studies* 50, no.7 (November 1998): 1229–44.

26. Taras Kuzio, "Transition in Post-Communist States: Triple or Quadruple?" *Politics* 21, no. 3 (September 2001): 169–78.

27. Orest Subtelny, "The Ambiguities of National Identity: The Case of Ukraine," in *Ukraine: The Search for a National Identity*, ed. Sharon L.Wolchik, and Volodymyr Zviglyanich (Lanham, Md.: Rowman & Littlefield, 2000), 1–10; Kataryna Wolczuk, "History, Europe and the 'National Idea': The Official Narrative of National Identity in Ukraine," *Nationalities Papers* 28, no. 4 (December 2000): 671–94; Stephen Shulman, "The Contours of Civic and Ethnic National Identification in Ukraine," *Europe-Asia Studies* 56, no. 1 ( January 2004): 35–56.

28. V. A. Kodin, "Imena na karte goroda (problemy okhrany istoritcheskoj toponimiki Khar'kova) (Names on the city's map [the problem of the preservation of the historic toponymy of Kharkov]), in *Kul'turna spadshchyna Slobozhanshchyny: Za materialamy konferentcii 5 Slobozhans'ki tchytannia* (Kharkiv, 2003), 115–18; Yana Soldatenko, "Robespierre v Kharkove ne pojavlialsia, no ulitca jego imeni ostalas" (Robespierre never was in Kharkov, but the street named after him still exists), *Vetchernii Khar'kov*, July 31, 2003; Svatenko Volodymyr, "Dopoky tce tryvatyme?" (How long will this continue?), http://maidan.org.ua/static/mai/1110894486.html.

29. Sergey Miroshnichenko, "Pereimenovany gorodskie ulitcy" (Urban streets are renamed), *Sobytie,* July 6, 1993.

30. This was erected April 26, 2001, in the central core of the city.

31. This was erected May 15, 2003, in the central core of the city.

32. This was erected December 13, 2002, on the city's outskirts.

33. This was erected July 28, 2000, on the city's outskirts.

34. This was one of the first public trials doctored by the Soviet secret police—the NKVD—that ushered in an epoch of Great Terror. It took place in Kharkiv in 1929.

35. K. Kevorkian, *Pervaya Stolitca: Rasskazy o gorode, publitcystika, otcherki* (The First Capital: Tales about the city, pamphlets, essays) (Kharkiv: Folio, 2002).

36. Recently, in his commentary on some real or imagined territorial claims of a small country that is a neighbor to Russia, Vladimir Putin, the then–Russian president, used a quotation from this novel.

37. Ryabchuk Mykola, "Shcherbitski Forever; Part 1: Marking of Political Space," *Krytyka* 5 (2003).

38. Vladimir Kaganskii, "Sovetskoe prostranstvo: Nashe nasledstvo" (Soviet space is our heritage), *Russkii zhurnal,* http://www.russ.ru/culture/20040820_kag.html.

39. R. Serbyn, "Velyka vitchyzniana vijna: Soviets'kyj mit v ukrains'kykh shatakh" (The Great Patriotic War: The Soviet myth in Ukrainian clothes), *Suchasnist'* 6 (2001): 63–88.

40. Miroshnichenko, "Pereimenovany gorodskie ulitcy."

41. B. V. Dubin, "'Krovavaja voina' i 'velikaja pobeda'" ("Bloody war" and the "great victory"), *Otehestvennye zapiski* 5 (2004).

42. See Terry Martin, *The Affirmative Action Empire: Nations and Nationalism in the Soviet Union, 1923–1939* (Ithaca, N.Y.: Cornell University Press, 2001), 432–59.

43. Mikhail Krasikov, "Slovo nie vorobey," *Vremia,* August 1, 2002.

44. T. Zhurzhenko, "Cross-Border Cooperation and the Transformation of Regional Identities in the Ukrainian-Russian Borderlands: Towards a Euroregion, 'Slobozhanshchyna'? Part 1," *Nationalities Papers,* no.1 (2004): 207–32; no. 2 (2004): 497–51; P. W. Rodgers, "Contestation and Negotiation: Regionalism and the Politics of School Textbooks in Ukraine's Eastern Borderlands," *Nations and Nationalism* 12, no. 4 (October 2006): 681–98; P. W. Rogers, "A Study of Identity Change in the Eastern Borderlands of Ukraine," DPhil thesis, Faculty of Social Sciences, University of Birmingham, 2005; Ray Taras, Olga Filipova, and Nelly Pobeda, "Ukraine's Transnationals, Far-Away Locals and Xenophobes: The Prospects for Europeanness," *Europe-Asia Studies* 56, no. 6 (September 2004): 835–36.

45. L. Bilaniuk, *Language Politics and Cultural Correction in Ukraine* (Ithaca, N.Y.: Cornell University Press, 2005), 175; G. Grinchenko, V. Kravchenko, O. Misiezdov, and O. Tytar, "Natcional'no-kul'turna identytchnist' meshkantcia "kontaktnoi zony" (National-cultural identity of "contact zones" residents), *Skhid-Zakhid* 8 (2006):161–84.

# 9

# L'viv in Search of Its Identity: Transformations of the City's Public Space

*Liliana Hentosh and Bohdan Tscherkes*

L'viv is a city that has been known throughout history under many variations of its name—L'viv, Lemberg, Leopolis, Lwow, Lvov, and L'viv again.[1] Each name reflects to a great extent the different periods of the city's turbulent history, and the different political/state entities that have governed it. From the very beginning in the thirteenth century, L'viv has represented cultural diversity. The city's different cultural and ethnic communities—such as Ruthenians, Poles, Germans, Jews, Armenians, and Hungarians—have played an important role in its life from the very beginning. These diverse cultures, religions, languages, and traditions were the building blocks of its image and identity.

In the fourteenth century, L'viv became incorporated into the Polish Crown. The development of the city's economic life as well as its government were subordinated to the premises of the Magdeburg Law.[2] During the fourteenth century, the city's planning scheme underwent radical transformations, which were heavily influenced by the Magdeburg Law's regulations (figure 9.1).[3]

Figure 9.1. Market (Rynok) Square. Photograph by Liliana Hentosh.

It could be said that L'viv's modern history started when it became part of the vast Hapsburg Empire and the center of its easternmost province. The Austrian administration introduced considerable changes in the city, among others in its appearance, by demolishing the medieval fortifications and building in their place a system of parks and avenues. These reconstructions were carried out in about 1825 before similar work was done in the Imperial capital, Vienna, itself.[4] For L'viv, the last decade of Hapsburg rule (1905–14) was a time of economic prosperity, when the city looked more like a cosmopolitan metropolis, always ready to absorb new trends in architecture and urban planning.[5]

## Changes in the City's Identity during Soviet Rule

The main groups of L'viv's population—Poles, Ukrainians, and Jews—went through crucial changes during Austrian rule. In the second half of the nineteenth century, they vigorously engaged in the nation-building process. In Polish, Ukrainian, and Jewish nation building, L'viv played a very important role. This contributed to the Ukrainian and Polish national mythologies: for the Poles, the city became a semper fidelis, the bastion of Polish culture; for the Ukrainians, it became a Ukrainian Piedmont. The rather liberal rules of the Hapsburg Dynasty provided these national communities with sufficiently good conditions for their development. The years before World War I were the last ones of relatively peaceful relations among the city's different national groups.[6] This peaceful, multiethnic L'viv ceased to exist after the collapse of the Austro-Hungarian Empire, and the multicultural city met its end as the result of World War II.

During World War II, L'viv did not suffer damage or destruction, and the city's architecture was left almost intact. But in that war, L'viv lost from 80 percent[7] to 90 percent[8] of its population, as a result of the Nazi Holocaust, Ukrainian-Polish ethnic violence, Soviet resettlements of Poles, and deportations of Ukrainians condemned for their resistance to the Soviet regime. New people came to the city, which in fifty years claimed it as their native city.[9] These newcomers could be divided into three main groups: (1) Ukrainians from the villages and towns of Western Ukraine (this group, which was the most numerous one, represented traditional Ukrainian culture); (2) Ukrainians from the villages and cities of Eastern Ukraine, which before the war had been the Ukrainian Soviet Socialist Republic (this group often demonstrated strong ties with Ukrainian folk culture and traditions, but at the same time was deeply Sovietized); and (3) Russians and non-Russians from the other republics of the Soviet Union (this group, more than the previous one, was the transmitter of the Soviet culture and way of life).[10]

As a result of these demographic transformations,[11] L'viv for the first time in its history became an almost entirely homogeneous city. Though still having an important Russian minority, during Soviet times it became a predominantly Ukrainian city, often called the "secret capital of Ukraine" or "the most Ukrainian city," that is, the most Ukrainian-speaking city in Ukraine, a distinction it retains to this day. The city's multicultural heritage, which could be easily traced in its architecture and in the fabric of its downtown area, is a challenge for its population; its past cultural diversity is prompting them to consider whether to accept and incorporate this heritage as a part of their own legacy or to reject it as something irrelevant and even alien. The question of how Ukrainian L'viv is responding to this multicultural quest at a time when the Ukrainian identity is in the process of making and remaking itself is an important one. Therefore, it could be very promising to analyze the cultural reorientation that took place in the city during the post-Soviet years in close relation with the process of building the modern Ukrainian national identity.

It could be said that during the last decade of Soviet rule, the Ukrainian identity in Western Ukraine developed as a strong denial of the Soviet, and at the same time of the Russian, idea.[12] The national identity of the Ukrainians of L'viv is their most important identity, according to sociological surveys,[13] and the Ukrainian identity of L'viv's Ukrainians is the most clearcut, most developed type of Ukrainian identity in contemporary Ukraine. In L'viv (and in Western Ukraine), Ukrainian nationalism has played a much more significant mobilizing role than in any other region of Ukraine.[14]

The almost five decades of Soviet rule changed L'viv's appearance. For the first time, the city was transformed into an industrial center, and many new enterprises, deeply integrated into Soviet industry, were built in it. The great number of workers required for this growing industry created a demand for cheap housing facilities. New houses built according to Soviet standards started to surround the prewar city. Soviet incursions into the historic city center were rather limited, and Soviet planners and architects were more interested in the theoretical planning of the major "Soviet" reconstruction of L'viv's old center than in its practical implementation. Thankfully, the great part of their plans remained on paper. One major plan was "to reorganize" in 1972 the area of the former Austrian military fortification from the mid-1850s.[15] Another one, even more pretentious and much more dangerous for the integrity of the historic center, was to erect a monument to Vladimir Lenin in the middle of the oldest part of the city center (dating from the fourteenth and fifteenth centuries) on the site of the artificial hill commemorating the Lublin Union (1569).[16]

Soviet dominance manifested itself in its most vivid form in the city's public spaces; "proper" Soviet street names, numerous monuments, commemoratory plaques, steles, Soviet symbols, and pieces of visual propaganda were on almost every square and corner (figure 9.2). At the same time, monuments closely connected to the city's "inappropriate" prewar history were neglected,[17] for example, many of L'viv's churches and the famous Lychakiv Cemetery. The policy of glasnost, introduced by Mikhail Gorbachev during the last Soviet years, opened the door to changes. The de-Sovietization of L'viv's public spaces started before Ukraine's Independence in 1991—in fact in 1988, when the first initiatives of the youth organization called the Lion Society (Tovarystvo Leva) were undertaken. These initiatives at first looked quite politically "innocent," but they actually had a very powerful anti-Soviet meaning. Probably the most important action was to take care of Lychakiv Cemetery; they decided to clean and to restore some of the monuments there, including the monument to the Pol-

Figure 9.2. An example of Soviet visual propaganda from the 1980s. Photograph from the personal archive of Bohdan Tscherkes.

ish freedom fighters who died in 1918–20 and whose Pantheon was destroyed by the Soviet authorities.

The next step in de-Sovietization was introduced by a decision of the Society of the Ukrainian Language, which was formed as an independent civic initiative in L'viv in 1988. This organization successfully put pressure on the City Council to change the Russian-language signs in L'viv (the Russification of the city had come hand in hand with Sovietization). The first one to be changed was a big neon sign reading "Lvov" above the city's main bus terminal.[18] The Ukrainian national blue-and-yellow flag, which was banned during Soviet times as a symbol of "reactionary bourgeois nationalism," appeared publicly for the first time in Ukraine during an April 1989 meeting to commemorate the third anniversary of the Chernobyl disaster. One scholar who paid special attention to the events in L'viv in 1987–90 very appropriately called these events a "Central European Renaissance." All these activities focused on a critical reassessment of the Soviet Communist reality, on building the first public organizations beyond state or party control, on reviving local Ukrainian culture and tradition, and on taking care of the monuments from the pre-Soviet, non-Ukrainian past. At the same time, they had a hidden agenda: to rediscover the place of L'viv in Central Europe.

## A Radical Approach to the City's Soviet Legacy

L'viv's very important contribution to the dismantling of the Soviet Union and its energetic support for the idea of Ukrainian independence made it an example of how to deal radically with the visible marks of the Soviet past. The most symbolic act of breaking with that past was the unprecedented decision of the first freely and democratically elected City Council to tear down the monument to Lenin. The act of erecting this monument, as well as its demolition, both had important meanings. At first it was planned to erect the monument to Lenin at the top of the High Castle,[19] but it was ultimately built in 1952 in front of the city's landmark Opera House. Before World War II, a few steps from that spot, a monument to the Polish king Jan III Sobieski had been situated (this monument was transferred to Poland—to Gdańsk—in 1950). The glamorous, eclectic Opera House from the turn of the twentieth century represented quite a different past of L'viv from the one represented by the Lenin statue in front of it. The famous Soviet sculptor Sergei Merkulov from Moscow designed the Lenin monument for L'viv. By offering a modestly scaled bust of Lenin, the sculptor was apparently trying to avoid a conflict with the surrounding architectural environment.[20] In September 1990, the deputies of the City Council were the first in the Ukrainian Socialist Republic and in the whole USSR to dismantle a monument to Lenin. Thousands of the city's inhabitants waited at the City Council Building and around the monument for that decision as well as indispensable for the demolition equipment. The figure of Lenin was torn down that very day in the presence of these thousands of people (figure 9.3). In a few months, the plaza in front of the Opera House was rebuilt, and it now serves as the site for the city's Christmas tree. During the events of the "Orange Revolution," it became a place for demonstrations.[21]

The next to go were the monuments to Yaroslav Halan, the Communist writer and anti-Catholic pamphleteer, and to Nikolai Kuznetsov, the war hero

Figure 9.3. The last minutes of the monument to Lenin before it was torn down, September 14, 1990. Photograph from the personal archive of Bohdan Tscherkes.

and officer of the NKVD (the Soviet secret police).[22] The life story of these two figures, immortalized by the Soviet authorities in bronze, aroused deeply negative attitudes among local Ukrainians. Both monuments had little artistic value. Within a short time, small parks were built where the big, full-figured monuments had stood. With Ukrainian Independence, the process of dismantling the Soviet-era monuments, plaques, and propaganda billboards accelerated. Today, L'viv has few monuments left from Soviet times, and those that remain memorialize World War II rather than Soviet nation building. The most important one is a memorial complex and cemetery for the Soviet soldiers who lost their lives in L'viv during World War II, called the Hill of Glory (Holm Slavy). It was designed by the architect Ivan Persikov and completed in 1952.[23] To build this complex and the adjoining plaza, the graves of thousands of Austrian soldiers were destroyed. Today the complex has lost its former meaning as a place for the solemn celebration of Victory Day (May 9), Soviet Army Day (February 23), the Day of the Liberation of L'viv (July 27), and Komsomol and pioneer special events. Over the years of Ukrainian Independence, this monumental complex has been neglected and is slowly decaying. Some other monuments and museums to the Soviet Army, such as the complex and the museum to the Carpathian military district, have been dismantled. One that survived, partly because it was considered too complicated to dismantle, is a monument to the Soviet Army, the "Monument of Glory" (built in 1970) on Stryiska Street, outside the bounds of the historic center.

There are several monuments to famous personalities of Ukrainian culture and literature from pre-Soviet times—such as the monument to Ivan Franko (opened in 1964; sculptors, V. Borysenko, D. Krvavytch, E. Mysko, and V. Odrehivskyi)—which were built during Soviet times. The Franko monument did not lose its meaning for the local population. Situated on a plaza opposite the city's university, the monument was a place of protest meetings in the late 1980s, and it became a gathering place for almost daily student demonstrations during the Orange Revolution.

## Attempts to Assert the City's Ukrainian Past and Ukrainian Present

In 1990, the freely elected city deputies started the process of changing the names of city's streets and squares.[24] For that purpose, a special group of experts (mainly professional historians) was formed as the Committee on Culture and National Revival. This group researched, consulted, and offered possible new names for the consideration of the deputies.[25] The process of renaming started in 1990, and the expert group worked up to 1997, but the major part of renaming was done at the beginning of 1990s. The first to be renamed were those streets closely related to Communism or the Communist Party—streets named after Lenin, Marx, Engels, and Dzerzhynsky. In some cases, the renaming was done in a way to manifest an opposite views or ideology. For example, the name of Friedrich Engels Street was changed to Evhen Konovalets, after the founder of the Organization of Ukrainian Nationalists (OUN), who had been murdered by the NKVD in 1938.

The swift and profound de-Sovietization in L'viv and in Western Ukraine could be seen as a process that laid the ground for European integration. The liberation from the Soviet past, especially from its visible marks, demonstrated the desire to break with the totalitarian past, to build a democratic society, and to live according to different ideas and values. In this sense, the de-Sovietization in L'viv of the late 1980s and early 1990s was an important component of the European orientation of the city, whose residents, according to many different surveys, are the most pro–European Union and pro-NATO citizens of Ukraine.

To create a Ukrainian image of the city, new names were often chosen from pre-Soviet Ukrainian history, or from the history of Galicia and Western Ukraine or L'viv. The names of Ukrainian national activists and of the leaders of the OUN and the Ukrainian Insurgent Army (known as the UPA), which fought the Soviets in the mid-1940s, were the most popular choices. Some of the new names stirred up controversy in the rest of Ukraine. One of L'viv's central streets was named after Stepan Bandera, a leader of the OUN, who is regarded with particular hostility in Eastern Ukraine.[26]

Often, the anti-Soviet approach went hand in hand with animosity toward Russia. Thus, the streets named after the famous Russian poets Alexander Pushkin and Mikhail Lermontov were renamed, the former Lermontov Street getting the name of Dzhokhar Dudaev, the founder and leader of the Chechen separatist movement.[27] This particular renaming caused an official Russian protest, and Russian and East Ukrainian media started to portray L'viv as an aggressively anti-Russian city. The city's deputies tried to balance their decisions; some Russian names survived on the city map, usually those of people who were politically neutral (e.g., the scientist Ivan Pavlov) or who were known for their sympathies toward Ukraine or Galicia (the writer Vladimir Korolenko). Among the thirty-three Russian names given to the city's streets or left unchanged, only one was taken from post-1917 Soviet Russian history.[28]

Certain streets had their prewar names returned, generally those whose names had a direct connection to the city's toponymy. For example, the former Lenin Street got back its old name of Lychakivska, which derives from the name of the former L'viv outskirts, Lychakiv. A few streets could be reminiscent of the powerful Polish cultural presence in the city before World War II. Besides the streets named after Nikolai Kopernik (Copernicus), Tadeusz Kosciuszko, and Adam Mickiewicz, there is the street of Alexander Fredro. The Ukrainian authorities returned the prewar name, partly because the Polish playwright Fredro was a grandfather to the Greek-Catholic metropolitan Andrei Sheptytskyi, to whom the Ukrainians of L'viv pay special respect. Some well known from city folklore names did not make a comeback. The best example is Akademichna Street (now Shevchenko Avenue); this name is known and used even by the people of younger generation but will probably soon be lost.

As a result of the activity of the city's deputies, each name on the city map was scrutinized, and in a very short time the great majority of the city's streets and squares were renamed. The main efforts were put into the de-Sovietization and Ukrainization of the city's topography. Here, the desire to stress the Ukrainian history of the city became obvious.[29] In many cases, the city's multicultural past was not chosen as point of reflection, and even L'viv's own history was to some extent neglected in favor of more attractive historical topics, for example, Kievan Rus' and Cossackdom. One can find streets named after Prince Volodymyr and Princess Olga of Kyiv, and after the Cossack leader M. Kryvonis, whose troops besieged L'viv and showed no mercy toward the city and its inhabitants. A more reflective and balanced approach obviously would require more time and effort. Nevertheless, some steps have been taken to reflect the city's multicultural history; together with Russian and Polish names, three Jewish names are on the city map.

The first years of Ukrainian Independence witnessed a renaissance of Ukrainian culture, which had been suppressed during the decades of Soviet power. The freedom to develop native culture gave a tremendous boost to many from the artistic milieu. The Ukrainians of L'viv, who considered themselves the most nationally orientated citizens of Ukraine, expected affirmative action on the state level to promote the Ukrainian language and culture. But Ukrainian presidents Leonid Kravchuk and especially Leonid Kuchma, along with their governments, were reluctant to support such special programs. Only some steps were made in education; for example, the number of schools with Ukrainian as the language of instruction increased significantly. In L'viv, the local and regional authorities proposed and conducted their own programs to support Ukrainian culture and education.

The local authorities as well as the Ukrainian inhabitants of L'viv regarded a very important part of such efforts to be the transformation of the city's public spaces. For many years, the Ukrainians in L'viv had been forbidden to erect a monument to the Ukrainian poet Taras Shevchenko. The Soviet authorities had feared that the unveiling of such a monument would arouse nationalist feelings. The decision to construct a monument to Shevchenko was adopted in 1987, and the first regional competition took place in 1988; forty groups of authors offered their projects to the committee, but none was chosen. The next republican (all-Ukrainian) competition took place in 1989, which raised even more active public discussion, but the committee at first did not support any of the projects. At this point, however, to speed up the building of the monument, the local authorities asked the committee to make a choice. Under these circumstances, the committee recommended the project of two young L'viv sculptors, V. Suhorskyi and A. Suhorskyi. Their project consisted of two parts: the figure of the poet himself, and a 12-meter-high stele called the "Wave of National Revival" rising up behind him and to his right (figure 9.4).

The building of the monument to Shevchenko was financially supported by the Ukrainian diaspora, and the project was constructed not in L'viv but in Buenos Aires, before being installed in L'viv.[30] The site in L'viv was chosen very successfully: in the beautiful plaza between the Opera House and the inspiring monument to the Polish poet Adam Mickiewicz erected in 1905. The first part of the monument, the figure of the poet, was unveiled on the first anniversary of Independence Day in 1992 and was a remarkable event; thousands attended. The next part, the "Wave of National Revival," was erected in 1995 and became a dominant point in the city's landscape. From the viewer's perspective, this 12-meter-high stele stands to the left of Shevchenko's monument and is decorated by relief figures of heroes from his poetry; dominant among them are Cossacks, because the Cossack epics form a very important part of Shevchenko's literary heritage (see figure 9.4). The accentuation of the Cossack myth stressed the pan-Ukrainian idea and made it present in the center of Western Ukraine. The plaza constructed

Figure 9.4. The monument to Taras Shevchenko on Freedom Avenue, built in 1992–95. Sculptors: V. Suhorskyi and A. Suhorskyi. Photograph by Liliana Hentosh.

around the monument to Shevchenko gave the city a new place for meetings, celebrations, and even concerts.

Among the several monuments in the central part of L'viv constructed during the years of Independence, the monument to Myhailo Hrushevskyi serves a quite obvious nation-building and state-building function. This monument was constructed in alignment with the monument to Shevchenko at the end of the Shevchenko Avenue, on a small plaza, which before the war was decorated by a monument to Alexander Fredro. The Shevchenko monument was unveiled in 1994 during the first presidential election campaign in independent Ukraine (figure 9.5). Its designers (sculptors, D. Krvavych, M. Posikira, and L. Yaremchuk; architect, V. Kamenshchyk) opted for very traditional approach by creating a sitting figure of Hrushevskyi, whose presence on Shevchenko Avenue is very significant, because he was the author of the monumental *History of Ukraine Rus'*, which delineated the continuity of Ukrainian history from ancient to modern times as well as its separate development from Russia's, and who was also the first president of the independent Ukrainian People's Republic (1917–18).

Figure 9.5. The monument to Myhailo Hrushevskyi, built in 1994. Sculptors: D. Krvavych, M. Posikira, and L. Yaremchuk. Architect: V. Kamenshchyk. Photograph by Liliana Hentosh.

Some monuments are more closely connected to the prewar history of L'viv and Galicia. One of these is a monument to Markian Shashkevych, unveiled in 1990 (sculptors, D. Krvavych and M. Posikira). The very romantic figure of young Shashkevych remind the viewer of his achievements as a leading figure of the Ukrainian Revival of the middle of the nineteenth century; his activity was very much influenced by and was typical for nineteenth-century Central European national awakening. His monument, therefore, asserts the idea of L'viv's belonging to the Central European cultural space.

A monument closely connected to the cultural, social, and political emancipation of the Galician Ukrainians is that to Prosvita (Enlightenment), the organization founded in 1868 by the Ukrainian elite for the education and emancipation of the Ukrainian peasantry in Galicia. This monument, again, is very traditional in form and approach (sculptor, V. Yarych). It was unveiled in 1993 to commemorate the one-hundred-twenty-fifth anniversary of Prosvita—an important remembrance in stressing local history and traditions, particularly those of independent civic institutions, now deemed important for a post-Soviet city trying to rebuild its civil society.

Among the other monuments unveiled over the years of Independence, two are dedicated to the severe losses of the city's inhabitants in and immediately after World War II. The first monument, to the victims of Communist repression unveiled in 1997 (sculptors, P. Shtaer and R. Syvenkyi), memorializes the victims of different nationalities killed by the Soviet regime in L'viv. This monument tries to convey the tragedy of innocent victims, killed without mercy in an NKVD prison housed in the building next door to the monument. The other monument commemorates the victims of the Holocaust in L'viv, and it was built in proximity to what was L'viv's Jewish Ghetto. This monument became an important and powerful reminder of the city's lost multicultural past, which was once home to a large Jewish community.[31]

Among the other monuments constructed in L'viv, one worth mentioning was the monument to the Ukrainian painter Ivan Trush. In this case, the monument itself attracts attention. Without visually powerful means or an important historical background, it very simply builds a bridge between the city's past and present inhabitants. Trush appears as a gentlemen in an old-fashioned hat and bow-tie and with an umbrella as walking stick, standing on the ground close to the park's entrance. It is a nice illustration of the way of life in a past epoch (sculptor, S. Oleshko, 1996).

The favorite way for the local authorities and local artists to assert the Ukrainian cultural dominance in L'viv has to install commemorative plaques. Some very important buildings have more than one plaque (e.g., the main building of L'viv National University). Some of these plaques have artistic value and do not provoke dissonance with the surrounding architecture. Others, rather big and decorated with bas-reliefs and almost-life-size figures, look quite out of place. Such plaques have been put up commemorating a number of Ukrainian politicians, artists, church leaders, writers, poets, scientists, athletes, heroes of the OUN, and so on—often without a proper assessment of their appropriateness and artistic value.

## Religious Revival and Multicultural History

During the years of Ukrainian Independence, L'viv has regained buildings, places, and monuments of religious devotion that had been ruined, neglected, or closed to the public in Soviet times. This process has taken time, effort, and money, because all these churches, chapels, and sacral monuments, which were numerous in prewar L'viv, needed serious renovation. In some cases, losses could not be recovered. Prewar L'viv was an administrative center for three church hierarchies under the pope that were associated with different nationalities: the Roman Catholic archbishop and metropolitan (Polish), the Greek Catholic archbishop and metropolitan (Ukrainian), and the Armenian Catholic archbishop and metropolitan (Armenian). The role and authority of these Catholic churches in the life of the city's different national communities were of real importance.[32]

The years of Ukrainian Independence became a time of religious revival in the city. Even during Soviet times, L'viv itself and Western Ukraine were known as one of the most religious regions of the Soviet Union. Today the reclaimed religious experience for many has become a search for spirituality or a return to national traditions that were banned in Soviet times. The churches, especially the Greek Catholic Church, also experienced severe repression and took part in the anti-Soviet resistance. In independent Ukrainian L'viv, the Greek Catholic Church started to play the dominant role,[33] which before the war had belonged to the Roman Catholic Church. Some traditions were common to all three above-mentioned churches. One of these is the cult of the Virgin Mary, regarded as the patroness of the city. Prewar L'viv had more than a dozen churches dedicated to the Virgin Mary, among them two cathedrals—one Roman Catholic and one Armenian Catholic. One important public place for centuries dedicated to the Virgin Mary's cult was a small plaza in the center of the city adorned by a statue of the Virgin. The Soviet authorities took the statue away, and in 1954 in its place erected a fountain designed by the architect A. Konsulov. In 1997, the plaza regained its prewar look—the statue of the Virgin Mary was returned (figure 9.6).

The plaza with this statue has become a very popular place of devotion, which often is used for public religious services. It is quite usual to see people there praying. Another well-known site of the Virgin Mary's veneration starting in the eighteenth century was recently rebuilt: a chapel on Lychakivska Street. A few years ago, the image of the Virgin Mary on the external wall of the Roman Catholic cathedral was restored. Numerous figures of the Virgin Mary were again put in the niches of old buildings, which had stood empty during Soviet times (e.g., on Drukarska Street). These places now are decorated with flowers and are cared for by the inhabitants, not by the clergy. The return of such places to their original function can be seen as the return of the former religious/Catholic identity of the city.

As to the churches, a very important issue should be addressed: that 90 percent of the churches have changed their formal affiliation. The majority of former churches of the Roman Catholic Church now belong to the

Figure 9.6. From left to right: A prewar statue of the Virgin Mary; sculptor: J. N. Hauttmann, 1859; from an old postcard. A fountain designed by A. Konsulov to replace the demolished statue of the Virgin Mary in 1954; from an old postcard. The reconstructed statue of the Virgin Mary returned to its prewar site in 1997. From the personal archive of Bohdan Tscherkes.

Ukrainian Greek Catholic Church or to one of the three Orthodox Church bodies in Ukraine. The Ukrainian Greek Catholic Church shares the Eastern/Byzantine/Greek Rite with the Orthodox churches. To adapt the church premises to the needs of the Eastern rite, several major changes have been made in all former Roman Catholic churches. An important requirement to conduct the Liturgy according to the Eastern Rite is to have a separate space in the altar part of the church separated by the "Lord's Gates," decorated by an array of icons. This meant some reconstruction and redecorating of the interior of many of L'viv's churches. Different objects of Ukrainian folk art, especially embroideries and lace, also decorated some churches. In this way, the baroque churches were given a "Ukrainian touch." It seems that for the majority of congregants, such Ukrainian decorations, usually done by older, pious women, are important for them in connecting with church buildings that formerly belonged to others.

## The Ukrainization of L'viv's Public Space

The powerful stream of changes during L'viv's Independence years have been aimed at transforming its public spaces to make them Ukrainian. "Ukrainization" was a natural response to the persecution of Ukrainian culture during Soviet times, and it reflects the demographic profile of the city: The Ukrainians are the most numerous group of city's population. In independent Ukraine, many of Ukrainian residents, as well as the local authorities and representatives of cultural and academic elites, started to carry on what Rogers Brubaker called a "compensatory project of using state power [in the case of L'viv and Western Ukraine, it is more correct to talk about the regional and city's authorities] to promote the core nation's specific ... interests."[34]

In such projects, however, very often the pan-Ukrainian idea won over local Galician distinctiveness. The Ukrainians in L'viv, while asserting the city's Ukrainian identity, opted for topics, issues, and ideas popular throughout Ukraine. A vivid example of this is the incorporation of Cossack heritage. In L'viv, the city the Cossacks besieged, several streets have been named after Cossack leaders, and monuments (e.g., one to Ivan Pidkova) and plaques (the plaque to the hetman Bohdan Hmelnytskyi on the wall of the Jesuit Collegium, where he studied) were unveiled. Such glorification could only be explained by a desire to build up the city's all-Ukrainian unity and Ukrainian identity.

Although it is possible to find and/or construct a common attitude toward the history of the seventeenth century, it is much harder to do the same with the history of the last century. In L'viv, the particularly Ukrainian twentieth-century experience of Western Ukraine has been privileged and reflected in the public space of L'viv; streets have been named after Ukrainian nationalists leaders, and a monument to Stepan Bandera was recently unveiled. Over the first years of "Ukrainization," much from the multicultural past has been forgotten; only a few streets retain the names of famous Poles or Jews. There has been no monument (except the monument to the Holocaust victims) or museum devoted to representatives of non-Ukrainian nationalities. The plaque honoring the well-known Jewish writer Sholem Aleichem, on the building where he lived, is one of the few reminders of the former Jewish presence in the city.

Conversely, the Ukrainization of L'viv's public space has not been a smooth, homogeneous process. Ukrainian identity itself is in the course of being reshaped. And the Ukrainians of L'viv could contribute their particular experiences—not only the experience of their strong ethnolinguistic distinctiveness but also the experience of living in a multicultural, multireligious milieu. "Ukrainization" is rather a tendency, which, it seems, has two main currents. These currents or trends do not exist in an absolutely pure form. The first one could be called the pan-Ukrainian, and the second could be seen as one focused on Western Ukrainian history and traditions.

The reconsideration of local history and traditions and their use in the transformation of the city's public space have opened a different perspective. The choices of topics, issues, and symbols common with other Central European and European nations have played an important role in stressing the European experience of Western Ukrainians in comparison with the rest of Ukraine. An example of this trend is the monument to the founder of the city of L'viv, the prince of Galicia and Volhynia, Danylo Halytskyi. This monument, which was unveiled in 2002 (sculptors, V. Yarych and Y. Churylyk), has a very traditional iconography: a knight on horseback, whose clothes and armor are in the Kievan Rus' tradition. But instead of the more historically accurate title "prince," the title "king" was put on the pedestal of the monument in reference to Halytskyi: "King Danylo" (figure 9.7). Danylo Halytskyi bore the title "king" only briefly, during a short-lived alliance with Rome. The choice of the title could demonstrate the desire to stress the European orientation of contemporary L'viv and even to reconsider the historical figure of Danylo Halytskyi as one interested in integrating the city into Western European civilization.[35]

Figure 9.7. A monument to King Danylo Halitskyi, built in 2002. Sculptors: V. Yarych and Y. Churylyk. Photograph by Liliana Hentosh.

## The Multicultural Heritage and Future of L'viv

During the past five or six years, the growing interest among the city's academia, writers, and artists in its multicultural past of the city has been manifested in conferences and roundtable discussions, exhibitions, articles, and journals. The considerable interest in the city's multicultural, multiethnic, and multiconfessional past can be seen in the activity of the independent cultural journal *Ï* (e.g., in its seminars and in an issue dedicated to the L'viv "Genius Loci: L'viv, Leopolis, Lwow, Lemberg"), which is sponsored by the artistic society Dzyga of the Institute of the City's Development. Several well-known modern Ukrainian writers and poets have reflected on these issues, among them Yuri Andruhovych.[36] The popular local newspaper *Postup* (Progress) has published a number of articles dealing in different ways with multiculturalism, with the European orientation of L'viv in both the past and present, and especially with its regional identity. In these discussions, conferences, newspaper articles, and books, one important question has been touched upon: the local and regional identity, of which important features are considered to be the multicultural experience and pro-European orientation of Western Ukrainians and Galicians.

Such interest in the multicultural past has focused, not surprisingly, on Hapsburg times. L'viv's times of economic and cultural prosperity, as well as the relatively peaceful interethnic relations within the Austro-Hungarian Empire, are now considered a Golden Age. Books and articles dealing with the history of the Hapsburg Empire have become popular among the inhabitants of L'viv. The Hapsburg era has become an inspiration for interior designers; several coffee shops and restaurants have been decorated in imitation of the Viennese fin de siècle. A few of them, such as Amadeus and Blue Bottle, even have art with the likeness of Emperor Francis Joseph and various Imperial symbols. Some even serve dishes associated with the different provinces of the Hapsburg Empire. The owners of the well-known restaurant and coffee shop Café Vienna not only decorated its walls with old images of L'viv but also decided to put at the entrance a statue of Jaroslav Hasek's literary hero—the Good Soldier Schweik. The figure of Schweik resting on a chair has become a popular tourist attraction (figure 9.8).

A few years ago, a group of young intellectuals and artists was considering building a monument to Emperor Francis Joseph.[37] Such an idea would illustrate not only the nostalgia or simple idealization of the past but also the assessment of the Hapsburg heritage as crucial for the European

Figure 9.8. A monument to Yaroslav Hasek's literary hero, the Good Soldier Schweik, erected in 2000. Sculptor: P. Shtaer. Photograph by Liliana Hentosh.

orientation of L'viv. According to surveys, the great majority of L'viv's inhabitants favor European integration for Ukraine. Usually, these ideas are articulated and supported by the younger generation. The same milieu has supported a more balanced approach to the complicated issue of Ukrainian-Polish relations, such as the opening of the Polish Pantheon at Lychakiv Cemetery.[38] When young people from the Lion Society started to clean and renovate the Pantheon, they had no idea that this particular cemetery would soon became a major issue in Polish-Ukrainian relations. Radical nationalist organizations from both sides stirred up controversy over the text of the memorial plaque on the front of the Pantheon. But in any case, the Pantheon to Polish soldiers was rebuilt and reopened in 2005, and it is situated in close proximity to a memorial to the Ukrainian heroes who died in the struggle for independence (figure 9.9). Such an approach to the complicated Ukrainian-Polish past could be an example of recognizing the city's past multicultural diversity as a part of its legacy that is important for its people today.

L'viv's multicultural heritage has become an important element in attempts to construct a regional Galician identity,[39] and it is often used to stress the uniqueness of L'viv and its region in Ukraine. This trend has been developing in contemporary L'viv and Galicia during the past few years. The representatives of this trend—mainly artists, scholars, and writers—are often successful in dealing with the city's non-Ukrainian past in their writing and art. Yet its presence in the city's public space is not yet very substantial. Several conferences and seminars in L'viv, both Ukrainian and international, have been dedicated to regionalism. Interest in regionalism could be seen as common trend in Western European countries, where discussions of such problems as well as practical steps that stipulate the development of regional peculiarities have become popular with the development of the European Union.

UNESCO recognized the historic center of L'viv in 1998 by placing it on the World Heritage List. But UNESCO's acclamation did not secure the substantial help needed to preserve the city's architectural monuments. UNESCO's representatives could not persuade local leaders to pay more attention to the dilapidated buildings and churches, demolished statues, falling-apart elements of Baroque decoration, and neglected centuries-old parks. Today, some of the city's leaders in academia, nongovernmental organizations, and business are trying to raise public awareness and to initiate small independent preservation projects.[40]

Quite recently, the newly elected Ukrainian president, Viktor Yushchenko, declared European integration to be a strategic objective of Ukrainian for-

Figure 9.9. The Pantheon to Polish soldiers, reopened in 2005. Photograph by Liliana Hentosh.

eign policy. At the local level in L'viv, this new course of the Ukrainian government toward closer ties with Europe are understood in deferent ways by L'viv's leaders. Some, like L'viv's mayor, Lubomyr Buniak, are thinking of new commercial projects (some of them are even dangerous for the integrity of the city's historic center) to attract tourists and boost local businesses as a way to build L'viv's European future.[41] Others, including many representatives of academia and nongovernmental organizations, are pointing out the importance of preserving L'viv's architecture, which reflects its historical connections with European cultural developments. Therefore, the preservation of monuments to L'viv's multicultural past that commemorate the city's lost diversity could help build a more open, transnational society that is much more predisposed to integration processes.

In modern times, L'viv has been associated with Austrian and Polish, rather than Ukrainian, traditions and cultures. Over past fifteen years, the city has been experiencing serious changes in its identity. Its public spaces demonstrate this in obvious ways. The radical break with the Soviet past cleared traces of the Soviet era out of these public spaces, especially from the historic center. Today, L'viv's public spaces are becoming very Ukrainian in character; they are laden with symbols and myths, which are intended to legitimize the idea of Ukrainian independence. This "Ukrainization" of public spaces has not been a smooth and homogeneous process. Different points of reference have been used: (1) Ukrainian history and the pan-Ukrainian idea, and (2) the history of Western Ukraine and its traditions. The latter has accentuated regional differences and influenced the construction of local/L'vivite and regional/Galician identities among the city inhabitants.[42] The reassessment of the cultural diversity of L'viv's past is going on, and the idea that this former cultural diversity is important for the city's identity and for the identity of its current populace is gaining support. These tendencies are becoming apparent in changes made to the city's public space as well.

## Notes

1. Traditionally, it has been thought that the city was founded in 1256, when the city of L'viv for the first time was mentioned in the Galician-Volhynian Chronicle. The city was founded by the Volhynian-Galician prince Danylo and named after his son Lev (Leo). "Lev" is a Ruthenian/Ukrainian first name and means "lion." The name of the city—"L'viv" in Ruthenian/Ukrainian, "Leopolis" in Latin, "Lemberg" in German, "Lwów" in Polish, "Lvov" in Russian—could be translated as "City of the Lion." A lion is on the city's coat of arms and is widely used as a decorative element throughout its downtown.

2. Officially, the Magdeburg Law was introduced or, as some historians would say, reintroduced in 1356 by the Polish king Casimir III.

3. Ihor Zhuk, "The Architecture of Lviv from the Thirteenth to the Twentieth Centuries," in *Lviv: A City in the Crosscurrents of Culture,* Harvard Ukrainian Studies 24, Special Issue, ed. John Czaplicka (Cambridge, Mass.: Harvard University Press, 2002), 99.

4. "'Kraków i Lwów: Pomiędzy prowincja, a metropolią,' Panel Discussion on November 15, 2002," in *Kraków i Lwów w cywilizacji europejskiej: Materiały międzynarodowej konferencji zorganizowanej w dniach 15–16 listopada 2002,* ed. Jacek Purchla (Krakow: Antykwa, 2003), 184.

5. Jacek Purhla, "Kraków i Lwów: Zmienność relacji w XIX I XX wieku," in *Kraków i Lwów w cywilizacji europejskiej,* ed. Purchla, 87.

6. Philipp Ther, "War versus Peace: Interethnic Relations in Lviv during the First Half of the Twentieth Century," in *Lviv,* ed. Czaplicka, 251–84.

7. Jaroslaw Hrycak, "Lwów w Europie środka," in *Kraków i Lwów w cywilizacji europejskiej,* ed. Purchla, 28.

8. Bohdan Tscherkes, "Stalinist Visions for the Urban Transformation of Lviv, 1939–1955," in *Lviv,* ed. Czaplicka, 205–22.

9. A total of 64 percent of today's city population were born in L'viv, but only 33 percent are second-generation inhabitants. See O. Drul', "Asymiliatsiini ta akul'turatsiini protsesy u L'vovi," *Nezalezhnyi kulturolohichnyi chasopys "I"* 23 (2001): 182–83.

10. Aleksandra Matyukhina, *W sovietckim Lwowie: Życie codzienne miasta w latach 1944–1990* (Krakow: Wydawnictwo Uniwersytetu Jagiellońskiego, 2000), 13–22.

11. A detailed analysis of the demographic transformations was done by Victor Susak, "The Ethnic and National Changes in the Composition of L'viv's Population, 1944–2000," MA thesis, L'viv National University, 2001.

12. The Ukrainian identity in Galicia / Western Ukraine from the middle of the nineteenth century up to World War II had been forming in opposition, first of all, to the Polish idea. During Soviet times, the situation changed; the Russians became the most important "others."

13. In 1994, the Institute for Historical Research at L'viv National University started a project titled "Lviv—Donetsk" to study the development of group identities in modern Ukraine. A survey in L'viv showed that the Ukrainian identity is regarded as the most important and the most popular one—73 to 74 percent of respondents chose the Ukrainian identity as their number one preferred identity from a list of different group identities. See Yaroslav Hrytsak, "National Identities in Post-Soviet Ukraine: The Case of Lviv and Donetsk," in *Cultures and Nations of Central and Eastern Europe: Essays in Honor of Roman Szporluk*, ed. Z. Gitelman, L. Hajda, J.-P. Himka, and R. Solchanyk (Cambridge, Mass.: Harvard University Press, 1999), 267.

14. A very important collection of essays on modern Ukrainian nationalism, nation building, and national identity by Yaroslav Hrytsak was published recently: Yaroslav Hrytsak, *Strasti za natsionalizmom: Istorychni eseii* (Kyiv: Krytyka, 2004), 145, 196.

15. Ihor Okonchenko and Olha Okonchenko, "L'vivs'ka tsytadel': L'viv Пьвів Leopolis Lwow Lemberg—Genius Loci," *Nezalezhnyi kulturolohichnyi chasopys "Ï"* 28 ( 2004): 272–79.

16. Tscherkes, "Stalinist Visions," 212–13.

17. A "proper," ideologically correct, history of the city was produced by a group of Soviet historians in 1984; the book was even formally edited by the secretary of the city's Communist Party Committee, V. Sekretariuk. See V. Sekretariuk, ed., *Istoriia L'vova* (Kyiv: Naukova dumka, 1984).

18. Padraic Kenney, "Lviv's Central European Renaissance," in *Lviv*, ed. Czaplicka, 303–12.

19. This is the highest of the hills surrounding the city and the former site of a medieval Galician fortress.

20. Tscherkes, "Stalinist Visions," 214.

21. The mass protests and demonstrations against the falsified elections of November 21, 2004, and in support of democracy and the Ukrainian opposition leader Viktor Yushchenko, got the name "Orange Revolution" because of the orange color of the opposition's banners, symbols, and flags.

22. The monument to Kuznetsov actually was taken down and then presented to his native town of Kuznetsov in the Sverdlovskii region of Russia in 1993.

23. On I. Persikov and the Hill of Glory, see Tscherkes, "Stalinist Visions," 213.

24. A very detailed study of the process of renaming L'viv's streets and squares has been presented by Yaroslav Hrytsak and Victor Susak, "Constructing a National City: The Case of L'viv," in *Composing Urban History and the Constitution of Civic Identities*, ed. John J. Czaplicka and Blair A. Ruble (Washington and Baltimore: Woodrow Wilson Center Press and Johns Hopkins University Press, 2003), 140–64.

25. For more details on the experts' previous experience, the work of the group, and proposals that were offered to the deputies, as well as the acceptance or rejection of new

names in some particular cases, see Hrytsak and Susak, "Constructing a National City," 151–55.

26. On the OUN and UPA, see Philipp Ther, "War versus Peace: Interethnic Relations in Lviv during the First Half of the Twentieth Century," *Harvard Ukrainian Studies* 24, nos. 1–4 (2000). Also see Yaroslav Hrytsak, *Strasti za natsionalizmom: Istorychni eseii* (Kyiv: Krytyka, 2004), 131.

27. Hrytsak and Susak, "Constructing a National City," stated that apparently the renaming of Lermontov and Pushkin streets was done without the experts' consent. The decision was made by the City Council.

28. One street was named after Andrei Sakharov immediately after his death.

29. The majority of names refer to modern Ukrainian history of the nineteenth and twentieth centuries. The premodern national history is represented by the old Rus' (14 streets), and Cossacks (32 streets). The Ukrainian national Revival of the nineteenth century is reflected in the names of streets and plaza given after 58 Galicianers and 67 non-Galicianers. The largest group of names (202) refers to twentieth-century nation building and Ukrainian nationalism. Hrytsak and Susak, "Constructing a National City," 154.

30. Vasyl' Ivanytskyi, an activist in the Ukrainian diaspora in Argentina and Canada, chaired the fund-raising committee. He was head of a similar fundraising committee while the monument to Taras Shevchenko was being built in Buenos Aires. He got special credentials from L'viv's mayor, Vasyl' Shpitser, to financially manage the construction of the monument. Mayor Shpitser and Ivanytskyi both acted to speed up the building of the monument.

31. The Jewish community of L'viv perished in 1942–43, and now only their public buildings (e.g., the Jewish hospital and synagogue) and a small number of streets (e.g., one named after the famous Jewish philanthropist Jakob Rappoport) are reminiscent of their important role in the city's life.

32. Liliana Hentosh, "Rites and Religions: Pages from the History of Inter-denominational and Inter-Ethnic Relations in Twentieth-Century Lviv," in *Lviv,* ed. Czaplicka, 171–204.

33. The Greek Catholic Church came into being in 1596 as a synthesis of Eastern and Western Christianity. At the turn of the twentieth century, this Church went through a process of Ukrainization and was dissolved in 1946 and persecuted by the Soviet authorities as an outpost of Ukrainian nationalism. Now this Church uses the official name the Ukrainian Greek Catholic Church or the Ukrainian Catholic Church.

34. Rogers Brubaker, *Nationalism Reframed: Nationhood and the National Question in the New Europe* (Cambridge: Cambridge University Press, 1996), 104. In the case of Ukraine, this is true only for the western part of the country.

35. The construction of the monument to Danylo Halytskyi stimulated discussions on his historical role. In 2003, the popular newspaper *Postup* (Progress) published chapters from *The History of the Kingdom of Galicia from Ancient Times up to 1264*. In 2004, this book was published under the same title. The author of this book was trying to present his interpretation of the first centuries of the history of Galicia. He made a special effort to stress the Western orientation of Galicia, through ties with the Hungarian dynasty and the Catholic Church. The author was trying to depict the Galician aristocracy as noble knights fighting against the tyranny coming from the East, from Kyiv and Volhynia. Prince Danylo was from the Kievan dynasty and from Volhynia, which was his inherited principality. In the book, he was depicted as a cruel usurper of the Galician throne and his alliance with Pope Innocent IV is described as a short-term political strat-

egy. The author of the book decided to stay anonymous and to use the name of the literary hero in the novel *Perversions* by Yuri Andruhovych. The book has artistic value; it is illustrated with woodcuts by two well-known L'viv painters, Volodymyr Kostyrko and Evhen Ravskyi. The woodcuts from the book were presented at an exhibition at the artistic society Dzyga. This book became a manifestation of the group of intellectual and artists who are supporting the idea of Galician identity. Volodymyr Kostyrko, a very talented painter from the younger generation, is considered the author of the book.

36. George G. Grabowicz, "Mythologizing Lviv/Lwów: Echoes of Presence and Absence," in *Lviv,* ed. Czaplicka, 313–42. Hryhorii Hrabovych, *Tesksty ta masky* (Kyiv: Krytyka, 2005), 155–81.

37. In 2000, a group of young intellectuals and artists gathered to discuss the project of a monument to the emperor at the artistic society Dzyga. A few days later, the city's mayor got the call from highest authorities in Kyiv, severely criticizing the idea as separatist. The project never materialized.

38. The Pantheon at Lychakiv Cemetery was built to bury and honor Poles who died in defense of Polish L'viv in 1918–20. In 1920, the Polish troops struggled with the Bolsheviks. The problem is that those Poles who died in 1918 fought against Ukrainians over L'viv. The prewar Pantheon was constructed to stress the Polish victory over Ukrainians. Soviet authorities destroyed the Pantheon. The Pantheon was successfully rebuilt from 1993 to 2002. But the Polish side insisted on the absolutely accurate rebuilding of the Pantheon, including the text of the plaque, which L'viv's City Council and some Ukrainian organizations considered an indignity. The text praised the heroic defenders of L'viv, who gave their lives for Poland's greatness. The Pantheon was ready in 2003, but the opening ceremony was postponed mainly because of the disputed text. After several rounds of talks in Warsaw, Kyiv, and L'viv, a compromise was recently reached. The City Council of L'viv adopted the final version of the Pantheon's design and the text on the commemorative plaque. The Pantheon was solemnly opened on June 24, 2005; both the Ukrainian and Polish presidents took part in the ceremony.

39. For a discussion of the regional Galician identity, see Ola Hnatiuk, *Pożegnanie z imperium: Ukraińskie dyskusje o toż samości* (Lublin, 2003); Mykola Riabchuk, *Dvi Ukraiiny* (Kyiv: Krytyka, 2003); and Yaroslav Hrytsak, *Strasti za natsionalizmom* (Kyiv: Krytyka, 2004).

40. This included very vocal nongovernmental organizations, e.g., the Foundation for the Preservation of L'viv's Historical and Architectural Legacy and its founder and leader, Andrii Saliuk. But often the City Council and L'viv's mayor, Liubomyr Buniak, did not find common language with them.

41. One such commercial project is to rebuild, or rather to build, the High Castle, the old castle from thirteenth and fourteenth centuries, which was completely destroyed centuries ago. There is no credible historical evidence for how this castle actually looked, but this did not stop Mayor Buniak and the City Council from voting in favor of its construction. A group of the city's deputies, nongovernmental organization leaders, scholars from the Ukrainian Academy of Science, and Shevchenko's Scientific Society criticized the mayor's idea and started a public campaign against the decision of the mayor and City Council to rebuild the castle.

42. According to the survey, 69.6 percent of the inhabitants of L'viv have chosen "L'vivite" as their number two preferred identity from a list of ten different group identities. See Hrytsak, "National Identities in Post-Soviet Ukraine," 267.

# 10

# Łódź in the Postcommunist Era: In Search of a New Identity

*Joanna Michlic*

Since the fall of Communism, Łódź, the second-largest city of Poland, numbering 800,000 inhabitants, has embarked on a process of cultural reorientation. This process aims at reshaping it into a forward-looking twenty-first century European city. A close look at this process reveals that the turn toward a postcommunist, optimistic, and European future seems heavily dependent on a return to the city's precommunist past—to what might be called the archeological project of rediscovering the local pre-1939 multiethnic and multicultural heritage. This phenomenon has two aspects: a positive reinterpretation and reevaluation of the pre-1939 heritage; and an actual revitalization of this heritage in the present and the future. Currently, effort related to the former aspect is much more advanced than effort related to the latter. In fact, there is a clear discrepancy between the level of positive reevaluation and endorsement of this heritage and the scope of its revitalization. This is not to say that the revitalization of the city's multicultural heritage has not taken place but that the major projects still exist in the form of architectural plans rather than entirely completed works.

This chapter provides a short overview of Łódź's cultural reorientation, which first began in the 1990s. It discusses the origins of this process and the various forms it is taking, from cultural discourse and cultural events to the renovation of the city's historic buildings and the erection of its new monuments. It also briefly discusses major projects to revitalizate historical areas, such as the Old Market (Stary Rynek).

What are the guiding principles behind the city's cultural reorientation? How do its authorities and local cultural elites define the rediscovery of its pre-1939 multicultural heritage? What are the dimensions of this process? And to what extent can this project be realized in a city that underwent major, irreversible demographic transformations as a result of World War II and the Communist era? These are some of the questions this chapter seeks to address.

## Łódź between the Past and the Present

In 1423, the Polish king, Władysław Jagiełło (1386–1434), granted the village of Łódź the status of a town, yet Łódź does not have the famous urban history common to other major Polish cities such as Gdańsk (Danzig), Kraków, and Wrocław (Breslau).[1] Łódź was a small, underdeveloped rural town during the First Polish Republic, and it remained so under Prussian rule between the 1790s and 1815. In 1809, when a small Jewish community settled in the town, its total population was 430.[2] In 1810, the number of residents slightly increased, reaching 514.[3]

The lack of a well-developed urban history before 1800 has had an impact both on Łódź's image and self-image. A complex of "historical inferiority" seemed to haunt the city until very recently.[4] It was for a long time perceived as an undesirable tourist destination, unlikely to be visited by Polish or foreign tourists. It was, perhaps, the only major Polish city to be scarcely noted in tourist guides to Poland.[5] Advocates of the city's post-1989 cultural reorientation aim to put an end to "Łódź's complex of historical inferiority" and its reputation as an undesirable destination for tourists. Their goal is to evoke pride in its history among its local population. In fact, generating pride in its pre-1939 heritage constitutes one of the main underlying principles of its ongoing project of cultural reorientation.

However, this is a complex project that involves major reassessments of Łódź's late-nineteenth and early-twentieth-century history. Characteristically, this period is now seen to constitute "the Golden Age" of this "young city," which became popularly known as the "Polish Manchester" and "the Promised Land." However, this chapter in the city's history was not always perceived as its "Golden Age." The first negative assessment of the industrialized city emerged at the end of the nineteenth century. The negative imagery generated during that period would receive further elaboration during the Communist era of 1945 to 1989. The Communists viewed the urban-industrial bourgeoisie and their culture as antithetical to the working classes they championed; the city's multiethnic and multicultural past had no place in the Communist version of its history and would be largely forgotten. Therefore, the city's post-1989 cultural reorientation is based on a retelling of its history from a new perspective that affirms its bourgeois, capitalist, multiethnic, and multicultural heritage. It is useful to review that heritage and its previous reception in both national and Communist contexts before considering the contemporary pattern of reception.

## The "Rebirth" and the "Golden Age"

Between the 1870s and 1890s, Łódź experienced its "Golden Age," a direct outcome of the city's "second birth" or "rebirth" in the first half of the nineteenth century. In the aftermath of the Treaty of Vienna (1815), the city fell under the Russian Empire, and this date marks the beginning of the "second birth" or "rebirth" of what was then a small town. On August 18, 1820, Rajmund Rembieliński (1774–1841), chairman of the Commission for Mazovia Province, issued a decree endorsing the development of textile industries in the town and its modernization. Rembieliński, who was also a poet and a veteran of Tadeusz Kościuszko's Uprising of 1794, realized that to implement the decree of August 18, the town needed an influx of entrepreneurs and businessmen with expertise in, and experience of, the textile industry.

Rembieliński invited newcomers from German and Czech lands to settle in Łódź and offered them tax concessions and state support to sell their goods on the vast Russian market. His efforts were strengthened by the visit to Łódź in 1825 of Tsar Aleksander I, who gave personal encouragement for the town's industrial development. The first entrepreneurs arrived in Łódź from the late 1820s to the 1850s. Berlin-born Ludwig Geyer (1805–69) arrived from Neugersdorf in Saxony in 1826; Karol Scheibler (1820–88) arrived from Monschau in 1853; and Kalmanowicz Poznański, a garment merchant (1785–1856), arrived in 1834 from the small village of Kowale near Włocławek in the Kujawy region. Geyer and Scheibler were later to acquire the nicknames "the Kings of the Cotton and Linen Empires of Łódź." Recently Geyer, Scheibler, and Israel Kalmonowicz Poznański (1833–1900), the son of Kalmanowicz Poznański, were officially granted the status of the founding fathers of Łódź's textile industry.[6] Their recognition is one of the key manifestations of the positive reevaluation of the city's capitalist and bourgeois heritage.

Between the 1850s and 1890s, Łódź underwent a rapid process of modernization. In 1864, it received its first telegraph station. In 1869, the first gas lamps appeared on its streets. In 1866, it acquired a railway connection on the important route between Warsaw and Vienna; and in 1898, its first electric tram was driven down its streets.[7] This first tram to appear on Polish territories under Russian administration gave the city a reputation for being a pioneer of modernization. In the post-1989 period, the characteristics of modernity became one important aspect of the city's newly constructed, postcommunist identity.

Between the 1850s and 1890s, the process of building up the textile empire would lend Łódź an enduring character. This empire employed one-quarter of all workers living in the area of Poland that was incorporated into the Russian Empire, a fact that contributed to the image of Łódź as the capital of workers and of the working-class movement. The major factories of Poznański, Geyer, Scheibler, Silberstein, Heinzl, and Kunitzer employed up to 7,000 workers.[8] The Communists would selectively emphasize aspects of this working-class history and imagery, which were key to their narrative of Łódź's past.

In contrast with other cities in Poland, Łódź became one of the most rapidly growing cities in late-nineteenth-century Europe. Its population was 16,000 in 1850, increased to 321,000 by 1900, and reached 600,000 in 1914 on the eve of War World I. Its speed of urbanization was comparable to that of American cities during the late nineteenth century. The "rediscovery" of these patterns of growth after 1989 has led to comparisons of Łódź with New York. These comparisons have not only pointed to the degree and speed at which the two cities grew; they have also noted their similar urban features, such as a grid layout of streets.

By the end of the nineteenth century, Łódź formed a rich mosaic of peoples, cultures, and religions, giving it a unique character. Germans, Jews, and Poles constituted its three main ethnic communities. Czech and French entrepreneurs and Russians, who were mostly administrators and official representatives of the Russian government, constituted smaller groups in the vibrant, multicultural local society.[9]

The unique constellation of textile factories, workers' housing, and industrialist palaces with gardens, created in the city between the 1850s and 1890s, are the key markers of Łódź's "Golden Age."[10] The industrialists' built palaces, houses, and tombs in historicist and modern architectural styles ranging from Classical to neo-Gothic, and from neo-Romanesque to Art Nouveau. These monumental edifices gave the city a unique aesthetic character.[11]

The "Golden Age" also manifested itself in the urbanization of large sections of the city on both sides of Piotrkowska Street, in the Śródmieście District. First laid down in 1821, this street of four kilometers in length would come to symbolize the strong presence of a prosperous urban bourgeoisie by the end of the nineteenth century.[12] The street offered expensive and luxurious European goods to its new "aristocracy." This nineteenth-century history of the rapid development of Piotrkowska Street epitomizes the transformation of Łódź from a small town into a modern industrial metropolis with unique architectural features and a European flair.

## Łódź as the "Bad City"

However, just as the city was leaving the era of the "Golden Age," negative images began to be associated with it. By the first decade of the twentieth century, it had acquired the reputation of "the bad city" (*złe miasto*), an epithet that reflected a new evaluation of its expansive capitalist, industrial, modern, and urban character. This negative image crystallized in certain circles among ethnic Polish cultural elites, whose sharp criticism of the industrial metropolis was rooted in Polish conservative and aristocratic traditions that idealized a country lifestyle as opposed to Western capitalist and urban influences, and saw the city as a source of "social and cultural evil." In 1907 Zygmunt Bartkiewicz (1867–1944), a popular Roman Catholic journalist and writer associated with the Polish nationalistic movement National Democracy (Endecja), coined the term " bad city."[13] In a series of essays, "Złe miasto," first published in the journal *Światło* that same year, he portrayed Łódź as a place of ruthless capitalist exploitation of the working class—an exploitation that generated poverty, corruption, and a lack of morals among the workers. According to Bartkiewicz, this capitalist exploitation had also led to social conflicts and to an eruption of violence and death in the city.

Bartkiewicz observed at close quarters the end of the Revolution of 1905–7, a revolution that had swept over major cities of the Russian Empire and that had not omitted Łódź.[14] By the end of 1907, 322 people had been killed and 400 injured in the city. During the events of 1905–7, the working class of Łódź constituted the largest concentration of workers in the *entire* Russian Empire. The ranks of workers were composed largely of ethnic Poles of peasant lineage, although there was substantial Jewish contingent as well. Jewish and German industrialists, whose ancestors had been invited to Łódź in the second and third decades of the nineteenth century, were the main owners of the textile factories.

Bartkiewicz viewed such wide social and economic conflicts, which erupted during the Revolution of 1905–7, only through the lens of a national conflict in which rich Jews and Germans exploited poor (ethnic) Poles. His views were simplistic and rooted in anti-Jewish and anti-German prejudices. Therefore, he saw the solution to the misery of the working class in the ideology of Polish organic nationalism.[15] He opposed the multicultural character of the city and wished that Łódź could become a homogenous society based only on Catholic cultural traditions. As a traditional Roman Catholic, he was also critical of new trends within the Polish Roman Catholic Church such as the emergence of the Mariavite Church, founded in 1906 to promote the renewal of the clergy's spiritual life. The popularity of the Mariavite Church, which became a denomination separate from the Catholic Church, was strong among the working and middle classes in Łódź in the last decade of the nineteenth century and first decade of the twentieth.[16]

The Polish Nobel Prize writer Władysław Reymont (1867–1925) portrayed late-nineteenth-century Łódź in a similar way. In his well-known novel *The Promised Land* (1899) (*Ziemia obiecana*), he depicted the key founders of the city's industrialization—the Lodzermenschen—as " ruthless, corrupt capitalists and exploiters who possess the mentality of liars."[17] In a manner similar to Bartkiewicz, Reymont negatively portrayed the Jewish and German characters in his novel to vent his strong ethnic and religious prejudices. Andrzej Wajda (1926–), the distinguished Polish film director, made a film based on Reymont's novel that appeared in 1975 under the same title.[18] Although Wajda toned down Reymont's negative attitudes toward Lodzermenschen and gave perhaps slightly friendlier interpretations to some of the characters who were not of Polish ethnicity, his film did not escape the major weaknesses of Reymont's novel. The film, no doubt a close adaptation of the novel, does not project any positive images of Łódź as a multicultural industrial metropolis. In the film, anti-Jewish and anti-German prejudices still constitute an integral part of the city's history. As in the book, the city appears to devour its inhabitants.

## Łódź in the Post-1945 Socialist Era

In the Communist period, officials provided Marxist interpretations of Łódź's pre-1918 local history. These interpretations reinforced the negative images of the bourgeois, industrialist, and capitalist past while glorifying the ethos born of the city's working-class past. This glorified history of the urban working class provided a platform from which to project the image of Łódź as a modern Socialist metropolis, whose affordable clothes and other goods attracted shoppers from all over Poland. The metropolis promoted by the Communists included the modernist architecture of bleak shopping centers and apartment blocks, such as one dubbed by the locals "Manhattan," built in the heart of the once-stylish Piotrkowska Street in the 1970s. Thus, cheap clothes, female weavers, factory chimneys, and the gray skies above the factories became keys to the iconography of post-1945 Socialist Łódź.

The Communists succeeded in removing Łódź's multiethnic and multicultural heritage from official histories and excluding it from public memory. History textbooks, tourist guidebooks, and commemorative practices all ignored that heritage. The great majority of nineteenth-century factories, palaces, and villas, which survived World War II intact, were nationalized in the early postwar period and came to house the various institutions and organizations of the Communist state. No information about their provenance —or their founders, former owners, and architects—was displayed on the buildings. The preservation of historic buildings was neglected to a great extent, in spite of the fact that in the 1970s these buildings were officially recognized as part of the protected historic urban heritage. City officials, architects, and urban planners often ignored the recommendations of art historians regarding greater care for the city's unique urban character. In the 1970s and in 1981, art historians held three major conferences in Łódź on its nineteenth-century architecture and on the unique character of this architecture in Poland.[19]

Some of Łódź's historic buildings were demolished in the 1960s, 1970s, and 1980s as new plans were implemented to expand the local transportation network. Among the buildings destroyed in the 1970s were the exceptional complex of the first weavers' houses at 173–232 Piotrkowska Street, which dated back to 1825–26. During this same period, planners demolished one of the treasures of Art Nouveau architecture, the 1902 train station, Łódź Kaliska, and replaced it with a bleak-looking modern structure. Despite such planning, the Art Nouveau buildings at 93 Avenue of Tadeusz

Kościuszko and at 156 and 164 Piotrkowska Street escaped demolition.[20] However, as was the case with many precious historical buildings, neither their interiors nor their exteriors were renovated. Thus the material heritage of Łódź's "Golden Age" was sentenced to physical as well symbolic oblivion. The enforced homogeneity of local society after 1945 also seems to have played an important role in the process leading to the obliteration of the city's pre-1918 multiethnic and multicultural heritage. The absence of knowledge of this heritage was the direct result of the Communists' positive reinterpretation of the social changes in Poland caused by World War II and the postwar transfers of populations. The Communists viewed the resulting ethnic and cultural homogeneity of postwar Poland as a desirable development. This can be interpreted as a sign of Communist adherence to the legacy of organic Polish nationalism, whose exclusivist tendencies had constituted a major political, social, and cultural force in Poland before 1939. In the Communist era, this fusion of Polish ethnic nationalism and Communism reached its peak between 1968 and 1969. One of its outcomes was the anti-Semitic purge of 1968–69, which did not pass over Łódź. In fact, the local press conducted one of the most avidly vicious anti-Semitic campaigns in all Poland.[21]

## Łódź's Pre-1918 Heritage and the Process of Forging the City's Postcommunist Identity

In the 1990s, local political and cultural elites began to challenge and deconstruct the negative image of pre-1918 Łódź by introducing positive re-reinterpretations of its pre-1918 bourgeois and the multiethnic heritage. They insisted that this heritage should constitute the central feature of the new postcommunist identity of the city, and they called upon local inhabitants to endorse this project accordingly. In this process, the nineteenth-century Lodzermenschen suddenly become positive and attractive figures whose qualities, achievements, and life's visions are ones that contemporary local society should be both proud of and wish to emulate.

The endorsement of Łódź's pre-1918 heritage as a part of the new local identity is symptomatic of a more general national reorientation that has been taking place in Poland since the fall of Communism: a turn to the culture of civic nationalism. This orientation has been gaining strength in Poland particularly since the second half of the 1990s and in the early 2000s. The endorsement also expresses changing attitudes toward the cultures of capitalism and the bourgeoisie, and toward a free market economy. However, because the reorientation is a totally new social and cultural phenomenon, it is difficult at present to estimate its impact on the local population. At this stage, there is a lack of available data about how it is affecting the transformation of Łódź into a postindustrial and bourgeois European city, and about how the city's inhabitants—of both the old and young generations—view this. However, some historical and demographic factors may constitute an obstacle to a swift, widespread local reorientation. The majority of the city's inhabitants have a working-class background, which may well make the adoption of a bourgeois ethos and heritage more difficult.

Łódź certainly lacks a strong and affluent middle class. Furthermore, the 1990s brought about a sudden and devastating decrease in textile production. Many obsolete factories, including the most important Poltex Factory (the pre-1945 factory of Izrael K. Poznański), were closed down because no funds were available to purchase new technologies and because the major importer of Łódź's textiles—the Soviet Union—was declining. This resulted in a persistently high level of unemployment among the city's population, particularly women. Unemployment reached a high of 8.4 percent in 1995 and slightly decreased to 7.9 percent in 2002.[22] Thus, one can at present point to the glaring discrepancy between attempts to forge a new identity for Łódź as a city of dynamic and successful Lodzermenschen, and the social and economic position of the city's average residents. One can argue that narrowing this discrepancy will depend on the city authority's ability to generate funds to support the postindustrial development and hence social transformation of the local population; which in turn might lead to the expansion of the local middle class, and perhaps to the re-creation of a more multicultural social makeup. Only then could the privileged narrative of the bourgeoisie and the city's multicultural history be accepted as authentic on a wider scale.

The post-1989 positive reinterpretations of Łódź's pre-1918 past have three interrelated features. The first is the endorsement of the pre-1918 past as an essential part of the city's historical traditions, with the ongoing construction of its postcommunist identity being based on the concept of the present continuity of these traditions. This suggests that the present is treated as "the New Zero Time," totally disconnected from the Socialist past, and is instead connected to the past of the city's "Golden Age." This also indicates the presence of an intense nostalgia and hunger for "a new rebirth" and "a New Golden Age" for the city among its political and cultural elites.

The second feature is the emphasis on the exceptionally modern character of Łódź's pre-1918 heritage on regional and national levels. The new and growing literature on old Łódź, such as tourist guidebooks and popular histories, concentrates on the special and exceptional features of the city's material historical culture.[23] The image of old Łódź as a modern city is also projected onto the present. However, this tendency to re-create the image of contemporary Łódź as the pioneer of modernization does not seem to be entirely realistic, and sometimes it even collides with the idea of the preservation of the pre-1918 heritage. For example, in the 1990s, the historical building that housed the city's Philharmonic Orchestra—the place where the famous pianists Artur Rubinstein (1887–1982) and Ignacy Paderewski (1860–1941) gave concerts in interwar Poland—was demolished. This demolition occurred despite opposition from the city's chief conservator of monuments, who argued that the building, designed in 1886 by the well-known architect Otto Gehlig, could be renovated. The building was replaced with a new glass-and-steel structure that reflected the latest trends in world architecture.[24] This is a good illustration of the tensions between the preservation of the urban nineteenth-century heritage and the desires of architects to belong to the avant-garde.

The third and final feature of positive reinterpretations of Łódź's pre-1918 past is an emphasis on its European roots and on the European character of its pre-1918 heritage. The rediscovery of this heritage seems to be understood as a tool for the transformation of contemporary Łódź into a "truly" European city. For example, the city takes pride in the fact that it has joined European cities in the Art Nouveau Network sponsored by the European Union. This gives it a special status vis-à-vis other major Polish cities that lack Art Nouveau architecture.[25]

In public speeches and interviews, local officials have expressed positive reinterpretations of Łódź's pre-1918 heritage. These pronouncements also reveal the extent to which this heritage is treated instrumentally as a means of gaining support for the city's ongoing social and economic transformation. For example, in an interview given in 1996 to one of the major national papers, Marek Czekalski, a former president of Łódź from 1994 to1998, stated:

> From the beginning as President, I was searching for an idea on how to revitalize Łódź. Local history became the source of my inspiration. I have read a great number of books about old Łódź and have selected those elements from its history that constitute chief markers of Łódź's

identity. Local traditions are one of the best assets of the city. The present inhabitants of Łódź have inherited the memory of an urban center which developed in a rapid manner, was inclusive of people of various nationalities, and was open toward foreign capital. . . . I think that those traditions are good for our times, since like one and a half centuries ago, we too are witnessing a major transformation.[26]

Positive reevaluations of Łódź's multiethnic past are found in the growing number of popular and scholarly publications on the local Jewish and German heritage that began to flourish in the 1990s and the 2000s.[27] In these publications, which are of varying quality, there is for the first time a visible tendency to view the city's multiethnic past as both local and Polish in a civic sense. A similar tendency is also visible in those sections of the official city Web site dedicated to the promotion of local tourism and in the local section of *Gazeta Wyborcza,* which runs special columns dedicated to the city's multicultural and multiethnic history. These include "Postcards from Łódź" and "A Multicultural Map of Łódź."[28] Information about the city's multicultural and multiethnic aspects also appears in the local section of *Gazeta Wyborcza,* under rubrics such as "Nostalgic Łódź" and "Old and New Łódź."[29] The tendency of publications to print the name "Łódź" in each of the four major languages spoken in the city before 1981—Polish, German, Yiddish, and Russian—also helps conjure up this multicultural past.[30]

The positive re-reinterpretations of the pre-1918 heritage also appear in slogans and credos that accompany major cultural events, such as the recently established Festival of Dialogue between Four Cultures,[31] which has taken place in Łódź at the end of September and beginning of October every year since 2001. The first festival in 2001 was promoted as an event in which history could be both relived in the present and become a part of the future. As Witold Knychalski, chairman of the first festival, expressed it:

> Everything starts with dialogue. Where there is none, nothing can be built. Łódź, a town erected in the nineteenth century at a rate faster than New York's, sprang to life just because dialogue between four nations proved possible; just as was the dialogue between their four cultures. In my dream about a major Łódź-based Cultural Festival of a European dimension, I have reached into the past, to the dialogue between the Four Cultures. This has led to the establishment of this truly unique town on a European scale. Although located at the very heart of Poland, Łódź was a multinational place of Poles, Jews, Germans, and Russians, living,

working, and building their "Promised Land" together. The Festival of Dialogue between Four Cultures reaches to the past to establish the link with the future; to launch a new brand of Poland, the country in which the Festival is held, and with Łódź the venue for the event.[32]

In the festival's second year, 2002, its organizers stressed not only the continuity of Łódź's pre-1918 heritage in both the present and future but also insisted that the festival allowed for a reliving of the European dimension of the city and for its transformation into a European metropolis. As in the previous year, in the evaluation of the relationships among Poles, Jews, Germans, and Russians, the organizers were careful not to mention any historical developments that might indicate any political, social, cultural, or economic tensions and conflicts among the various ethnic groups. Instead, they underscored those aspects of these relationships that were based on tolerance, local solidarity, and unity, and were rooted in the concept of living and sharing one place. This avoidance of any challenging historical conflicts indicates the difficulty of integrating the more complicated aspects of Łódź's multicultural history into present narratives about its past. Similarly enthusiastic slogans evoking local solidarity and tolerance, backed up with carefully selected historical images, have accompanied the most recent festivals.

The Festival of Dialogue between Four Cultures is organized by the Society for Dialogue between Cultures, Łódź—Land of the Future, Polish Television S.A., and the Municipal Office. The festival has this credo:

> Łódź, capital city of our region in the heart of Poland, is a magical city. It owes its specific character to a mix of four cultures, four nations, and many mentalities that became one. It is the only city in Europe to originate from the efforts and special qualities of its inhabitants who sought a new place to live, thus creating their own "small Motherland." Four nations built this city from the very beginning. Poles, Jews, Germans, and Russians all came here as immigrants seeking a New Land. They lived next to one another and together went through periods of prosperity and tragedy. It was a melting pot of nations, customs, and national characteristics. For almost two hundred years, these four nations were able to find a common way of living. They learnt to be tolerant and to respect each other. The Unified Europe toward which we are now making our way took its first steps in Łódź. This spirit has been present since those old times in Łódź.[33]

The introduction of a new slogan, "Łódź—Dobre Miasto" (Łódź—the Good City) expresses Łódź's firm and urgent desire to break away from its old negative associations. This slogan has recently been propagated by *Tygiel Kultury* (Melting Pot), which is the main cultural monthly published in the city. Its first issue appeared in January 1996.[34] From its inception, *Tygiel Kultury* has advocated the incorporation of the pre-1939 multicultural heritage into the present and future local identity. Zbigniew Nowak, its editor in chief, has devoted many special editions to the city's multicultural heritage, to the local social and cultural history of Jews and Germans, and to discussions about the city's contemporary identity.[35] In fact *Tygiel Kultury* is the chief intellectual forum for debates about the city's past and contemporary identities. This monthly publication voices salient reflections about the responsibility of contemporary local elites to preserve the local multiethnic heritage. It also invites former inhabitants of the city from before 1939, now living in Israel, Germany, and the United States, to present their points of view on past and contemporary images of Łódź, and on the preservation of the local heritage. Its editors and local contributors seem to be immersed in a process of profound rediscovery of the pre-1939 past, a past in which Łódź appears to be an exciting book full of fascinating but forgotten and "unknown" places and characters, to be discovered anew and integrated into contemporary representations. The assumption accompanying these ideas is that local history has to be retold anew.

Perhaps the most visually powerful example of the integration of the multicultural past into Łódź's city space is a series of cast iron sculptures of its famous former inhabitants, commissioned throughout the last decade and sited at various sites along Piotrkowska Street.[36] The first sculpture erected was that of Julian Tuwin (1894–1953) sitting on a bench. Tuwin, born into a Jewish family in Łódź, was one of the most creative and best-known Polish poets of the twentieth century. The sculpture was erected in the 1990s in the middle section of 104 Piotrkowska Street, next to the city's Municipal Offices. A second sculpture, of Artur Rubinstein, is located not far from that of Tuwin. Like the poet, Rubinstein was born in Łódź. His likeness stands next the house where he once lived. In 2002, a sculptural rendering of Łódź's famous industrialists—Izrael Kalman Poznański, Karol Scheibler, and Ludwik Grohman—appeared in the lower part of Piotrkowska Street near Jaracza Street.

Another powerful, albeit impermanent, attempt to reclaim a multicultural past that also reflects on its destruction is the photographic installation *Windows of Bałuty*, by Paweł Herzog.[37] This moving work is a collage of contemporary photos of the district of Bałuty and original wartime photos of Jews working in the Bałuty section of the infamous Łódź ghetto that the Germans established on February 8, 1940. In his introduction to the exhibit, the artist declares that his aim is to "awaken" the inhabitants of Łódź and to inspire them to reflect upon the tragic forgotten history of this old part of the city, which before World War II was the suburb of the Jewish working class.[38] This installation allows one to contemplate the abrupt end of the vibrant multicultural community of Łódź.

In the aftermath of the Nazis' invasion of Łódź on September 8, 1939, they renamed the city Litzmannstadt and incorporated it into the Warthegau region (Kraj Warty). During the Nazi period, Łódź became an "antimulticultural and antimultiethnic city." Many Poles were expelled to the General Government (Generalna Gubernia), and the Nazis subjected the remaining ethnic Poles to severe discrimination. The local Jewish population was confined to the ghetto located in the districts of Bałuty, Stare Miasto, and Marysin. Only a small group of local Jews, numbering 5,000 to 8,000, survived the ghetto. This number stands in sharp contrast to the size of the prewar local Jewish community, which on the eve of World War II constituted one-third of the city's population and was estimated at 230,000. Herzog's photographs were exhibited in a section of the Poznański industrial complex, the so-called Manufaktura on Ogrodowa Street. The exhibit accompanied the official commemorations of the sixtieth anniversary of the liquidation of the Łódź Ghetto. These commemorations took place at the end of August 2004.[39]

The mayor of Łódź, Jerzy Kropiwnicki, organized the sixtieth anniversary of the liquidation of the Łódź Ghetto as a major, widely publicized, and international four-day set of ceremonies. In contrast to the commemorations surrounding the fiftieth anniversary of the ghetto's liquidation in 1994, which memorialized the Jewish community of Łódź with a single sculpture depicting Moses with the Decalogue—a figuration strongly criticized for its irrelevance—the sixtieth-anniversary ceremonies created many permanent and acclaimed commemorative sites in the city.[40] The train station, Radegast Banhof, where the main commemorative event took place on August 29, was renovated before the event. In the same area, a new monument in the form of a red brick hall with an attached column in memory of the victims of the Holocaust was erected on the initiatives of the mayor and the City Council. This monument was modeled after the monument in the Valley of Jewish Communities at the Yad Vashem Memorial Center in

Jerusalem. The names of all the cities and towns of Poland, Germany, Austria, and the Czech and Slovak regions, from where Jews were brought to the Łódź Ghetto are inscribed in both Polish and Hebrew on the hall's interior walls. An additional commemorative plaque to the memory of Roma victims, who were transported from Austria by the Nazis, was also erected.

A park located along Wojska Polskiego Street dedicated to the survivors of the Łódź Ghetto is another site of lasting commemoration. On August 30, 2004, a group of survivors of the ghetto along with members of their families planted 350 trees in this 6-hectare large park. Halina Elczewska, one of the ghetto's survivors, was the initiator of this "living monument."[41] Her role exemplifies the recent involvement of the remaining members of Łódź's Jewish community in local commemorative practices and the preservation of the city's Jewish sites. The Foundation Monumentum Iudaicum Lodzense, established in 1995 with the support of the organization, based in Israel, of the former residents of Łódź, represents another example of the involvement of the city's former Jewish inhabitants in the preservation of Jewish sites, such as the cemetery on Bracka Street, the largest Jewish cemetery in Europe.[42] The city authorities regularly support these initiatives.

Various buildings and areas, which once belonged to the ghetto and which represent important chapters in its history, were marked for the commemorative ceremonies. Maps and information about the ghetto and commemorative events were also widely circulated among the local population. In 2005, the city also planned to introduce a permanent exhibit on the former territory of the ghetto, titled "In the Footsteps of the Litzmannstadt Ghetto."

A drawing by Abramek Koplowicz, who was transported to Auschwitz with his parents as a thirteen-year-old child in August 1944, served as the logo for all the publications and signposts related to the commemorative ceremonies.[43] Zbigniew Nowak and the late Zbigniew Dominiak, two editors in chief of *Tygiel Kultury*, "discovered" Abramek's thirteen wartime poems and drawings in 1990 in a forgotten collection of archival documents, and, together with Koplowicz's half-brother, they initiated the idea of giving his name to one street in the city. The City Council and mayor approved their project, and a newly built modern complex of condominiums in one of the fashionable districts of the city was named after him in the late 1990s. Koplowicz became the "city's new hero" during the commemorative events of 2004. For example, representatives of the City Council visited his street to pay tribute to his memory.[44] These commemorative events represent a successful attempt to integrate the memory of Łódź's once-vibrant Jewish community into the city's urban space, local history, and contemporary identity.

## Rediscovering and Revitalizing Urban Heritage

Publications and cultural events constitute the major venues for propagating a rediscovery of Łódź's multicultural past. However, the actual renovation and revitalization of the architecture and sites embodying the city's multicultural heritage has been relatively modest. The implementation of projects devoted to material culture began in the second half of the 1990s, but the major projects still await full realization. Their completion depends on receiving sufficient funds from various sources, including the European Union and foreign and domestic private investors. The present situation indicates that the city has not yet collected sufficient funds to put its plans for the major historical areas into effect. Even projects already approved by the City Council and mayor are struggling to find sponsors.

One such a project is the revitalization of the Old Market (Stary Rynek) and the surrounding areas along Franciszkańska, Północna, Zachodnia, Lutomierska, and Wojska Polskiego streets, right up to Church Square (Kościelny Plac).[45] This is the oldest part of nineteenth-century Łódź, and the place where the main center of Jewish life was established in 1825. Advocates of the revitalization of the Old Market, united in the grassroots Association of the Friends of the Old Market, aim at renovating the entire infrastructure of the area and introducing new monuments and institutions that would memorialize the pre-1939 heritage. For example, on the Western side of the Old Market, they plan to decorate the buildings with paintings depicting the pioneers of industrial Łódź: Israel Kalman Poznański, Robert Biederman, Karol Gotleib Anstadt, Abraham Prussak, Herman Konsztad, Zygmund Jarociński, Edward Heineman-Jarecki, Samuel Jezechiel Saltzman, Józef Dobraciński, Samuel Barciński, and Gottfried Eckert.[46]

On the eastern side of the Old Market, they plan to introduce paintings depicting the six leading authorities of the different religions that formed the social and cultural landscape of pre-1939 Łódź, including, among others, the bishop of the Orthodox Church, Jerzy Korenistow; Rabbi Eliash Chaim Maizel; and a representative of the Lutheran Church, the Reverend Rudold Gustaw Gundlach.[47]

On Północna Street, they plan to set up a Museum of the History of the Electric Trams of Łódź. This project, which aims to emphasize one of the most modern aspects of nineteenth-century Łódź, is modeled on the concept of museums of transport found in other European cities. Advocates of this revitalization project also plan to establish a Center for Education about the Holocaust on Północna Street. This indicates a growing interest in education against racism, xenophobia, and anti-Semitism in a city that not so long ago had the reputation of being infamous for its anti-Semitic graffiti.

Another project that depends heavily on garnering sufficient funds for its realization is the revitalization of Księży Młyn, the unique historical complex and so-called kingdom of Karol Wilhelm Scheibler. Księży Młyn was built in the late 1860s and the 1870s. It consists of three main urban features: workers' housing, which provided housing to 321 families and which was modeled on workers' housing, built by artisans such as the one at Bedford Park near London (1875); the four-story cotton mill factory, built in red brick and in the style of a fortress; and the residential area of the Herbst villa and the surrounding garden at 72 Przędzelniana Street. This villa was named after Edward Herbst, the husband of Matylda, who was Scheibler's eldest daughter. Scheibler also built a school for the children of his factory workers and other employers in 1876, a shop for his workers in 1877, and a workers' hospital in 1886, which functions as a hospital to this day. The city has agreed to cover the costs of renovating four of the eighteen two-story buildings, which Scheibler had constructed for the most outstanding and productive workers and managers of his factory, and he has been looking for investors who would finance the project's remaining structures.[48]

The project of revitalizing the Manufactura, the large complex and so-called kingdom of Israel Poznański, at 17 Ogrodowa Street, also suffered at the beginning from a similar lack of funding, though it is the most advanced revitalization project in the city.[49] Like Scheibler's industrial complex, Poznański's Manufaktura comprises a factory built in the style of a red brick fortress, workers' housing based on Ogrodowa Street, and the formerly residential Poznański Palace at the corner of Ogrodowa and Zachodnia streets, now housing the Museum of the History of Łódź. This is the largest postindustrial complex in Łódź. It is located on 270,000 square meters. The revitalization of all the buildings belonging to this complex began in the spring of 1999. The project was completed at the end of 2005. The city takes pride in this project, advertising it as the "biggest project of urban revitalization in Central Europe" and as "a city in a city."[50] The project aims to transform

Poznański's Manufaktura into a recreational and commercial center that will serve the local community. Its advocates also hope that it will generate interest on a wider national level. In a preliminary advertising flier, the city has announced the creation of an American-style shopping mall, a giant car dealership, a home-and-garden center, a multiscreen cinema complex, a Museum of Modern Arts, a Museum of Science and Technology for children, a bowling alley, a hotel, and a Heritage Museum of Poznański's Manufactura. The city has also stressed the European roots behind the inspiration for the revitalization of the Poznański industrial buildings complex. They underscore that this project emulates four successful revitalization projects that have already been completed in Central Europe: the Vitra Design Museum in Berlin; the MEO Contemporary Art Collection in Budapest; the Stilwerks Arts Centre in Hamburg; and a hotel converted from an old water tower, built between 1868 and 1872, in the town of Wasserturm.[51]

The recently completed renovation project of the oldest Orthodox church building in Łódź, the Church of Saint Aleksander Newski, located at the corner of Kiliński and Narutowicza streets, is a good example of the inclusion into the local heritage of a building that for a long time was associated with Russian rule. This Orthodox church was built in 1884 according to the design of the city's chief architect, Hilary Majewski, who also designed Poznański's Manufaktura. Only in the early 2000s has this Russian Orthodox church been identified as an important historic landmark and tourist attraction for the city.[52]

The City Office recently also announced the implementation of a new project known as "tourist paths" to celebrate Łódź's multicultural past. These four paths are in the process of preparation: "Palaces and Residences of Łódź," "German Łódź," "Jewish Łódź," and "Industrial Architecture of Łódź."[53] These projects aim to raise the level of historical knowledge about the city among the its residents by introducing permanent signposts and metal maps attached to walls. This project has yet to be implemented, so it is too early to comment on its possible acceptance and popularity by local society and by domestic and foreign tourists. It is also difficult to comment on the aesthetic aspects of the signposts and maps, and on the scale of their integration into the urban landscape.

The most advanced renovations of historic buildings are visible on Piotrkowska Street, the most expensive and best-maintained street in Łódź, with many shops offering famous European designer brands. Renovations have also taken place on T. Kościuszki Avenue, which runs parallel to Piotrkowska Street. Generally, it is new private owners who are responsible for restoring the exteriors and interiors of buildings. But in the late 1990s and the beginning of the 2000s, the city also carried out a number of important renovations of historic buildings recognized as architectural jewels. For example, in 1998, it renovated the facade of the five-story building at 143 Piotrkowska Street, built in 1898 by the respected nineteenth-century architect David Lande, a member of the local Jewish community.[54]

Yet on leaving Piotrkowska Street for other areas, the impression one might receive is of entering a quite different world—one of crumbling historic buildings; of tired worn-down facades, with accretions of a half century of grime; of places where no one seems to care about the past or present; of decayed, graffiti-lined streets; of unrenovated interior cobblestone courtyards where small children play football; and, above all, of a lasting impression of emptiness, absence, and the unheralded passing of time. One can find plenty of all the above in Śródmieście, the oldest section of Łódź's suburbs, which reveals the extent to which the destruction of this city in the post-1939 periods still has an impact on its contemporary identity. These urban spaces reveal how difficult it is to bring about a new and much desired "rebirth" and "Golden Age" to match the historical "rebirth" and "the Golden Age." Could contemporary Łódź become once again the new Promised Land? And for whom, given that it is a city of departed historical communities and, moreover, of limited economic opportunities—a place from which young people tend to depart for Warsaw and abroad?

Here, the overarching pertinent realities are that, in marked contrast to the nineteenth century city, twenty-first-century Łódź is almost totally ethnically homogenous—and far from being an affluent metropolis. The city's political and cultural elites have turned to the pre-1939 past to conceive and create a new postcommunist, forward-looking European entity, where bourgeois and multicultural narratives are privileged. In this way, moral and social aspects—taking responsibility for the multicultural past and saving it from oblivion through memorialization and symbolic integration into official history and contemporary identity—are mixed with more pragmatic aspects—soliciting financial and technological aid among foreign institutions and investors, including from those communities whose ancestors once lived in the city.[55]

Łódź's effort to forge a new identity of place does not necessary need to end in failure—although, given the enormous changes in the city's social and cultural landscapes in the post-1939 periods, and given the presence of a void of meaning in the city, one cannot escape from reflecting that this project has salient limitations. Łódź's rediscovery and successful integration of its pre-1918 multicultural and bourgeois past depends on the reception of this project by local society at large. Are the urban spaces dedicated to the celebration of the city's multicultural past and to commemorating that past's tragic disappearance meaningful not only to local political and cultural elites but to non-elites as well? Time alone may tell whether Łódź's bourgeois, multiethnic, and multicultural past will be accepted by its inhabitants as an essential part of their heritage—and a key aspect of their future identity.

## Notes

1. See Henryk Poselt, *Łódc do roku 1825: Kalendarium—Łódź* (Łódź: Wydawnictwo Piątek Trzynastego, 2003), 7. Despite many popular publications, there is an evident lack of scholarly books about the political, social, and cultural history of Łódź.

2. Ibid., 24.

3. Ibid., 25.

4. Representatives of local cultural elites stress that the low self-esteem found among residents in the city is caused by a historical inferiority complex. E.g., Marian Panek, the chairman of the Restoration Plan of the Old Market in Łódź, made the quoted comment to the author of this chapter in a communication of January 2005.

5. Foreign tourists who plan to visit the city are acutely aware of the lack of information about the city in travel books on Poland. See, e.g., the comments of Christopher Phelps, "Being There," *Chronicle of Higher Education,* December 23, 2004, 7; and Karol Schlögel, "W poszukiwaniu 'Ziemi Obiecanej,'" *Tygiel Kultury,* no. 4 (1997): 10.

6. On the history of the industrialist families of Łódź, see Leszek Skrzydło, *Rody fabrykanckie,* vols. 1 and 2 (Łódź: Oficyna Bibliofilów, 2000).

7. Schlögel, "W poszukiwaniu "Ziemi Obiecanej," 12.

8. Ibid., 12.

9. For a rare and interesting account of the relationship between the various ethnic and cultural groups that lived in the city, see the essays of Henryk Vimard, a French journalist who visited Łódź in 1910. Henryk Vimard, *Łódź: Polski Manszester* (Łódź: Biblioteka Tygla, 2001; reprint).

10. On the history of entertainment in Łódź during the Golden Age, see Wacław Pawlak, *Minionych zabaw czar czyli czas wolny i rozrywka w dawnej Łodzi* (Łódź: Oficyna Bibliofilów, 2001)

11. On the history of Łódź's nineteenth-century architecture, see, e.g., Stephen Muthesius and Irena Poplawska, "Poland's Manchester: 19th Century Industrial and Domestic Architecture in Łódź," *Journal of the Society of Architectural Historians* (United States) 35 (June 1986): 148–60.

12. The first established section of Piotrkowska Street ran between Plac Kościelny and Stary Rynek—the oldest part of the city. Today this section is called Pojezierska Street. See Poselt, *Łódź do roku 1825,* 28. There is still a lack of comprehensive urban studies on Łódź.

13. Zygmund Bartkiewicz's "Złe miasto" was published in 1911 and was reprinted

in 2001 by the Biblioteka Tygiel Kultury. For information about Bartkiewicz, see the introduction by Andrzej Kempa to the reprint *Złe miasto* (Łódź: Biblioteka Tygiel Kultury, 2001), 5–11.

14. On the responses of city's industrialists to the Revolution of 1905–7, see Andreas R. Hofmann, "The Biedermanns in the 1905 Revolution: A Case Study in Entrepreneurs' Responses to Social Turmoil in Łódź," *SEER* 82, no. 1 (2004): 27–49. On the history of the Revolution of 1905–7, see, e.g., Robert E. Blobaum, *Rewolucja: Russian Poland. 1904–1907* (Ithaca, N.Y.: Cornell University Press, 1995).

15. For a different account of the Revolution of 1905–7 in Łódź, see the reports written by the left-wing Russian journalist Iwan Timkowskij-Kostin, "Miasto proletariuszy." These reports first appeared in Polish newspapers in 1907 and were republished by Biblioteka Tygla Kultury in 2001.

16. On the history of the Mariavate Church, see Marek Budziarek, *Łódzki bedeker wyznaniowy* (Łódź: Oficyna Bibliofilów, 1998), 33; and Jerzy Dzieciuchowicz et al., *Rola wyznań religijnych w kształtowaniu przestrzeni miejskiej Łodzi* (Łódź: Wydawnictwo Uniwersytetu Łódzkiego, 2004), 106–8.

17. Karol Borowiecki, Maks Baum, and Moryc Welt are the three protagonists who represent the Lodzermenschen type in Reymont's Ziemia Obiecana. Reymont, first, published *Ziemia obiecana* in parts in editions in the newspaper *Kurier Warszawski* (1897–98). *Ziemia obiecana* appeared as an entire volume in 1899 and was republished in the interwar and post-1945 periods. See Władysław Reymont, *Ziemia obiecana*, 2 vols. (Warsaw: PIW, 1970). For an English translation, see Władysław Reymont, *The Promised Land* (New York: Alfred A. Knopf, 1927).

18. There is no critical comparison of Reymont's book with Wajda's film *Ziemia obiecana*. For interesting reflections on the subject, see Urszula Dzieciątkowska, "W poszukiwaniu Łódzkiej wizji," *Tygiel Kultury*, no. 4 (1997): 18–27. For an interesting review of Wajda's film, which discusses the problem of antiminority prejudice, see Omer Bartov, *The "Jew" in Cinema: From the Golem to Don't Touch My Holocaust* (Bloomington: Indiana University Press, 2005), 24–27.

19. Polish art historians organized the first two conferences, which took place in 1971 and 1979. The third conference, which took place in 1981, was an international scholarly event. During the third conference, scholars acknowledged the pre-1918 heritage to be an example of a unique industrial architecture in Europe. See Krzysztof Stefański, "Zagrożone dziedzictwo," *Tygiel Kultury*, nos. 1–3 (2003): 18.

20. Ibid., 18–19.

21. On the anti-Semitic campaign of 1968–69, see, e.g., Dariusz Stola, *Kampania antysyjonistyczna* (Warsaw: Instytut Studiów Politycznych Polskiej Akademii Nauk, 2000); and the interview with Alina Margolis-Edelman, "Jestem nigdzie," *Tygiel Kultury*, no. 3 (1998): 18–24.

22. See *Uproszczony lokalny program rewitalizacji wybranych terenów śródmiejskich oraz pofabrycznych Łodzi na lata 2004–2006* (Łódź: Konsorcjum pro-Revita, 2005), 18; available at http://www.prorevita.pl.

23. See, e.g., Marek Budziarek et al., *Łódź nasze miasto* (Łódź: Oficyna Bibliofilów, 2000).

24. See Stefański, "Zagrożone dziedzictwo,"19.

25. See Joanna Podolska, "Łódź: Kobieta secesyjna," *Gazeta Wyborcza*, November 7, 2004, Section: Miasto Łódź; http://maista.gazeta.pl/Łódź/2029020,35136,238067.html.

26. See Wojciech Górski's interview with President Marek Czekalski, "Nieznana ziema," *Magazyn Rzeczpospolitej,* no. 12 (1996): 2.

27. See, e.g., Krystyna Radziszewska and Krzysztof Wożniak, eds., *Pod jednym dachem: Niemcy oraz ich polscy i żydowscy sąsiedzi w wieku XIX i XII* (Łódź: Wydawnictwo Literackie, 2002); Andrzej Machejek, ed., *Żydzi Łódźcy* (Łódź: Wydawnictwo Hamal, 2004); Andrzej Kempa and Marek Szukalak, *Żydzi dawnej Łodzi: Słownik biograficzny Żydów Łódzkich oraz z Łodzią związanych,* vol. 1 (Łódź: Oficyna Bibliofilów, 2001); Joanna Podolska and Jacek Walicki, *Przewodnik po cmentarzu żydowskim w Łodzi* (Łódź: Oficyna Bibliofilów, 2002); and Wojciech Gorecki, *Łódź przeżyła Katharsis* (Łódź: Biblioteka Tygla Kultury, 1998).

28. See http://www.uml. Łódź.pl and http://miasta.gazeta.pl/Łódź.

29. See http://miasta.gazeta.pl/Łódź.

30. See the title page of Marek Budziarek et al., *Łódź: Miasto czterech kultur* (Łódź: Urząd Miasta Łodzi, 2004).

31. For information about past and future Festivals of Dialogue between Four Cultures, see http://www.4kultury.pl/indexen.php/s+preamble.

32. See the statement of Witold Knychalski, chairman of the first festival, September 27–October 6, 2001; http://www.4kultury.pl/indexen.php/s+preamble.

33. See the statement signed by the Festival Bureau on behalf of the organizers of the second festival, September 27–October 6, 2001; http://www.4kultury.pl/indexen.php/s=f2002.

34. On the history and ethos of *Tygiel Kultury,* see http://free.ngo.pl./tygiel.

35. See *Tygiel Kultury,* issue nos. 4–6 (2004), dedicated to the history of the Łódź ghetto and pre-1939 Jewish Łódź; issue nos. 1–3 (2003); issue no. 4 (1997), which contains articles on the identity of Łódź in different chronological periods; and issue nos. 1–3 (2002), also dedicated to a discussion of the city's identity.

36. The city also erected the sculpture of Władysław Reymont, sitting on a trunk, at 137 Piotrkowska Street. This sculpture stands as symbol of the city's pride in the Polish writer who was a recipient of Nobel Prize and who wrote about Łódź. Of course there is a clear tension between the vision of Reymont's Łódź and the vision of the city represented by the other figures of the iron sculptures on display on Piotrkowska Street.

37. For a selection of Herzog's photos see, the appendix to *Tygiel Kultury,* nos. 4–6 (2004): 2–5.

38. Ibid., 6.

39. See the Program of the Commemoration of the Sixtieth Anniversary of the Liquidation of the Litzmannstadt Ghetto in Łódź.

40. Aleksander Klugman, a former resident of Łódź, wrote a critical article about the commemorative events of the Fiftieth Anniversary of the Łódź Ghetto; see Aleksander Klugman, "Czy w Łodzi mieszkali kiedys Żydzi?" *Tygiel Kultury,* nos. 1–3 (2002): 30–38. Also see the discussion preceding the ceremony unveiling the monument on November 6, 1995: Mieczysław Gumola, "Odczytanie z kamienia: Pomnik Dekalogu," *Kronika Miasta Łodzi* 2 (2004): 38–44.

41. See two brief reports, "Drzewka w parku ocalałych," and "Drzewka nie pozwolv zapomnieć," *Dziennik Łódzki,* September 31, 2004.

42. On the history and activities of the Foundation Monumentum Iudaicum Lodzense, see its Web site, http://www.Łódźjews.org.

43. The drawing and poems of Abramek Koplowicz were published in *Tygiel Kultury,* nos. 4–6 (2004): 40–51.

44. I am grateful to Zbigniew Nowak, editor in chief of *Tygiel Kultury,* for giving me the letter of Eliezer Grynfeld, half-brother of Abramek Koplowicz. In the letter, Grynfeld movingly describes the sudden and unexpected rediscovery of Abramek Koplowicz by representatives of the City Office.

45. See Marian Panek, "The Project of Revitalization of the Old Market in Łódź," http://www.staremiasto.Łódź.pl and http://www.turystyka.Łódź.pl. I thank Panek, chairman of the Association of the Friends of the Old City, for providing me with the copy of the project.

46. Ibid., 5.

47. Ibid., 7. On the history of various religions and sacral architecture in Łódź, see Dzieciuchowicz et al., *Rola wyznań.*

48. See the conversation of Luiza Skawińska with the chief architect of Łódź, Piotr Biliński, "Aby miasto rosło w siłę, a ludzie żyli dostatnio . . . ," *Tygiel Kultury,* no. 4 (1997): 47.

49. See *Uproszczony lokalny program rewitalizacji,* 15.

50. See the two-page flier *Manufaktura News: A City in the City.* I thank the employees of the Department of Promotion, Tourism, and International Cooperation of the City of Łódź for supplying me with this flier.

51. Ibid., 2.

52. See the description of this church on the Web site of the City Office in the Tourism section, http://www.uml.Łódź.pl/indeksik.php3?menu2=6&zapytanie=6,02.02,17; and Budziarek et al., *Łódź,* 106–10.

53. I received this information in January 2005 from the Urbanization Office, affiliated with the City Office.

54. See the entry on the history of this neo-Renaissance building at http://www.uml.Łódź.pl.

55. A good illustration of the instrumental aspect of the rediscovery of the multicultural past are the comments of Jerzy Kropiwnicki, mayor of city, made before his trip to Tel Aviv with twenty-two local businesspeople. At the beginning of January 2005, Kropiwnicki stated: "It is high time that the relationship between Łódź and Tel Aviv was cultivated not only on the social and cultural level but also on the economic level." See "'Przegląd Wydarzeń,' Z Misją do Izraela, Urząd Miasta Łodzi," January 3, 2005; available at http://www.uml.Łódź.pl.

# 11

# Szczecin's Identity after 1989: A Local Turn

*Jan Musekamp*

The city of Szczecin (German: Stettin) is one of the largest cities in Poland, but at the same time it is one of the most indistinct on most Poles' mental maps. One reason is its location: Szczecin is in the extreme northwestern corner of the country, on the border with Germany and about forty-five miles south of the Baltic Sea. Being a highly centralized state after 1945, Poland was not focused on its periphery; in the eyes of many Szczecinians today, the focus has not changed since the fall of Communism.[1]

For Szczecin and its inhabitants, the conclusion of World War II signaled a caesura, from which Szczecin could not recover for a long time. Forced both by the advance of the Red Army in April 1945 and the decisions made at the Potsdam Conference, which ceded German Eastern Territories, the entire (German) population of about 400,000 had to leave their hometown of Stettin. The westward shift of the Polish borders made Stettin, henceforth Szczecin, a frontier city. By 1947, Szczecin was a mostly homogeneous Polish town. Still, having been destroyed during the war,[2] it lacked both inhabitants and a reconstructed city center.

Communist propaganda often claimed that, "after almost one hundred years of Swedish and two hundred years of Prussian rule, . . . Szczecin had returned to the Motherland."[3] As everywhere in the so-called Regained Territories of the People's Republic of Poland, the city's German history could not objectively be discussed for forty-five years. The new Polish settlers of Szczecin, who had arrived from all over prewar Poland (and especially from nearby Wielkopolska, or Great Poland), were presented with a history that stressed the importance of their city as an eighth-century Slavonic trading post, and that it had been part of the Polish state for a short period during the Eleventh Century, having been ruled by the Slavonic Griffin dukes of Pomerania until 1637. Polish postwar historiography underlined the fact that the Pomeranian rulers were conscious of their Slavonic roots. At the same time, the fact that Szczecin had belonged to the Holy Roman Empire as part of the German nation was marginalized. Szczecin's connections to the Polish crown and its conflicts with the electors of Brandenburg were core themes of the Polish narrative that was created after the war. More objective historiography reveals that, in fact, the dukes tried to keep their independence by maneuvering between Brandenburg, Poland, and Sweden. Moreover, German and Polish historians unanimously agree that the peak of Pomeranians' political importance was achieved under Bogislaw X (1454–1523), who unified all Pomeranian duchies and made Szczecin the capital of the state. By contrast, new Polish historiography stresses the city's history as part of the independent Pomeranian Duchy. As a result, many of the new inhabitants of Szczecin could not feel "at home" with their history. The fact is that the 83 years of Swedish and 225 years of Prussian and German rule (following the extinction of the Griffins) was not openly discussed and, even if it was, it would have been seen as a historical low point.

As in the case of Wrocław,[4] a feeling of temporality was widespread in Szczecin, particularly in the first decades after the war. This was, by and large, a result of its proximity to the border, which was not definitively recognized by Germany until 1990. Situated predominantly west of the so-called Oder-Neisse line and a walkable distance from the German border, Szczecinians were susceptible to all kinds of rumors about an eastward shift of the German border. The feeling of constant threat was partially alleviated with Nikita Khrushchev's visit to Szczecin in 1959 and the treaty between West Germany and Poland in 1970. This feeling was completely alleviated with the recognition of the Polish western border by a reunified Germany in 1990.

Ironically, Szczecin's location—next to Germany and close to West Berlin, with its abundant international contact due to its harbor—contributed to forming a society that was much more open to change than other Polish cities. In that regard, it might not be quite as surprising that the strikes and demonstrations of the 1970s and 1980s, which led to the Solidarity movement and, ultimately, the fall of Communism in Poland and Europe, first broke out in the harbor cities of Gdańsk and Szczecin.

Szczecin's intellectuals already started to discuss the terra incognita of prewar German Stettin in the 1980s. This process was accelerated by the changes of 1989. The formation of a new civic identity in a Polish city with Slavonic and German roots was concomitant with a variety of transnational and regional events. As evidence for this formation of a new identity, this chapter presents the celebrations of the city's different historical anniversaries, the reevaluation of a historical urban district, the honoring of a German mayor, and discussions about new monuments.

## Seven Hundred Fifty Years or Sixty Years? Anniversaries

In democratic societies, official celebrations of anniversaries provide excellent information about a city's identity. This is certainly true for Szczecin after 1989, where commemorative practice demanded that locals determine which historical events are worth remembering and which layers of the city's history are better left buried.

Communism had hardly vanished when an important date in local history was approaching: the granting of Magdeburg municipal rights to Szczecin under Pomeranian duke Barnim I in 1243. Before 1989, the importance of this date could not be expressed because it would acknowledge the city's historical connection to Germany and the ensuing influx of (now-missing) German-speaking settlers, who transformed the city and assimilated its Slavonic-speaking inhabitants. The truth is that Szczecin was not the only city with such ties, because even the unquestionably Polish city of Cracow had been granted Magdeburg municipal rights. By 1993, a majority of the Szczecin City Council—most originating from the Solidarity-movement—were unconcerned about the German origin of the rights and passed a law on February 19 decreeing that the celebration of the seven-hundred-fiftieth anniversary of the granting of municipal rights to Szczecin was an "occasion to present the performance of our town and its history."[5] This decision was controversial, but the public had been carefully conditioned for the enterprise; a special commission under the guidance of a well-known historian, Gerard Labuda, was created to discuss the preparations for this anniversary.[6] Nevertheless, some Szczecinians accused the council of celebrating the Germanness of the city.[7] Officials had to stress that, although Germans would be invited, preparations and festivities lay exclusively in Polish hands.[8]

However, the director of the Szczecin National Museum at the time—a respected archeologist and decade-long researcher of Szczecin's Slavonic past—did not approve of the jubilee. Instead of the Magdeburg commemoration, he advocated celebrating what he called the "Szczecin millennium," because there had been a flourishing Slavonic settlement in the territory by the tenth century.[9] The first postwar Polish mayor, Piotr Zaremba, considered another date the actual birthday of Szczecin, namely 1945, when the Polish administration took over the city.[10] Other opponents of the anniversary stressed the high costs of the festival, but Szczecin's city fathers calculated that those celebrations would attract tourism and business from Poland and abroad, thus promoting Szczecin as a jewel in the center of Europe.[11]

Another point, however, was just as significant as the notion of Szczecin's Europeanness in these debates about commemorative practice. The City Council president, Jan Otto, mentioned when reporting about the preparations for the anniversary that when Barnim I granted Szczecin municipal rights, the city gained a certain level of autonomy from the monarch. In many ways, 1989 signified a move toward the periphery, because that year would be seen as an end of Warsaw's rule over its "provinces" through the reestablishment of elected local self-governing bodies.[12] The celebrations offer evidence of an adjustment in Szczecin's cultural memory, which had been limited to the events of its Slavonic history before 1989.[13]

The commemoration began on April 2, 1993, and lasted several months, with expositions, lectures, and conferences. It was evident that these events increased Szczecinians' interest in their city's prewar history. In an exhibition on grand Szczecinians, not only the Polish but also German heroes of the city were presented.[14]

And what about Szczecin's distinctively *Polish* anniversaries? Like other cities that had been within the Soviet sphere of influence, only one anniversary connected to local history had been regularly celebrated, the liberation by the Soviet Army, which in Szczecin's case fell on April 26, 1945. The arrival of the first Polish administration four days later and the definitive takeover by Poland on July 5, 1945, had never been a significant part of the celebration of Szczecin's "return to the Motherland." But the character of these anniversaries changed after 1989. Given that there had been open criticism of the Soviet Union for having dismantled large parts of

Szczecin's economic potential,[15] after the fall of Communism, mainly July 5 was routinely celebrated.

In 1995, the fiftieth anniversary of Polish rule in Szczecin was celebrated at the Central Cemetery on April 26, the date when the fighting ended in Szczecin. Mayor Bartłomej Sochański honored those killed in action and, perhaps for the first time in the city's commemorative history, mentioned the suffering of the German population as well. On April 29, the voivodship's (region's) Parliament held a jubilee meeting in the castle, where the German consul general was invited.[16] Nevertheless, in the special July 1, 1995, edition of Szczecin's oldest newspaper, *Kurier Szczeciński* (edited and paid for by the municipality), any mention of the fate of the Germans who had been forced to leave their hometown of Stettin in the first years of Polish rule was curiously absent. In his foreword, Sochański mentions the city's sense of belonging to Europe, but he returns to all-too-familiar rhetoric when talking about the return of Szczecin to Poland in 1945.[17] The special edition addresses different aspects of postwar Szczecin, portraying Poles as pioneers and heroes in the years after the war—many of whom were still alive. For the editors of the jubilee edition, the consciousness of living in a city with a multicultural past did not seem to be of great importance; they considered the anniversary to be an exclusively Polish one, unrelated to Stettin.

Still, on the fiftieth anniversary of the Szczecin National Museum (a museum with a long history in the prewar Stadtmuseum), a collection of antique art objects and copies of renaissance bronze sculptures, which had been transported to Warsaw in 1948 by order of the government, were returned to Szczecin. In 1913, the Stettin industrialist and art patron Heinrich Dohrn offered these exhibits to the newly erected Stadtmuseum. The museum's officials expressed their pride about the returned objects, underlining the fact that Dohrn had been a valued son of the city.[18] Paradoxically, the highlight of the Polish museum's fiftieth anniversary was the return and exhibition of objects belonging to the prewar German museum—tangible evidence of the so-called return of history after 1989.

In 2005, the sixtieth anniversary of Polish Szczecin was celebrated. This time, 1945 was not considered to be the starting point of the city's history. In contrast to the fiftieth anniversary, one can clearly see a development from a polonocentric view toward one that included "multiple historical perspectives."[19]

Although many civic organizations—from the fire brigade to the elementary schools—celebrated their sixtieth anniversaries, the Pomeranian Library

(Książnica Pomorska) self-confidently celebrated one hundred twenty-five years of existence, thus overcoming the 1945 caesura.[20] The National Museum prepared an exposition presenting the life of ordinary Szczecinians over the sixty years since the war,[21] all the while not forgetting about the Germans and other minorities in the city. The first exhibit is a freight car placed inside the gallery depicting Szczecin's central station in the 1940s. On the track, the belongings of people were represented—those leaving (Germans) and those arriving (Poles from different parts of the country, Polish Jews returning from exile in the Soviet Union, Ukrainians expelled from their homes in southeastern Poland, and Greeks and Macedonians escaping from the civil war in their home country).[22] This new acceptance of Szczecin's multicultural past, as in Wrocław,[23] can be seen as a reaction against the narrative of the homogeneous Polish nation-state that had prevailed after 1945.

## The Podzamcze District: The New Old Town

As a result of air raids in 1944, Szczecin's medieval center on the Oder River had been destroyed almost completely and only a few historic buildings, such as the Old Town Hall and the castle, remained (albeit heavily damaged). They were rebuilt during the decades after the war. As a former residence of the Slavonic Griffin dynasty, Szczecin's castle played a crucial roll in Communist-era Polish nationalist propaganda.[24] The inauguration of various memorial plaques and monuments as well as the exposition of the Pomeranian Dukes' crypt transformed the castle into a classical realm of memory (*lieu de mémoire*).[25] The castle served as a pantheon of Polish Szczecin, constructing a link to the city's Slavonic past and giving the inhabitants a sense of continuity.[26]

Szczecin's first postwar Polish mayor, Piotr Zaremba, was a city planner with a modern concept of how to rebuild the former German city. He did not want to restore destroyed quarters in order to return to the status quo of 1939. He planned to benefit from the destruction of large parts of the city to "erect a new city, continuing the valuable traditions of the old town but leaving behind all that implied long foreign [German] rule."[27] As a result, the postwar rebuilding of the old town led to a new modern quarter, following modernist principles of "light, air and sun." During postwar reconstruction, the old street network was preserved, but modern residential buildings were constructed, as in other European cities destroyed during the war. Although this concept differed from the reconstruction of Wrocław or

Gdańsk, the result was similar, because purely residential areas replaced the mixed areas of flats, businesses, and restaurants that had previously dominated those neighborhoods (figures 11.1 and 11.2).

Realizing another modern idea in city planning, in 1949, Zaremba completed construction of the highway-like "Oder Artery" on the rubble of the destroyed area on the river bank.[28] Despite ephemeral plans to erect skyscrapers, the space between the new residential areas and the highway remained empty until 1995; the ruins had served as a brick quarry for the reconstruction of Warsaw. In the 1980s, the northern part of the historical old town was affected by the construction of another controversial traffic project, the Castle Route (Trasa Zamkowa), connecting the city center with the right bank quarters by means of a monstrous viaduct. Altogether, these measures led to a complete change of the quarter's function. Before 1943, this district had been a business center with a direct connection to the river. After 1945, Szczecin was literally cut off from the river by the highway and the empty space. Like Wrocław and Gdańsk (even today), prewar Stettin had lived in symbiosis with the river, and the newly erected residential neighborhood did not correspond with the Old Town's prewar function.

In 1983, Szczecin decided to launch a competition to revitalize the eastern part of the old city, the so-called Podzamcze District. The winner was an architect and city planner, Stanisław Latour of Szczecin Technical University. He proposed keeping the old street network but erecting new buildings upon the old foundations. His hope was that these buildings would revive both the prewar atmosphere as well as the function of the quarter, returning the neighborhood to a residential, business, and recreational district (figure 11.3). Its dimensions would equal to historical sizes; the facades, however, would be in individual, postmodern styles.[29] For Szczecin, these plans were quite revolutionary, especially in their ambition to recreate the prewar German town's history, architecture, and lifestyle. Due to Poland's chronic economic crisis throughout the 1980s and beginning 1990s, this project was not immediately realized. But political changes finally brought economic changes and, in 1995, the Podzamcze Housing Cooperative laid the foundations for buildings on the first block to be built. Unlike earlier reconstruction projects in Gdańsk and Wrocław, only two of the facades follow historic forms. Next to the reconstructed Old Town Hall, two tenements have been adorned with Baroque facades based on prewar photographs, thus creating a link to the city's past (this kind of rebuilding can be observed throughout Central Europe and is usually called the second wave of reconstruction) (figure 11.4).[30]

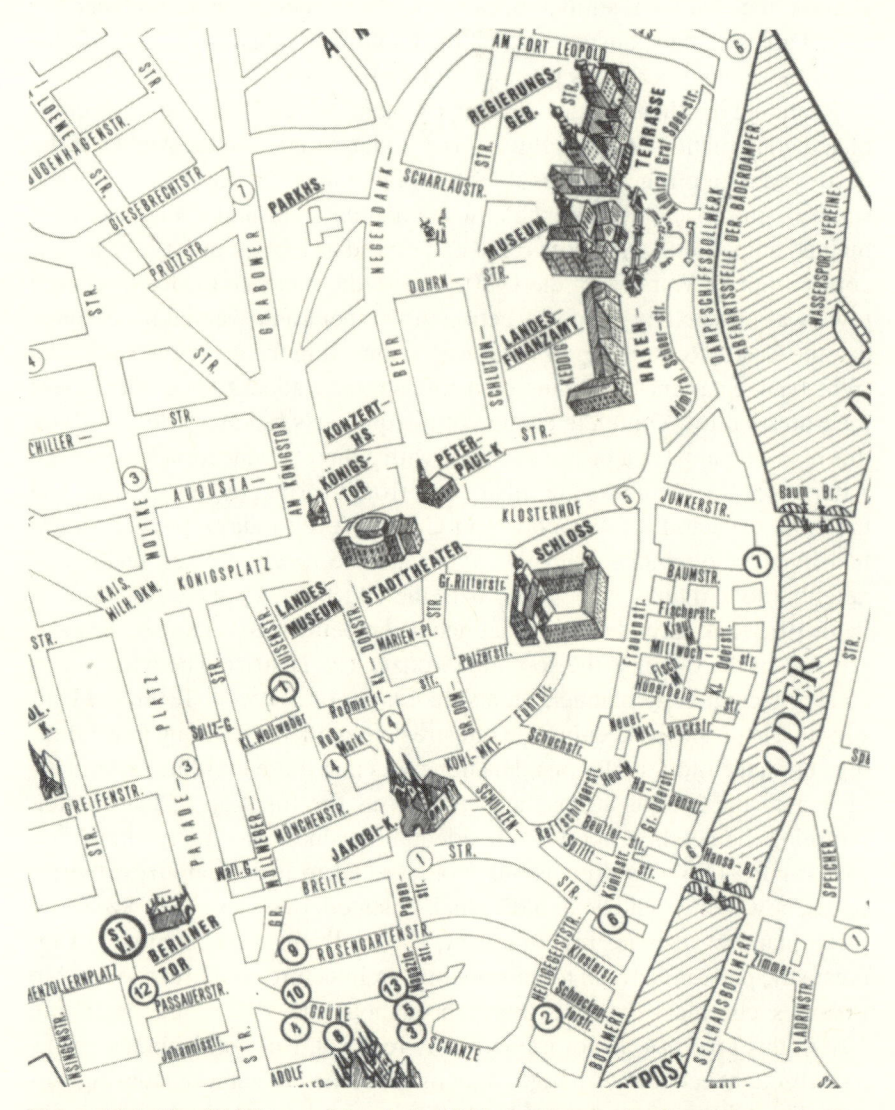

Figure 11.1. The Old Town of Stettin in 1942. A close-meshed road network characterized the old city center on the Oder River. North of the castle ("Schloss") is the Hakenterrasse. Drawing from *Stettin: Kurze Stadtgeschichte,* edited by Jan M. Piskorski, Bogdan Wachowiak, and Edward Włodarczyk (Poznań: Poznańskie Towarzystwo Przyjaciół Nauk, 1998), back cover; used by permission.

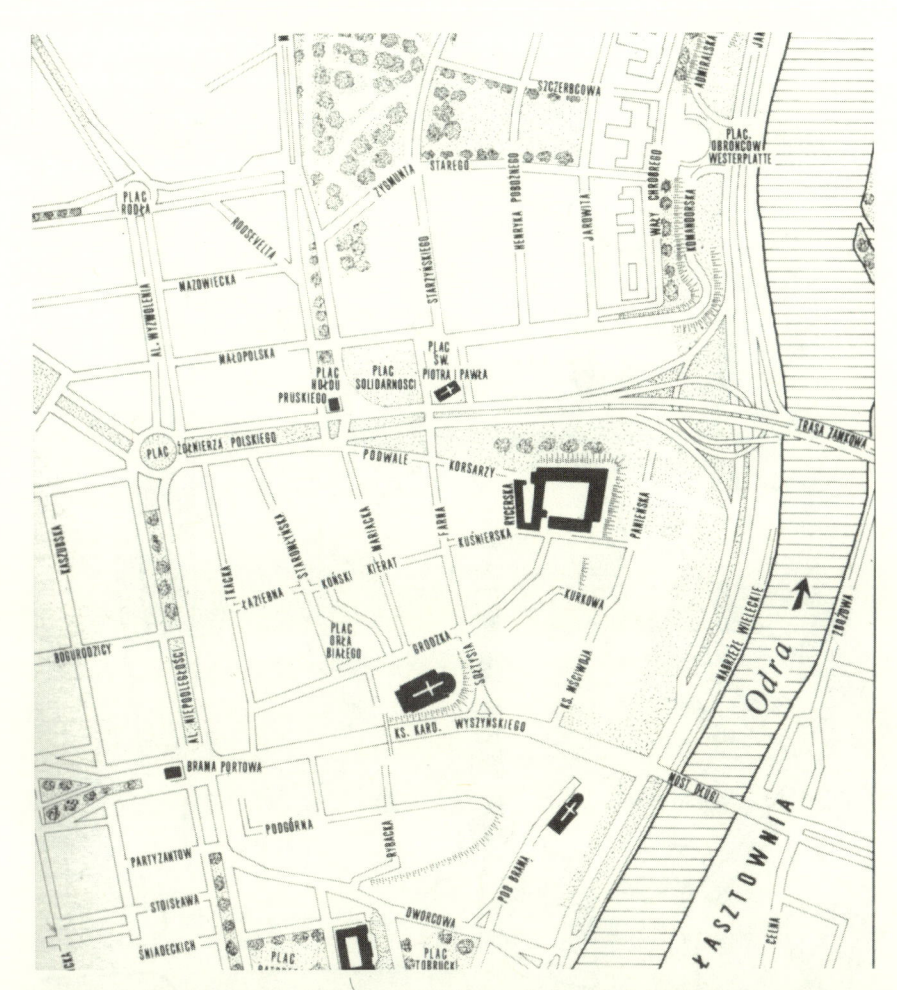

Figure 11.2. The historic Old Town of Szczecin in 1995. Only the western part of the district has been rebuilt. The "Oder Artery" separates the city from the river. West of the highway, a considerable part of the district remained vacant until 1995. Drawing from *Stettin: Kurze Stadtgeschichte,* edited by Jan M. Piskorski, Bogdan Wachowiak, and Edward Włodarczyk (Poznań: Poznańskie Towarzystwo Przyjaciół Nauk, 1998), page 137; used by permission.

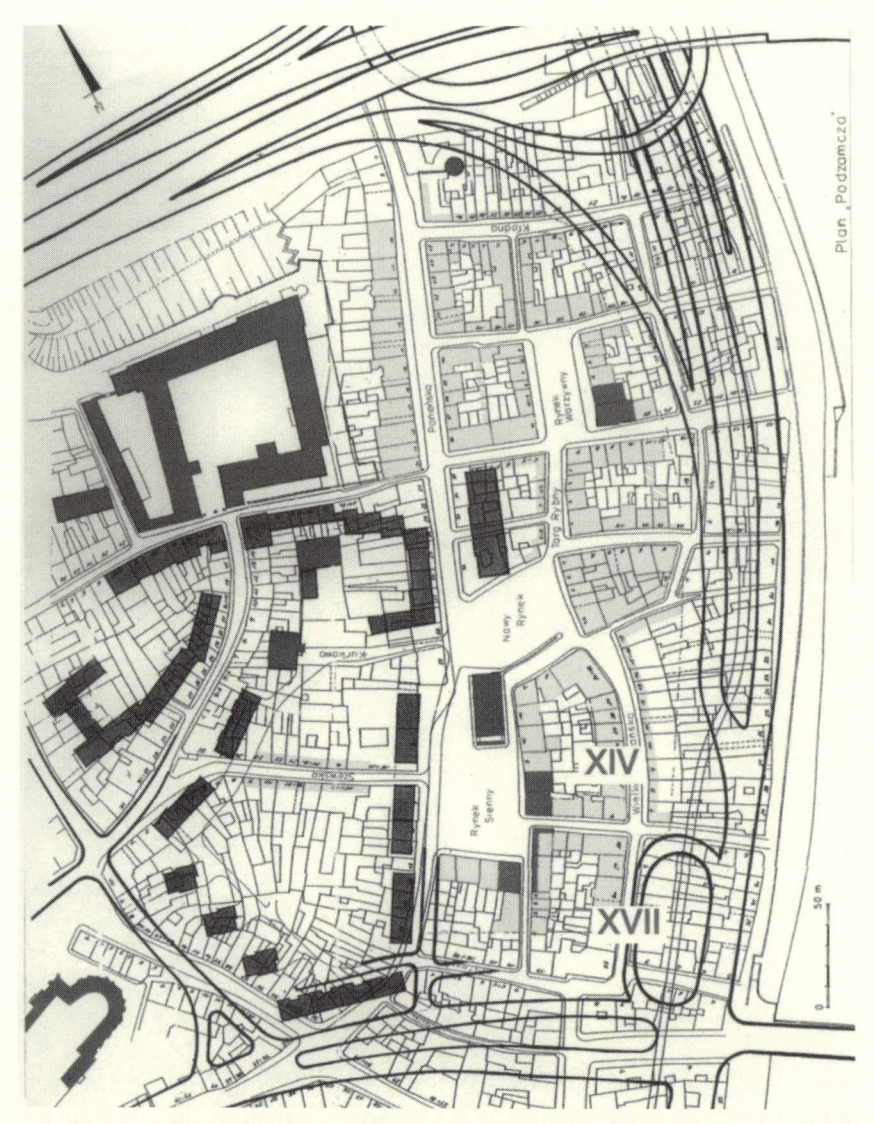

Figure 11.3. The Podzamcze District. The prewar district, compactly built, is being partly reconstructed (shown by the gray-shaded areas). An up ramp (at the top of the drawing) and the Oder Artery (at the right side of the drawing) have amputated the historic Old Town from its surroundings. Drawing from *Szczecińskie Podzamcze: Staromiejska dzielnica nadodrzańska i jej odbudowa —kwartały XIV i XVII,* by Maciej Słomiński (Szczecin: Spółdzielnia Mieszkaniowa "Podzamcze," 1998); used by permission.

Figure 11.4. The Podzamcze District in 2003 (block XVII), divided from the Oder River by the Oder Artery. The castle is visible in the background. Photograph by Jan Musekamp.

The population received the new quarter of residential buildings, offices, pubs, and restaurants enthusiastically. One of the new residents stated that after rebuilding the Old Town, Szczecinians would no longer have to take second place in competing with old town atmospheres in Gdańsk, Wrocław, Poznań, or Cracow. "Sometimes dreams come true. . . . Szczecin can boast of its new Old Town."[31] Ultimately, the Podzamcze District became a tourist magnet. Especially German visitors, often prewar inhabitants, admired the project, which they considered a return to history.

Unfortunately, the housing cooperative that organized the reconstruction project ran into financial problems following the economic crisis of 2001, which affected all of Poland. The Szczecin shipyards were hit especially hard. Having finished four of the ten blocks, the cooperative announced bankruptcy in mid-2002, leaving behind angry investors and unfinished construction sites.[32] All sites and buildings came under private ownership, which did not prove beneficial to the plan. Some flats remain uninhabited, and a couple of tenements have yet to be finished, while still other sites await development. These "eyesores" deter tourists, for obvious reasons.[33] At the moment, the vivid old town atmosphere that the city planners had hoped to create is perceptible only in patches throughout the district. Nevertheless, Szczecin is planning a return to its prewar roots by revitalizing the area around its old heart, the Oder River. The Oder Artery is to be replaced by an annex to the Podzamcze District, returning to the historic street network that had been destroyed by the highway.[34]

## Mayor Hermann Haken: German or Szczecinian?

Revolutions imply radical changes in a country's memorial landscape. After 1989, most Polish cities had a "facelift." Not only did the market economy lead to a more colorful city image; it involved changing street names and monuments. The act of replacing street names reflects the citizens' new views of their past; they are a mirror of the collective memory. According to Maurice Halbwachs, this "collective memory . . . adapts the image of ancient facts to the beliefs and spiritual needs of the present."[35]

After 1989, street names in Szczecin referring to Communist ideology were generally replaced by heroes of the interwar period or the national resistance of World War II. Thus, Red Army Street was renamed Monte Cassino Street, Marian Buczek Street became Józef Piłsudski Street, and so on.[36] But the landscape is not only the returning to Polish national history, previously oppressed by the Communist system, but is also commemorating local heroes, linking topography with local heritage. As more and more Szczecin pioneers of great merit die, the city honors them by naming streets after them. One of the last local heroes commemorated in that way was Lieutenant Hieronim Kupczyk, who was killed in action in Iraq in 2003.[37]

More remarkable is the act of commemorating German Szczecinians. On December 17, 2001, the Szczecin City Council decided to name a newly built roundabout in the western part of the city after the former German mayor of Stettin, Hermann Haken, who had been in office from 1878 to 1907.[38] By honoring Haken, the members of the council explicitly acknowledged the city's German legacy. It was Haken who had forced the erection of the famous "Hakenterrasse" (Polish: "Wały Chrobrego"), a group of historicist, representative buildings in the northern part of the Old Town (figure 11.5). In 1945, the undestroyed Hakenterrasse was the first residence of the Polish administration. Of course, in 1945, a Polish flavor was asserted when it was given the name of Poland's first king, Bolesław Chrobry, who had

Figure 11.5. The Wały Chrobrego (formerly Hakenterrasse) National Museum and administration buildings, symbolizing the continuity from prewar Stettin to postwar Szczecin. Photograph by Jan Musekamp.

reigned over the territory of Szczecin. Today's Wały Chrobrego is the home of the National Museum (the former Stadtmuseum), the voivodship administration (the former German provincial administration), and the Sea Academy. The buildings' functions show the continuity between German Stettin and Polish Szczecin; the whole complex has become an example of the multicultural roots of the city.

But the council's decision to commemorate a German mayor was not accepted by everyone. When it came to a vote, twenty-two voted for the change to Haken, but eighteen were against the idea. This controversy reverberated in the society at large; public discussions about Haken are an excellent example of the reorientation, or "local turn," of the Szczecin collective identity and a change in the self-identification of its citizens.[39]

Like the two other Szczecin newspapers, the local edition of Poland's leading newspaper, the *Gazeta Wyborcza,* started to commit itself to increasing information about German Stettin after 1989. When publishing the results of the "Szczecinian of the Century" public poll in 2000, the *Gazeta Wyborcza* poignantly titled its article, the "Pro-German Szczecin."[40] Although Piotr Zaremba took first place in the poll, Hermann Haken and his successor Friedrich Ackermann followed in second and third place. The author's motivation stemmed from the fact that Szczecinians had come to recognize that the most beautiful buildings in the city were those that had survived since German times. Second, the German winners of the voting had ruled before 1933, and thus could not be connected to the National Socialists. Third, Szczecin's postwar history was quite short and characterized by a lack of heroes. Zaremba was, truth be told, the only strong and popular Polish mayor. The most important reason is Szczecin's search for a local identity. This process is exacerbated by the city's inferiority complex, which was caused by its peripheral, border-zone location, as well as by Warsaw's domineering rule, both before and after 1989. Uncovering the German layers of the city's history was seen as helping to reassert Szczecin's strength within Poland.

The poll was a sensation; not only did it open a forum for discussion about the city's German past to a broader public, but it was also much more effective than any of the anniversary celebrations. The poll allowed Szczecinians to redefine their identity by accepting the prewar history of the city as their own.[41] Previously, only a small circle of specialists and enthusiasts dealt with the German cultural heritage, including conservationists, art historians, and a few historians. Their valuable contribution consisted of new research on Szczecin's history, with an outstanding Polish-German coproduction about Szczecin's first years after World War II.[42] After the voting, the *Gazeta Wyborcza* proposed adding Haken (and Ackermann) to the register of possible street names, an idea that was accepted by the Committee of Public Order and Self-Government. In September 2001, a majority of the committee decided to recommend that the City Council name the roundabout after Haken. One commissioner stressed the importance of that decision for the appropriation of a Szczecinian historic memory: "We have to build up a feeling of local identity, Haken lived in this city and co-created it." In the end, only one commissioner rejected the project, fearing that the decision would give rise to negative emotions, especially among the elderly population.[43]

The committee's statement was published and subsequently led to a broad discussion. A kind of "Hakenomania" broke out; a sensation erupted when a local historian identified a damaged tombstone at the city's Central Cemetery as Haken's last resting place.[44] In November 2001, right before the final voting in the City Council, readers of the *Gazeta Wyborcza* began sending letters praising and, at times, criticizing the proposal. The Catholic association Civitas Christiana and some other right-wing organizations (having grown to be quite strong in Poland) proposed to name the roundabout after the Polish pioneers, who had settled Szczecin after 1945, thus returning to pre-1989 Communist propaganda: "Maybe Haken is a symbol of Szczecin, but of the German one. We cannot accept such a figure. . . . It is the Polishness of these lands we have to promote."[45] Szczecin's professor of history, Edward Włodarczyk, replied, "We should honor those people who did something for this city. Haken deserves it as much as the Polish pioneers of Szczecin. . . . What is the problem about Haken being a German? If we would like to be correct in national terms, we should build a Polish water network next to the German one." The Polish Patriotic Association, Kontra 2000, complained about an ongoing "Germanization" of the city. The association polemicized, "If the roundabout will be named after Haken, we shall [soon] propose renaming some square into 'Hitlerplatz.'"[46] Another reader's letter compared the situation of Szczecin with those of L'viv (Polish: Lwów; German: Lemberg), which was the birthplace of many Szczecin inhabitants: "We sing songs about Lwów, . . . visit the cities of our forefathers, but forbid Europe from remembering its great persons."[47]

On November 26, 2001, the City Council planned to decide about the matter. The press called this decision, "an exam in Europeanness," alluding to Poland's forthcoming membership in the European Union. By restoring the memory of Haken, local identity would be enforced, and it would be based on the prewar, German history of the city, as well.[48] In spite of the committee's straightforward decision and despite positive public opinion, the City Council did not decide about the issue until three weeks later, as scheduled. Protests from some organizations made council members hesitate. Another flood of angry letters arrived at the *Gazeta Wyborcza,* complaining about the provincialism of Szczecin and the missed chance to show the Europeanness and openness of the city. In the end, Haken's advocates were victorious. The press was enthusiastic about the council members' courage and the new, "modern, European face" of Szczecin, which would find its identity in its local history—a history not necessarily Polish.[49] Such an unprecedented case of commemorative practice regarding the city's history is not faultless. Such enthusiasm also suffered a setback in the following years, as enthusiasm for the European Union was in decline. In 2000, the League of Expellees (Bund der Vertriebenen), a notorious organization of expellees from former Eastern Territories of Germany, established a foundation in order to erect a Berlin "Center against Expulsions" (Zentrum gegen Vertreibungen).[50] Discussions about this center had already exacted its heavy toll on Polish-German relations, when in 2003 the Prussian Claims Society (Preußische Treuhand), an organization of radical German expellees, started to threaten Poles with lawsuits relating settlement claims. These claims, though backed by a minuscule group of activists, caused enormous damage in Polish-German relations and led to disillusionment on the side of Poles concerning Germany.[51] In Szczecin, which is only two hours away from Germany's capital, Berlin, these feelings were even deeper. In the wake of growing skepticism about Germany and irrational fears about the European Union, the mayor of Szczecin, Marian Jurczyk, was elected in November 2002, partly because of his nationalistic rhetoric.[52] Haken came to play a role in this drama as well; during renovations of the National Museum on Wały Chrobrego (the former Hakenterrasse) in September 2003, some prewar street names cut in sandstone on the building's facade were uncovered. Among them was the German inscription "Haken-Terrasse." This discovery revived the "Haken discussions"—was Haken only a Stettin hero or a Szczecin hero, as well? Backed by its readers, the *Gazeta Wyborcza* started a campaign to renovate the plate in order to publicly expose it. But it proved to be a bad time to expose the German legacies in Szczecin; in a fierce discussion, the museum's director, as well as the already-mentioned Włodarczyk, stood against the *Gazeta Wyborcza*, arguing that the inscription should be inventoried but then hidden under plaster. The arguments against exposure varied. The museum's director argued that the German street sign would lead to ambiguity concerning signposting: "For the museum, the question of the plate is not a conservational problem . . . but a legal one, for it would violate the competences of local self-administration deciding about the street names in Szczecin."[53] Two professors of history from Szczecin University backed the director, citing preexisting examples of positive Polish-German cooperation for the sign's obsoleteness, and warning against creating a precedent that would strengthen German revisionists' claims (like those of the "Prussian Claims Society").[54] In this case, it seems as if not only German-Polish relations but also the local identity had been suffering.

## Local Heroes: Monuments after 1989

Monuments connect past and present. They also represent officially approved images of history. For centuries, the destruction of monuments had been an instrument to demonstrate the power of the conqueror, symbolizing the destruction of existing traditions and liberation from the past.[55] On the one hand, tradition was destroyed; on the other hand, new traditions were created.

When Poles took over Stettin, not only were former inhabitants expelled from the city but also everything that looked German was eradicated. As in Wrocław and Gdańsk, a plethora of monuments testifying to the cities' German past were removed, often "outdoing" street names and thousands of inscriptions in their commemorative value. In Szczecin, the monument to Emperor Frederick III was destroyed in 1945, creating a void until 1960, when the national poet Adam Mickiewicz filled it—a German national hero was replaced by a Polish one. After 1989, memorial landscapes were almost certain to change with the times. Although no monuments were destroyed (aberrantly, neither Lenin nor Marx found his way to distant Szczecin), locals were discontented with their memorial landscape. Generally speaking, they only had national, religious, or abstract heroes, such as Mickiewicz, the Virgin Mary, and the postwar Szczecinians, symbolically immortalized by huge eagles located in Szczecin's largest park next to the New Town Hall.

Looking for a new self-image, Szczecinians could be proud of two historical events that occurred in postwar Szczecin, namely, the workers' uprisings of 1970 and 1980. In both Poland and abroad, Lech Wałęsa and his Solidarity movement in Gdańsk are well-known historical, anticommunist figures. That protests and demonstrations were held in Szczecin, similar in extent and consequence to those in Gdańsk, is not well known.[56] Even in 2005, when celebrating the twenty-fifth anniversary of the founding of Solidarity, the world generally looked to Gdańsk, leaving Szczecin (once again) on the sidelines—a fact that certainly did not improve Szczecinians' self-image.

With activists of the Solidarity movement in power, plans arose to build a monument to commemorate the protests of December 1970, when the ruling Communist Party's headquarters in Szczecin had been burnt down and the state militia had killed sixteen people. In 1996, after several years of discussions, the City Council decided to build a monument. An appropriate December 1970 Committee had already been convened two years earlier, and the design of the monument was to be determined by an open competition.[57] In 1998, the Polish Architects' Association arranged a competition. The winner was a young team from Szczecin, planning to create a hundred so-called phantoms that would represent the demonstrating masses. Experts cited this solution as "evidence of dealing with this subject very responsibly, without melodramatics."[58] It seemed as though everyone would be satisfied.

But the members of the committee, having initially agreed on the project, changed their minds two years later. Among other problems, they wanted a cross to symbolize the killed workers. They also complained that the design was too small compared with the Solidarity monument in Gdańsk.[59] Therefore the City Council decided to realize another project, called *The Wave*. The monument was to be opened in December 2001, but that deadline could not be met because, disgusted by the way that the winners of the competition had been treated,[60] the designer of *The Wave* withdrew his project.[61]

In the coming years, fierce discussions brought about several changes in the concept and appearance of the monument. In 2002, a new competition was arranged, with *Paths through Life* taking the ribbon. *Paths through Life* envisioned sixteen interrupted paths that symbolized the sixteen victims of the 1970 protests. However, once again, the committee disagreed with the outcome of the competition. Its honorary chairman, Marian Jurczyk, the leader of the protests in 1980 and newly elected mayor, preferred another design, the so-called *Workers' Pieta*, which would be realized by an artist who did not participate in either of the two competitions.[62] The model of the *Pieta*, with a worker holding a wounded or killed person in his arms, reminded many of Socialist realism of the Stalinist era. Szczecinian artists were disgusted, denouncing the project as banal. The editors of the *Gazeta Wyborcza* called it "one of the most ridiculous and, at the same time, one of the most terrible ideas of Mayor Jurczyk." The *Pieta* caused a heated discussion among Szczecinians.[63] The council's Commission of Culture rejected the project. In its opinion, not only should workers be able to identify with the monument but all Szczecinians who participated in the protests, workers as well as teachers, students, and the like. "No one holds a monopoly on Szczecin's history outside of its inhabitants," stated the chairman of the commission, Paweł Bartnik.[64]

Finally, in December 2004, the commission employed the sculptor Czesław Dźwigaj from Cracow to make his proposal for a monument. Szczecin's mayor selected a huge sculpture called *Angel of Freedom*, which, as the title suggests, depicts an angel holding a crown of thorns in his hands. The original draft had to be changed various times to calm down some of the fiercest critics, variously comparing the *Angel* to a monstrance, a character from a fantasy film, or a hussar with an accordion.[65] The City Council finally approved the *Angel* as a monument commemorating not only the events of December 1970 but also those of August 1980.[66] The majority of the council was not convinced of the artistic value of the sculpture, but they were tired of the endless discussions, especially with regard to the victims: "I finally voted for the *Angel* because I recognized that it was a disgrace that there was no monument yet," as one council member stated; another added: "I do not like Dźwigaj's *Angel,* but I recognized this never-ending discussion as being enough."[67] On August 28, 2005—exactly twenty-five years after the beginning of the 1980 strikes and after more than a decade of fierce discussions—the participants in the 1970 and 1980 protests inaugurated the controversial *Angel of Freedom.*[68] In the end, the mere construction proved to be more important than its actual appearance (figure 11.6).

Monuments erected during the lifetime of the heroes they honor are most often heavily disputed. However, despite harsh criticism during its creation, and the blatant personal ambitions of the city's mayor, the *Angel* is likely to be integrated into Szczecin's memorial landscape with relative ease. For the Szczecinians' identity, the protests of 1970 and 1980 seem to be the most outstanding historical events, a reason to be proud of the city.

Another monument did not cause any trouble among Szczecinians, but it would have surely burdened the relations between Szczecin and Warsaw. As mentioned above, some prewar Stettin art objects were returned to Szczecin from Warsaw in 1995. An integral part of the prewar collection were copies of renaissance sculptures, including the monumental bronze horse statue of the knight Bartolomeo Colleoni, which had adorned the second floor of the Stadtmuseum. The original statue, located on the square near Saint John's and Saint Paul's Church in Venice, is an excellent example of renaissance art. After World War II, it was transported to Warsaw even before the rest of the collection. In 1946, the Warsaw Help Committee in Szczecin came up with the idea of presenting the Colleoni to Warsaw,[69] which had lost most of its monuments due to its total destruction. Despite transportation problems, the Colleoni arrived in Warsaw, where no one knew where to install it. It was only in 1949 when it found a place in the courtyard of Warsaw's newly rebuilt Academy of Fine Arts.[70]

Some Szczecinians had never forgotten that their cultural objects had been taken away. In 1990, after the reestablishment of local self-government, a long fight for the return of the Colleoni began. Antoni Adamczak, a local tourist guide, wrote the City Council an open letter proposing to replace the so-called Gratitude Monument, honoring the Soviet soldiers who had liberated the city, with the Colleoni statue. Interest grew as more and more people and institutions wanted to return the monument for the planned seven-hundred-fiftieth anniversary in 1993. But the Academy of Fine Arts was not willing to give up the sculpture, because it had gained such popu-

Figure 11.6. The *Angel of Freedom* on Inauguration Day, August 28, 2005, commemorating the 1970 and 1980 uprisings. Photograph from the Szczecin City Council.

larity as a student meeting point. In 1998, the mayor of Szczecin held talks with the Academy of Fine Arts, which offered to commission a copy of the Colleoni—even the costs were calculated.[71]

In 2001, the fight for the Colleoni's return was finally successful. In the newly established Internet forums of the *Gazeta Wyborcza,* a discussion about the Colleoni once again launched by posing the question "Is it worth one more try?" and asking the newspaper to support these efforts. This forum set off an avalanche:[72] In the following months, Szczecin's newspapers overwhelmingly supported those fighting for the Colleoni's return.[73] The Colleoni came to be a monument that would decide the city's identity.[74] With more and more Szczecinians protesting, the Academy of Fine Arts finally had to surrender. In September 2001, the academy's director declared his willingness to return the equestrian statue, on the condition that Szczecin would raise enough funds to make a copy for the academy.[75] The Szczecin community and institutions were mobilized, enough funds were raised after a mere eight months, and Warsaw was paid for a copy of the Colleoni.[76] Meanwhile, a dispute had emerged over where to install the reclaimed sculpture. Its prewar place was the museum, but now the community wanted him to decorate a representative square. Although the previously mentioned Gratitude Monument was not removed, an empty space opposite of the latter was prepared for the Colleoni. On August 31, 2001, the Colleoni monument was inaugurated festively by an entourage in historic costumes announcing the Colleoni's unveiling; there was even a special guest from Bergamo who had been invited as a descendant of Colleoni (figure 11.7).[77]

The Colleoni united Szczecinians in their will to oppose Poland's capital. One could generally say that the Szczecin community saw Warsaw as patronizing to the country's periphery. At the same time, fighting (successfully) for the Colleoni's return could help ease Szczecin's chronic inferiority complex. But for most Szczecinians, it was the opposition against Warsaw that molded this proto-identity; discovering a part of prewar, German Stettin actually took second place. Interestingly enough, the monument did not return to the museum, where it had been before. By setting it in a busy square, its importance grew significantly as compared with its prewar position. At the same time, by installing it opposite the hated Soviet monument, it poignantly contrapositions the city's past commemorative landscape with its future. Indeed, the Colleoni has advanced as a symbol of Szczecinian unification today. Just before parliamentary elections in September 2005, the candidates of the six major political parties held a meeting at the Colleoni

Figure 11.7. The monument to the knight Bartolomeo Colleoni at its new site in 2006. Photograph by Jan Musekamp.

monument to express there positive intentions in the Szczecin region, despite political differences.[78]

It is worth briefly analyzing one other monument, which no longer exists in the urban landscape, namely Stettin's symbol, Sedina. This female figure is an allegory of the city of Stettin and had been part of a monumental fountain in front of the so-called Red Town Hall. In 1898, this fountain was erected by the well-known sculptor Ludwig Manzel, on the occasion of the opening of Stettin's free harbor. A bronze Sedina was steadying herself on a sail and an anchor, symbolizing the city's maritime traditions. At her feet was placed the trade god, Mercury, and maritime gods steering a boat, symbolizing the power and wealth of the city (figure 11.8).[79] Sometime between 1943 and 1945, the bronze elements vanished, probably meeting their fate to be melted down for war matériel. After 1945, only the sandstone pedestal and the fountain had survived. Some years after the war, an anchor was displayed in this space, continuing the maritime traditions of the Sedina (figure 11.9). The prewar allegorical monument, however, was never replaced.

Figure 11.8. The prewar Sedina monument (Manzelbrunnen), an allegory of how the city's wealth is based on trade and shipping. From a historic postcard, used by permission of www.sedina.pl/.

By the 1950s, people were conscious of the void resulting from Sedina's absence.[80] Even before the Colleoni's comeback to Szczecin, some Szczecinians started thinking about putting up a copy of the lost Sedina. In the mid-1990s, Mayor Bartłomiej Sochański thought about cofinancing a Sedina reconstruction from the city's budget. But at the time, the erection of other monuments connected with the Polish history of Szczecin took center stage; financing a "German" monument at that time would likely have caused protests. It was council member Arkadiusz Litwiński who was most active in reestablishing this monument, which, according to him, was nei-

Figure 11.9. The Sedina monument today. The anchor symbolizes the city's link to the sea. Photograph by Jan Musekamp.

ther a symbol of Polishness or Germanness but of the city.[81] The *Gazeta Wyborcza* did a great deal to return its central symbol to Szczecin, and it appealed to the community to find out more about the monument's whereabouts.[82] Until 2005, its fate could not be uncovered, but a growing number of Szczecinians began to support the initiative. After the Colleoni's return, enthusiasm about a possible reconstruction of the Sedina rose. In June 2004, a Sedina Reconstruction Committee was founded with the National Museum's director, Lech Karwowski, as secretary, and an association of businesspeople as patrons. The committee plans to raise funds for an accurate copy of the original Sedina.[83] And with the mayor supporting the reconstruction, it seems to be only a question of time when the city's allegorical figure returns. On an Internet forum, people expressed their satisfaction about this. If a decision is made, this symbol of German Stettin might become the central symbol of Polish Szczecin, thus overcoming the caesura of 1945: "The Sedina monument is a symbol of Szczecin, our town, and we must remember that it has been German. What's the problem? We have to care of beautiful things—all of them don't have to be Polish."[84]

## Conclusions

Celebrating different anniversaries, revaluating historical city quarters, renaming streets, erecting new monuments, and fighting for lost ones—all have one thing in common: They reflect a community's changing civic identity and self-consciousness. Just as in Riga or Kaliningrad, this "archeology of the local" in Szczecin has been able to reinforce local and communal identities, thus constituting "a means to self-enfranchisement."[85]

The revaluation of a prewar city quarter in Szczecin does not necessarily mean a true appreciation of its former German inhabitants. After all, it was not the "German" quarter that had been restored but a "historical" quarter, one that could also be linked to the city's Slavonic past. The act of admitting a citizen of German Stettin to the pantheon of local collective memory has a different quality. It expresses the manifestation of a new self-consciousness. In the case of the Sedina, Szczecinians felt that their identity was lacking an important element of a prewar, local history. Artur Daniel Liskowacki, being a "pioneer" in linking Stettin and Szczecin by means of literature,[86] called the Szczecinians' enthusiasm for the Colleoni's return "a meaningful manifestation of the growing hunger for identity."[87] Nevertheless, as the discussions about German inscriptions show, the actual condition of Polish-German relations is able to help or hinder Szczecin's "soul searching."

The 2005 anniversary shows that today's inhabitants of Szczecin still have closer relations with Polish Szczecin than with German Stettin—even if less so than in 1995. This can be explained by the fact that their parents and grandparents came here after 1945, formed the city, and transmitted their relations on to the next generations, creating a communicative memory based on postwar historical events.[88] But as fewer and fewer eyewitnesses of Szczecin's Polish pioneer years survive, the caesura between the histories of the German city and the Polish city is becoming increasingly blurred. Third- and fourth-generation Szczecinians are fascinated by their city's German history as much as by its Polish history. Young Szczecinians have created a Web homepage for sharing comprehensive information about their city's past—a past that is not solely determined by 1945.[89]

This process appears to be more advanced in Wrocław and Gdańsk than in Szczecin. There are multiple reasons. Even today, Szczecin's location right at the frontier has an impact, and many people still fear a "German return," albeit economically and not politically. In addition, the universities of Wrocław and Gdańsk have stronger traditions than that of Szczecin, which was established only in 1984 and is not able to exert as much intellectual influence.

One might even venture to say that Wrocław's Europeanness and multiculturalism form an artificial facade, hiding discussions about German and Prussian heritage for a later date. In that regard, Szczecin may be more advanced. It is already a self-confident city, even if it is finding its place in a *region* but not on a *border*. In conclusion, a growing number of Szczecinians no longer perceive themselves in a national color but a local one; in the words of John Czaplicka, "The urban narratives are now composed in closer alignment with the specificity of space."[90]

## Notes

1. There are striking parallels to the situation of Kaliningrad. Both cities were considered the westernmost outposts of their states.
2. For an overview of Szczecin's history, see Jan M. Piskorski, Bogdan Wachowiak, and Edward Włodarczyk, *A Short History of Szczecin* (Poznań: Poznańskie Towarzystwo Przyjaciół Nauk, 2002).
3. Henryk Mąka, *Szczecin* (Poznań: Wydawnictwo Poznańskie, 1972), 5.
4. See chapter 3 in this volume by Gregor Thum.
5. See http://www.szczecin.pl/prawo/rada/1993/ur464_93.html.
6. Wojciech Lizak, "Niechciany jubileusz," *Polityka* (Warsaw), February 13, 1993.
7. Sylwia Ptak, "Będzie drogo, ale hucznie: Rozmowa ze Zbigniewem Zalewskim, wiceprezydentem Szczecina," *Przegląd Tygodniowy,* March 4, 1993.
8. "Prezentacja Szczecina Europie: Jubileusz 750-lecia praw miejskich—wielką szansą," *Kurier Szczeciński,* March 22–24, 1993.
9. Wojciech Lizak, "Niechciany jubileusz," *Polityka,* February 13, 1993.
10. Piotr Zaremba, "Moje miasto," *Kurier Szczeciński,* March 22, 1993.
11. "Szczecin tu, teraz i w XXI wieku, Rozmowa z prezydentem miasta dr. Władysławem Lisewskim," *Kurier Szczeciński,* April 2–4, 1993.
12. "750-lecie nadania Szczecinowi praw miejskich," *Kurier Szczeciński,* January 19, 1993.
13. See Jan Assmann, *Das kulturelle Gedächtnis: Schrift, Erinnerung und politische Identität in frühen Hochkulturen* (Munich: Beck Verlag, 1999), 52.
14. Hipolit Żegadło, "Wielcy Szczecinianie: Wystawa 750-lecia," *Kurier Szczeciński,* April 28, 1993.
15. For detailed information about the Soviet Army's dismantling the economy, see Ryszard Techman, *Armia Radziecka w gospodarce morskiej Pomorza Zachodniego w latach 1945–1956* (Poznań: Wydawnictwo Poznańskiego Towarzystwa Przyjaciół Nauk, 2003).

16. Bogdan Twardochleb, "Z biegiem dni...," *Pogranicza* (Szczecin), 1995, 159.
17. "50 lat polskiego Szczecina," *Kurier jubileuszowy,* January 7, 1995.
18. Jadwiga Najdowa, "Sprawozdanie z działalności Muzeum Narodowego w Szczecinie w roku 1995. In *Materiały Zachodniopomorskie* 41 (1995): 464.
19. John J. Czaplicka, "Urban History after a Return to Local Self-Determination: Local History and Civic Identity," in *Composing Urban History and the Constitution of Civic Identities,* ed. John J. Czaplicka and Blair A. Ruble (Washington and Baltimore: Woodrow Wilson Center Press and Johns Hopkins University Press, 2003), 374.
20. See the library's Web site, http://www.ksiaznica.szczecin.pl.
21. This exposition was in the museum building at 3 Wały Chrobrego Street from July 5, 2005, to June 30, 2007.
22. See the precedent exposition "The Homeland of Many" (Ojczyzna wielu) in Szczecin's National Museum, June 28, 2002–March 31, 2005.
23. See chapter 3 in this volume by Thum.
24. On the importance of the Szczecin castle, see Jan Musekamp, "Der Königsplatz (plac Żołnierza Polskiego) in Stettin als Beispiel kultureller Aneignung nach 1945," in *Wiedergewonnene Geschichte: Zur Aneignung von Vergangenheit in den Zwischenräumen Mitteleuropas,* ed. Peter Oliver Loew, Christian Pletzing, and Thomas Serrier (Darmstadt: Harrassowitz Verlag, 2006), 19–35.
25. See Pierre Nora's concept of memorial landscapes and realms of memory ("lieux de mémoire"): Pierre Nora, "Entre Mémoire et Histoire: La problématique des lieux," in *Lieux de mémoire,* vol. 1, *La République,* ed. Pierre Nora (Paris: Gallimard, 1984), xvii–xlii.
26. Nora, "Entre Mémoire," xvii; Aleida Assmann, *Erinnerungsräume: Formen und Wandlungen des kulturellen Gedächtnisses* (Munich: Beck Verlag, 1999), 309.
27. Piotr Zaremba, *Wspomnienia prezydenta Szczecina, 1945–1950,* 2nd ed. (Poznań: Wydawnictwo Poznańskie, 1980), 421.
28. For a concise description of the city planners' reorganization of Szczecin's old town, see Jörg Hackmann, "Stettin: Zur Wirkung der deutsch-polnischen Grenze auf die Stadtentwicklung nach 1945," in *Grenzen und Grenzräume in der deutschen und polnischen Geschichte: Scheidelinie oder Begegnungsraum?* ed. Georg Stöber and Robert Maier (Hannover: Verlag Hahnsche Buchhandlung, 2000), 217–34.
29. For a description of the planning in detail, see Jolanta Barańska, Stanisław Latour, and Lucjan Jan Lipiński, *Modelowe przykłady rewaloryzacji wybranych zespołów zabytkowych na Pomorzu Zachodnim* (Szczecin: Wydawnictwo uczelniane Politechniki Szczecińskiej, 1990), 211–41.
30. For a description of the Podzamcze reconstruction, see Grzegorz Stiasny, "Rekonstrukcja nastroju," *Architektura-Murator* (Warsaw), 1999, 22–29 (English summary included); Maciej Słomiński, *Szczecińskie Podzamcze: Staromiejska dzielnica nadodrzańska i jej odbudowa—kwartały XIV i XVII* (Szczecin: Spółdzielnia Mieszkaniowa "Podzamcze," 1998).
31. Michał Janosz, "Odrodzenie starówki," *Gazeta Wyborcza Szczecin,* May 4, 2001, Szczecin insert.
32. Zarząd wyczerpany, "Podzamcze w likwidacji," *Gazeta Wyborcza Szczecin,* June 28, 2002, Szczecin insert.
33. "Kto skończy te domy. Podzamcze: Co dalej z kamienicami przy Panieńskiej," *Gazeta Wyborcza Szczecin,* January 11, 2006, Szczecin insert; Andrzej Kulej, "Polnische Wirtschaft," *Gazeta Wyborcza Szczecin,* June 10, 2005, Szczecin insert.

34. Kinga Konieczny, "Sercem Szczecina jest rzeka: Rozmowa z prof. Stanisławem Latourem, architektem," *Gazeta Wyborcza Szczecin,* February 24, 2003, Szczecin insert; Dariusz Gorajski, "Deptak nad Odrą?" *Gazeta Wyborcza Szczecin,* January 5, 2006, Szczecin insert.

35. Maurice Halbwachs, *La Topographie légendaire des Évangiles: Étude de mémoire collective* (Paris: Presses Universitaires de France, 1971; orig. pub. 1941), 7, quoted after Barry Schwartz, "The Social Context of Commemoration: A Study in Collective Memory," *Social Forces,* no. 82 (1982): 377.

36. See http://www.szczecin.pl/prawo/rada/1991/1991_XIV_125.html.

37. Sebastian Wołosz, "Montaż z poślizgiem proceduralnym: Tabliczki na ul. ppłk. Kupczyka," *Gazeta Wyborcza Szczecin,* May 19, 2004, Szczecin insert.

38. See http://www.szczecin.pl/prawo/rada/2001/ur974_2001.htm. At the same time, a park in the city center was named after Haken's successor, Friedrich Ackermann.

39. See Assmann, *Das kulturelle Gedächtnis,* 132.

40. Jerzy Sawka, "Polski Szczecin proniemiecki," *Gazeta Wyborcza* (Warsaw), January 25, 2000.

41. Nora, "Entre Mémoire," xxix.

42. Ostseeakademie Lübeck-Travemünde and Instytut Historii Uniwersytetu Szczecińskiego, eds., *Stettin 1945–1946: Dokumente–Erinnerungen. Szczecin 1945–1946— Dokumenty–Wspomnienia* (Rostock: Hinstorff Verlag, 1995).

43. Kinga Konieczny, "Rondo Hakena: Nasze miasto odzyskuje pamięć," *Gazeta na Pomorzu,* September 15–16, 2001, Szczecin insert.

44. "Odkrycie grobu Hakena," *Gazeta na Pomorzu,* November 2, 2001, Szczecin insert.

45. Zbigniew Roragiewski, "Nie będzie Niemiec: On jest też nasz," *Gazeta na Pomorzu,* November 10–11, 2001, Szczecin insert.

46. "Nie Niemcowi: Rondo Hakena—Protest Kontry," *Gazeta Wyborcza Szczecin,* November 21, 2001, Szczecin insert.

47. Zbigniew Rymarczuk, "Haken a my," *Gazeta Wyborcza Szczecin,* November 14, 2001, Szczecin insert.

48. Jerzy Sawka, "Egzamin z Europy: Radni o niemieckich burmistrzach," *Gazeta Wyborcza Szczecin,* November 26, 2001, Szczecin insert.

49. Jerzy Sawka, "Nasi Niemcy," *Gazeta Wyborcza Szczecin,* December 18, 2001, Szczecin insert.

50. Concerning the activities of the foundation, see Stiftung "Zentrum gegen Vertreibungen," available at http://www.z-g-v.de/ (including English version).

51. More on German-Polish relationship of the last years, see Jan M. Piskorski, *Vertreibung und deutsch-polnische Geschichte—Eine Streitschrift* (Osnabrück: Fibre Verlag, 2005).

52. Jurczyk was the leading figure of Szczecin's Solidarity uprising in 1980.

53. Lech Karwowski, "Oświadczenie Muzeum Narodowego," *Gazeta Wyborcza Szczecin,* September 27–28, 2003, Szczecin insert.

54. Edward Włodarczyk and Włodzimierz Stępiński, "Napisy trzeba zachować, ale przykryć," *Gazeta Wyborcza Szczecin,* October 16, 2003, Szczecin insert.

55. Winfried Speitkamp, "Denkmalsturz und Symbolkonflikt in der modernen Geschichte: Eine Einleitung," in *Denkmalsturz: Zur Konfliktgeschichte politischer Symbolik,* ed. Winfried Speitkamp (Göttingen: Verlag Vandenhoeck und Ruprecht, 1997), 6, 12–13.

56. See Artur Daniel Liskowacki, "Pionierzy i kondotierzy," *Gazeta Wyborcza*, January 26–27, 2002.
57. See http://www.szczecin.pl/prawo/rada/1996/1996_xxii_261.html.
58. Małgorzata Anusewicz, "Konkurs rozstrzygnięty, realizacja projektu niebawem," *Pogranicza* (Szczecin), 1999, 90–93.
59. Michał Rembas, "Brak detali i nie ma krzyża," *Gazeta Wyborcza Szczecin*, January 30, 2001, Szczecin insert.
60. See http://www.szczecin.pl/prawo/rada/2001/ur793_2001.htm.
61. Michał Rembas, "Honor architekta," *Gazeta Wyborcza Szczecin*, April 4, 2001, Szczecin insert.
62. Michał Rembas and Kinga Konieczny, "Pieta, nie ścieżki. Pomnik Grudnia '70: Zaskakująca procedura," *Gazeta Wyborcza Szczecin*, December 13–14, 2003, Szczecin insert.
63. Jolanta Kowalewska, "Poronin / Jerzy Sawka, Kontrowersyjna Pieta," *Gazeta Wyborcza Szczecin*, July 15, 2004, Szczecin insert.
64. Kinga Konieczny and Wojciech Jachim, "To bunt całego miasta. Radni przeciwko 'Robotniczej Piecie,'" *Gazeta Wyborcza Szczecin*, September 10, 2001, Szczecin insert.
65. Jerzy Połowniak, "Anioł czy kwiat magnolii? Rozmowy o pomniku Grudnia '70," *Gazeta Wyborcza Szczecin*, January 12, 2005, Szczecin insert.
66. Jerzy Połowniak, "Anioł populizmu," *Gazeta Wyborcza Szczecin*, January 11, 2005, Szczecin insert.
67. "Anioł populizmu," *Gazeta Wyborcza Szczecin*, January 11, 2005, Szczecin insert.
68. For a complete record of the inauguration speeches, see "Uroczyte odsłonięcie pomnika upmiętniającego Ofiary Grudnia 1970," http://bip.um.szczecin.pl/showpage?chapter=11376.
69. See Archiwum Państwowe w Szczecinie, Urząd Wojewódzki Szczciński 5078, 19 (letter of November 12, 1946, to Warsaw Help Committee).
70. "Posągi ze Szczecina ozdobią dziedziniec Akademii Sztuk Pięknych w Warszawie," *Kurier Szczeciński*, August 4, 1949.
71. See http://www.kroki.ps.pl/colleoni/proby.html.
72. See http://forum.gazeta.pl/forum/72,2.html?f=12&w=206951&v=2&s=0.
73. See Ewa Podgajna, "Colleoni, wróć!" *Gazeta Wyborcza Szczecin*, May 17, 2001, Szczecin insert.
74. Maciej Kowalewski, "Symbol miasta," *Gazeta Wyborcza Szczecin*, June 2–3, 2001, Szczecin insert.
75. Ewa Podgajna, "Kondotier wróci," *Gazeta Wyborcza Szczecin*, September 13, 2001, Szczecin insert.
76. Ewa Podgajna, "Pomnik już nasz," *Gazeta Wyborcza Szczecin*, May 17, 2002, Szczecin insert.
77. Magdalena Szymków, "To było zupełne zaskoczenie: Potomek Colleoniego w Szczecinie," *Gazeta Wyborcza Szczecin*, August 30, 2002, Szczecin insert.
78. "Twarz przy twarzy, dłonie w dłoniach," *Gazeta Wyborcza Szczecin*, September 21, 2005, Szczecin insert.
79. Ewa Gwiazdowska, "Pomnik-wodotrysk zw. Sedina-Brunner [*sic*] (Manzel-Brunnen)," in *Encyklopedia Szczecina*, vol. 2, ed. Tadeusz Białecki (Szczecin: Instytut Historii, Uniwersytet Szczeciński, Zakład Historii Pomorza Zachodniego, 2000), 154.

80. See Czesław Piskorski and Bolesław Rajkowski, *Jeden dzień w Szczecinie: Informator* (Szczecin: Prezydium Rady Okręgu Towarzystwa Rozwoju Ziem Zachodnich, 1959), 10.

81. Andrzej Kraśnicki, "To symbol miasta: Rozmowa z Arkadiuszem Litwińskim," *Gazeta Wyborcza Szczecin,* December 23–26, 2000, Szczecin insert.

82. Andrzej Kraśnicki, "Prawie jak przed wojną," *Gazeta Wyborcza Szczecin,* December 27, 2000, Szczecin insert.

83. See http://www.sedina.pl/modules.php?op=modload&name=News&file=article&sid=26.

84. "Krista57," February 2, 2005, http://forum.gazeta.pl/forum/72,2.html?f=70&w=20428575&a=20433385.

85. John J. Czaplicka, "The Archeology of the Local: Introduction," in *Composing Urban History,* ed. John J. Czaplicka and Ruble, 25, 27.

86. See Artur Daniel Liskowacki, *Ulice Szczecina* (Szczecin: Wydawnictwo Promocyjne "Albatros," 1995); and Artur Daniel Liskowacki, *Eine kleine* (Szczecin: Wydawnictwo, 2001). The latter almost obtained the most important Polish literature prize, Nike.

87. Artur Daniel Liskowacki, "Pionierzy i kondotierzy," *Gazeta Wyborcza Warszawa,* January 26–27, 2002.

88. Assmann, *Das kulturelle Gedächtnis,* 50.

89. See http://www.sedina.pl.

90. Czaplicka, "Urban History after a Return to Local Self-Determination," 372.

# Conclusion: Cities after the Fall
*Nida Gelazis, Blair A. Ruble, and John Czaplicka*

In 1997, the Commission of the European Union issued its proposed Agenda 2000, which outlined a series of objectives that would simultaneously deepen the interconnectedness of the European Union's member states and widen its current borders through an enlargement plan to embrace postcommunist Europe. The Commission's plan seemed counterintuitive: Why would the EU attempt to address two of the most controversial and challenging issues at once? The agenda was controversial because it seemed to defy the deep divisions between those member states that supported further integration and those that believed deepening would only bring further restrictions on state and individual activity. The issue of EU enlargement created even more problems, because the cultural, political, and economic disparities created by the Iron Curtain still seemed so wide that it was difficult to imagine how to bring the two sides together.

The Commission of the European Union responded by asserting that these two objectives were complementary and would reinforce each other, forming the "twin engines" that would propel the EU to a new level of integration. Though this rhetoric seemed like wishful thinking at the time, in the years to follow, the assertion that the two objectives complemented each other seemed to play itself out. Working at cross purposes, Euroskeptics and European integrationists fueled the opposite "engines," enabling the EU to move forward on both initiatives. For example, while enlargement skeptics worked at raising barriers to accession by advocating tougher EU legislation (deepening), Euroskeptics pushed for enlargement (widening) as a way to water down the Union.

The complementarity of the two objectives held even when there was no ulterior motive. For example, in the process of pursuing the enlargement policy, which involved measuring postcommunist countries' compliance with European norms, the EU member states became aware that their norms were not always clear enough to be transferable, which prompted the adoption of new European directives and legislation, including a new Charter for Human Rights. In this way, issue by issue and country by country, the EU has during the past decade both deepened its basis for integration and substantially widened its borders, growing from fifteen members in 1997 to twenty-seven in 2007.

It is one thing to see this trend in political, economic, and legal terms, but culture and values would seem much more difficult to define among the EU members in the West, let alone transfer to the East. Yet even in this sphere, there is an argument that enlargement helped to better define European identity. In this case, perhaps this process worked from East to West; in their attempt to prove their "Europeanness," it has been posited that postcommunist countries began to imitate European culture and values in their attempts to assimilate.[1] Through this process of imitation, postcommunist Europe may have helped to define European culture and values—in all its often contradictory forms. From this perspective, the chapters in this volume contribute to the growing literature in search of a European identity and demos.

## The Return of the Nation-State

From a certain perspective, one can view the "fall" of communism as a triumph of the nation-state. As this book has shown, the cities in the "new" countries of the former Soviet Union have felt pressure to build a cohesive national identity against a backdrop of seemingly arbitrary border shifts, wars, and countless waves of migration that transformed their ethnic character. This has been a reflex prompted as much by a rejection of communist cosmopolitanism as it has been an imitation of the stable narratives that protect the integrity of nation-states in Western Europe. The reinforcement of such narratives has been a strong motivation for modifying and adding to the material culture of postcommunist cities. The choice of integral narratives has presented difficulties in cities with histories inhabited by multiple cultures, peoples, and religions.

L'viv, which has been known by a half dozen names throughout its long history, exemplifies just such a city, for its physical and symbolic character has been shaped by a multiplicity of cultures, religions, languages, and traditions. Significantly, the city has been a major administrative center for three church hierarchies—the Polish-oriented Roman Catholic Church, the Ukrainian-oriented Greek Catholic Church, and the Armenian Catholic Church—and has been home to a vibrant Jewish community. In chapter 9, Liliana Hentosh and Bohdan Tscherkes explore the significance of this complex legacy in the process of defining public space in the aftermath of Ukrainian Independence. In L'viv, a multicultural approach to history has come into conflict with the Ukrainian state-building exercise, leading to conflict over the naming and meaning of various streets and public spaces throughout the city. Any reconsideration of local history and traditions is further complicated by the city's violent twentieth-century history, which has left this once cosmopolitan, multiethnic city the domain of just one ethnic group—the Ukrainians. Hentosh and Tscherkes demonstrate how the Ukrainianization of a city with strong historical associations with Armenians, Austrians, Jews, Poles, and Russians can go relatively smoothly even when only Ukrainians remain.

The need to create national institutions in postindependence Vilnius, combined with the city's complex history, have compelled local and national leaders to impose a new vision of Lithuanian identity onto the cityscape. Unlike the other two Baltic states, with their capitals of Tallinn and Riga, Lithuania had lost its capital to Poland before it lost its independence in 1940. Vilnius had been annexed by a newly reconstituted Poland shortly after World War I, so that the Lithuanian edifices of modern state power during the interwar years were to be found not in Vilnius but in Kaunas. As Irena Vaisvilaite describes in chapter 1, local leaders began to inscribe a Lithuanian narrative into Vilnius during the late Soviet era, which was further ramped up after Independence. Decisions had to be made about where the president of Lithuania was to live in the reclaimed historic capital, and about which monuments would be rebuilt or retained to represent the newly reconstituted nation-state. Such decisions necessarily involved a re-invention of the past as Vilnius had been an administrative center rather than a capital for centuries. Old monuments could be reerected, restored, and recreated. The buildings housing the major branches of the new Lithuanian state had to somehow find a home in structures that spoke of a Russian Imperial past, Polish rule, and Soviet domination.

In chapter 8, Volodymyr Kravchenko explores the difficulty of establishing a national narrative in a cityscape that reflects the realities of a place caught on the borderland where two nations intersect and intermingle. Kharkiv is a city that holds profound meaning for both Russians and for Ukrainians. Those meanings, however, diverge widely. For Russians, Kharkiv was a key outpost in the nation's subjugation of the "Wild Steppe." By contrast, for Ukrainians, Kharkiv was a center of treason and dissent, because it served as the capital of Soviet Ukraine following the Bolshevik Revolution and remained an important Soviet industrial center before Independence. Following 1991, efforts were made to systematically remove the physical and nominal signs of the city's prominent Soviet past. Yet rather than physically rebuild the city, the local administration simply renamed institutions, buildings, streets, and entire neighborhoods. But how to do so in a way that established ties to a Ukrainian past that was often secondary to the Russian and even Soviet pasts? Kravchenko reveals that this effort is highly dependent on national Ukrainian politics, with the events of the "Orange Revolution" opening up the possibility for a new national narrative that transcends the divisions of the past.

## From Communist Cosmopolitanism to European Multiculturalism

The rebounding of national identity is clearly evident throughout postcommunist Europe. In their efforts to reenter history, city leaders have worked to reinforce—and to some degree reinvent—stable national narratives so as to insulate themselves from the recent nationless pasts or to make a case for their inclusion in Western Europe's family of nations. Yet maintaining a grip on a single national historical narrative was not easy, because they could not be protected from democracy's chaos. Competing historical narratives arose almost as soon as one was embraced, and thus unity on a single story was practically impossible to achieve.

Far from being a failure, such challenges to any singular, monolithic national identity should be seen as further evidence that postcommunist

Europe has been moving closer to Western Europe, where decades of continued migration, further transnational integration, and a new appreciation for multiculturalism and diversity have changed the tone of national narratives substantially since the end of World War II. Interestingly, in postcommunist Europe, some of these multicultural challenges to nationalist-driven histories have appeared in the absence of actual multiculturalism; ethnic groups that had shared cities with members of the titular nation have long since disappeared from these cities through large-scale migration, expulsion, or ethnic cleansing. The motivations behind challenging the nationalist narrative with multicultural histories have been as varied as the histories themselves. Several chapters in this volume offer important insights into these motivations and the subsequent contests over history.

Rather than offering an opportunity for embracing Polish nationalism, the fall of Communism had an opposite effect in the border town of Szczecin, as Jan Musekamp explains in chapter 11. During the communist period, historians and city planners colluded to conceal as much as possible the fact that the city had in been part of Germany before its transfer to Poland in 1945. As a result, the proverbial clock on the street of communist Szczecin was turned back several centuries to a time when the territory was inhabited primarily by Slavs. A new openness to debate in the postcommunist period has lifted the taboo of ignoring the city's multicultural past, and Germans and Jews have been brought back into the local historical narratives. Moreover, by asserting the city's German connection, Szczecinians have been able to overcome, in part, their feelings of inferiority toward Warsaw, which had dominated them for decades.

In describing the revival of Łódź in chapter 10, Joanna Michlic notes how difficult it is to revive a city by harking back to a "golden age" in which multiple cultures contributed to the flowering of a city. Histories may provide a motif and motivation for emulation and further development, and may even help to instill a will toward tolerance of other cultures (a facet of liberal cosmopolitanism), but those histories are also starkly reminiscent of loss and the impossibility of return. This is especially true in the case of Łódź, which was once a microcosm of Europe in its mix of four cultures: German, Jewish, Polish, and Russian. Once the ethnic mix was changed and the economic basis for integration disappeared, urban revival became fraught with contradictions.

There are also many instances in which embracing multiculturalism does not mean embracing all the historic ethnic groups represented in a city's past. Following certain historical narrative threads inherently involves choosing one interpretation over another, or one historical period rather than another. These choices are deeply political. We can see this in Gregor Thum's observations in chapter 3 about the positive reception and rearticulation of a Hapsburg past in Wrocław. Though it is being done in the spirit of multiculturalism, this attempt at accentuating the city's Hapsburg past is contradicted by the contemporary failure to recognize its Prussian heritage—a heritage that is quite evident in its modern infrastructure and buildings. In Vilnius, one notes how discovering the influence of multiple European nations in the archaeological excavation of the Grand Duke's Palace went hand in hand with denying Polish cultural influences.

In the Baltic capitals of Tallinn and Riga, Russian language and culture were not among the more celebrated historical aspects of a European and multicultural past. The Danish, Swedish, and German historical contributions had easier access through the multicultural door to recognition. Referring to a cosmopolitanism made evident or projected into architectural styles, Jörg Hackmann demonstrates in chapter 4 how the particular modernist architecture of Tallinn serves to lend that city an "international" image that has aligned it variously with the larger region of Europe (the North), although the architecture itself—in its various classical modernist, restorationist, and postmodern articulations—has been largely designed by Estonian architects.

## Making European Aspirations Visible

Tallinn's choice to highlight its Nordic rather than Russian heritage is by no means unique or unexpected. In the contest over which interpretation of history will find material expression in a particular postcommunist city, a popular determinant for choosing between available options involves asking which interpretation of history will help link this city to a future to which its inhabitants aspire. A common response has been to choose the option that would bring the city closer to a united Europe.

Making historical connections to the rest of Europe or "relocating" into a larger Europe has seemed to be a way of justifying the inclusion of postcommunist Europe into Western political structures and a means to insinuate "Western" values and orientation into a local context. It is no coincidence that it has been during the postcommunist period that the search for the "true" center of Europe has become highly contested. It is also the case that many of the contestants for this title are located in the region considered by this volume.

At a regional level, several cities have worked at promoting the fact that they were originally part of Germany or the Hapsburg Empire—both of which are unquestionably "European." At another level, cities have pointed to their inclusion in the geographical extension of historic European economic and cultural spheres of influence, such as the Hanseatic League, or to their European traditions in philosophy, religion, and architecture.

In chapter 11, Musekamp posits that Szczecin's proximity to the German border made it more open to change than other Polish cities. It should come as no surprise, he writes, that Szeczcin was one of the cities where strikes and demonstrations broke out in the 1970s and 1980s. Yet he also chronicles the tension between Szczecin's opposing identities; its leaders and social groups have alternately masked its German past to strengthen its links to Poland and celebrated its ties to the West to establish Poland's European credentials.

Considering Russia's European credentials, in chapter 2 Nicolai Petro offers an analysis of the "Novgorod myth," which has given that city a conceptual framework to "identify itself with Europe, while preserving a distinctly Russian cultural identity." This myth amounts to a delicate balancing act that recalls nascent democratic traditions and the economic integration into a larger Europe of a peculiarly Old Russian city. This act is taking place in a Russia that is recognizing its European ties but remaining apart from Europe in a recrudescence of Great Power aspirations. The question Petro poses is about the viability of a historic model for a European identity within Russia. Where emulating the model has contemporary concrete results, such as the inclusion of Novgorod in a revived Hanseatic League, it shows its viability.

The species of Russian/European identity being cultivated in contemporary Kaliningrad is of quite a different nature and poses the question about historical models quite differently. In her treatment of the issue in chapter 7, Olga Sezneva points to the formation of a hybrid identity, which attempts to incorporate the essentially foreign German past of the city's former identity as Königsberg. The city's European credentials are found in the physical remnants of its expulsed culture and population, in its geographic location (both actual and mythic), and in the pride taken in its contributions to European culture. The current populace thus would seem to want to integrate the past into a genealogy of place that includes identifying them as Russian *and* European. And the city's recent settlers are assuming the identity of the place and relocating themselves and the city at the center of Europe.

In many of the cities discussed in this volume, one can see a similar tendency: Tallinn, by virtue of its architecture, finds its way into the heart of Northern Europe. L'viv gravitates to its Hapsburg heritage and its place in Central Europe. Wrocław does the same. Łódź gravitates to its place in an industrial heartland of the continent. In a sense, these cities are making up for their earlier "displacement" in "Eastern Europe," a region that had been defined through a political ideology that suppressed all local (i.e., place-based) self-determinations. The movement taking place in these cities is centripetal, moving from a perceived periphery toward a perceived center called Europe. The motive forces behind this movement are Europe's economic prosperity, its cultural vitality, and its successful political institutions. As demonstrated by the chapters in this volume, this movement toward the center of Europe is being propelled by myriad mythic, historic, and contemporary factors.

There is also almost always a clear temporal dimension to these reorientations and "relocations." Each locality, each city finds its unique path to the center of Europe—whether a particular era, a period style in architecture, archaeological discoveries, or postmodernist skyscrapers. One can view some of the cities' commemorative restorations as a way of selecting and restoring an era of urban history that would most closely associate the city with the rest of Europe. In the same vein, one could view the structures built with the impetus of postsocialist capitalism as an alignment with the future of Europe. Preservation, restoration, reconstruction, and new construction are all means of reorienting the postcommunist city and lending it an image or character linking it with either historical or modern concepts of "Europe."

## Embracing Capitalism and Democracy

In addition to planned and imposed changes in the postcommunist landscapes of the cities featured in this volume, the seemingly independent forces of capitalism and democracy have also left their marks. Postcommunist Europe has set out to adopt the political system and market organization of the West, and these ideological and legal changes have found concrete expression in the material culture of each city. Ironically, some of the so-called EU fifteen have expressed fear that the twelve new member states do not share their European social values, given their shrinking public sectors and strong embrace of the neoliberal economic paradigm. Yet the EU has created these neoliberal "tigers" by encouraging postcommunist governments to liberalize their markets and quickly shrink their state budgets to encourage economic growth. These new values are being expressed in the cities considered here through proliferating shopping centers, skyscrapers, and office parks.

In Tallinn, the postsocialist emergence of a market economy has proven to be an all-powerful force driving urban design. Hackmann notes that if Soviet plans for the design of the city were plans that seldom came to fruition, then the postsocialist plans of the 1990s hardly deserved to be called plans at all. Rather, these plans seemed more a documentation of the incursions of market forces into the urban fabric. In many cases, these incursions did not take into account concerns about preserving the city's historic structures and fabric.

Like many European cities, Vilnius faces the complex task of fitting contemporary urban functions into a premodern urban form. Vaisvilaite emphasizes the difficulty of creating a fully functional modern city while simultaneously historically preserving a medieval city. In the case of Vilnius, the response has been to relocate its new functions—whether related to the governance of the newly independent state or to the commercial requirements of its capitalist economy—to the periphery. This arrangement leaves as yet unanswered the function of the historic Old Town, which may evolve into little more than a tourist destination, with glass office towers and shopping centers glowering on the horizon.

Even without the impetus of EU accession, post-Soviet cities have been transformed by capitalism. In chapter 6, Karl Qualls explains the unexpected links in Sevastopol between the rise of multiculturalism and capitalism. During the "Orange Revolution," the city's historical sympathy for Russia meant that Viktor Yanukovich was extremely popular and, in typical Soviet style, ran his campaign from Nakhimov Square in the old Communist city center. By contrast, Viktor Yushchenko's youthful campaign, which was meant to turn all of Ukraine toward the West, was launched from a tent in front of the local McDonald's. Although this location was advantageous because the American restaurant is a meeting place for the city's youth, it did allow many to question the sources of Yushchenko's campaign financing. Nevertheless, as Qualls points out, in the juxtaposition between Yanokovich in Nakhimov Square and Yushchenko in front of McDonald's, "the contrast between old and new could not have been clearer."

With the return to Crimea by the ethnic Tatars, a certain amount of ethnotourism has mushroomed in the region. Tourists can now go to Sevastopol to see not only the city's military heritage but also what is left of the region's history as a bustling multicultural port, which was home to Muslim Tatars, Jewish Karaites, Orthodox Greeks, and Russians. Although part of the draw is Crimea's uniqueness in contrast to the rest of Europe, the ostentatious consumerism that has emerged to cater to the new tourists seems to indicate that the city has certainly adopted capitalist values from the West, even if it does not identify with the rest of the continent.

Despite its very Old World location on the site of the ancient settlements surrounding the Black Sea, Odessa is a young city—considerably younger than most of the other cities included in this volume, as Oleg Gubar and Patricia Herlihy explain in chapter 5. Founded by Imperial decree on May 27, 1794, Odessa became an American-style frontier town of long and straight avenues offering broad vistas of rampant, not-always-licit land speculation; of cosmopolitan freedom; and of a forgiving attitude toward sins of all nature. In 1803, Catherine the Great's grandson, Tsar Alexander I (1801–25), named the Duc de Richelieu, a great-nephew of the famed cardinal—a thirty-six-year-old Frenchman who had fled the Revolution in his own country—to preside over the increasingly rambunctious frontier town in the far southwestern reaches of his empire. Over the course of the next eleven years, Richelieu secured Odessa's fate as a place in between. Odessa became—and would remain—a raucous, wide-open, randy patch of earth through which the grain riches of Ukraine's and Russia's vast Black Earth steppe would pass to reach the outside world.

Odessa became a cosmopolitan city, and more; it remained a place where different people sought their destinies together. Not everyone greeted diversity warmly in either city, with fierce anti-Jewish pogroms erupting a century ago. Nonetheless, Odessa has remained a city that, in the end, has proven to be more tolerant than not; and, certainly, more accepting of diversity than most cities in the world. Odessa has gloried in the carnavalesque, in the turn of profit, and in the most pragmatic view of life. In their city infused with moral skepticism and tolerance for the various ambiguities and peccadilloes of life, Odessits spend little time worrying about symbolic and ideological purity.

Not surprisingly, then, the local authorities in Odessa viewed the collapse of the Soviet regime not as an opportunity to reorient their city within an independent Ukraine but as a moment to pursue mammon as aggressively as possible. The result, as Gubar and Herlihy reveal, has been a devastating lack of concern for preserving the physical, historic city. Instead, local nostalgia for the past is expressed through a continuing commitment to a metaphysical past—an "Odessa myth"—even as the physical city languishes unkempt awaiting bulldozers to move in to realize the next phantasmagorical project of some local real estate baron. Self-delusion, abetted by an unbridled quest for profit, evidently is more fun than the hard work required to save the city as place, in addition to embracing it as myth.

The uneven ways in which the cities examined in this volume have changed belies the fact that the cities' formerly authoritarian countries are still unaccustomed to and not completely comfortable with the often wild, mismatched, and disproportionate results of capitalist and democratic choices. Efforts to bring decisions about identity, city planning, and monuments to public debate show that, at a certain level, societies understand the value of democratic processes. In the case of Szczecin, however, city leaders were hesitant to relinquish complete control to democratic outcomes. This was clear when the City Council faced the question of how to build a memorial to commemorate the labor demonstrations that took place in Szczecin in the 1970s and 1980s, which helped to dismantle communism. Musekamp described the drama in detail, with the mayor and council repeatedly overturning the vote of the responsible committee after not one but two open competitions on the design of the memorial were organized. In the end, a popular sculptor was commissioned directly by the mayor, and the statue he designed, though heavily criticized, now stands in a prominent square in the city center.

Vaisvilaite chronicles the disputes over the fate of Cathedral Square in Vilnius, where the interests of archeologists intent on resurrecting a glorious national past conflicted with those of a government intent on creating a glorious national present in the form of a Presidential Palace and Office. A compromise was found, with the former Bishop's Palace coming to serve as the symbolic center of the new presidential republic. Similar battles broke out over how to preserve and develop the Old Town, often placing private owners at odds with preservationists. These conflicts were further complicated by the necessity of balancing an urban heritage, embracing multiple cultures, with the demands of twenty-first-century nation building.

## The Search for a European Demos

Through its process of self-rediscovery, each city explored in this volume is simultaneously helping to answer a larger question: What does it mean to be European? The residents of postcommunist cities are engaged in redefining their identities among the many that are available to them. They are taking inspiration from any number of historical moments, but also from the ideals to which they aspire. In each city, debates rage over the conflicting interpretations of which cultural monument, building, and/or historical period best represents the city's past, present, and future.

At the same time, a similar debate is being conducted at the supranational level to determine what, if any, European culture exists that would serve to unite the continent through a European demos. It would seem to be an impossible task to unite the people of this continent, with its extremely diverse mix of languages, religions, cuisines, and traditions. In exasperation at the task (along with fear that the EU system may collapse without it), a number of scholars have argued that the creation of a single demos is unnecessary for the European Union to survive. But in skipping over this complex task, we risk abandoning our Enlightenment ideals of what is needed to create a modern democracy and leave unanswered the critiques of the European Union's "democratic deficit."

Rather than abandoning the project of searching for a European demos, this volume offers hope that there may be a way of comprehending this demos through the shared histories, identities, and aspirations of the people living in the continent's postcommunist cities. The complexity of city planners' and builders' tasks, as explained in the preceding chapters, reveals the wider web of complex urban interconnections throughout Europe. Throughout time, layers of cultural sediment have left their mark on the continent's postcommunist cities. As their inhabitants have begun to uncover, evaluate, and make choices about what to discard and what to preserve, new patterns of historical and cultural belonging have begun to emerge. In their hopeful search to better define themselves as Europeans, the people of postcommunist Europe's cities may have inadvertently started to unlock the puzzle of what unites all Europeans.

## Note

1. David Laitin asserts that "the pressures of peripheralisation will induce East Europeans self-consciously to promote a deepening of a European culture that West Europeans themselves have less motivation to foster." David Laitin, "Culture and National Identity: 'The East' and European Integration," *West European Politics* 29, no. 1 (January 2006): 78.

# Contributors

**John Czaplicka** is currently an affiliate of the Center for European Studies at Harvard University and cochair of the European Cities Study Group. He has taught at Hamburg University, Harvard University, and Humboldt University in Berlin. His past publications have focused on the pictorial imagery of Berlin, Americanism in Germany, the art of exile artists, and commemorative practices in Germany and Central Europe. His current projects include Divided Cities/Divided Histories, which compares the historical imagery of five cities in Central Europe, Berlin, Gdansk, L'viv, Riga, and Vilnius; and he is preparing a monograph on the concept of cultural landscape. His publications include an edited collection of essays on the city of L'viv (2005) and a coedited collection of essays on composing urban history (2004). Among his current projects are an intellectual portrait of the German-American scholar Hugo Münsterberg and further studies of the postcommunist urban landscape.

**Nida Gelazis** is currently the program associate and editor for the East European Studies Program at the Woodrow Wilson International Center for Scholars. She received a BA in political science from the University of Chicago and an LLM in comparative European and international law from the European University Institute. She previously was the managing editor of the *East European Constitutional Review* at the University of Chicago Law School and was on the staff of the Constitutional and Legislative Policy Institute in Budapest. She was also a research associate at the Robert Schuman Centre for Advanced Studies of the European University Institute.

**Oleg Gubar** is a journalist and historian of the city and region of Odessa. He contributes to several Odessa newspapers and magazines, including the journal *Deribasovskaia-Rishel'evskaia,* of which he is an editor. He graduated from Odessa State University, where he studied geology, geography, and archeology. He has published dozens of articles, pamphlets, and monographs on the history of Odessa. His chapter on the history of Odessa appears in *Odessa Memories* (University of Washington Press, 2003). His latest work is a monograph on the history of planning in Odessa based on the archival records of the Urban Planning Committees. Another of his volumes, a collection on these archival records that is the second in a series, will be published in 2008.

**Jörg Hackmann** is an acting professor of East European history at the University of Greifswald and visiting scholar at the University of Chicago. He specializes in the history of Poland and the Baltic region. His research focuses on historical cultures, civil society, and nation building. His recent publications include *Die Ordnung des Raums: Mentale Karten in der Ostseeregion,* coedited with Norbert Gotz and Jan Hecker-Stampehl (Wissenschafts-Verlag, 2006); *Nordosteuropa als Geschichtsregion,* coedited with Robert Schweitzer (Schmidt-Römhild, 2006); *Civil Society in the Baltic Sea Region,* coedited with Norbert Gotz (Ashgate, 2003); and "Mapping Baltic History: The Concept of North Eastern Europe," in a 2002 special issue of the *Journal of Baltic Studies.*

**Liliana Hentosh** is a senior research associate at the Institute for Historical research of L'viv National University. Among her academic interests are the history of the Catholic Church, interdenominational relations in Ukraine, and the history of L'viv. She has participated in numerous research projects on the modern history of Western Ukraine and L'viv. During the past decade, she has published numerous articles and essays on the history of the Catholic Church and the history of interethnic and interdenominational relations. She recently published the book *The Vatican and Challenges of Modernity: The East-European Politics of Pope Benedict XV and Ukrainian-Polish Conflict in Galicia, 1914–1923* (VNTL-Klasyka, 2006).

**Patricia Herlihy** is the Louise Wyant Professor at Emmanuel College, Boston. At Brown University, she is also an adjunct research professor at the Watson Institute for International Studies and professor emerita of history. She is the author of *Odessa: A History, 1794–1914* (Harvard University Press, 1986); she contributed a historical essay to *Odessa Memories* (University of Washington Press, 2003), which she also coedited with Nicolas Iljine; and she has written numerous articles on Odessa. She is also the author of *The Alcoholic Empire: Vodka and Politics in Late Imperial Russia* (Oxford University Press, 2002).

**Volodymyr Kravchenko** is a professor and head of the Department of Ukrainian Studies at V. N. Karazin National University in Kharkiv. He specializes in the history of Ukrainian historical writing, in the history of the National University, and the history of the city of Kharkiv, especially from the end of the eighteenth to the beginning of the twenty-first century. He is the author of numerous articles on renowned Ukrainian historians, such as Dmytro Bahalii, and on various aspects of Ukrainian and Russian interpretations of Ukrainian history at the beginning of the nineteenth century. He also serves as a director of the Kowalsky Eastern Ukrainian Institute, which is affiliated with the Canadian Institute of Ukrainian Studies at the University of Alberta, and as the editor in chief of the journal *Skhid-Zakhid* (East-West).

**Joanna Michlic** is an associate professor in the Department of History and chair of Holocaust studies and ethical values at Lehigh University. Her major publications include the *Neighbors Respond: The Controversy about Jedwabne,* coedited with Antony Polonsky (Princeton University Press, 2004); and *Poland's Threatening Other: The Image of the Jew from 1880 to the Present* (University of Nebraska Press, 2006). She is currently working on a monograph, *The Social History of Jewish Children in Poland: Survival and Identity, 1945–1949.*

**Jan Musekamp** is an assistant professor of Eastern European history at the European University, Viadrina Frankfurt (Oder). He specializes in the history of forced migrations, with an emphasis on cultural appropriation in the multiethnic cities of Central and Eastern Europe, and on the history of mobility in the nineteenth and twentieth centuries. In recent years, he has published numerous articles on Szczecin and Brno in the twentieth century.

**Nicolai N. Petro** is a professor of political science at the University of Rhode Island. He specializes in Russian politics and foreign policy, with an emphasis on culture and religion. He has published numerous essays and articles. His most recent book is *Crafting Democracy* (Cornell University Press, 2005), which is based on two years working and living in the Russian region of Novgorod.

**Karl D. Qualls** is an associate professor and chair of the Department of History at Dickinson College. He specializes in Soviet urban reconstruction and modern states' plans for transforming societies. He has published several articles on the rebuilding of Sevastopol after World War II, and he is now completing a monograph on this topic. He is currently investigating the lives of the Spanish children exiled to the Soviet Union during the Spanish Civil War.

**Blair A. Ruble** is currently the director of the Kennan Institute of the Woodrow Wilson International Center for Scholars, where he also serves as director of the Comparative Urban Studies Program. He previously served at the Social Science Research Council (1985–89) and the National Council for Soviet and East European Research (1982–85). He received his MA and PhD in political science from the University of Toronto (1973, 1977), and an AB degree with highest honors in political science from the University of North Carolina at Chapel Hill (1971). He is a native of New York City. He has edited a dozen volumes and written five monographs. His book-length works include a trilogy examining the fate of Russian provincial cities during the twentieth century: *Leningrad: Shaping a Soviet City* (University of California Press, 1990); *Money Sings! The Changing Politics of Urban Space in Post-Soviet Yaroslavl* (Woodrow Wilson Center Press and Cambridge University Press, 1995); and *Second Metropolis: Pragmatic Pluralism in Gilded Age Chicago, Silver Age Moscow, and Meiji Osaka* (Woodrow Wilson Center Press and Johns Hopkins University Press, 2001). His most recent monograph is *Creating Diversity Capital: Transnational Migrants in Montreal, Washington, and Kyiv* (Woodrow Wilson Center Press and Johns Hopkins University Press, 2005), which examines the changes in such cities as Montreal, Washington, and Kyiv brought about by the recent arrival of large transnational communities.

**Olga Sezneva** is the Harper Fellow and the Collegiate Assistant Professor at the University of Chicago. Her research interests lie at the intersection of migration, social memory, and political changes. The book she currently is working on, *Contingent Place, Tenacious Homeland,* follows the transformation of the German city of Königsberg into the Soviet, and recently Russian, city of Kaliningrad after World War II. The book follows different strategies of forging a collective past, the goals they accomplish, and the transformation of these strategies in the context of social change. Her publications include "We Have Never Been German: The Economy of Digging in Russian Kaliningrad," in *Practicing Culture,* edited by Craig Calhoun and Richard Sennett (Routledge, 2007).

**Gregor Thum** is a research fellow at the Freiburg Institute for Advanced Studies. He specializes in modern Central European history, with an emphasis on German–East Central European relations. His first book, *Die fremde Stadt: Breslau 1945* (Siedler, 2003), examines the cultural transformation of German Breslau into Polish Wrocław after the border and population shifts of 1945. He is currently writing a book on the history of German imperial ambitions in East Central Europe since 1800.

**Bohdan Tscherkes** is a professor and director of the Institute of Architecture at L'viv National Technical University and a guest professor at the Technical University in Vienna. He specializes in city planning and the history of architecture. He has a special interest in the post-Soviet transformations of Eastern Europe. He has participated in numerous state and regional expert committees. During the past decade, he has published numerous articles, essays, and reports.

**Irena Vaisvilaite** is an associate professor in the Department of History at Vilnius University. She received her PhD from M. V. Lomonosov Moscow State University. Her dissertation focused on Baroque architecture during the era of the Lithuanian Grand Duchy. She has taught at the Vilnius Art Institute and chaired the Lithuanian Art and Culture Institute's Art History Department. She defended her dissertation on the Lithuanian Catholic Church under Nazi and Soviet rule at the Pontifical Gregorian University. She specializes in seventeenth- to twenty-first-century Central European cultural history. She also serves as an adviser to Lithuanian president Valdas Adamkus, heading the Culture, Science, and Education Group.

# Index

*Figures, notes, and tables are denoted by f, n, and t following the page number.*

Aalto, Alvar, 134*n*41, 135*n*70
Ackermann, Friedrich, 318
Adamczak, Antoni, 323
Adnan, Kivan, 152
Alchevs'ky, Oleksii, 237
Aleichem, Sholem, 163*n*4, 271
Alexander I (Tsar), 56, 283, 344
Alexander II (Tsar), 56
Alexy II (Patriarch), 178
Altmäe, Riina, 112, 113*f*
Alver, Andres, 121
Andreyev, Vasily, 61–62
Andriukaitis, Vytenis, 52*n*25
Andruhovych, Yuri, 272, 278*n*35
*Angel of Freedom* (monument in Szczecin), 322–23, 324*f*
anniversaries. *See* festivals and fairs
Ansel'm, I.A., 149
Anstadt, Karol Gotleib, 296
anticommunism, 63, 92–95
Antinis, Robertas, 28
anti-Semitism, 88, 172, 191*n*8, 288, 297. *See also* Jews
apartments and residential buildings: in Kharkiv, 227, 234, 235*f;* in Łódź, 285, 287; in L'viv, 258; in Odessa, 146, 148–50; in Szczecin, 315–16; in Tallinn, 108, 120, 125–26, 127*f,* 132*n*9; in Vilnius, 30, 36, 44, 51*n*9; in Wrocław, 79. *See also* real estate markets
archeologists and archeological excavations: in Novgorod, 67; in Odessa, 155; in Tallinn, 128; in Vilnius, 32–34; in Wrocław, 81, 82–83
architecture: in Central and Eastern Europe, 196; in Kaliningrad, 198, 199, 203–4, 207–9, 212; in Kharkiv, 223, 224*f,* 226–27, 228*f,* 234; in Łódź, 287–88, 290, 298–99, 300*n*11; in L'viv, 275; in Odessa, 148–49, 153–55, 163; as political culture, 3, 12*n*3; in Sevastopol, 170, 172–73; in Tallinn, 106, 107–8, 111–18, 120–31, 132*n*10, 133*n*23, 136*n*82; in Vilnius, 23, 28–29, 44; in Wrocław, 77, 79, 93–95. *See also* skyscrapers and high-rise buildings
Art Nouveau, 106, 131*n*3, 287, 290
artworks and galleries: in Kharkiv, 244, 246*f;* in L'viv, 270; in Szczecin, 309, 323, 325; in Vilnius, 24, 25. *See also* museums
Assmann, Jan, 80

Babel', I.E., 141, 157
Bachmann, Klaus, 97
Bahaliy, Dmytro, 225, 237

353

## Index

Balčiūnas, Vytautas, 27
Bandera, Stepan, 263, 271
Barciński, Samuel, 296
Barnim I (duke), 307, 308
Bartkiewicz, Zygmunt, 285–86, 300n13
Bartnik, Paweł, 322
Bashmet, Iurii, 244, 245f
Batiuskov, K.N., 141
bazaars. See marketplaces and market squares
Belinsky, Vissarion, 222
Berlin (Germany), 87
Bernardazzi, Aleksandr, 149
*beskhozyaistvennost* (mismanagement), 203, 215n15. See also mismanagement, public
Biederman, Robert, 296
Blodek, L'ev, 149
Boffo, Francesco, 143f, 145
Bogdanas, Konstantinas, 24
Bogislaw X (ruler), 306
Boitsev, Anatoly, 66
Bolesław Chrobry, 316–17
Bolsheviks. See Communists and Communist Party
Bonhoeffer, Dietrich, 85, 98
books and periodicals: on Hapsburg Empire, 273; on Łódź, 300n1; on Vilnius, 23, 51n5; on Wrocław, 82. See also libraries; media
borders and borderlands, 2–3, 5, 231–49
Born, Max, 85
bourgeoisie: in Łódź, 283, 285, 288–89, 299–300; in Wrocław, 82–85
Boym, Svetlana, 13n7, 196
Brandenburg-Ansbach, Albrecht von, 208
Brandt, Willy, 80
Brazauskas, Algirdas, 33
Brėdikis, Vytautas, 27
Breslau. See Wrocław
bridges: in Tallinn, 128; in Vilnius, 45, 47f
Brubaker, Rogers, 270
Bruns, Dmitri, 133n23
Bubyr, Aleksei, 110, 110f, 131n3

Budziarek, Marek, 301n15
Buniak, Lubomyr, 275, 279nn40–41
business centers. See commercialization and commercial purposes

cafés. See restaurants and cafés
Cambiaggio, Luigi, 145
Cannes Architecture and Investment Fair, 44
capitalism, 4, 10–12, 284, 285, 289, 342–45
Casimir III (King), 276n2
castles and palaces: Bishop's Palace of Vilnius, 21, 33, 52n18, 345; Grand Duke's Palace (Vilnius), 3, 4, 32–33; Lower Vilnius Castle, 18, 32–33, 51n14; in L'viv, 260, 277n19, 279n41; Palace of the Sovereigns (Vilnius), 33–34, 34f, 35, 38–39; Presidential Palace (Vilnius), 52n18; in Szczecin, 310, 331n24; Trakei Castle (Vilnius), 52n16; Upper Vilnius Castle, 45, 48f; Vorontsov Palace (Odessa), 142, 143f
Cathedral of Saint Sophia (Novgorod), 54, 55f, 58, 59f, 60
cathedrals. See churches and cathedrals
Catherine II, 137, 138f, 157
Catherine the Great, 169, 344
Catholic Church: in Łódź, 286; in L'viv, 268–70, 278n33; in Vilnius, 20, 21
Čekanauskas, Vytautas, 27
celebrations. See festivals and fairs
cemeteries: in Łódź, 295; in L'viv, 258, 274, 279n38; in Wrocław, 78–79
chapels. See churches and cathedrals
Charter for Human Rights (EU), 336
Chernobyl disaster, 237, 259
Chernoivanenko, Oleg, 157
Chernoivanov, Oleg, 138f
Chichibabin, Boris, 236
Chizhov, N., 138–39
Chrobry, Boleslaw, 97–98
churches and cathedrals: Cathedral of Saint Sophia (Novgorod), 54, 55f, 58, 59f, 60; Church of Saint John the Baptist (Novgorod), 62f; in

Kaliningrad, 210, 212; in L'viv, 268–70; in Odessa, 152–55*f*; Saint John's Cathedral (Wrocław), 84; in Sevastopol, 172, 176–78, 185, 192*n*28; in Tallinn, 108, 132*n*16; in Vilnius, 18, 21, 24, 36, 52*n*20, 345; in Wrocław, 83. *See also* Mariavite Church; Orthodox Church; synagogues

city plans. *See* maps and city plans

city walls in Vilnius, 38–39, 41

Club of the Merry and Witty (KVN), 142

Colleoni, Bartolomeo, 323, 325–26, 326*f*, 329

commercialization and commercial purposes: in Kaliningrad, 206–7; in Kharkiv, 223, 224*f*, 232–33; in Łódź, 283–84, 289; in L'viv, 258; in postcommunist cities, 9–10; in Sevastopol, 179–83, 184*f*, 189; in Tallinn, 120, 121*f*, 122*f*, 123–24, 128; in Vilnius, 36, 37, 40–41. *See also* trade (commercial)

Communists and Communist Party: Central Committee Building (Tallinn), 114, 133*n*28; in Kaliningrad, 199; in Kharkiv, 226; in Łódź, 283, 284, 287–88; in L'viv, 267; and memories, 196; in Novgorod, 60, 63; in Odessa, 142; in Poland, 81; in Sevastopol, 187, 189; in Szczecin, 306, 316; in Tallinn, 114. *See also* anticommunism; ideologies

concert halls. *See* cultural centers

Copernicus (Nikolai Kopernik), 263

Cossacks, 219–20, 237, 247, 251*n*3, 265, 270

Council of Europe, 45

Crimea (region), 173–74, 175, 184

Crimean War, 170, 177, 178–79

cuisine. *See* restaurants and cafés

cultural centers: in Łódź, 290; in Odessa, 152, 156*f*; in Tallinn, 125, 126*f*, 133*n*31

Czaplicka, John, 1, 107, 133*n*20, 330, 335

Czekalski, Marek, 290–91

Dall'Aqua, Gaetano, 145

Danzig. *See* Gdańsk

Danzig Corridor, 199

Davies, Norman, 82

*Death in Breslau* (Krajewski), 85

demos, 345–46

deportations. *See* migrations

Deribas, F., 146

Derzhavin, Gavrila, 224

De-Voland, François, 143, 145

Diaghilev, Sergey, 185, 187

Dialog project (Novgorod), 68, 70

*Dingęs Vilnius* (*Vanished Vilnius*) (Drėma), 35

Dingsdale, Alan, 12*n*2

Dirgėla, Petras, 24

diversity and multiculturalism: in Łódź, 281, 283, 287–88, 289, 299–300, 303*n*55; in L'viv, 255, 257, 264, 268–70, 272–76; in Novgorod, 54; in Odessa, 137, 138–39, 150, 151–52, 163*nn*5–6; in postcommunist cities, 338–40; in Sevastopol, 172; in Soviet Union, 164*n*10; in Szczecin, 310, 330; in Wrocław, 96–97. *See also* ethnicities; heritage and heritage protection

Dobkin, Mikhail, 241

Dobranciński, Józef, 296

Dohrn, Heinrich, 309

Dominiak, Zbigniew, 295

Drėma, Vladas, 35, 39

Dudaev, Dzhokhar, 263

Dzerzhinsky, Felix, 236, 249

Dźwigaj, Czesław, 322–23

Earle, Hobart, 153

earthquakes, 173, 191*n*11

Eckert, Gottfried, 296

Eduards, Boris, 138*f*

education and learning: in Kharkiv, 221–22, 225; in L'viv, 264; in Novgorod, 55–56, 60, 64, 67; in Szczecin, 330

Eesti Muinsuskaitseselts (Estonian Monuments' Protection Society), 133*n*32

Egorov, Vladimir, 201
*Ehituskunst (Art of Building)* on Estonian architecture, 118, 135*n*57
Elczewska, Halina, 295
Ellan-Blakytny, Vasyl', 237
embassies in Vilnius, 29–30, 51*n*8, 51*n*10, 51*n*11
empires. *See* Hapsburg Empire
Engels, Friedrich, 262
entertainment facilities. *See* sports and entertainment facilities
Estonian Monuments' Protection Society (Eesti Muinsuskaitseselts), 133*n*32
Eteriia, Filiki, 156
ethnicities: in Eastern Europe, 8; in Kaliningrad, 201, 202; in Kharkiv, 223–24; in Łódź, 284, 291–92, 299, 300*n*9; in L'viv, 255, 276*n*9, 277*n*11; in Sevastopol, 183–87, 186*f*, 189–90, 193*n*46; in Tallinn, 107, 114–15, 131*n*5, 132*n*7; in Ukraine, 197. *See also* diversity and multiculturalism
ethnographic villages, 207
Eugenie, Saint, 242
European Commission, 67
Europeanization, 197
European Union: and Art Nouveau Network, 290; and Baltic cities, 11; and capitalism, 342–43; and demos, 346; and Eastern European cities, 3; and enlargement, 335–36; and Estonia, 125; and Europeanization, 197; and Kaliningrad, 200; and Lithuania, 49; and Łódź, 296; and Poland, 76, 319, 320; and Russia, 71; and Ukraine, 175, 185, 187–88, 262; and Wrocław, 95, 99
excavations. *See* archeologists and archeological excavations

fairs. *See* festivals and fairs
fast food chains. *See* restaurants and cafés
Father Fedor (fictional character), 239–40
festivals and fairs: in Kharkiv, 244–45, 247; in Łódź, 291–92, 302*n*31; in Novgorod, 60; in Szczecin, 307–10, 329; in Vilnius, 41, 42, 49
Finland, architecture in, 130–31
Finno-Ugric (ethnic group), 54
*The First Capital* (Kevorkyan), 239
*The First Republic* (film), 64
Fish Village project (Kaliningrad), 205, 206–9, 213
flats. *See* apartments and residential buildings
fleets. *See* navies and fleets
Fonsiorovskii, Felix, 149
forced migrations. *See* migrations
Foucault, Michel, 3
Francis Joseph I (Emperor), 273, 279*n*37
Franko, Ivan, 262
Frapolli, Francesco, 145, 147*f*
Frapolli, Giovanni, 145
Frederick III (Emperor), 321
Fredro, Alexander, 89, 90*f*, 91, 263, 266
Frunze, Mikhail, 170–71
Fydrych, Waldermar, 92

Galicia (region), 274, 276, 277*n*12, 278*n*35
galleries. *See* artworks and galleries
Garden, Busolt, 210, 211
gardens. *See* parks and green spaces
*Gazeta Wyborcza* (Polish newspaper): on Colleoni monument, 325; on Łódź, 291; on Sedina monument, 328; on Szczecin, 317, 318, 319, 320, 322; on Wrocław's millennium, 85
Gdańsk (Poland), 321, 322
Gediminas, Grand Duke, 18, 30–31, 31*f*, 32
Gehlig, Otto, 290
Gelazis, Nida, 1, 335
genealogy of Kaliningrad, 211–14
geography of Kaliningrad, 198–200
Germans: and Kaliningrad, 197–98, 200, 201, 203, 204–5, 215*n*11; from Kazakhstan, 13*n*5; in Łódź, 283–84, 286, 291, 292–93; in Reval/Tallinn, 110; in Szczecin, 305–10, 316–21,

328–30, 332*n*51; in Vilnius, 18; in Wrocław, 75–77, 78–81, 84–88, 96–97
Geyer, Ludwig, 283–84
ghettos: in Łódź, 294–95, 302*n*40; in L'viv, 267; in Vilnius, 20, 23. *See also* Jews
glasnost, 35, 258. *See also* perestroika
Golden Age (Łódź), 283–85, 288, 289, 299, 300*n*10, 339
*Golden Child* (monument), 160
Golden Duke Film Festival, 142
Golozatyi, Hetman, 161–62
Good Soldier Schweik (fictional character), 273, 273*f*
Gorbachev, Mikhail, 35, 150, 258
Gorky, Maxim, 21
graveyards. *See* cemeteries
green spaces. *See* parks and green spaces
Grimm, D.I., 177
Grohman, Ludwik, 293
Gross, Jan, 88
Grynfeld, Eliezer, 303*n*44
Gubar, Oleg, 6, 137, 344
Gundlach, Gustaw, 296

Haber, Fritz, 85
Habermann, Eugen, 116, 117*f*
Hackmann, Jörg, 10, 105, 134*n*36, 340, 343
Haken, Hermann, 316–20
Hakenterrasse. *See* Wały Chrobrego
Halan, Yaroslav, 260–61
Halbwachs, Maurice, 316
Hallas-Murula, Karin, 127, 132*n*10
Halytskyi, Danylo, 271, 272*f*, 278*n*35
handicrafts in Vilnius, 40, 41
Hanseatic League, 5, 54, 70, 151, 341
*Happy-Go-Lucky Guys* (film), 141
Hapsburg Empire, 95–96, 256–57, 273, 340, 341
harbor and port areas, 118, 123–24, 140*f*, 145, 146*f*. *See also* navies and fleets
Harvey, David, 209
Hasek, Jaroslav, 273, 273*f*
Hausen, Marika, 132*n*14

*haydamak* (participant in Ukrainian uprising), 225, 252*n*17
*Heimatschutz* (protection of homeland), 105
Heineman-Jarecki, Edward, 296
Heinzl, Juliusz, 284
Heitmann, Friedrich, 210, 214
Hentosh, Liliana, 10, 255, 337
Herbst, Edward, 297
heritage and heritage protection: in Eastern Europe, 2; under Gorbachev, 35; in Łódź, 281, 282–83, 287–300, 301*n*19; in L'viv, 257, 272–76; and modernization, 105; in Novgorod, 61, 65, 67; in Sevastopol, 171–72; in Vilnius, 36–43, 50, 52*n*21. *See also* diversity and multiculturalism
Herlihy, Patricia, 6, 137, 163*n*1, 165*n*26, 344
Herzen, Alexander, 236
Herzl, Theodor, 42
Herzog, Paweł, 293, 294
heterotopy, 3, 12*n*4
Hetmanate (Ukrainian region), 220–21, 222
high-rise buildings. *See* skyscrapers and high-rise buildings
historic preservation. *See* restoration work
history. *See* political history
*The History of the Kingdom of Galicia from Ancient Times up to 1264* (Kostyrko), 278*n*35
*History of Ukrainian Rus'* (Hrushevskyi), 266
Holocaust and Holocaust survivors: in Baltic region, 125; in Łódź, 294, 297; in L'viv, 257, 267; memorial in Kharkiv, 237; in Wrocław, 88. *See also* Jews
Holtei, Karl von, 85, 98
Honchar, Oles', 238
hotels: in Kaliningrad, 209; in Tallinn, 109, 112, 112*f*, 114, 120–23, 122*f*, 124*f*; in Vilnius, 25, 36, 45
houses of worship. *See* churches and cathedrals; mosques; synagogues

housing. *See* apartments and residential buildings
Hrushevskyi, Myhailo, 266, 266*f*
Hrytsak, Yaroslav, 277*n*14, 277*n*24, 278*n*27
Hulak-Artemovsky, Petro, 226, 252*n*22
humor, 141–42
Hvylovy, Mykola, 237

*Ì* (Ukrainian cultural journal) on L'viv, 272
icons. *See* artworks and galleries
identities: and architecture, 196; in Kaliningrad, 200–205, 212; in Kharkiv, 222, 223, 236, 238, 241, 250; in Łódź, 288–96, 299; in L'viv, 256–60, 270–71, 274, 275–76, 277*nn*12–13, 279*n*42; and nation-states, 336; in Novgorod, 67, 70, 71; in Odessa, 150; and political economy, 197; and postcommunist cities, 11–12, 338–39, 345–46, 346*n*1; in Sevastopol, 168, 170, 171, 183, 187, 189–90; in Szczecin, 305–34; in Tallinn, 130; in Vilnius, 17, 27; in Wrocław, 76, 81
ideologies: and Odessa, 141, 151; and Sevastopol, 170–71; and skyscrapers, 49; and Vilnius's Old Town, 35; in Wrocław, 81. *See also* Communists and Communist Party
Il'f, Ilia, 141, 157, 159, 240
industries and industrialization. *See* commercialization and commercial purposes
inferiority complexes, 282, 300*n*4, 318
Innocent IV (Pope), 278*n*35
inscriptions in Wrocław, 77, 79, 85, 86*f*
Istomin, Vladimir, 177
Ivan III (Grand Prince), 56
Ivan the Terrible (Tsar), 57*f*
Ivanytskyi, Vasyl', 278*n*30

Jagiełło, Władysław, 282
Jan Kazimierz University, 89
Jarociński, Zygmund, 296

Jasudytė, Ramutė, 24
Jews: in Kharkiv, 231; in Łódź, 282, 286, 291, 292–96; in L'viv, 197, 264, 267, 271, 278*n*31, 337; in Odessa, 137, 141, 152–53; in Sevastopol, 172, 190*n*7; in Szczecin, 310, 339; in Vilnius, 8, 13*n*8, 18–19, 20–21, 23, 39–41, 40*f*, 42, 52*n*24; in Wrocław, 87–88, 96. *See also* anti-Semitism; ghettos; Holocaust and Holocaust survivors
Johanson, Herbert, 116, 117*f*
John Paul II (Pope), 95, 178
jubilees. *See* festivals and fairs
Jugendstil. *See* Art Nouveau
Jurczyk, Marian, 320, 322, 332*n*52

Kaasik, Veljo, 129
Kabiol'skii, Vil'gel'm, 149
Kagansky, Vladimir, 60, 71
Kaliningrad (Russia), 195–215, 341; Fish Village/Lomse Project, 206–7, 213; future of past in, 213–14; genealogy of, 211–14; geography of, 198–200; identity in, 4, 5, 200–205; Luisenwahl Project, 209–11, 213, 214; and politics of location, 205–12; reconstruction in, 211–12; and Szczecin, 330*n*1; "theater of architecture" in, 207–9
*Kaliningradskaya Pravda* on Germans in Kaliningrad, 215*n*11
Kallas, Toivo, 112
Kallion, Valmi, 133*n*23
Kalm, Mart, 120, 126, 127, 133*n*27, 133*n*31
Kangropool, Rasmus, 133*n*23
Kant, Immanuel, 4, 207, 208, 213
Karaite (ethnic group), 18
Kararskii, Aleksandr, 169
Karazin, Vasilij, 222, 225, 226, 241
Karp, Raine, 112, 113*f*, 114–15, 115*f*, 129
Karwowski, Lech, 328
Kasperavičienė, Birutė, 27
Kašuba, Vytautas, 31, 31*f*
Kataev, Valentin, 160

*Katedra* (*The Cathedral*)
 (Marcinkevičius), 24
Katyn massacre (1940), 92
Kaunas (Lithuania), 19, 28–29, 337
Kayserling, Caroline-Amalia, 208–9
Kazak, Anatolii, 140
Kersten, Rein, 112
Kevorkyan, Konstantin, 239
Kharkiv (Ukraine), 219–53, 338;
 beginnings of, 220–21; borderland
 status of, 5, 231–49; and Russian
 Empire, 221–26, 250; and Soviet
 Empire, 8, 10, 226–31, 250
*Kharkiv's History in 250 Years since Its Foundation* (series of publications), 225
Kharko (Cossack figure), 247, 249
Khdanov, Andrei, 236
Khmelnytsky, Bohdan, 220–21, 229, 251*n*3
Kholodnaia, Vera, 160, 162*f*
Khrushchev, Nikita, 234, 306
Kievan Rus', 58
Kirikov, Boris Mikhailovich, 131*n*3
Klugman, Aleksander, 302*n*40
Kmieliauskas, Vytautas, 24
Kniaznik, Alexander, 160*f*, 161
Kniephof (Prussia), 206
Knychalski, Witold, 291–92
Kodres, Krista, 132*n*7, 136*n*82
Kominek, Bolesław (Cardinal), 87
Königsberg. *See* Kaliningrad
Konopińska, Joanna, 79
Konovalets, Evhen, 262
Konsulov, A., 269
Konsztad, Herman, 296
Kopernik, Nikolai (Copernicus), 263
Koplowicz, Abramek, 295, 302*n*43, 303*n*44
Korenistow, Jerzy, 296
Kornilov, Vladimir, 177
Korsunov, Alexander, 66, 71
Kościuszko, Tadeusz, 263, 283
Kostomarov, Mykola, 224–25, 226, 252*n*16
Kostyrko, Volodymyr, 278*n*35

Kotli, Alar, 116
Kozachinsky, 157
Krajewski, Marek, 85
Kramarev, M., 146
Krastiņš, Jānis, 131*n*3
Kravchenko, Volodymyr, 5, 8, 10, 219, 338
Kravchuk, Leonid, 264
Kresy (Polish eastern territories), 88, 89, 91–92
Kŕopiwnicki, Jerzy, 294, 303*n*55
Krūminis, Bronius, 27
Krushel'nyts'ky, Mar'an, 237
Kryvonis, M., 264
Kuchma, Leonid, 174, 177, 240, 241, 247, 264
Kühnert, Ernst, 132*n*18
Kunitzer, Juliusz, 284
Künnapu, Vilen, 121, 122, 124*f*, 129
Kupczyk, Hieronim, 316
Kuprin, Alexandr, 157
Kurba, Les', 237
*Kurier Szczeciński* (Polish newspaper) on Germans in Szczecin, 309
Kushnarev, Evgeniy, 249
Kuusik, Edgar, 118
Kuznetsov, Nikolai, 260–61, 277*n*22
Kvitka-Osnovianenko, Hryhory, 222, 226, 237, 238, 251*n*8
KVN (Club of the Merry and Witty), 142
Kyiv (Ukraine), 56, 151, 168

Labuda, Gerard, 307
Łagiewski, Maciej, 87
Laitin, David, 346*n*1
Lande, David, 299
Lapin, Leo, 118, 129
Lashkarev, L., 146
Latour, Stanisław, 311
Law on Immovable Cultural Heritage (Lithuania), 36, 37
Law on Local Governance of 1990 (Lithuania), 36
Law on Presidential Elections of 1992 (Lithuania), 51*n*12

Law on the Takeover of Property of Lithuanian Communist Party and Communist Organizations of 1991 (Lithuania), 51n7
Lazarev, M.P., 171, 177
learning. *See* education and learning
Lefebvre, Henri, 3, 12n4
Lenin, Vladimir: and Estonian Parliament Building, 116; and Kharkiv, 229, 231f, 243; and L'viv, 258, 260, 261f; and Sevastopol, 167, 170, 171; and street names, 62; and Vilnius, 21, 31
Leopold I (Emperor), 95
Lermontov, Mikhail, 224, 263
libraries: in Lithuania, 51n5; in Szczecin, 309–10; in Tallinn, 114, 115f, 133n31
Likhachev, Dmitry, 58
Lindgren, Armas, 110, 111f
Liskowacki, Artur Daniel, 329
Litwiński, Arkadiusz, 327
Łódź (Poland), 281–303, 339, 342; as "bad city," 285–86, 300n13; past and present in, 6, 282–83, 299–300; post-1945 socialist era in, 287–88; postcommunist identity of, 288–96, 299; pre-1918 heritage of, 288–96, 299–300, 301n19; rebirth and Golden Age of, 283–85, 288, 299, 300n10, 339; urban heritage of, 296–300
Lodzermenschen (Łódź's industrial founders), 286, 288, 289, 301n17
Lomonosov, Mikhail, 241
Lomonosov, Nevsky, 241
Lomse Project (Kaliningrad), 206–7
Lönn, Wivi, 110, 111f
Lõoke, Marika, 118, 119f
*Lord Novgorod the Great* (film), 64
Louise of Prussia (Queen), 210, 214
Luisenwahl Project (Kaliningrad), 205, 209–11, 213, 214
Luzhkov, Iurii, 175
L'viv (Ukraine), 255–79, 337, 342; future of, 272–76; and identity during Soviet rule, 256–60, 275–76; multiculturalism in, 255, 257, 264, 268–70, 272–76; Polish expellees from, 88; religious revival in, 268–70; Soviet legacy of, 260–62, 275; and Szczecin, 319; Ukrainian past and present of, 10, 262–68, 276n1; Ukrainization of public space, 270–71, 275–76; and Wrocław, 88–92
Lwów. *See* L'viv

Maciejwska, Beata, 85
Magdeburg and Magdeburg Law, 255, 256f, 276n2, 307–8
Maiorov, A.I., 149
Maizel, Eliash Chaim, 296
*Maja (House)* (periodical) on Estonian architecture, 123, 135n57
Majewski, Hilary, 298
malls. *See* shops and shopping centers
mansions. *See* apartments and residential buildings
Manzel, Ludwig, 326
maps and city plans: of L'viv, 263–64; name changes on, 7; of Odessa, 143, 144f, 145; of Sevastopol, 186f; of Szczecin, 311, 312–14f
Marazli, Grigorii, 156
Marcinkevičius, Justinas, 24
Mariavite Church, 286, 301n15
market economy. *See* capitalism
marketplaces and market squares: in Kaliningrad, 211; in Kharkiv, 233, 233f; in Łódź, 296; in L'viv, 256f; in Novgorod, 55, 55f; Nowy Targ (Wrocław), 93–95; in Odessa, 146, 147f; in postcommunist cities, 9–10; in Wrocław, 83, 83f, 84, 89, 90f, 93–95, 296. *See also* Rynek; trade (commercial)
Martha the Magistrate, 64
Marx, Karl, 170–71
Masel'skiy, Alexander, 240
Matveeva, Svetlana, 67
media: in Kharkiv, 239; in Novgorod, 64; in Sevastopol, 178, 179, 188. *See also* books and periodicals
Memel (Prussia), 199, 214n7

memorials. *See* monuments
memories: and Communism, 196; and Kaliningrad, 200, 202; and Novgorod, 53–58; purging of, 6; and Szczecin, 329, 331n25; and Wrocław, 77–80, 87, 99
Menachem-Mendle (fictional character), 138, 163n4
*Mercury* (brig), 169
Merkulov, Sergei, 260
Meshkov, Iurii, 173–74, 191n14
Mesner, Eduard, 149
metro stations in Kharkiv, 240–41, 243, 244, 245
Michlic, Joanna, 6, 281, 339
Mickiewicz, Adam, 156, 263, 265, 321
migrations, 6, 87, 91, 97, 200, 339
Mihnovs'ky, Mykola, 237
Millennium Program of 2001 (Lithuania), 34–35
Mindaugas, King, 33
Mirlikiiskii, Saint Nicholas, 152, 154f
mismanagement, public, 203, 204. See also *beskhozyaistvennost* (mismanagement)
modernization: of Kharkiv, 221, 226, 233–34; of Łódź, 284, 290; of Novgorod, 63; of Vilnius, 25
monasteries. *See* churches and cathedrals
Monument Restoration and Design Institute (Vilnius), 23
monuments: in Kharkiv, 224–25, 229, 231f, 232f, 236–43, 239f, 242f, 244, 247, 249; in Łódź, 294; in L'viv, 258–62, 264–68, 265f, 269, 271, 275; in Novgorod, 57f; in Odessa, 142–43, 156–63; preservation of, 105; in Sevastopol, 169, 170, 183, 190; in Szczecin, 320–29; in Tallinn, 115; in Vilnius, 18, 26–27, 28, 30–32, 31f, 38, 42–43; in Wrocław, 77–78, 85, 87, 89, 90f, 92–93, 97–99
*Monument to the Reader* (sculpture), 157
Moorehouse, Roger, 82
Morandi, Francesco, 145
Moscow (Russia): architecture in, 106; and Novgorod, 55–56, 61, 71; and Sevastopol, 168. *See also* Muscovy
mosques, 172, 184
movie theaters. *See* sports and entertainment facilities
Mudry, Yaroslov, 241
multiculturalism. *See* diversity and multiculturalism
Murray, John, 190n5
Muscovy, 56, 58. *See also* Moscow
Musekamp, Jan, 305, 331n24, 339, 341, 345
museums: in Łódź, 297, 298; in L'viv, 261–62; National Art Museum (Vilnius), 34, 52n20; in Odessa, 142; in Szczecin, 309–10, 320, 331n21; in Tallinn, 118, 124–25, 125f, 135n70; in Vilnius, 8, 13n8, 32, 41; in Wrocław, 85, 87. *See also* artworks and galleries
myths and mythology: and Kharkiv, 225, 227, 229, 239, 247; and L'viv, 256–57, 275–76; and Novgorod, 53, 56, 58, 60–61, 65–66, 71; and Odessa, 6, 137–65; and postcommunist cities, 4; and Wrocław, 76, 78–79, 80–81, 83–84, 91–92, 97–98. *See also* narratives; symbols and symbolism

Nakhimov, P.S., 171, 177, 188
*namestnik* (Ukrainian provincial leader), 224, 251n14
Napoleon, 210
narratives: Czaplicka on, 330; in Kharkiv, 237; and nation-states, 337; and postcommunist cities, 3–6, 338; and Sevastopol, 169–70, 190n2; in Socialist period, 196; and Wrocław, 4, 80–82. *See also* myths and mythology
Nasvytis, Algimantas, 29
Nasvytis, Vytautas, 29
nationalism and nationality: in Łódź, 286, 288; in Tallinn, 107–8, 115–18, 130; in Vilnius, 19. *See also* nation building

nation building: in L'viv, 256, 266, 277*n*14; in postcommunist countries, 336–38; in Vilnius, 30–35. *See also* nationalism and nationality
nation-states. *See* nation building
NATO. *See* North Atlantic Treaty Organization
navies and fleets, 169–70, 171, 174–75, 189, 190, 191*n*18. *See also* harbor and port areas
Nazis: in Łódź, 294–95; in Sevastopol, 169, 177; in Vilnius, 20, 23; in Wrocław, 85, 96
Neizvestny, Ernst, 160
Neris River, 25–26, 25–26*f*, 45, 52*n*26
Nevsky, Alexander, 241, 247
newspapers. *See* media
new town areas in Vilnius, 21, 25, 27, 49
Nora, Pierre, 331*n*25
North Atlantic Treaty Organization (NATO): and Baltic states, 11, 125; and Lithuania, 49; and Ukraine, 174, 175, 185, 188, 262
Novgorod (Russia), 53–74, 341; creating better past, 58–63; medieval city as modern political symbol, 58–66; policies in, 63–65; political unity in, 65–66; reintegration into Europe, 5, 67–71; in Russia's memory, 53–58; symbols in, 58–66
*Novgorod* (newspaper) on republican Novgorod, 61
Novgorod Interregional Institute for the Social Sciences, 64–65
The Novgorod Project: A Leap into Postindustrial Society, 63–64
Novgorod State University, 63, 73*n*30
Nowak, Zbigniew, 293, 295, 303*n*44
Nowicki, Stanisław, 79
Nowy Targ (New Market in Wrocław), 93–95

Ochin, Oleg, 61
Oder Artery (Szczecin), 311, 313*f*, 314*f*, 315*f*, 316
Odessa (Ukraine), 137–65, 344–45; myth of, 6, 138–43, 150–63; shaping of, 143–50
Odessa Philharmonic Orchestra, 153
Odra River (Oder), 83
office buildings. *See* commercialization and commercial purposes; skyscrapers and high-rise buildings
Ojari, Andres, 127*f*
Okas, Jüri, 118, 119*f*
old town areas: in Szczecin, 310–16, 312*f*, 313*f*, 331*n*28; in Tallinn, 108, 117; in Vilnius, 21, 22*f*, 23, 25, 27, 30, 35–43; in Wrocław, 82–83, 84, 93
Olga of Kyiv (Princess), 264
Orange Alternative (Polish anarchic movement), 92–93, 94*f*
Orange Revolution, 157, 187, 247, 248*f*, 249, 260, 277*n*21, 338
*The Orange That Saved Odessa* (sculpture), 157–58
Orthodox Church: in Kaliningrad, 198; in Kharkiv, 220, 241–42, 242*f*, 247; in Łódź, 298; in L'viv, 270; in Novgorod, 60–61; in Odessa, 152, 152*f*, 153; in Sevastopol, 176, 178, 179, 185, 190; in Vilnius, 18–19, 20, 21. *See also* churches and cathedrals
Ossolineum (Polish cultural institution), 89
Otto, Jan, 308

Paderewski, Ignacy, 290
Padrik, Ain, 121, 122, 124*f*
palaces. *See* castles and palaces
*Panorama of Racławice* (painting), 89, 92
Pantheon to Polish soldiers (L'viv), 274, 275*f*, 279*n*38
parks and green spaces: in Odessa, 157; in Vilnius, 41, 43–44, 50; in Wrocław, 78–79
parliaments. *See* Riigikogu Hoone; Seimas
*Paths through Life* (monument in Szczecin), 322
patriotism, 239, 240

Paul I (Emperor), 157
Paustovskii, K.G., 141
Pawlak, Wacław, 300*n*10
pedestrian zones: in Kaliningrad, 212; in Vilnius, 50
Peil, Indrek, 125*f*
Peil, Ülo, 118, 124, 129
perestroika, 27, 35, 58, 158–59, 236–37. *See also* glasnost
Persikov, Ivan, 261
Petro, Nicolai N., 5, 6, 53, 341
Petrov, Evgeny, 141, 157, 159, 240
Philip (Duke of Edinburgh), 178
Piłsudski, Jozef, 20
Piotrowska Street (Łódź), 285, 300*n*12, 302*n*36
Piskorski, Jan M., 332*n*51
plaques, commemorative. *See* monuments
Podzamcze District (Szczecin), 310–16, 314*f*, 315*f*, 331*n*30
*Pogodalis* (Dirgėla), 24–25
Poles and Poland: and borders, 2–3; and L'viv, 256–57, 271, 274, 279*n*38; and Vilnius, 19–21, 24, 42; and Wrocław, 77–80, 88–92, 97
political history: of postcommunist cities, 196–97; of Vilnius, 17–18
*Politics and Place-Names: Changing Names in the Late Soviet Period* (Murray), 190*n*5
*polky* (military-administrative units), 219–20
Pomerania (region), 306
Popadin, Alexander, 205
Poplawska, Irena, 300*n*11
Poplawska, Muthesius, 300*n*11
Port, Mart, 112
ports. *See* harbor and port areas
postindustrialism, 63–64
postmodernism in Tallinn, 114, 130, 131
*Postup* (*Progress*) (newspaper): on Galician history, 278*n*35; on L'viv, 272
Potebnia, Oleksandr, 226, 252*n*21
*Potemkin* (battleship), 158

Potsdam Conference (1945), 77, 80, 305
Poznań, Wrocławian descendants from, 89
Poznański, Izrael Kalman, 293, 296, 297
Poznański, Kalmanowicz, 283–84
Preobrazhenskii, Mikhail, 108
preservation. *See* restoration work
private residences. *See* apartments and residential buildings
privatization: in Kharkiv, 233; in Vilnius, 36, 37, 43
*The Promised Land* (*Ziemia Obiecana*) (Reymont), 286, 301*n*17
propaganda: and L'viv, 258, 259*f*; and restoration projects, 35; and Szczecin, 306, 319; and Wrocław, 76, 78, 81
Pro Wratslavia, 98
Prusak, Mikhail, 63, 65–66, 73*n*33
Prussak, Abraham, 296
Prussia and Prussians: and Kaliningrad, 198–99, 205–6; and Szczecin, 306; and Wrocław, 96, 101*n*30
*The Prussian Roots of the Russian Tree* (mural), 209, 213
publications. *See* books and periodicals
public spaces. *See* urban spaces
Pushkin, Aleksandr, 138, 141, 157, 159*f*, 224, 263
Pushkin, O.P., 163*n*5
Putin, Vladimir, 71, 177, 253*n*36
Puusepp, Raud, 129

Qualls, Karl D., 5, 167, 343
Quedlinburg Convent, 35

Rabinovich, 157, 158*f*
radio plant, Tallinn, 118, 119*f*
*The Rape of Europe* (sculpture), 160
Rauch, Christian Daniel, 210
Ravskyi, Evhen, 278*n*35
real estate markets: in Kaliningrad, 211; in Odessa, 148. *See also* apartments and residential buildings
reconstruction: in Kaliningrad, 198, 211–12; in Odessa, 142, 155; in postcommunist cities, 4–5; in Vilnius,

reconstruction (*continued*)
3, 4, 27, 33, 37, 39–41; in Warsaw, 78; in Wrocław, 78, 83, 84, 93–95. *See also* restoration work
"Recovered Lands," 76, 79, 97, 98
reforms in Novgorod, 53, 56, 61, 63
religion. *See* Catholic Church; churches and cathedrals; Mariavite Church; mosques; Orthodox Church; synagogues
Rembieliński, Rajmund, 283
renaming. *See* street names; town squares
renovation. *See* modernization; restoration work
residential buildings. *See* apartments and residential buildings
restaurants and cafés: in Kaliningrad, 207; in L'viv, 273; in Odessa, 139*f*; in Sevastopol, 179, 181, 183; in Vilnius, 36, 37, 38*f*, 42, 49, 51*n*11; in Wrocław, 84, 91
restoration work: in Kaliningrad, 204–5; in L'viv, 275; in Sevastopol, 176, 177–78; in Tallinn, 115–21, 130, 133*n*32; in Vilnius, 20, 21, 23–24, 33–35, 38–39; in Wrocław, 88. *See also* reconstruction
Reval (Estonia): and Germans, 110; medieval structure of, 108; tourism in, 106–7; urban history of, 109–10. *See also* Tallinn
revitalization: in Łódź, 281–82, 297–98; in Szczecin, 311
revivals, historic: in L'viv, 268–70; in postcommunist cities, 195; in Vilnius, 41–42, 52*n*17; in Wrocław, 78
Revolution of 1905–7, 286, 301*n*15
Reymont, Władysław, 286, 301*nn*17–18, 302*n*36
Ribas, Joseph de, 145, 159, 160*f*
Richelieu, Duc de, 146, 147*f*, 158, 159, 344
Riga (Latvia), 106, 111, 131*n*3
Riigikogu Hoone (Estonian Parliament Building), 116, 117*f*

Roma (ethnic group), 295
Romanovna, Ekaterina, 202–3
"The Route from the Varangians to the Greeks" (Novgorodian project), 70
Rubinstein, Artur, 290, 293
Ruble, Blair A., 1, 335
Russia and Russians: and Kaliningrad, 200–204, 213; and Kharkiv, 220–26, 249, 250; and Łódź, 283, 285–86, 292; and L'viv, 257–58; and Sevastopol, 168–75, 178, 189–90; and Vilnius, 18–19, 20, 42. *See also* Soviet Union
Rutenians (ethnic group), 18
Rynek (Wrocław's market square), 83, 83*f*, 84, 89, 90*f*
Ryzhkov, Vladimir, 58

Saarinen, Eliel, 108–9, 110, 116, 117–18, 132*n*14
sailors. *See* navies and fleets
Saint Petersburg (Russia), 106, 156–57
Sakharov, Andrei, 278*n*28
Saks, Aare, 120
Saliuk, Andrii, 279*n*40
Saltzman, Samuel Jezechiel, 296
Scheibler, Karol Wilhelm, 283–84, 293, 297
Scherbitskiy, Vladimir, 240
Schiller, Friedrich, 85
schools. *See* education and learning
Scudieri, Giovanni, 145
sculptures. *See* artworks and galleries
Sedina (monument in Szczecin), 326–29, 327*f*, 328*f*
Seimas (Lithuanian Parliament), 29, 32, 37, 51*n*13
self-government in Novgorod, 56, 65, 66, 73*n*30
Sepmann, Henno, 112
Sevastopol (Ukraine), 167–93, 343; commercialization of space in, 179–83, 184*f*; ethnicity and tourism in, 183–87, 186*f*, 189–90, 193*n*46; importance of past in, 5, 168–73, 189–90; post-Soviet Ukrainianization

of, 173–79, 189, 190; and 2004
presidential campaign, 187–89
Sezneva, Olga, 5, 195, 341
Shashkevych, Markian, 267
Shcherbinin, Count, 241, 247, 249
Sheptytskyi, Andrei, 263
Shevchenko, Ignatii, 176
Shevchenko, Taras: and Kharkiv, 225, 227, 230*f*, 238, 250; and L'viv, 264–66, 265*f*, 278*n*30; and Sevastopol, 168, 175–76
Shmidt, Valer'ian, 149
shops and shopping centers: in Kaliningrad, 212; in Kharkiv, 233–34, 234*f*; in Łódź, 287, 298; in Novgorod, 55; in Sevastopol, 179–81, 180*f*, 182*f*, 183*f*; in Tallinn, 120, 121–23, 123*f*, 128; in Vilnius, 37–38, 44; in Wrocław, 84
Shpitser, Vasyl', 278*n*30
Shubina, Svetlana, 67
Shumulson, I.L., 177
Silberstein, Markus, 284
Silesia (Polish region), 84
Sillaste, Henno, 120
Skovoroda, Hryhorii, 224, 225, 237, 251*n*15
skyscrapers and high-rise buildings: in Kharkiv, 227, 229*f*; in Tallinn, 111–12, 112*f*, 120; in Vilnius, 45, 47*f*, 49; and Westernization, 167. *See also* architecture
Sloboda (Ukrainian region), 220, 221, 222, 226, 236, 238, 250*n*1
Smirnov, Victor, 64, 73*n*33
Soans, Anton, 118
Sobieski, Jan III, 260
Sochański, Bartłomej, 309, 327
Solidarity movement, 92–93, 307, 321–22, 332*n*52
Soroka, Vladimir, 73*n*30
sovereignty: in Lithuania, 33; in Novgorod, 54
Soviet Union: and Eastern European borders, 2–3; and Kaliningrad, 199;

and Kharkiv, 226–31, 242–44, 250; and Lithuania, 51*n*15; and L'viv, 256–62, 275, 277*n*17; multiculturalism of, 164*n*10; and Novgorod, 58; and Odessa, 141–43; and postsocialist era, 8–9; and Sevastopol, 173, 176, 191*n*12; and Tallinn, 116; and Vilnius, 20–21, 27–28; and Wrocław, 92. *See also* Russia and Russians
Spilka vyzvolennia Ukrainy trial (Union for the Liberation of Ukraine), 237, 253*n*34
sports and entertainment facilities: in Tallinn, 112, 113*f*, 114; in Vilnius, 44–45, 49. *See also* theaters
Sreznevskii, Izmail, 226, 252*n*20
stadiums. *See* sports and entertainment facilities
Stadnitsky, Arseny, 59*f*
Stalin, Joseph, 21, 236
State Heritage Protection Commission (Lithuania), 37
statues. *See* monuments
Stein, Edith, 85, 98
Stepanov, Nikolai, 161
Stettin. *See* Szczecin
stores. *See* shops and shopping centers
Strasbourg (France), 67, 69*f*
Strauss, Anselm, 1, 6, 12*n*1
street names: in Kharkiv, 224–25, 227, 236, 243; in Łódź, 295; in L'viv, 258, 259, 262–64, 271, 277*nn*24–25, 278*nn*27–29, 278*n*31; in Novgorod, 61–63, 62*f*, 73*n*25; in postcommunist cities, 7; in Sevastopol, 170–71, 176, 189, 190, 190*n*5; in Szczecin, 316, 320; in Vilnius, 21, 28; and Westernization, 168; in Wrocław, 77, 78
subway stations. *See* metro stations
Sud'ina, Taisia, 161
Suhorskyi, A., 264
Suhorskyi, V., 264
Susak, Victor, 277*n*11, 277*n*24, 278*n*27
Suvorov, Alexander, 209

Sweden: and Novgorod, 56; and Szczecin, 306; and Vilnius, 51*n*8
*Światło* (Polish journal) on Łódź as "bad city," 285
symbols and symbolism: in Kharkiv, 236, 237, 238, 241, 243, 244; in L'viv, 260, 275–76; in Novgorod, 58–66; postsocialist, 10, 11; and Strauss, 1; in Szczecin, 319; in Tallinn, 116; in Vilnius, 28–29. *See also* myths and mythology
synagogues: in Odessa, 152; in Vilnius, 40; in Wrocław, 88
Szczecin (Poland), 305–34, 339, 341; anniversary of, 307–10, 329; and Haken, 316–20; and L'viv, 319; monuments in, 320–29, 345; old town in, 310–16, 312*f*, 313*f*, 331*n*28; Podzamcze District in, 310–16, 314*f*, 315*f*, 331*n*30

Tallinn (Estonia), 105–36, 340, 342–43; architecture in, 106, 107–8, 111–18, 120–31, 132*n*10, 133*n*23, 136*n*82; nationalism and nationality, 107–8, 115–18; restoration of nationality in, 115–18, 130; spaces in, 118–20, 131; time and location of, 10, 105–7, 131; twofold history of, 108–11, 109*f*; urban development in, 126–28, 130, 135*n*64
Tallinn Tan (group of architects), 129
Tartars (ethnic group): in Sevastopol, 172, 183–84, 197, 343–44; in Vilnius, 18, 42
Tchaikovsky, Pyotr, 224
television. *See* media
Teutonic Order, 116, 206
theaters: in Odessa, 148; in Tallinn, 110, 110*f*, 111*f*, 116–17. *See also* sports and entertainment facilities
Thum, Gregor, 4, 75, 340
Timkowskij-Kostin, Iwan, 301*n*15
Tokarev, Aleksandr, 159, 159*f*, 161, 161*f*, 162*f*
Toricelli, Giordano I., 145, 149

Torkarev, Aleksandr, 157
tourists and tourism: in Kaliningrad, 206, 213; in Łódź, 282, 291, 298, 300*n*5; in L'viv, 275; and New Hanseatic League, 70; in Novgorod, 64, 68, 68*f*, 69*f*; in Odessa, 154–55; in Sevastopol, 178–79, 183–87, 186*f*, 189–90, 193*n*46, 343–44; in Szczecin, 308, 315–16; in Tallinn, 106, 128; in Vilnius, 23, 37, 41, 44
town halls: in Riga, 111; in Vilnius, 18, 19*f*; in Wrocław, 84
town meetings. *See veche*
town squares: in Kharkiv, 236, 237–38; in L'viv, 262, 277*n*24; in Odessa, 145*f*; in Sevastopol, 171; in Vilnius, 21, 31–32, 39, 45, 46*f*, 49
trade (commercial): in Novgorod, 54–56, 55*f*, 70; in Odessa, 148. *See also* commercialization and commercial purposes; marketplaces and market squares
training programs. *See* education and learning
Traskov, Vladimir, 161
Treaty of Friendship and Cooperation of 1997 (Russia/Ukraine), 174
Trubetskoi, Eugene, 53
Trummal, Tiit, 121, 127
Trush, Ivan, 267
Tscherkes, Bohdan, 10, 255, 337
Tsereteli, Zurab, 247
Tumanskii, V.I., 141
Tuwin, Julian, 293
*The Twelve Chairs* (Il'f and Petrov), 159, 239–40
"two great defenses," 169–70
Two-Plus-Four Agreement (1990), 76
*Two Soldiers* (film), 141, 157
*Tygiel Kultury* (*Melting Pot*) (journal): and Koplowicz, 295, 302*n*43, 303*n*44; on Łódź, 293, 302*n*35

Ukraine and Ukrainians: in L'viv, 10, 256–57, 262–68, 270–71, 275–76,

276n1; and Sevastopol, 173–79, 189, 190
United Nations Educational, Scientific and Cultural Organization (UNESCO): and L'viv, 274; and Odessa, 142–43; and Riga, 131n3; and Tallinn, 108; and Vilnius, 39, 43
United States, Lithuanian views of, 49
universities. *See* education and learning; *individual universities by name*
University of Vilnius, 20, 24
University of Wrocław, 95–96
urban development: in Kaliningrad, 205, 211–14; in Kharkiv, 222–23, 226–27; postcommunist, 8–9, 195–96; in Tallinn, 126–28, 130, 135n64; in Vilnius, 17, 44
urban spaces: in Kaliningrad, 208; in Kharkiv, 234; in L'viv, 258, 264, 270–71, 275–76; in Sevastopol, 179–89, 184f, 188, 193n39; in Tallinn, 118–20, 131; in Vilnius, 25; in Wrocław, 79–80, 84
Urbel, Emil, 129
USSR. *See* Soviet Union
Utesov, Leonid, 140, 159
Utochin, Sergei, 159, 161f, 165n26

*Vaba Eesti Ehitab* (*Free Estonia Is Building*), 123
Vaisvilaite, Irena, 8, 17, 343, 345
*vaivadija* (Lithuanian province), 19
Valiuškis, Gediminas, 27
Vallner, Siiri, 124, 125f
Vanished Vilnius program, 29
Vapaavuori, Pekka, 129
Vashchenko, Grigoriy, 240
Vasil'ev, Nikolai, 110, 110f
Vasyukov, Vadim, 175
Veche (electoral association), 61
*veche* (town meetings), 54, 64, 66
*Veche* (newspaper) on Novgorod myth, 60
villas. *See* apartments and residential buildings

Vilna Gaon Museum of Jewish Culture, 41
Vilnius (Lithuania), 17–52, 337–38, 343; before 1990, 8, 18–27, 50; as administrative center, 18–30; as capital, 18–30, 43–50; and nation building, 30–35; old town, 21, 22f, 23, 25, 27, 30, 35–43; as regional center, 43–50
Vimard, Henryk, 300n9
Virgin Mary, cult of, 268–69, 269f, 321
Vladimir the Great (Grand Prince), 176, 177
Vasilij Nazarevic Karazin National University, 225, 241, 247
Volodymyr (Prince), 264
Vsevolozhskii, N.S., 163n5
Vysotskiy, Vladimir, 240
Vytautas, Duke, 28

Wajda, Andrzej, 286, 301n18
Wałęsa, Lech, 321
walls. *See* city walls
Wały Chrobrego (Szczecin), 316–17, 317f, 320, 331n21
Warnke, Martin, 12n3
Warsaw (Poland): and art objects in Szczecin, 323, 325; bourgeoisie in, 84; Brandt's visit to, 80–81; reconstruction in, 78; Wrocławian descendants from, 89
*The Wave* (monument in Szczecin), 322
"Wave of National Revival" (stele in L'viv), 265
*White Sails Gleam* (Kataev), 160
Wilhelm I (Emperor), 98
Wilno. *See* Vilnius
*Windows of Bałuty* (photographic installation), 293–94
Włodarczyk, Edward, 319
*Workers' Pieta* (monument in Szczecin), 322
World Heritage List (UNESCO), 39, 108, 131n3, 274
World Trade Organization (WTO), 71

Wrocław (Poland), 75–101, 340, 342; as anticommunist city, 92–95; as bourgeois city, 82–85; as European city, 95–97, 98–99; as German city, 84–88; and L'viv, 88–92; modes of memory in, 77–80, 87, 99; narrative in, 4, 80–82; Polish expellees in, 88–92; Polishness of, 77–80, 97
Wrzesiński, Wojciech, 75–76

Yanin, Valentin, 56, 58
Yanukovich, Viktor, 188, 343
Yeltsin, Boris, 174
Yushchenko, Viktor, 157, 187–89, 193$n$40, 274–75, 277$n$21, 343

Zabłocka-Kos, Agnieszka, 95, 101$n$30
Zalman, Elijahu ben Solomon, 13$n$8, 42, 43$f$
Zaremba, Piotr, 308, 310–11, 318
Zawada, Andrzej, 81
Zdrojewski, Bogdan, 82
Zubrus, Vytautas, 27
Zybura, Marek, 81